Business Policy, Planning, and Strategy

Business Policy, Planning, and Strategy

F.T. HANER

University of Delaware

WINTHROP PUBLISHERS, INC.
Cambridge, Massachusetts

Library of Congress Cataloging in Publication Data

Haner, Frederick Theodore,
    Business policy, planning, and strategy.

    Includes bibliographies and index.
    1. Industrial management. 2. Planning.
3. Decisionmaking. I. Title.
HD31.H313 658.4 75-41451
ISBN O-87626-096-2

© *1976 by Winthrop Publishers, Inc.*
    17 Dunster Street, Cambridge, Massachusetts 02138

10 9 8 7 6 5 4 3 2 1

To my children, Lynn and Mark

Contents

Preface

Business Policy, Planning, and Strategy is intended for the capstone course offered to college seniors. While many students will go on to careers solely within a chosen profession, their performance is likely to be improved by knowledge of: (1) what occurs in upper levels of management, and (2) how other professions contribute to accomplishing both their objectives and those of the company.

The concept for this book came from twenty years of line and staff experience in executive management and from five years of teaching the policy course to undergraduate students. The approach involves combining the case method used by many colleges with the principles and theory required for case solutions in the capstone course. Competing books, for the most part, either have very limited text material or contain chapters on policy at the functional level which are repetitious of content in other business courses.

The objectives for this book have been to achieve a balance between text and cases, to concentrate the material on the most modern methods for achieving company goals, and to bridge the gap between theory and application in actual operations wherever possible.

An example of the material included to accomplish these objectives is top management's use of the computer in strategic decision making. This tool assists in making good decisions faster by reducing errors originating with quality of information and by gaining improved perspective on available alternatives. More executives are introducing computerized techniques because of the scope of their responsibilities.

Social responsibility is discussed from the perspective of the potential conflict which exists between obligations to the community and those to shareholders expecting maximum profits. Minority race training programs and pollution control are examples of projects which often lose priority when a company encounters a sharp increase in global competition, shorter product life cycles, and general difficulty in retaining profit margins.

This book also deals with management in a period of inflation and shortages. Energy, other basic materials, and several product components become difficult to obtain at prices which yield a sufficient profit to the companies which consume and/or process them. Trade-offs between supply substitutes and the cost of supplies to keep operations going illustrate another example of important decision variables involved in achieving objectives.

The major components of this book describe the fundamentals of how executive management defines and carries out its responsibilities:

Part 1, The Foundation for Executive Management, forms a five-block foundation needed by executive management to plan and formulate strategy successfully. While roles, responsibilities, policies, organizational designs, and information systems are discussed separately in the chapters, each company needs the optimum combination of the five to perform at its best. Cases are used to illustrate specifics, and a comprehensive case serves to integrate the material for the student.

Part 2, Fundamental Techniques in Planning and Strategy Formulation, describes techniques to achieve growth in profits and other company goals. Material in the five chapters represents the core of executive management activity. Cases involve situations which illustrate some of the steps to take and modifications to make in the process of realizing actual success from application of the techniques. Finally, a comprehensive case which builds on information given in previous cases on the company in Chapters Two and Eight allows the student to apply the techniques.

Part 3, Realizing Plans and Strategies, involves methods employed by executive management to achieve objectives in their plans and strategies. Special situations encountered in acquisitions, international business, inflation, and shortages, are covered. The last chapter describes portions of executive life in the corporation including the entrance of minorities and women at the top. Cases illustrate the impact of management competence on company performance and develop understanding of control methods which prevent or minimize potentially serious problems.

An overall picture evolves from *Business Policy, Planning, and Strategy*. Designed for a semester, but adaptable to the quarter system, the student gains insight on how executive management plans, organizes, operates, and responds to problems, and copes with outside influences. Cases add reality and the human dimension to the theory of what should occur.

Considerable assistance has been received in completing the book. The cooperation of the University of Delaware was critical in testing and revising the manuscript during the summer of 1973, the spring and fall of 1974, and the fall of 1975. Parallel to this testing, an editorial team composed of business executives commented on the material. Finally, reviewers arranged by the publisher provided important perspective, especially Art Elkins of the University of Massachusetts, offered constructive suggestions on manuscript organization. Continuing contributions were made by research assistants Tres Birdsall, Bill Davis, and Dick Foster, and others provided information for aspects of the text and cases.

Business Policy, Planning, and Strategy

Introduction

Primarily, this book is a study of top-level company managers who direct and coordinate others in their organization in order to achieve company goals. It is a struggle to become a member of this elite group of executives. Comparatively few people succeed. Usually, it takes a minimum of 15 years for a college graduate to gain a threshold position such as director of planning or general manager of a small subsidiary company. However, there are important reasons for studying this exclusive group of executives at an early stage in a person's career.

1. People are more likely to succeed in their first jobs in accounting, finance, marketing, personnel, production, and so on if they have perspective on what is happening at higher levels of a business organization. Accordingly, the job of controlling cash or making a sale takes on greater significance, and the individual's role in planning makes more sense. Even at a lower level in the firm the individual becomes part of a company team with a basic purpose.

2. People refine their business skills with experience. This book attempts to describe how to handle responsibilities as the individual is progressively promoted to positions that require more than knowledge of a specific function.

3. An employee's image begins to form the day the person is interviewed. The individual's appearance, personality, and behavior while carrying out responsibilities contribute to the rate of progress within the organization. It is important to: (a) be aware of success factors; (b) develop personal assets, and (c) minimize exposure of personal weaknesses.

People are promoted until they reach a level in the organization beyond which they are limited by their skills and personal characteristics. Alert students will begin in college to push this level as high as possible. Knowing what is important is critical in the process of improving your management potential. The remaining steps are up to the individual.

The Foundation for Executive Management

The first five chapters form a foundation needed by executive management to plan and formulate strategy successfully. While the roles, responsibilities, policy, organizational design, and information systems are discussed separately in the chapters, each company needs the optimum combination of the five to perform at its best.

PART ONE

The Role of Executive Management

The decision makers who shape policies, plans, and strategies are identified, and the source of their authority is clarified. A review of the decision-making process, problem-solving systems, and the functions of managing follow. Finally, the social constraints confronting executives are discussed. The chapter orients the student to the responsibilities of a general manager in contrast to those of people specializing in accounting, marketing, production, and so on.

At the top of management is a group of people who must interpret the shareholders' wishes and translate them into realistic objectives for the business. They must transmit the objectives throughout the organization and integrate the activities of other employees to achieve optimum profit performance. They must direct, guide, and coordinate current operations. However, a major portion of their time is spent planning the future. In this book, these individuals and their staff will be identified as *executive management*.

Figure 1–1 illustrates that the source of management authority comes from the shareholders. Shareholders elect a board of directors to act on their behalf in delegating specific powers and responsibilities to the chief executive officer (CEO). The CEO in turn delegates authority to people at lower levels in the organization. Regardless of the mistakes made by others, the chief executive officer is ultimately responsible for company performance.

In many firms the power of shareholders has been diluted by the existence of large numbers of small investors. Furthermore, shares are often traded on stock exchanges to earn a short-term profit rather than being held for long-term investment. Except in instances where substantial blocks of stock are still controlled by individuals, firms, trusts, mutual funds, and so on (with these blocks retained as investments), the board of directors assumes the authority it has had

1

Figure 1–1. Executive Management's Place in the Organization

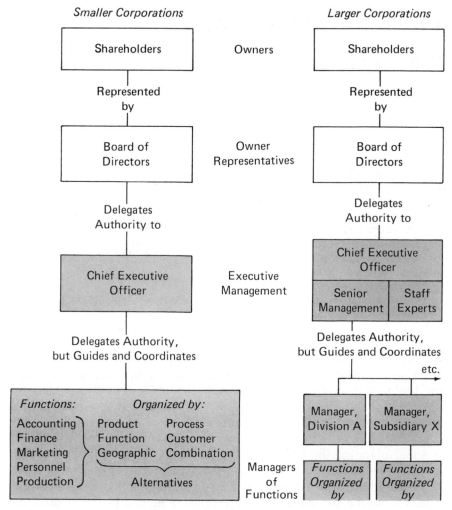

Smaller Corporations

Larger Corporations

| Shareholders | Owners | Shareholders |

Represented by

| Board of Directors | Owner Representatives | Board of Directors |

Delegates Authority to

Executive Management

Chief Executive Officer

Senior Management | Staff Experts

Delegates Authority, but Guides and Coordinates

etc.

Functions: *Organized by:*

Accounting   Product   Process
Finance   Function   Customer
Marketing   Geographic   Combination
Personnel
Production   Alternatives

Managers of Functions

Manager, Division A | Manager, Subsidiary X

Functions Organized by | *Functions Organized by*

traditionally without direction from shareholders. Division managers play a role in executive management and usually are part of the third tier. In large companies managers of functions are pushed back to the fourth tier and are not considered part of executive management.

Executive management realizes its objectives by:

1. Directing, influencing, and coordinating divisional and functional personnel running existing operations.
2. Formulating strategies that capitalize on opportunities and minimize problems.
3. Establishing long-range plans to assure a high level of future performance.

Most chief executive officers have a distinct style of leadership. Therefore, objectives are most fully realized by attracting executive management people who are compatible with the CEO's approach to managing.

TREND IN BOARD OF DIRECTORS' COMPOSITION AND FUNCTIONS

While the responsibility for managing the corporation rests with executive management, considerable authority remains with the board of directors in their primary role as trustee for the shareholders. In order to act on behalf and in the best interest of the owners, board members must have:

1. A broad base of knowledge that can guide decision making.
2. Sincerity and loyalty to the corporation and shareholders to guarantee that knowledge is directed toward achieving company objectives.

Individual directors sometimes interpret their appointments as representing a faction of the shareholders or special interest groups. This is considered a mistake by most executives, because it can create situations in which directors are acting in the interest of small groups at the expense of the overall company.

Most boards exercise their responsibility in two major areas: counsel to executive management and approval on the following categories of decisions:

1. Disposition of assets exceeding the discretionary limit[1] of management including expansion, acquisitions, mergers, and divestitures.
2. Objectives and plans that significantly change the direction of company operations.
3. Changes in the capital structure including financing plans.
4. Major policy decisions such as those affecting dividends, labor unions, government relations, and so on.
5. Important personnel changes involving officers and new projects.
6. Items pertaining to sensitive company situations such as community programs.

In the first half of the 1900s board members were frequently important shareholders or individuals strongly influenced by the

[1] This limit could range from $5,000 to $500,000 depending on the size of the company.

owners. This tradition is rapidly disappearing. Most boards are now composed of prominent executives from outside industries, members of management, and representatives of the banking community. This combination results in boards with high technical and management expertise. However, it also results in weak communications between shareholders and board members. Consequently, decisions are sometimes made based on what directors think is best and not necessarily on what the shareholders want.

Figure 1—1 (see p. 6) portrays the theoretical role of directors acting on behalf of owners. However, today in American corporations, there are areas of potential conflict between the interests of directors and those of shareholders. This conflict is present when the chairman of the board is also chief executive officer. In this situation the individual has the dual role of heading the organizational component representing both owners and managers. It is a difficult assignment requiring an individual with extraordinary integrity to avoid subordinating the desires of the shareholders. Another conflict arises when board members are selected from firms and banks conducting business with the company. There is an opportunity for their company's gain at the expense of the shareholders.

Other problems arise when the board of directors decides on detailed matters that properly should be undertaken by company executives. When the board initiates such actions, it is a warning signal that some components in the company's organization are out of balance and are not functioning as intended. However, the usual situation is conscientious acceptance of the proper level of responsibility by board members to act on behalf of shareholders, even when communication between the two groups is weak.

THE IMPACT OF PROFESSIONAL MANAGEMENT

In the early years of the American capitalistic system, company owners were also the managers. There was no conflict between the investor's demand for an adequate return on capital and the day-to-day demands of running the business. They were one and the same. In the 1970s, a single shareholder or executive owns sufficient stock to control a business much less often. Too, the latitude of decision making by management has been narrowed by economic forces and laws and regulations enforced by government.

The result of widely distributed ownership of companies is increased power by *executive management*. Board members are appointed because of their distinguished reputations in managing businesses and not because they own or represent shares in the company. If professional management strongly influences the selection of the board of directors, some observers foresee the following problem areas.

1. Board of director composition may be manipulated to minimize interference with top management decisions and to advance special interests rather than those of the shareholders.

2. Rate of return on capital could be adversely affected by overreaction to pressures by minority groups, consumer groups, students, ecologists, and so on. Investment in projects with low profits and an excessive amount of time and resources allocated to community needs might hurt performance.

3. Compensation, stock options, bonuses, and benefits such as cars and social clubs for management may exceed what investors think are necessary incentives for expected performance.

4. Risk taking may vary from what owners feel is justified for profit objectives. For example, ventures in foreign countries and/or diversification into new fields may be challenging to management. However, these decisions may result in operating losses and dissipation of the owner's capital.

5. Distribution of after-tax earnings and the dividend policy could become an issue. Management may decide on a plowback program that lessens or terminates dividends. To realize a cash return on their investment, stockholders might be forced to sell their shares if a market exists.

On the positive side, widely distributed ownership of the major firms within the economy provides for effective public pressure on industry, which could not otherwise exist. Mutual funds, bank trusts, labor union and other pension funds, insurance companies, foundations, and so on invest on behalf of the public. A combination of owners prevents excesses resembling those during the days of the empire builders in American business when monopolies manipulated the consumer and earned extraordinary profits by deceiving the public. Public opinion can be focused on problem areas, and the results are often more efficient than government regulation. For example, in the period 1968–72 institutional investors representing thousands of individuals responded to public pressure and influenced management through the power of their large holdings to allocate more capital and time toward eliminating pollution, conserving natural resources, and aiding the community.

In addition to private sector constraints, the government acts as a check against excesses in business practices. Figure 1–2 summarizes the extent to which local, state, and federal agencies can affect the business system. Such agencies react to pressures from citizens, special interest organizations, competitors, and so on, and pass laws

Figure 1-2. Government Pressure on Business

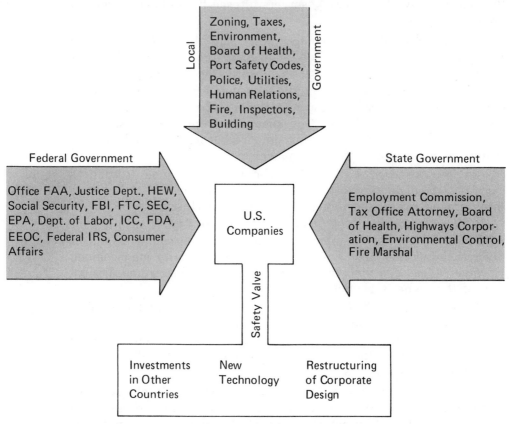

Local Government

Zoning, Taxes, Environment, Board of Health, Port Safety Codes, Police, Utilities, Human Relations, Fire, Inspectors, Building

Federal Government

Office FAA, Justice Dept., HEW, Social Security, FBI, FTC, SEC, EPA, Dept. of Labor, ICC, FDA, EEOC, Federal IRS, Consumer Affairs

U.S. Companies

State Government

Employment Commission, Tax Office Attorney, Board of Health, Highways Corporation, Environmental Control, Fire Marshal

Safety Valve

Investments in Other Countries

New Technology

Restructuring of Corporate Design

or use indirect methods to encourage management to make decisions that correspond more closely with public needs. Frequently, the reaction of executive management is allocation of more funds to projects that minimize government interference and achieve company objectives at the same time.

Professional Managers

Professional managers working in the 1970s have two important characteristics:

1. They are well trained and obtain positions in executive management on the basis of job performance rather than relationships with shareholders or significant share ownership.

2. They have fewer conflicts of interest when deciding on matters related to social responsibility than do owners with capital invested in the business.

While their careers depend on meeting profit goals and share appreciation objectives, these managers are more likely to make decisions that weigh interests of the public than were managers in previous decades.

Another factor that affects the performance of professional managers is the increasing complexity of large companies and the resulting scope of responsibilities. As a company expands, more and more important positions are needed to manage efficiently major components of the organization, including staff experts to advise on decision making. As a result, authority is delegated to several people. A manager's success is usually dependent on the person's ability to work with a variety of personalities having varying degrees of power.

DECISION MAKING BY EXECUTIVE MANAGEMENT

The basic elements in decision making are the same for minor and major business problems. Figure 1−3 illustrates a decision-making approach used to reach a decision with a high probability of being successful. It is important to understand that alternative courses of action must exist. Otherwise, there is not a decision to be made but only an act to be carried out.

For example, assume that an executive manager has been bypassed in a promotion situation. The individual must decide between the alternatives of continuing with the present company with less than anticipated opportunity for advancement or looking for a position in another company. The person decides to stay and is fired after a few months. At that time the manager has no alternatives and must find a job. While looking, the individual may develop more than one offer that results in another decision.

Most business situations are considerably more complex than the problem areas in Figure 1−3. Moreover, in many cases it is not certain whether the correct decision was made until long after the results are known. Executive management frequently asks, "What would have happened if we had implemented alternative 'B' instead of 'A'?" The worst situation is when a 'C' or 'D' existed, and the company did not know of these possibilities. A thorough investigation phase is critical to developing the full range of opportunities, estimating the risk of each, and selecting the optimum course of action.

Once the problem areas in Figure 1−3 are known, the probability of making the correct decision can be increased greatly. In most cases, interpreting symptoms as the cause of a problem, bending information to conform with a preconceived conclusion, and so on lead

Figure 1–3. Decision Making: Process and Problems

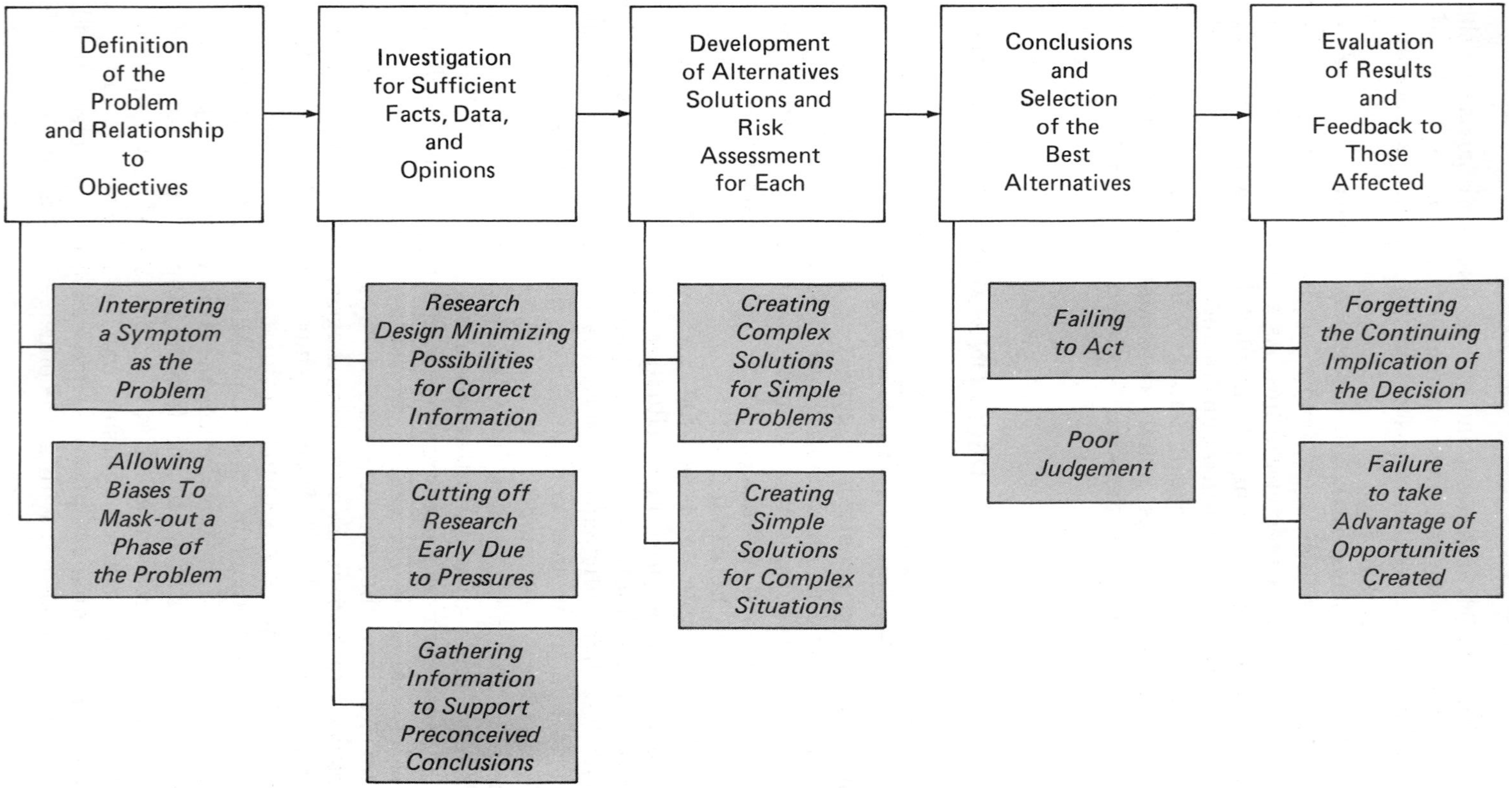

Definition of the Problem and Relationship to Objectives	Investigation for Sufficient Facts, Data, and Opinions	Development of Alternatives Solutions and Risk Assessment for Each	Conclusions and Selection of the Best Alternatives	Evaluation of Results and Feedback to Those Affected
Interpreting a Symptom as the Problem	Research Design Minimizing Possibilities for Correct Information	Creating Complex Solutions for Simple Problems	Failing to Act	Forgetting the Continuing Implication of the Decision
Allowing Biases To Mask-out a Phase of the Problem	Cutting off Research Early Due to Pressures	Creating Simple Solutions for Complex Situations	Poor Judgement	Failure to take Advantage of Opportunities Created
	Gathering Information to Support Preconceived Conclusions			

12

to poor decisions. Occasionally, an executive will select the optimum alternative for the wrong reasons.

One of the tactics used by company "politicians" is the art of *never* making a decision. The theory is that you cannot hurt your career if you never make a bad choice of alternatives. Taking full advantage of this theory, such people maneuver for the position of being able to: (1) accept credit for a good decision made by someone else, and (2) sidestep blame for a poor decision. If executive management could weed out all of the people using this tactic, there would be major personnel voids in many companies.

One of the most important contributions to company success by executive management is the creation of an environment in which managers are encouraged to make rather than avoid decisions. The approach used by top executives varies by situation, but usually includes:

1. Rewarding prompt correct decisions.
2. Counseling managers making the wrong choice of alternatives to help them identify problem areas such as those in Figure 1-3.
3. Updating decision performance notations on records of important personnel to isolate good decision makers from poor or political decision makers.
4. Warning offenders and citing situations in the records, before firing people for poor or no decision making.

The Framework for Decision Making by Executive Management

An executive, whether at the top or performing in a specific function, must be aware of responsibilities in order to make good decisions. Chapter Two will give the details of the responsibilities for executive management. Figure 1-4 indicates the general categories to which time is allocated, showing typical proportions.

The most significant characteristic of an executive management position is that more time is spent on planning future operations than in running the day-to-day business. This is because authority has been delegated to lower level managers to carry out specific components of previously designed plans. In addition, executive management must maintain perspective in order to: (1) judge performance; (2) compare alternative growth strategies; (3) make adjustments that could involve expansion for one division and contraction for another, and (4) allocate resources for new operations.

In small businesses the general manager is forced to take on several jobs that might be handled by line or staff personnel in larger

Figure 1-4. Management Time Allocation

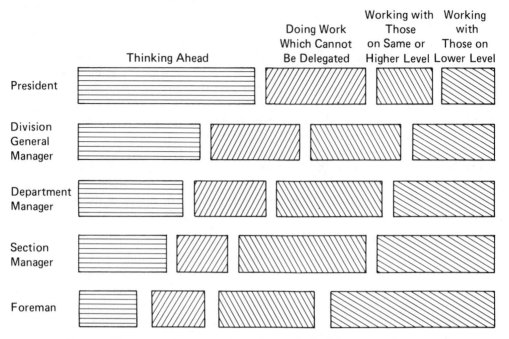

firms. Many small operations have failed because insufficient time was allocated to analysis of trends, planning, and adjusting for change.

Feedback plays a critical role in executive management decision making. A continuous flow of communications, not just data, is essential to inform executive management of what is happening in the company from the market place to plant operations. When this flow is filtered and/or distorted, executive management has a restricted information base on which to plot a company's future course. Alternatives for growth in earnings usually include some combination of internal expansion and external sources of profits such as acquisitions and mergers. If members of executive management do not have an accurate outlook on their firm's operations, it is highly probable they will make poor planning decisions.

Above average performance on decision making does not mean being 100% correct. Good managers make mistakes regularly. However, it is rare that they survive if mistakes lead to serious losses. Usually, less important matters are involved. In any case, *feedback* is essential to identifying a poor decision as soon as possible. In addition, conditions change and adjustments are required to gain the most from a given plan. Consequently, flow of current information from personnel knowledgeable of existing operations is vital to meeting short- and long-range objectives.

Successful operations depend on identifying existing and potential problems as well as pinpointing all opportunities. Corrective actions to prevent serious operating difficulties can then be initiated through the planning process and through executive directives.

Greater attention is being given to devising methods that reduce the probability of a problem being detected solely by the normal course of business or purely by chance. Serious setbacks have resulted from learning about a situation too late. The methods emerging are usually tailored to the needs of specific companies, but the fundamentals listed here are common to most problem-solving systems.

1. Objectives for each component of the business are defined in quantitative and qualitative statements. The objectives must result in minimal conflict between these organizational components, and each should have an attainable timetable. Usually there is a priority list established to give preference to objectives having the greatest impact on performance.

2. Every time a company plan[2] is revised, the objectives are reviewed to determine whether they are still appropriate. The decisions to retain, revise, or drop must be based on both accumulated knowledge by the reviewers and an information search that probes for problem areas. At this stage, comparisons of objectives and estimates of what is attainable can identify a problem (or an opportunity).

3. Assuming a problem is uncovered, the task of developing the best apparent solution is undertaken by going through systems analysis (generation of alternatives, evaluation of these alternatives, and selection of a course of action). The actions can range from a comprehensive strategy to isolated adjustments of operations. Parts of this course of action are normally reflected in the company plan.

4. The need for special action not covered in typical plans could be critical to actually solving the problem. Therefore, most problem-solving systems involve a communications plan designed to get required action. In addition to informing affected managers, a follow-up phase is included to assure that the solution receives proper attention.

5. Finally, it must be determined whether the solution selected is doing the needed job. A control mechanism in the course of action is required to monitor progress for either adjustments or a completely new approach.

---

[2] The reference to "company plan" pertains to any formal plan, short- or long-range, companywide or company segment.

Most of these fundamentals have been applied intuitively by successful managers for years. A well-run department has always had standards and objectives. These standards and objectives have been periodically reviewed and updated. In some cases very creative thinking was necessary to resolve problems identified in the process of improving efficiency and discovering new opportunities.

Today, however, the scope and complexity of business does not permit executive management simply to hope that their personnel will apply the fundamentals. Instead, a policy is often established to compel managers to follow a problem-solving system, and procedures are developed that guide the prescribed methods.

The Cycle of Planning, Organizing, Implementing, and Controlling

In many courses on management the student has studied the repetitive cycle of planning, organizing, implementing, and controlling. Often, this has been interpreted to mean that it is feasible to make a single adjustment in a plan, with the achievement of objectives as the result. This is a rare situation. The operating plan should be modified constantly to reflect current financial, market, and production information and also changes in assumptions on which the plan was based. Long-range plans must be revised regularly.

The decision-making process must be thought of as a continuous cycle. Figure 1-5 demonstrates that concept. Feedback leads to redefinition of the problem and objectives, information, and so on. More feedback on the modification requires additional adjustments necessary to achieve the needed balance in personnel, materials, and so on. Controlling the revised plan becomes difficult and new changes are necessary.

The objectives of these continuing adjustments are greater efficiency and increased profits. However, the opposite can occur as the result of excessive paperwork and lengthy committee meetings to coordinate changes. Executive management must use common sense in encouraging managers to make planning modifications. Employees can become frustrated with guidelines that are fluid. Comments like, "Don't bother with this plan. Wait five minutes and a new one will come down," are common in industry. Even with planning methods that permit major contributions by lower level management, insignificant adjustments can cause friction among managers on the same level of the organization and result in inefficiency and lower profits.

No convenient formula exists to indicate the exact number of changes. It depends on the company, the industry, and the degree to which executive management is informed.

Figure 1–5. The Continuous Cycle of Decision Making

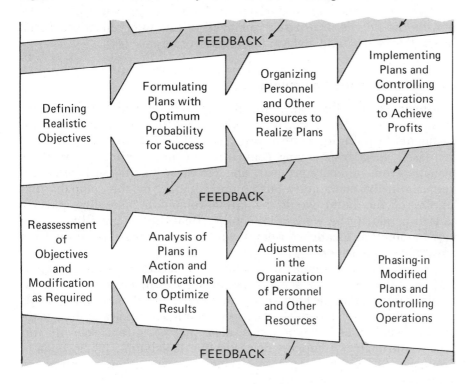

Social Constraints in Decision Making

Social responsibility is having an impact on decisions at each level of the management structure in Figure 1–1. The role of executive management in this problem area is to:

1. Identify social developments that could affect business.
2. Estimate how special interest groups supporting social causes could affect current operations and short- and long-range plans.
3. Devise strategies to: (a) cope with pressure groups; (b) attain company objectives, and (c) implement projects meeting social needs.
4. Develop external relations programs to optimize benefits from the strategies.
5. Monitor projects under the direction of other components in the organization for progress and timing, initiating control actions as required.

Executive management cannot please everyone when performing this portion of its role in decision making. The measure of success will be the degree of progress achieved in attaining objectives stated in strategies (#3) and external relations programs (#4).

Interaction with the Community

Business usually places social problems in two categories: (1) those having a direct impact on profit performance, including investments in pollution control projects with a low rate of return and increased costs from hiring comparatively low proficiency workers (usually from minority groups), and (2) those having serious consequences in the community but minimal impact on the company. Examples of the latter would be crime related to narcotics, poverty caused primarily by worker immobility (inability or unwillingness to move to another location for employment), and disease resulting from unsanitary conditions.

A few firms volunteer a minimum of resources, such as capital and executive time, to socially responsible projects and avoid excessive investments to help solve community problems. This attitude has motivated governments to convert voluntary programs into mandatory regulations. Communities also play a direct role in this process through: (1) support of restrictive legislation; (2) boycotts of products; (3) withholding the services of sympathetic contractors, suppliers, bankers, workers with special skills, and so on, and (4) moral persuasion through labor unions, churches, social clubs, and other organizations. Figure 1−6 shows the process usually selected by executive management in reacting to the community and other outside pressures.

Special Interest Groups

A special interest group can be either a formal or informal national or regional organization. Its purpose is to: (1) publicize the injustices, social problems, and so on caused by current policies, practices, and attitudes, and (2) take all actions feasible to change unfavorable situations. Financial support usually comes from contributions by sympathetic individuals, nonbusiness organizations, companies, and government. Formally organized groups often apply for special tax status and pay staff members to carry out objectives. Informal groups formed to correct a specific community problem usually have volunteer workers and very small budgets.

The range in size, power, financial backing, and effectiveness is immense. Executive management can easily misjudge the potential of

Figure 1-6. Handling Social Problems

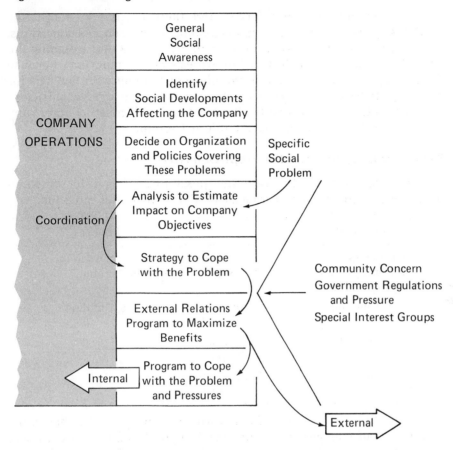

a group and allocate too much or too little toward responding to its demands. Part of the problem in a company's assessment of special interest groups often originates with: (1) emotions involved with the cause; (2) the group's limited knowledge of business; (3) the blend of biases, prejudices, and personality differences that divert attention from the issues, and (4) the degree of conflict between the cause of the problem and profit objectives.

Consequently, a communications breakdown is common. Parties involved miscalculate the positions being taken. Very little listening takes place. To achieve successful solutions, top business executives should emphasize a period of careful attention to written demands, to verbal criticisms, and to the ideas, suggestions, and reasoning of the group involved. Frequently, the opinions of the public, customers, suppliers, and others involved with the company are helpful to gauge degrees of compliance.

Complexity of Decision Making in Coping with Social Forces

The number of social forces and their frequently conflicting positions present executive management with complex decisions. Carrying out the step-by-step process in Figure 1—3 and weighing the benefits and costs of each decision are especially important, because the proper decision may not be popular nor the one with benefits for the immediate future. Executive management must have sufficient and accurate facts to justify its position, and must counter any adverse publicity from a special interest group.

Social Responsibility and the Profit Objective

The best way to illustrate the possibility of conflict between social responsibility and profits is to give a potential situation.

Project P		Project F
Electronic Pulse Conveyor System for Component Movement	Proposed Investment	Filtration System for Stream Pollution Control
$ 1 million	Amount Involved	$ 1 million
$200,000	After-tax Profits	$15,000
20%	Simple Rate of Return	1.5%

A cost/benefit analysis of each proposed investment is becoming a basic tool of management to be certain that all the facts are known. For example, in addition to the bare data, Project F may involve: (1) compliance with a state regulation; (2) community benefits, which when analyzed yield cash returns in lower personnel turnover, efficiency producing cooperation from neighboring utilities, and so on; (3) a strategy to avoid making a more costly expenditure or improve relations with a merger candidate, and so on, or (4) alienation of neighboring industry because of subsequent pressure on them to make similar expenditures.

Decisions based on qualitative as well as quantitative information regularly involve situations where profits and long-range competitive position are affected by accepted social responsibility. The public in the role of shareholders will complain about the low rate of return on investment at one moment, and lack of progress toward pollution control, minority race unrest, and so on at another time. In this environment executive management attempts to make decisions that minimize the impact on profits and maximize the social benefits.

Executive management receives its authority from the board of directors who represent the shareholders. Often, the board has a weak communications link with shareholders now that members are appointed for distinguished reputations in business rather than because they are owners or representatives of owners. These men and women are expected to have both knowledge that will contribute to the firm's growth and loyalty so that the knowledge is directed toward achieving company objectives. However, this is not always true.

Professional managers have gained power as ownership has become more widely distributed. Decision making frequently is controlled by company executives. Five areas of conflict between shareholder interests and management decision making can result from: (1) board manipulation; (2) overreaction to social pressures; (3) excessive compensation; (4) risk taking, and (5) contribution of earnings. These problem areas are being met by adjustments in the business system such as mutual and pension funds having sufficient influence to help protect the public. In the 1960s and 1970s government has also played an increasing role in preventing excesses.

The key elements of decision making include (1) definition of the problem; (2) research to uncover sufficient facts and opinions; (3) development of alternative solutions; (4) selection and implementation of the best solution, and (5) evaluation of results and feedback to those affected. Knowing the full range of alternatives is essential for making the correct decision. Corporate politicians frequently avoid decisions and commitments to a specific position. Instead, they maneuver to take credit for good decisions by others whenever possible.

Problem-solving systems have evolved from the need to identify problems before situations become serious and to assure an orderly approach to optimizing under the given conditions. The cycle of planning, organizing, implementing and controlling is continuous. Feedback permits adjustments to plans and increased efficiency. However, too frequent changes in a plan can frustrate personnel carrying out the details and cause loss of proficiency.

Decision making by executive management under social constraints involves five basic steps: (1) identifying social developments that can affect the company; (2) estimating the effect of special interest groups supporting the cause; (3) devising strategies to cope with the situation; (4) developing external relations programs to maximize benefits from the strategies, and (5) monitoring projects under the direction of others in the organization to assure progress.

The community has three principal methods of influencing business to listen on important issues. First, the government is alerted to the problem and pressures are exerted to enforce regulations. Second, government is pressured to pass new laws. Third, the public organizes boycotts, withholding of services, and moral persuasion.

DISCUSSION QUESTIONS

1. Give three examples of distinctly different composition in the membership of a corporation's board of directors.
2. Discuss the characteristics which professional managers must possess for the decade of the 1970s.
3. How does executive management create an environment that encourages managers to make decisions rather than avoid them?
4. Explain the need for feedback in the continuous cycle of decision making.
5. What is the relationship between the essential elements of decision making and the five basic steps in determining a company's social actions? How could cost/benefit analysis be involved?
6. Identify the problems that can originate with a company's assessment of special interest groups.

SUGGESTED READINGS AND BIBLIOGRAPHY

"Board: It's Obsolete Unless Over Hauled," *Business Week*. May 22, 1971, pp. 50–51.

"Business Week's Manual for Social Action," *Business Week*. May 20, 1972, p. 104.

"Change Invades the Board Room," *Fortune*. May, 1972, pp. 85:156–159.

Fabun, Don. *The Corporation as a Creative Environment*, Glencoe, 1972.

"G. M.: The Price of Being Responsible," *Fortune*. January, 1972, pp. 85:98.

Koontz, Harold. "The Corporate Board and Special Interests," *Business Horizon*. October, 1971, pp. 72–82.

Lawless, David J. *Effective Management, Social Psychological Approach*. Prentice-Hall, 1972.

Mace, M. L. "Directors," *Fortune*. February, 1972, pp. 35:157.

Mace, M. L. "Directors," *Business Week*. September 25, 1971, p. 14.

"Performance Audits by Outside Directors," *Business Review*. July, 1972, pp. 50:112–116.

"Picking the Best for the Board; Views of Executives," *Nations Business*. August, 1972, pp. 60–61.

"President and the Board of Directors," *Business Review*. March, 1972, pp. 50:37–49.

"Radicals in the Board Room?" *Forbes.* May 15, 1972, pp. 109:61—65.

Sethi, S. Prakash. *Business Corporations and the Black Man.* Chandler, 1970.

Stuart, Spencer A. "The Problem of the New Chief Executives," *Duns.* January, 1970, pp. 24—26.

Summer, Charles E. and Jeremiah J. O'Connell. *The Managerial Mind.* Irwin, 1973.

Vance, Stanley. "Black Power in the Board Room," *Business Horizon.* June, 1971, pp. 81—88.

"What's Best—Inside or Outside Directors?", *Iron Age.* December 3, 1970, p. 23.

"Who Opened That Window in the Board Room?", *Iron Age.* November 25, 1971, p. 27.

Responsibilities

Profits and factors that modify the responsibility to produce profits are identified. A discussion of other responsibilities emphasizes the contribution made to company performance by management knowing its responsibilities, individually and collectively, in order to set goals and policies, to plan and to formulate strategy.

Traditionally, the primary responsibility of executive management is to carry out the wishes of the shareholders. Knowing these wishes is complicated by the following factors:

2

1. The board of directors acts as a trustee of the shareholders. Theoretically, members should be able to communicate shareholder preferences to management. In Chapter One it was pointed out, however, that in reality the board offers expertise, influence, and perspective on company problems rather than a communications link with the owners.

2. The majority position of shareholders is difficult to determine without a survey. Large blocks of stock are often owned by mutual and pension funds, bank trusts, insurance companies, and so on, and these organizations exert considerable influence on decision making. Pressure from special interest groups, whose objective is to make their cause appear to reflect the majority opinion, may also be directed at management. In most cases it is very difficult to determine which position reflects the majority.

3. Many shares of most American corporations are bought and sold every day. The reasons behind each transaction are not known, but most analysts assume shareholders change their holdings to improve the financial return on their investment. Certainly there are

other reasons, but executive management has comparatively few letters and telephone calls as means of knowing specific preferences in goals, policies, and operations.

It can be seen that large corporations with thousands of shareholders have a very limited opportunity of knowing the exact wishes of its owners. As a result, goals and policies reflect traditional interpretations of what the shareholder wants and are changed very slowly to be certain that new approaches do not cause unexpected shareholder reactions.

PROFITS AS THE PRIMARY RESPONSIBILITY

The historical measure of success in business is after-tax profit. Profit provides the means for distributing dividends and generating appreciation in share value. It is the tangible reason people give for buying and selling shares. Profit gives management an index of performance. It is the basis of a company's relationship with banks and other financial institutions, and offers government a source of revenue from taxes on earnings. Profits have an immense impact on a company, the shareholder, and the community. It is natural for executive management to accept after-tax earnings on invested capital as its primary responsibility.

The question raised by business critics in the 1970s is to what extreme management should go to earn profits. The following divergent opinions portray the difficulties facing executive management in satisfying the shareholder's demand for profit performance on one hand and the demands of the public and government for social responsibility on the other.

"The purpose of business is profits. Profits must be the goal, the justification for corporate existence, and not viewed as a result."
John Handy, "The Successful Executive," Dun's, April, 1972, p. E24D.

"If in fact the primary or overriding purpose of business is to make a profit, then the free enterprise system should and will be self-destructive."
John Adam, Jr., "Put Profit in its Place," Harvard Business Review, March–April, 1973, p. 150.

The difference in these viewpoints is the degree to which: (1) the buyer, who is the source of cash inflow, should be satisfied for a given price, and (2) the community should benefit from corporate profits. The dilemma is further complicated in today's highly competitive environment by the fact that the buyer, the community citizen, and the shareholder can be one and the same.

Mr. Adam points out in his article that business has viewed marketing from the seller's goals and commitments rather than the consumer's needs. The primary goal of the seller has been, and will be, profits. However, success in the 1970s will depend on balancing this goal with goods and services that reflect the consumer perspective. Profit becomes most attackable when it is labeled, "The vigorous pursuit of heedless self-interest."

External Pressures Modifying Executive Responsibilities

1. Other changes are occurring in the American economy, which have a major influence on executive responsibilities. The public expects more from corporations. People are more highly educated and informed, and know quickly about corporate actions. Images of companies are constructed through the years from the bits of information supplied by news media. The result is tremendous pressure exerted on corporations by what is called *citizen power* to balance the profit motive with concern about the community in which they operate.[1]

2. Professional management is more willing to accede to public pressure. Most managers own very few of the total outstanding shares. Their entrepreneurial spirit is limited to using profits as a measure of performance. Managers themselves have developed a social consciousness. This induces them to undertake programs and projects for the community, which would not have been seriously considered by executive management in past decades. In the mid-1970s the net vector of public pressure shifted to a greater degree of compromise on social issues related to energy matters. However, professional managers continue to be concerned about isolated conditions in their communities.

3. Business is learning that free enterprise is a revocable privilege, not a given right. Excesses by corporations lead to interference from government, pressure groups, and the public. Daniel Bell says in *The Coming of the Post Industrial Society*:[2]

We in America are moving away from a society based on a private enterprise system toward one in which the most important economic decisions will be made at the political level in terms of consciously defined goals and priorities.

Experience in multinational business has also made clear that ex-

[1] *Profiles of Involvement*, by S. Nowland and D. R. Shayon in Philadelphia, 1972, is a basic reference for investigating the degree to which specific firms are reacting to social pressure. Quote used by permission of Chilton Book Company.

[2] From *The Coming of Post-Industrial Society: A Venture in Social Forecasting*, by Daniel Bell, © 1973 by Daniel Bell, Basic Books, Inc., Publishers, New York.

treme controls can convert a profitable company into a loss operation. This understanding has acted as a deterrent against unethical practices in some cases. It has also been an inducement to communicate more effectively reasons for certain actions to outside influences such as labor unions, local government, federal authorities, and so on. This change in ground rules for corporate behavior also results from the public recognizing that its role as both investor and consumer is best served by not tolerating previous practices. Robert Kay of the accounting firm, Touche, Ross and Co., characterizes the current mood: "There's a demand for lily-white hands in business".[3] Summarizing, American business is undergoing fundamental changes.

The result of the three pressures is that some companies are responding, formally or informally, by modifying their goals to reflect public pressure. This is leading to changes in executive management's interpretation of responsibilities. It is obvious the public will no longer accept unscrupulous practices and will use direct community pressure, the government, and organizations such as labor unions and financial institutions to stop or control such practices. What is certain is the reaction of the investor to decisions on behalf of the consumer and community, which threaten dividends and share appreciation.

EXAMPLE What would happen if American Motors adopted a strategy to scrap all facilities for making large cars performing at less than 25 miles per gallon and generating air pollution in excess of the most stringent Environmental Protection Agency standards? Assume that AMC management adopted this strategy based on consumer pressures for a car that would conserve energy resources, reduce highway congestion and parking problems, offset sharply increasing costs of operation, and minimize urban pollution significantly. Also assume that AMC forecasts were optimistic about an adequate portion of the buying public being ready to give up their comfortable big cars with everything automatic for the new type of economical transportation. However, some executives might be skeptical about the reliability of surveys on which the forecasts were based. In addition the company's analysis might indicate that the changeover would involve major losses and high unemployment during a 30-month transition period followed by profit recovery in the succeeding years.

Probably AMC executive management is certain that this type of automobile reflects what the consumer actually needs, and the community would gain significant benefits. However, before going ahead executive management would ask the following fundamental questions related to their responsibility:

1. Does the majority of shareholders agree that consumer and

[3] Reprinted from the April 14, 1973 issue of *Business Week* by special permission.

community benefits outweigh the medium-term impact on profits?

2. Will selling by shareholders who do not support the decision drive down the value of the shares to a point where a crisis of confidence is created among supporters?

3. Will the financial institutions, labor unions, and special interest groups originally agreeing with the basis for the decision withdraw support under pressure from minority segments of the public?

This situation illustrates the necessity of seeking the best combination of: (1) profits as the primary responsibility of executive management and, (2) needs of the consumer and community as important qualifying factors. Figure 2–1 demonstrates the factors that serve to balance overenthusiastic efforts to earn profits.

Figure 2–1. Achieving the Proper Balance

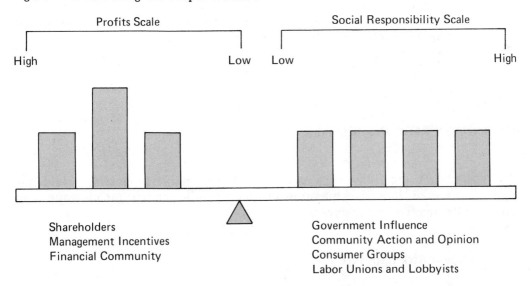

Other Possibilities for the Primary Responsibility

Profits are not always the primary responsibility of executive management, nor is concern about consumer needs. The following three situations modify or replace the profit motive:

1. Companies having a high rate of growth as a goal put minimum emphasis on short-term profits. Instead, after-tax cash flow and optimum equity and debt financing arrangements are primary responsibilities in order to have capital for plowback into investments that have a high probability of profits in the future. The shareholder, in this instance, accepts the potential of significant

share appreciation over a period of years in place of current dividends.

2. Owners with a tax problem at the company and/or individual level place emphasis on nontaxable corporate benefits, stability, and tax avoidance. It is a narrow line between this goal and stagnancy leading to losses and contraction. However, a surprising number of businesses are in this position, and executive management has an unusual challenge to avoid a drift toward losses.

3. Special situations include operations aimed at forms of philanthropy, research, community programs and projects, and specific interests such as car racing, hobbies, and artistic talents.

Many companies of all sizes consider *growth* as an overriding goal. This is usually defined as an annual rate of increase in earnings per share after taxes, which consistently exceeds an attainable figure such as 8%.

The situations described in #2 and #3 are usually found in smaller firms. They are not typical of large corporations. However, it can be seen from these examples of primary responsibilities that executive management must define the wishes of the majority of shareholders as carefully as possible.

SECONDARY RESPONSIBILITIES

When the framework created by the primary responsibility is determined, it is then possible to identify other important obligations of executive management.

Prudent Risk Exposure

Executive management is charged with the care of shareholder assets. On the other hand, its primary responsibility usually is to achieve continuing increases in profits. To grow, a company must incur risk because expansion and new ventures involve uncertainties. Therefore, it is necessary to select new investments that result in both profit increases and prudent risk exposure.

The process of risk assessment must include *'downside out' analysis*. This involves considering the worst combination of events that could occur and the net impact of these events on the new investment. The manager also determines the effect on the division and the overall company under these adverse conditions. Downside out analysis gives a "basement" to risk assessment and sometimes un-covers aspects that dampen enthusiasm about a venture.

No rule has been formulated on how far to go in risk exposure because the process of risk assessment is complex and usually in-volves intangibles. Many firms have strategies to maximize profits by minimizing caution about risk conditions (maximin). The opposite strategy would be much more conservative. It accepts the probability of minimum profits when continuously avoiding high-risk conditions (minimax).

The judgment and competence of executive management varies considerably from company to company. For example, an apparently high-risk investment yielding potentially high profits could be managed by one team of executives with ease while another might incur serious losses. A third management team might dismiss the proposal even before it reaches the stage of financial commitment.

The usual reason for needlessly exposing a company to risk that causes losses are managers misreading the implications of facts and forecasts, or not having adequate information. The student should know that it is not uncommon for highly successful executives to make a serious error in risk assessment and yet recover. Obviously, the careers of those who repeat errors of judgment will be hurt as will those of people involved in tragedies resulting in bankruptcies or a lasting impact on earnings.

Social Responsibility

Pressure is on corporations to make significant progress in the six areas given here:

1. Control of air, land, noise, and water pollution.
2. Policies and programs for employment, training, and promotions of minorities.
3. Solving community problems in education, crime, drugs, local issues, and so on.
4. Conservation of energy, natural resources, and public facili-ties.
5. Accurate descriptions of product characteristics and per-formance.
6. Addition of safety devices and warning signals in the produc-tive process and on products.[4]

---

[4] The Occupational Safety and Health Act of 1973 (OSHA) is considered to be extreme-ly important because of the expenditures required to comply with its many phases.

Figure 2-2. Balancing Capital Allocations

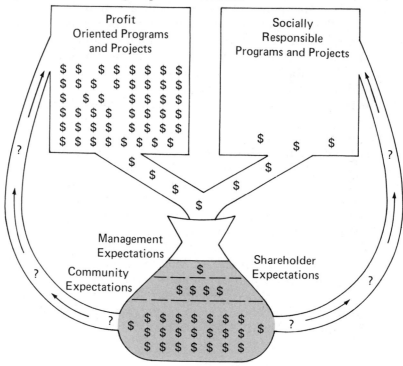

It is obvious that a company must make some compromises because of energy supply conditions but that it cannot divert all its resources to these programs and projects. Executive management has the responsibility to define how much effort and money can be applied to meeting social responsibility. Figure 2-2 illustrates the relationship between varying expectations for profits and choices of projects for capital allocations.

In some companies the planning process includes a social audit that results in a central store of information as to what various components of the organization have done and are proposing to undertake. Formal consideration of community obligations is necessary due to the laws and regulations being enforced by both the Environmental Protection Agency and local authorities. As described in Chapter One, future action is discretionary and ranges from programs and projects to avoid more laws and regulations to those that are wholly voluntary.

One of the greatest deterrents to more investment in social responsibility by American companies is the absence of a measure of social performance. It is highly probable that executive management would allocate more capital and time to social responsibility if their performance could be measured by the following equation:

$$\text{Earnings per share} + \text{Social earnings per share}$$
$$= \text{Performance of management}$$

Shareholders would want to compare the return on capital allocated to both type of earnings to be certain that American operations do not turn into profitless capitalism. Absence of profits would lead to a flight of capital from domestic business, expanded government investment to fill the void, and accelerated socialism in the United States.

The presence of a weighting factor highlights executive management's responsibility to the shareholder in making decisions about resource allocations to the six categories of social programs and projects. If the company proposes to spend considerable time and money on these items, shareholders should be informed of the probable impact on earnings. Then they have the option of selling their stock if, in their opinion, executive management is allocating excessive sums to social responsibility.

The Decision-Making Environment

Two broad categories are involved in the responsibility to create the optimum environment for decision making.

Minimizing Politics

Every company has some degree of politics. Power centers are created by the design of the organization. It is fundamentally important to direct the effort of these power centers toward the goals of the overall company. Goals of individuals should be assisted by and not conflict with those of the firm.

One of the primary motivations to minimize politics is to maintain communications. People become cautious when confronted by individuals who are unscrupulously using their positions to gain greater personal power and career advancement. Consequently, informal flow of information slows, and management efficiency suffers. The following quote from Marshall Dimock's *A Philosophy of Administration* clarifies the importance of preventing this situation.

A free flow of communication lets the individual become a source of creativity, spontaneity, flexibility, initiative, variation—all the things that keep institutions vital and growing. The individual is the origination, creative force, the group, the integrative, cooperative element. Without a clear channel of communications to this resource, the firm is less effective.

Another motivation for minimizing politics is to reduce the impact maneuvering plays on morale. Talented, competent people become dissatisfied when other members of management direct their efforts toward corporate games instead of creative strategies and problem solving. When low morale develops, it is not long before the better personnel find positions with other companies. As this occurs, the intensity of politics tends to increase because: (1) a greater portion of the remaining personnel play corporate games; (2) insecurity develops from a high rate of turnover, and (3) profit performance deteriorates and pressure for improvement builds from all directions, perpetuating the cycle.

Executive management has the responsibility to monitor the corporate environment and deal with employees who place personal ambition ahead of company goals. A harmonious atmosphere is essential. When politics begins to spread and departments are concerned primarily about their individual power and influence, an accelerating downward spiral intensifies.

Other Behavior Standards

It is the responsibility and obligation of executive management to set high standards of ethics and integrity. The behavior and moral principles shown at the top spread throughout the organization. If executives at the highest level in the company have questionable stan-

Figure 2–3. The "Halo Effect"

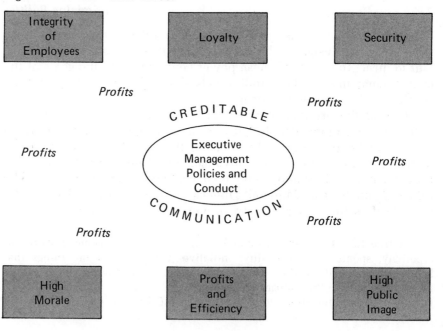

dards, the remainder of the employees will follow their example and initiate unethical practices. Some business critics have claimed it is necessary to behave like an undisciplined predator to achieve profit objectives. However, thousands of successful companies with honest management belie these allegations. The consequences of public exposure and possible prosecution of the company image are results of unethical and illegal practices. A political environment could be another. Loyalty, even speaking well of the organization, disappears because the company is not worthy of the statement of such emotion. Figure 2—3 illustrates the benefits of high standards of behavior.

Conflicts of Interest

As executives increase the number of their contacts outside the company, conflicts of interest can develop. *Business Week*[5] gives the following rules for avoiding this.

* Establish a conflict-of-interest committee composed of representatives from top management, to consider and implement rules governing the conduct not only of employees but of the company itself.
* Insist that key managers and employees in sensitive positions complete questionnaires at least once a year disavowing conflicts and disclosing associations that could lead to conflicts.
* Forbid employees to use inside information for personal profit, or to disclose it to such outsiders as banks, brokers, and institutional investors. Require executives to report periodically on any dealings in the company's stock.
* Avoid transactions between your company and any of its officers, directors, or major stockholders. Have any such deals scrutinized by impartial outsiders.
* Exercise caution in dealings between affiliated companies. At the least, have a committee of outside directors pass on transactions between a parent company and a subsidiary that has some public ownership.
* Steer clear of directors who serve on the boards of companies that compete with your company, even if the competition is in a minor, remote area. Some experts advise flat out against putting a broker or investment banker on your board.
* Set up an audit committee of outside directors. It is good insurance against top-level internal conflicts.
* Warn employees that paying bribes to secure business is as much against company rules as accepting them.

[5] Reprinted from April 14, 1973 issue of *Business Week* by special permission. © 1973 by McGraw-Hill, Inc.

* Do not sweep conflict-of-interest problems under the rug. If a law has been broken, turn the matter over to the proper law-enforcement authorities.

Fundamental Management Practices

Executive management has the responsibility to be certain that the most modern qualitative and quantitative techniques are being applied to the decision-making process. While this type of competence is expected from people at the top, old routines become deeply grooved here as well as at lower levels. New developments are often regarded suspiciously, especially if the new method requires knowledge not gained earlier in their career or taught when current top management was in college. Here are two recommended ways to avoid this pitfall and to build attitudes that are conducive to superior performance.

1. Maintain an open mind toward suggestions that depart from traditional methods and encourage innovation without significantly slowing the decision-making process.
2. Generate attitudes that place importance on anticipating problems and opportunities, and conceiving creative solutions through organizational designs and modern techniques, including computerized programs.

The environment created by an executive management team with these attitudes will lead to above average morale, improved communications, functional team relationships, and generally a higher probability of carrying out the primary responsibility. While less tangible than the management practices to be described, the two recommendations are considered critically important for executives fulfilling these obligations.

Formulating Policies, Plans, and Strategy

Executive management must provide operational leadership through a fundamental framework for decision making for all levels of the organization. The process charts steps resulting in a course of action for the company beginning with the present and extending several years into the future. While the framework should be regularly modified to reflect current developments, it becomes a basis for delegating authority and responsibilities to others in the company.

Stated here are the steps for which executive management is responsible in this area.

1. Goals must be established that determine the degree to which the company is dynamic and aggressive. Measures must be selected

that enable management to know whether or not goals are being achieved. These measures could be a combination of financial (earnings per share), marketing (sales volume), production (cost per unit), and other considerations appropriate to specific companies.

2. Policies are guidelines for the business and covet dividends and plowback, acquisitions and internal development, capital from equity and debts, and other items having a substantial effect on the business. Whether written formally in a company handbook or the net effect of verbal directives, policies also provide standards for behavior in carrying out responsibilities and a structure identifying an individual's specific limits in decision making.

3. Subsequent to setting goals and establishing policies, strategies must be formulated and integrated into short- and long-range plans. This involves changes through specific programs and projects, based on forecasts of existing operations. If strategies and plans are timely and creative, the company should consistently perform as well as or better than competitors and grow in size and profits.

Each of these steps will be explored in detail in subsequent chapters.

It is important to add that in the 1970s the process of formulating strategy and planning requires use of computer technology. Forecasting techniques, simulation, allocating resources through linear programming, and other quantitative methods save time, reduce the probability of error, and spark the conception of profit generating ideas. If executive management does not use these methods and adheres to past practices, performance could be jeopardized as competition in an industry intensifies.

The content of goals, policies, plans, and strategies depends on the competence and leadership of executive management. However, taking these steps creates a framework for the business and the basis on which the remainder of management makes day-to-day decisions.

Developing Managerial Competence

An important executive management responsibility is the development of managerial competence. This includes qualitative judgment as well as technical skills. There are three phases in the process of carrying out this responsibility: (1) employment practices; (2) training while employed, and (3) termination of individuals not performing to expected levels.

EMPLOYMENT PRACTICES It is comforting for managers at lower levels in the organization to know that they have an opportunity to be considered for openings before outsiders.

Top management positions to be filled by executives working with other companies are usually handled through executive search firms. They have access to computerized applicant banks and background data sorting to concentrate on those candidates with a high probability of being hired. Screening through interviews and testing is handled in a professional way by the search firm to improve the quality of individuals interviewed by company officials.

Executive management has a specific obligation to select people of the best possible quality, either from within or from the outside. To do this, they must know what they are looking for, using a carefully designed job description and organizational framework with responsibilities and interrelationships fully defined.

TRAINING PROGRAMS A broad range of training is offered by most corporations. Examples include tuition paid night school, company conducted programs on phases of the business or important skills, executive seminars at prominent universities, and other approaches such as pay incentives to obtain specific levels of professional expertise.

The investment in training should be evaluated as any other allocation of capital. There are some exceptions to this principle such as special programs for minorities. However, it is prudent for executive management to evaluate company paid training through a cost/benefit analysis that weighs tangible and intangible returns with direct and indirect costs.

Some training programs for executive management are part of compensation packages. For example, a regularly scheduled executive seminar in Florida or Switzerland could be the means of attracting and retaining key personnel. Sabbatical leaves are being granted to top managers to relieve work pressures and improve their knowledge of new methods. They spend six months at a university or on a personally designed research project that rebuilds their enthusiasm and vitality. In both Europe and the United States there are executive exchange programs between noncompeting companies to generate new ideas.

Simple availability of a development program, however, may not be enough. Individual managers must encourage subordinates to take advantage of the opportunities. Excessive workloads and feelings of insecurity about being replaced sometimes result in a manager placing obstacles in the way of some employees. Executive management must monitor, and encourage other managers to monitor, attitudes toward training programs and take those steps required to motivate full use of them.

TERMINATIONS The decision to fire an employee is important. Assuming there are no legalities limiting the decision such as in some foreign countries, the net result of the staying or leaving must be considered carefully. Regardless of annoyances and emotions, the questions must be asked,

"What are the grounds for dismissal?"

"To what degree will the performance of the department, division, etc., gain or lose by his or her departure?"

"Is there a qualified replacement?"

"Does the decision require redesign of the organization?"

Most people do not like the experience of firing a manager. It can, however, be the end of the development cycle for individuals who do not respond to company programs to increase competence and promote from within. Blockages in the organization create barriers for young executives who could be candidates for top management. A clearly defined policy for the termination procedure should exist including the early retirement alternative.

Updating the Organizational Design

It is essential to have an organizational structure that defines reporting relationships and the responsibilities of each person in the firm and that reflects current and anticipated operating conditions. Within this structure executives implementing plans and strategies know what is expected of them and who is going to carry out components of plans and strategies that are not undertaken by their sections and departments.

In a dynamic company, organizational change must occur in order to keep pace with operating conditions. To make the proper decisions at the correct times, centralized authority may be applicable in one part of the firm and decentralized authority in another. Knud Hansen, president of Hansen Elektronik A/S in Europe, thinks of the organization as the picture one sees through the viewfinder of a camera. You must refocus regularly to operate effectively.

On the other hand, major changes are unsettling to most managers. Also, there is often a period of low efficiency immediately after new relationships are established. While many corporations have completely reorganized in a short period of time such as one year, usually it is advisable to proceed at a slower pace. An organizational design is often included in long-range plans. New relationships are established gradually through steps that coincide with realizing specific components of the plan.

It is quite possible to nullify the gains resulting from developing management and installing benefits and incentive systems, when the organizational structure does not reflect operating needs. The upper levels of a company, which can make such decisions to restructure, have an obligation to maintain a practical, efficient organization.

Modernizing Information Systems

Earning profits through plans, strategies, competent managers, and an efficient organizational structure is dependent on the flow of information that keeps decision makers informed. Success in business frequently can be measured by the degree to which managers increase the probability of being correct by having adequate knowledge of operating details.

Executive management has two specific responsibilities related to information. *First*, within normal economic constraints, the most modern and practical information systems must be installed to provide the necessary facts for all members of the organization to make good decisions. *Second*, personal information systems that are adequate for their responsibilities must be maintained.

The creation of a first-class information system depends on establishing attitudes within the company that permit these four types of information to reach the right people.

1. Matters for which a superior may be held responsible.
2. Matters of controversy and disagreement that disrupt the harmony of the company.
3. Matters requiring approval, coordination, or advice.
4. Matters that should lead to changes in policies, plans, strategies, and organizational design.

Flow of this type of information permits evaluation that will lead to successful decisions.

SUMMARY

The primary responsibility of executive management is to carry out the wishes of the shareholder. This has been interpreted as maximizing after-tax profits. However, pressures reflecting the factors modifying interpretation of responsibilities are balancing the profit motive with concern for the consumer and the general public. Other interpretations of the primary responsibility include growth as measured by plowback and new investment rather than short-term profits, and special situations such as tax avoidance.

Factors modifying executive management's interpretation of its responsibilities include the following developments.

1. Consumers are being protected by government agencies, pressure groups acting on behalf of the community, and intensive global competition.

2. A more highly educated and informed public expects behavior and decision making by employees of corporations, which consider the welfare of the community in balance with profits.

3. Professional management, not having significant investment in the company, tends to be more receptive to social responsibilities than companies run by the owners or their appointed managers.

4. Business is learning that free enterprise is a privilege, not a right, and that unethical and illegal behavior leads to restrictive actions by government.

Secondary responsibilities include prudent management of company resources by avoiding excessive risk. Obligations to the public in the areas of pollution control, minority policies and programs, community problem solving, resource conservation, and leadership in government are important. The character of management behavior is another major responsibility and deals with minimizing company politics, promoting leadership in ethics and integrity, and avoiding conflicts of interest.

The attitude of executive management plays a major role in achieving productive and efficient business practices. An open mind toward suggestions and emphasis on anticipating problems and opportunities sets up the possibility of implementing the following operating responsibilities.

1. Goals must be established and policies updated. The sequence then involves short- and long-range plans to provide a framework for operations. Strategies are formulated to optimize performance as competitive conditions become clear.

2. Managerial competence must be continually developed through specific programs and policies such as promotion from within and training programs.

3. The organizational design must be updated at intervals to assure that reporting relationships and authority for decision making are in the proper places.

4. Modern information systems, such as those utilizing computerized microfilm, are required in today's intensely competitive environment in order to increase the probability of correct decisions.

The primary responsibility of executive management, that of carrying out the wishes of the shareholder, has not changed materially. However, ownership of American companies has changed. Consequently, there has been a shift from a 100% profit motivation to one including social responsibility and concern for consumer needs. Government, reflecting the mood of the public, has acted to give business incentive to accelerate this shift in emphasis.

DISCUSSION QUESTIONS

1. Is there an optimal balance between profit performance and social responsibility? How would you determine this balance?
2. Define social responsibility. Identify situations in which social responsibility replaces other responsibilities.
3. How is risk related to managerial responsibility?
4. What is the impact of a political environment in a company? If it exists, how would you correct it?
5. Is the best way to evaluate a training program on end results or the structure of the program? Explain your answer.
6. Firms have installed advanced information systems only to find out that newer more efficient systems are available. Discuss how you would handle this problem as a manager of a business.
7. Select a local company. Investigate the role played by its shareholders in establishing the primary responsibility of executive management. Discuss the results of your research.

SUGGESTED READINGS AND BIBLIOGRAPHY

Aaker, David A. and Day, George S. "Corporate Responses to Consumerism Pressures," *Harvard Business Review.* November—December, 1972, pp. 114—124.

Adam, John, Jr. "Put Profit in its Place," *Harvard Business Review.* March—April, 1973, pp. 150—158.

Blumberg, Phillip I. "Corporate Responsibility and the Environment," *The Conference Board Record.* April, 1971, pp. 42—47.

Burck, Gilbert. "The Hazards of 'Corporate Responsibility,'" *Fortune.* June, 1973, p. 114.

"Business Week's Manual for Social Action." *Business Week.* May 20, 1972, pp. 104—107.

"Conflict of Interest: The Moral Climate Changes," *Business Week.* April 14, 1973, pp. 55—60.

Curcuru, Edmond H. and Healey, James H. "The Multiple Roles of the Manager," *Business Horizons.* August, 1972, pp. 15—24.

Dimock, Marshall *A Philosophy of Administration.* 4th ed. Holt, Rinehart, and Winston, 1969.

Dodd, E. M., Jr. "For Whom are Corporate Managers Trustees?" *Harvard Law Review.* May 8, 1932, pp. 1154—1155.

"Explaining the Red Ink," *Industry Week.* March 29, 1971, pp. 43—46.

Gapay, Les. "SEC Moves to Force Corporations to Put More Financial Data in Their Annual Reports," *The Wall Street Journal.* January 11, 1974, p. 26.

Grayson, C. Jackson, Jr. "Eight Ways to Raise Productivity—and Profits," *Nation's Business.* November, 1972, pp. 30—36.

"How Ideas are Made into Products at 3M," *Business Week*. September 15, 1973, pp. 224–226.

Jacoby, N. H. "Corporate Power & Social Responsibility," Macmillan, 1973.

Jensen, Michael C. "The Corporate Political Squeeze," *The New York Times*. September 16, 1973.

Kruse, Thomas M. "Our Changing Society: The Challenge for Business," *Supervisory Management*. June, 1972, pp. 22–24.

Lindsay, Franklin A. "Management and the Total Environment," *Columbia Journal of World Business*. January–February, 1970, pp. 19–25.

Metzer and Colletti. "Does Profit Sharing Pay?" *Profit Sharing Research Foundation*, 1971, pp. vii–x.

Meyer, G. Dale. "Management and the Environment," *Academy of Management Journal*. March, 1967, pp. 119–127.

Nelson, Hale. "Post-Watergate: Implications for Business," a talk before the General Electric Co., Division Managers Meeting, September 26, 1973, pp. 1–18.

Parker, Jack S. "The Vital Need for Profit," The Executives' Club of Chicago, October 19, 1973, pp. 2–7.

Reilly, William P. "Do All the Good You Can," *S.A.M. Advanced Management Journal*. October, 1972, pp. 73–78.

"The First Attempts at a Corporate 'Social Audit,'" *Business Week*. September 23, 1972, pp. 88–92.

"The Annual Report Becomes A Confession," *Business Week*. April 21, 1973, pp. 44–46.

Thompson, Donald B. "Looking Beyond Today's Profits," *Industry Week*. February 5, 1973, pp. 41–48.

Walton, C. C. *Ethics and The Executive*. Prentice-Hall, 1969.

"Water Cleanup Becomes a Booming Industry," *Business Week*. April 7, 1973, pp. 50b–50g.

Case: A Redefinition of Responsibilities at Powerite Tools, Inc.

The case illustrates the conflicts that can arise regarding the responsibility to earn profits. Decision alternatives are affected by the founders of Powerite behaving as majority shareholders instead of professional managers. The situation involves a change in market conditions and the need for Powerite Tools to consider alternatives contrary to the principles that enabled the company to compete successfully in the past. Profit margins suddenly deteriorated in late 1974, and the causes seemed to be permanent rather than temporary.

BACKGROUND ON POWERITE

The company was started in 1954 by two Korean War veterans, Joseph J. Huggins and Richard D. Foster. With $100,000 of equity (savings, poker winnings, family loans, and $15,000 from Dick Foster's aunt) and $250,000 in bank loans,[1] they began in a small, rented factory. The first year they almost lost the business because of refusing to allow enough money to service their debt.

Instead of increasing prices, they turned to production methods that reduced costs substantially. This convinced the First National Bank of Chicago to restructure their loan, which could have been called on December 31, 1954. Because Powerite Tools offered only a quality portable, power-driven chain saw and a two-speed hand drill for a large but narrow market segment, Powerite was able to demonstrate quick results in both cost reduction and market expansion. In the late 1950s the company expanded to produce vibrating and rotary sanders, rotary and blade saws, drill presses, and lathes, all for the home workshop enthusiast who might want something "substantial."

The financial summary given here indicates Powerite's success

---

[1] The loan was a five year, 6½% demand note with equal principle repayments due at year-end in 1954–58. Interest was to be paid quarterly.

| | $000 | | | | | $000 |
	1974	1973	1972	1970	1965	1954
Net Sales	19,344	19,978	17,775	14,276	10,151	457
Powerite Line	16,104	16,788	15,115	12,751	10,151	457
Qualitite Line	3,240	3,190	2,660	1,525	—	—
After-tax Profits	1,743	1,976	1,881	1,505	1,223	(38)
Percent of Sales	9%	10%	10½%	10½%	12%	—
Long-term Loan Outstanding	175	350	525	875	1,750	250

through 1974. The sales performance of the two product lines are isolated for comparison.

The initial marketing area was in a 50-mile radius from the plant just west of Chicago. In 1960 it became a 250-mile radius, and expansion to a 400-mile radius was possible after a new plant was completed in 1965. A thrust into Oklahoma and Kansas opened a new area for growth in the early 1970s. Figure 2C−1 shows the normal price pattern within distribution channels (see p. 46).

Wholesalers doing business with Powerite Tools have been substantial organizations with the best retailers in their area of operation. Market relationships have been without serious problems. Being at the upper end of the quality scale and producing tools that actually achieved high performance standards, Powerite was able to be a dependable supplier that quickly replaced faulty merchandise and upheld guarantees. The company thought that the loyalty of these wholesalers was an important asset of the firm.

In addition, in 1966 Powerite started supplying Mooney Mart in Chicago with tools remade from rejects and returns from wholesalers under the name Qualitite. As Mooney Mart expanded they contracted with Powerite to supply a line of power hand tools including drills, sanders, and saws that would be the quality line from the discount store's viewpoint but a continuing outlet for Powerite rejects. Huggins and Foster had accumulated several ideas for a new production line that would permit low-cost assembly of carefully purchased parts. As a result, they were able to continue offering both a $20 price and excellent quality for the 3 items. In 1969 this put them in the position to say, "This marketing and product combination is the turning point. We're now in a position to double sales every 10 years." They were on the verge of exceeding their expectations in 1974 when the market for home power tools changed.

Inside Powerite

Executive management in the company consisted of 10 people. Figure 2C−2 shows the people in key positions in 1973 when the problem developed. Note that Joe Huggins and Dick Foster had succeeded in creating an office of the president where they shared responsibilities without friction. Either chief executive officer could run the company equally well if the other was not present. If the relationship continued under pressure, their rapport would be a great asset for Powerite.

THE MARKET SETBACK

The most valuable asset of Powerite in December, 1974 was feedback from the market. At that time, the following information came from regional sales managers.

1. Yamasuki Tools, formerly a discount supplier, has entered the mid-America market by establishing a Chicago regional service and sales office. With headquarters in Osaka, the company is a worldwide supplier of hand tools. Their potential penetration of the American market was based on a cleverly conceived campaign graphically illustrating points of superi-

Figure 2C–1. Market Structure and Pricing

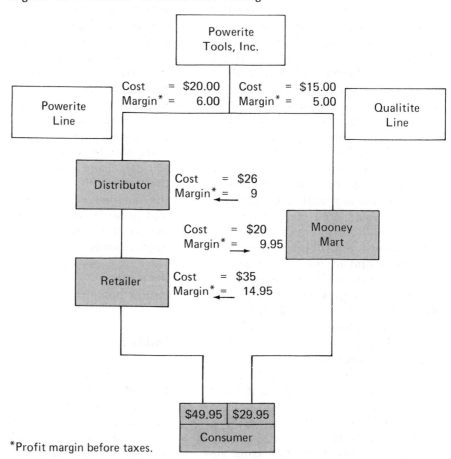

*Profit margin before taxes.

Figure 2C–2. Powerite's Organization

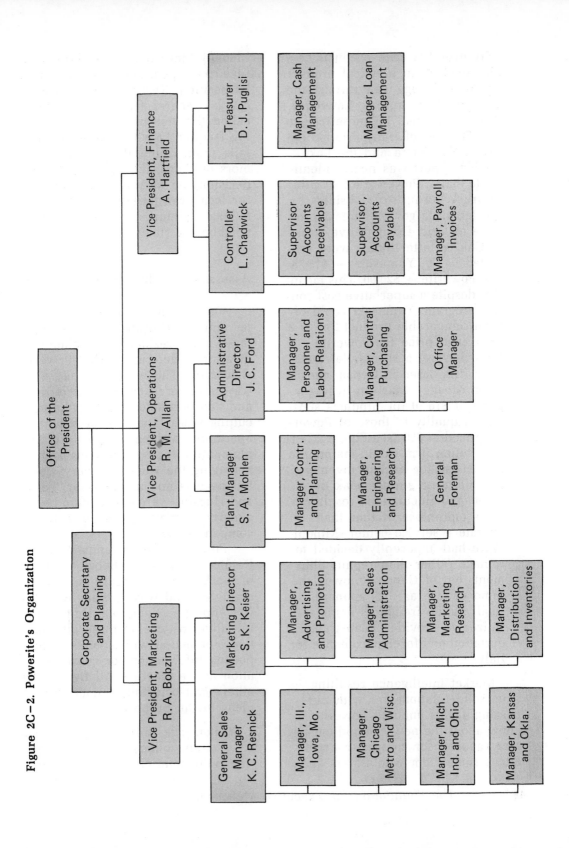

ority over Powerite products. Shipment of an identical product line into Chicago went through the Panama Canal and St. Lawrence Seaway on small Japanese freighters. The cost of transportation between Yokohama and the Lake Michigan port was nearly identical to that of Powerite for 40 miles by truck because of subsidies by the Japanese government to promote exports. Comparative costs in Chicago after duties were estimated to be: Yamasuki — $16.75 and Powerite — $20.00. This meant that despite a superlative cost control program, Yamasuki could offer a comparable product line at a breakeven price for Powerite.

2. Minoni-Ware, a substantial European firm based in Genoa, has offered Mooney Mart an average price of $16.50 for products similar in quality to those of Powerite priced at $20 (see Figure 2C–1). The Italian firm would maintain a warehouse for backup inventory in Chicago to supply peak demand and fluctuations resulting from guarantees. Rather than operate a service center, Minoni-Ware had apparently decided to replace rather than repair. Shipments out of Genoa followed the same pattern as the Japanese, small Italian freighters being subsidized to provide cheap transportation and foreign exchange for Italy.

Market intelligence resulting from solid relationships with purchasing agents enabled Powerite to know about the new competition before requests for contract renegotiations came from wholesalers and Mooney Mart. It gave Powerite some time, perhaps a month, to determine its position. Recognizing the urgency, the general sales manager had called the vice president of marketing frequently with additional details about wholesaler offers and rumors of Yamasuki and Minoni-Ware decisions on locations, commitments for local transportation, and expectations for market penetration into neighboring states.

Assessment of the Powerite Situation

On December 16, 1974, Dick Foster and Joe Huggins met with their three vice presidents and planning director to determine what Powerite should do. The two CEOs had always monitored central purchasing and had originated most of the cost-cutting ideas. The vice president of operations had been capable of implementing their suggestions and managing the workforce very well, but he was not an innovator. Foster and Huggins were expected to be the experts on matters related to the company's cost base.

Powerite was fortunate to have Rainer (Charley) A. Bobzin as head of marketing (see Figure 2C–2). His creative mind was at work with the first report on Yamasuki. He took the initiative to develop three alternatives for action with adequate supporting information for consideration at the meeting. All five of the others had contributed data and ideas to the proposals.

1. a. *Powerite Brand.* Fight Yamasuki and others penetrating the mid-America market for "up-

per end quality" on a price basis. This means being prepared to go to $19.00 per unit from $26.00 during 1975. Since the company was optimally efficient, quality must be cut to the level of the Qualitite brand. Lower cost components would result in a cost of $15.00 per unit including an extra allowance for rejects and repairs. A hard hitting advertising campaign would stress Powerite's reputation, emphasize a "buy American" approach, and show several scenes in which homeowners are sweating and developing blisters with manual tools because, "the Japanese (or Italians, and so on) don't have the replacement parts for my power drill (saw, sander, and so on)." No one outside the executive management level would know about the cutback in quality of the Powerite line.

b. *Qualitite Brand.* Force out the Italians with a price equalling contract renegotiation. Being assured of 100% of Mooney Mart's business is essential to the strategy. More rejects and returns are likely with the proposed Powerite line. This would increase availability of rebuilt units for sale to discount outlets. Also, the volume achieved by purchasing identical parts for the Powerite and Qualitite lines would permit discounts that would enable the company to achieve an average unit cost of $12.50 on Qualitite including increased costs for repairs and

adhering to any guarantees given to Mooney Mart. As a result, the profit margin per unit is less but the potential for increased volume is excellent.

Forecasts of operations indicate a decrease in after-tax profits in 1975 during the transition, but a resumption in growth as measured by sales and earnings of both lines in 1976. This alternative would strengthen the competitive position of Powerite Tools, Inc. and perhaps enable the company to expand geographically.

2. a. *Powerite Brand.* Create a new place in the market for the Powerite line by upgrading the product line. A minor increase in the cost to $26.00 per unit from $20.00 based on improved purchased components would yield a superior product. When combined with new industrial designs for housings, casings, and grips, the public could be expected to respond to "Super-Powerite." The price structure would be $39.00 to wholesalers instead of $26.00, $54.00 to retailers instead of $35.00, and an average price to the customer of $79.95. This gives the retailer an extra 5% margin (48% markup as compared to 43%) and an incentive to "push" the product.

A survey of 30% of retailers carrying Powerite and wholesalers dealing directly with construction contractors is the basis of marketing's sales forecast. The projections indicate an initial 15% drop in volume and a 18% decline in profits during 1975 and 1976 followed by recovery to 1974 levels in 1977. While this would be a drastic step, there is an important change occurring in the market for equipment used by professionals instead of "do-it-yourselfers." Stealing has become a serious cost problem for contractors. Many are switching to tools that will not stand up under normal usage over several years, but would last at least a year on the job.

b. *Qualitite Brand.* Concede on price only as required to retain a substantial portion of the Mooney Mart business, especially during the 1—2 year transition stage while the new Powerite line gains an improved share of the market. If volume with Mooney Mart declines, purchasing costs for both the Qualitite and Super-Powerite lines could increase and profit margins narrow. Therefore, it would greatly strengthen the company's competitive position against market entry by other foreign firms if a projected cost base of $12.50/unit could be achieved, as compared with $15.00 at present, by selling to other chains in the market area serviced by Powerite Tools, Inc. A line based on re-built Super-Powerites could assist in obtaining new contracts.

3. a. *Powerite.* Fight Yamasuki and others on the basis of quality rather than price. Redirect advertising, promotion, and direct sales to retain existing customers and develop new outlets in the existing sales territories. An increased profit margin should be given to wholesalers and retailers. Assuming no added marketing costs, this means cutting Powerite back to an average of $2.00 per unit profit margin before taxes, or a margin of 10% in 1975. (Costs remain at $20.00 per unit while the price to wholesalers is reduced to $22.00.) The intensive campaign would generate sufficient volume in subsequent years to reduce the average cost by $3.00. This would give a $5.00 margin on $17.00 of cost, or the same 30% ± being earned currently.

Choosing an Alternative

Everyone agreed that Alternative #2 was too great a risk to be the company's sole strategy. Powerite could be left with a very small market if the survey proved to be wrong. The idea had merit, and the Super-Powerite line could be market tested in 1976 after the company had resolved its present problem.

Everyone also agreed that Ken Resnick, general sales manager, must personally secure at least one other long-term order similar to the Mooney Mart contract as soon as possible. This should have been done in the early 1970s to hedge against a situation such as the present one, and Charley Bobzin accepted responsibility for this not occurring. It was critical in late 1974 to move quickly to reduce the opportunities for foreign firms to break into the market. In addition, added volume would regain some of the profit margin that might be conceded to Mooney Mart to keep out the Italians.

Aside from minor points such as the "Buy American" content of the advertising campaign, this was where general agreement stopped. The three vice presidents and the planning director were unanimous in selecting Alternative #1 as the only logical approach. The market, which had been rough for lower quality producers for over five years, was going to get cut throat at the upper end. Powerite's reputation with wholesalers and retailers would permit retention of most of the existing customers. With extra effort by Ken Resnick's sales force, the company would be expanding both volume and profits by the end of 1975. Bob Allan characterized the four executives' attitude by saying, "It's the kind of tough strategy the Japanese and Europeans will understand. We'll bounce them out of America."

Dick Foster and Joe Huggins had eliminated Alternative #1 from the beginning because of the fundamental point on which it was based: the public had to be deceived by stating or implying that the Powerite line for which the customer was paying approximately $20.00 more was superior to the Qualitite line when, in fact, they would be nearly identical. The founders, and still major shareholders,[2] felt that the reason they survived in 1954 was because they solved their problems by offering a better product for the price they had committed rather than deceiving their customers by cutting quality or increasing the price.

The two CEOs knew intuitively what had to be done, and discussion of the possibilities led them to take the following actions.

1. Quality was improved by new statistical quality control methods for inspection and testing. Machines had been designed for this purpose, rather than relying on personnel and possible delays, so that there would be a minimal impact on costs.
2. Housings, grips, and cords were modernized to give a streamlined appearance, obtain a better balance for handling by the user, and dissipate heat from extended use.
3. Criticisms in Yamasuki's promotions were corrected immediately. While 1 and 2 had little impact on costs, the combined result of the changes would give an initial average unit cost of $21.25.
4. The suggested improvements in margins at both the wholesaler and retailer levels were used as a good countertactic. However, Powerite did not indicate concessions were based on pressure from foreign competition but rather on product improvement that would lead to significantly increased volume. Sell to wholesalers at $24.00 per unit and recommend the consumer list price to continue at $49.95.
5. The sales force intensified efforts to increase volume. Incentive sys-

[2] Foster and Huggins sold 45% of the company in 1968 after registration on the Midwest Stock Exchange. In 1973 they sold another 30% of their original shareholdings when the stock price reached 14 times current earnings per share, the upward trend being contrary to the MSE index that year. In summary, 75% of outstanding shares is held by the public.

tems for sales representatives were designed to increase effective calls per week.

6. Advertising and promotion could be as hard hitting as marketing wished as long as it was honest. "Buy American", distance from the basic source of parts, defects in design, and other Powerite advantages were authorized.

Charley Bobzin and Austin Hartfield estimated that the company would lose money in 1975 and the first half of 1976 as a result of these decisions, and that it might not be feasible to gain the sales needed for profits in the remainder of the second year. Austin Hartfield reported that unit volume would have to increase 15% to offset the price cut to $24.00 and wage increases scheduled in mid-1975.

STUDENT PROBLEMS

The Chief Executive Officers, Dick Foster and Joe Huggins, behaved with what they believed to be integrity. However, the business has other shareholders, and the course of action developed from a combination of the three alternatives will probably result in losses during 1975 and part of 1976. Share value will decline and the company may pass dividends. Furthermore, willingness to give up majority ownership just before the trouble began could lead to accusations that Foster and Huggins knew about the threat of foreign competition.

Charley Bobzin maintains that advertising and promotion could be worded in a way that would not directly deceive the public. It is true that Powerite's past reputation would imply quality superior to products such as Qualitite. However, the company would not make these statements although the improvement in exterior appearance and tool balance might justify such words in the promotion.

Imagine that you own 1% of Powerite Tools, Inc. and have been accurately informed of the decision by the office of the president. Evaluate the company's proposed course of action from your point of view as a shareholder. As an investor who is not a speculator, determine answers to the following.

1. What is the outlook for dividends and share appreciation in 1975−76? Could the company fail? Assess the rate of growth in the 1977−80 period.

2. Is there a basis for a shareholder suit or an SEC action against Foster and Huggins for misleading the public in 1973 when the owner/managers sold 30% of their holdings? The premise would be that they knew competition would increase sharply and that foreign firms would be entering the market. Therefore, failure to disclose these probable events warrants a Securities Exchange Commission investigation.

3. Identify the best alternative other than the one made by Foster and Huggins. Can you accept the principles on which the most financially attractive decision is based? Would you modify Bobzin's #1 proposal? How?

Business Policy

Policy is defined, and the definition is expanded by giving examples of policies that might be set at various levels of the organization. Rules and directives of less permanence and importance are contrasted with guidelines that could have major impact on the company. Trends in business policies are considered. The chapter relates to policies as a framework for decisions by management, thereby strongly influencing the way executives fulfill their responsibilities.

At an American Management Association seminar participants from several large corporations were asked, "What is policy?" The answers were astonishing in that very few related to accepted definitions of policy. For example, one executive read pages of platitudes, such as hiring the best people and living by the Golden Rule. Others claimed policy to be another word for strategy, a decision rule, or statement of a company goal. The important point about these replies is that many managers do not have an understanding of what policy is. The definition given here is one derived from the contributions of several cooperating companies.

A *policy* is a statement, verbal, written or implied, of those principles and rules that are set by managerial leadership as guidelines and constraints for the organization's thought and action.

The purpose of policy is to enable management to relate properly the organization's work to its objectives. As a result, the existence of practical and comprehensive policies tends to increase efficiency. Decisions made within a policy framework have a higher probability of being synchronized with other decisions made within the company.

3

THE PERSONNEL WHO SET POLICY

Policies are set by management at various levels in the firm. Since authority and responsibility limit one's capacity to make policy decisions, the importance of the policy will normally depend on the individual's level in the organization. Recall that shareholders theoretically delegate their authority as owners to the board of directors, which acts on their behalf. In turn, the board delegates managerial authority and responsibility to the chief executive officer. Throughout the various levels of management the delegation process continues.

According to the definition, setting policy is limited to "managerial leadership." These words are intended to include levels of management that are lower in the organization than this text's definition for executive management. For practical reasons, determining policy is not solely the prerogative of the top executives. Some examples will clarify who can establish policies and the types of policy they can establish.

1. *Dividend policy* is ultimately decided at the board level because it determines how the shareholder will obtain a return on an investment—cash through generous dividends, share appreciation through a plowback policy, or some combination of the two.

2. In regard to growth objectives, executive management will establish the *capital allocation policy* for maintenance and expansion of existing facilities, proposed investments, internal development of new product lines, and other projects having a substantial influence on future performance.

3. The controller sets the *policy on relations with the Internal Revenue Service.*

4. The manager of sales administration determines *policy on coordination with customers* to balance shipments with orders.

In each example, a lower level of the organization is involved, as illustrated in Figure 3–1. In every case a rule is established to guide the course of action to be taken by subordinates. Some involve routine actions, and these policies are set by managers at lower levels. As actions become less routine and involve discretionary decisions that could affect the future of the company, guidelines and constraints are made in the upper levels of the organization. Some very important policies, such as the existence of short- and long-range plans, must be made by the chief executive officer. This individual has full responsibility for the company's performance.

Figure 3–1. The Personnel Who Set Company Policy

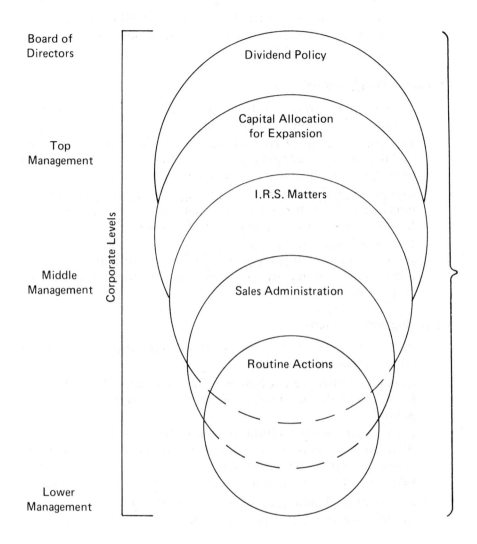

Organizational Responsibilities for Policy

Some examples of policies for a typical firm such as Powerite Tools, Inc. will clarify the meaning of this business term. These examples are given by the organizational component setting the policy.

Board of Directors

* Minimum dividend distribution of 30% of after-tax earnings.
* Plowback of cash remaining after dividends to realize the management goal of 8% per year for growth.

Executive Management

* Content of proposals to the board of directors on allocation of resources including financial plans.
* Types of channels of communication from and to all personnel, making certain managers are fully informed on phases of the operation affecting their responsibilities.
* Composition of plans, both short- and long-range, to coordinate decision making throughout the organization, and a mechanism for regular review and updating of content.
* Necessary authority, financial budgets and controls for personnel to carry out their responsibilities, and maintain an updated organizational structure that clarifies the nature of these responsibilities.

Marketing Management

* Product line decisions but in coordination with production and other departments.
* Communication system between line sales and management to have knowledge of developments in the market as rapidly as possible.
* Price guidelines permitting the sales department to be competitive in the industry, to achieve profit objectives, and to respond to market opportunities.
* Standards for advertising, promotion, and selling methods.
* Distribution channels that are the lowest cost alternatives, and provide for flexibility in distribution.

Production Management

* Approaches to cost control programs and cost reduction planning on all operations.
* Optimum combinations of modern manufacturing processes and facilities to realize cost objectives.
* Inventory levels at the raw material, semifinished, and finished product levels to meet fluctuations in customer demand but also avoid overcommitment of capital employed.
* Subcontracting the manufacture of components.

* Requirements to maximize productivity and avoid work stoppages.

Accounting Management

* Working capital requirements as affected by the timing of payables and the terms of payment of receivables.
* Audits by all outside parties including the Internal Revenue Service are to be supervised by the controller.

Other Functional Management

* Legal counsel which best combines company knowledge and legal competence.
* Programs of research on a continuing basis that yield new product lines commercially viable.
* Computer and peripheral hardware for automation, information systems, control devices, and aids to strategic decision making.

These policies result from managers creating guidelines that permit persons reporting to them to carry out their work without continually asking what to do. They are refined in content over time and provide a framework for managing the business.

Directives, Orders, Procedures, and Work Rules

The word *policy* is sometimes used for standing orders that pertain to the work of individuals at various levels of the organization. For example, a supervisor could decide whether workers in the typing pool may read at their desks when there is no work. In another situation a supervisor might determine that three defectives in a row indicate a machine is not set up properly. Most executives would refer to *company policy* when discussing limitations placed on the use of a club membership by their families, which is part of the compensation package. These and similar procedures, orders, and work rules are not policies. They are not sufficiently important to provide a framework for efficient achievement of company goals.

One-time restrictions such as who handles the cash in a transaction, procedures for handling an immense order from a supplier, and similar cases with a limited span are usually called *directives*. They are intended to specify who can do what under special circumstances. To determine the proper business term to apply, use the following test.

Policies provide a framework for and pertain to important company decisions over a period of years. Rules and constraints with a limited time span and/or guiding decisions and employee conduct on lesser matters are not policies.

None of the examples involving typing pools, work station practices, use of club memberships, purchasing procedures for a single transaction, and so on pass the test. On the other hand, guidelines on capital allocations, dividends, taxation, scope of product lines, and so on comply with all aspects of that test. Figure 3–2 concedes that a "gray" area can exist in the definition of what is important.

Figure 3–2. The Gray Area Resulting from Changing Definitions of What Is Important

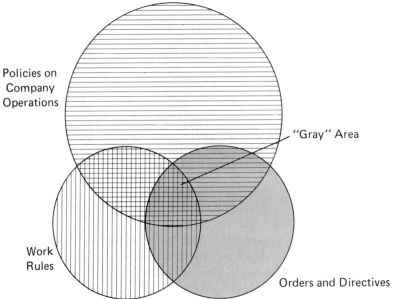

THE RELATIONSHIP OF POLICY TO PHILOSOPHIES, GOALS, PLANS, AND STRATEGIES

Business terms other than directives, orders, and so on are sometimes used carelessly. This results in confusion on what is actually meant. Guidelines and constraints have a great impact on decision making at all levels in the organization. Therefore, it is understandable that some executives tend to interchange policy with other fundamentals of managing. Let us examine areas of potential confusion.

Philosophies, Creeds, Principles, and Purpose

Before discussing these terms and relating them to policy, definitions are given here that synthesize those published by several companies.

A *philosophy* is a body of knowledge that provides a logical basis for thinking and actions within the organization. Company philosophy involves the reason for its existence and is expressed in principles. In the case of Powerite Tools it means the highest possible quality for a reasonable price with no variation in policies related to honesty in advertising, guarantees, and other factors influencing the consumer. The philosophy rigidly applies despite the short-term effect on profits.

A *creed* is used most often to express principles relating to ethics, integrity, community service, standards of leadership, rights of those involved, and similar subjects. Powerite Tools does not have a formal creed, but one could be derived from the information given in the Chapter Two case.

A *principle* is a truth accepted or professed as fundamental. It is also considered to be an accepted guide or rule of conduct, action, or thought and is often included in definitions of policy. The difference between use of principles in a philosophy or creed and those in policies is the breath of the truth involved, policy being more specific. For example, Alternative #1 proposed by vice president of marketing Bobzin violated a principle of honesty in Powerite Tool's philosophy.

Purpose is an overall aim for being and doing the fundamental reason for carrying out a business operation. Henry Ford II says that the social responsibility of the corporation has not changed for Ford Motor Company, and that this responsibility is " . . . to earn profits for shareholders by serving consumer wants with maximum efficiency. This is not the whole of the matter, but it is the heart of the matter . . . ."[1] Sperry Rand is less specific: "Making machines do more so man can do more. Not just a nice phrase, but a statement of corporate purpose."[2]

A hierarchy results from these definitions. A philosophy is made up of principles. These principles make up the basis for a policy framework. Management must work within the guidelines provided by policies.

Once proven, a philosophy will usually remain sacrosanct. Principles will change only with fundamental changes in the business en-

[1] Report to Shareholders, Ford Motor Company, Inc. May 1972. Used by permission of Ford Motor Company, Inc.
[2] Sperry Rand Corporation publications in 1973.

Figure 3–3. The Progression of a Philosophy

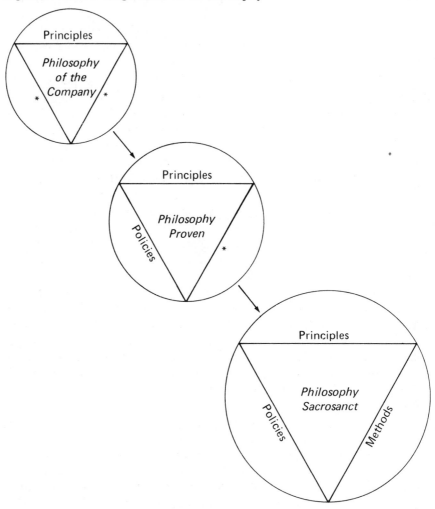

vironment and usually require board of director approval. Policies will be revised with business conditions, and methods will vary frequently. Figure 3–3 illustrates the progression from the rigidity of a philosophy to the flexibility of methods. Terms such as company philosophy, creed, mission, and so on imply broad statements intended to be applicable under a wide range of conditions over a period of several years. Managers carrying out specific responsibilities may not encounter a conflict with such statements during a lifetime with a firm. However, executive management, charged with charting a course of future action, may frequently refer to such statements for guidance.

Goals and Objectives

It is becoming clear that many business terms can be defined broadly or narrowly. With a change in scope, they can mean different things to different managers. Goals or objectives are good examples. This book uses the two words synonymously. However, some companies arbitrarily decide that one pertains to short-range and the other long-range. The word selected does not matter in their opinion as long as there is a decision to clarify usage within the firm. A general definition is given here.

A *goal* or *objective* is an end to be achieved, a future condition, or result to be accomplished in carrying out an activity.

Sir Geoffrey Vickers in *The Art of Judgment*[3] makes a distinction between: (1) goal setting and goal seeking, and (2) norm setting and norm holding. His opinion is that goals should be stated in terms that do not have a specific measure. This book does not support this distinction and believes the two are integral. The end to be achieved or result to be accomplished should be stated specifically according to the systems approach, which stresses measures of effectiveness to monitor progress toward the goal or objective.

It is clear that goals and objectives can be defined broadly and that a policy needs precision in order to be a rule or a guideline. Creative, aggressive business executives will find loopholes in policies as they do in laws if they are not carefully stated.

Plans and Strategies

Plans and strategies are management methods needing specific norms against which success can be measured. The exact approach to planning and formulating strategy varies from situation to situation and company to company. Important refinements of these methods have been developed in the 1970s, and changes will continue in order to reflect current conditions. As a result, plans and strategies are tools through which management can achieve specific company goals. Chapters Six through Ten discuss the nature of these methods in detail.

Policies guiding planning and strategy formulation are much less flexible than the methods. For example, the guideline for growth in XYZ, Inc. is a 5% annual increase in after-tax earnings developed mostly through internal research. Acquisitions are limited to sup-

[3] Vickers, Sir Geoffrey, *The Art of Judgment: A Study of Policy Making*, Chapman and Hall Limited, London; Basic Books, Inc., New York, 1965.

porting the exploitation of products and services resulting from company research. This policy could be in effect for several years, and a change would occur only in the absence of success. Even with disappointing results, executive management and/or the board of directors could decide that management methods are causing the problem rather than the policy, and that plans and strategies are not taking full advantage of market opportunities during the years involved.

Business Terms and Policy

Two conclusions can be drawn from this discussion on the relationship of policy to philosophies, goals, plans, and strategies.

1. There is a progression from the general to the specific as one goes from philosophies to methods, and in the same order, another progression from very infrequent change to complete flexibility. Figure 3—4 shows the relationships.
2. Usage and meaning of business terms varies widely from company to company, and can even confuse communications from division to division.

Figure 3—4. Analogy of the Terms

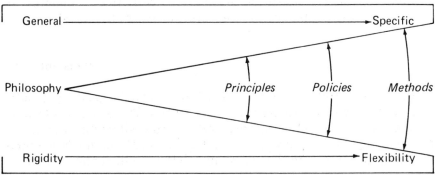

If a manager understands that there is a possibility that he or she and another executive are using the same words and thinking of a different meaning, or different words intending the same meaning, the incidence of conflict and confusion will be reduced.

To summarize, policies originate with philosophies and principles that express the reasons for a company's existence. They provide guidelines and constraints for day-to-day operations, and change when business conditions change sufficiently to adjust policies so that philosophies and principles can be maintained. The latitude of discretion in decision making is confined by these guidelines and, consequently, direction is given to company operations.

WRITTEN, VERBAL, AND IMPLIED POLICIES

The laws of a country are carefully worded, passed by governing bodies after considerable debate, and are published so that every citizen can adhere to the law. Despite this attention to detail, judges interpret laws differently. If this possibility exists in government, think of the variety of interpretations that may be given to business policy.

To minimize the incidence of verbal and implied policies conflicting with written policies, companies usually accumulate in a single book hundreds of guidelines for decision making originating throughout the firm. The keeper of this manual, who is frequently the corporate secretary, monitors additions and deletions to be certain they are consistent with: (1) each other; (2) philosophies and principles, and (3) laws and regulations. Sometimes the monitoring function involves a committee of executives and legal counsel.

The primary advantage of written policies is that they are tangible references for decision making. Access to these references is, therefore, necessary, and the keeper of the policy manual must provide copies to key executives. When distribution should be restricted, such as guidelines on allocation of after-tax profits, volumes can be made up to meet the needs of specific components of the organization.

Verbal and Implied Policies

Intangible guidelines can have both negative and positive effects. They are difficult to communicate. Also leadership, or lack of it, is reflected in unwritten policies. When top management is creative, dynamic, competent, and honest, personnel are inspired. It is better if the rules for guiding operations such as pricing and product development, or those on conduct such as coordination and ethical behavior, are written. However, they can be derived from example.

Smaller companies rarely have a formal policy manual. The scope of operations is reduced, and employees know what is acceptable and what is not. Easy access to top executives makes formalizing the guidelines unnecessary. In large corporations they are needed because layers of the organization separate the individual setting policy and the person running one of the affected departments.

In the absence of written policies, tradition guides many businesses. Decisions are made in the manner they were made in previous years. While there is slow adjustment to new conditions, tradition can be dangerous in a dynamic environment where at one extreme, decentralized authority may be required or, at the other extreme, the chief executive officer must decide. Some experts feel that an organization can respond to changes in the business environment faster when not bound by a manual that states the applicable policy.

However, most executives think it is better to work within a policy framework. They feel that the order resulting from this approach is more beneficial than the fluid atmosphere of having only verbal and implied policies.

Communicating Policies

An employee must know that a policy exists in order to adhere to it. A manual is a basic way to accomplish this objective. Content can be selectively controlled by various combinations of policies being distributed to the appropriate components of the organization. However, this formal approach rarely fulfills the need for communicating policies completely.

When no manual exists, or when it is outdated and not a reliable framework for decision making, conscious effort must be made by executive management to inform verbally or by implication from their actions. In this case there is considerable room for misinterpretation or convenient misunderstanding. On the other hand, there is flexibility in not being bound to written guidelines. Occasionally a manager can seize an opportunity that could have been eliminated by a formal policy but does not violate a philosophy or principle. An example would be a production manager at Powerite Tools buying used equipment and making a component very cheaply when the outdated written policy was to buy all components.

Despite a responsibility to maintain an updated policy framework for decision making, top management often finds it difficult to run the business and keep the manual current. Months and years pass before the changes are made, unless there is a system for regularly revising written policies.

It has been stated that defining policy and separating this term from other business terms are difficult tasks for some executives. However, communicating policy to all levels of the organization is sometimes an equal challenge. Realizing that it is important to performance is a basic first step. The concept is portrayed in Figure 3–5.

Figure 3−5. Communicating Policies

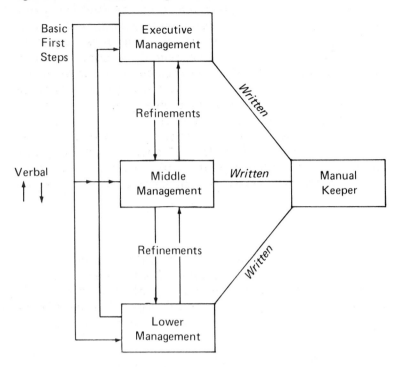

EXTERNAL AND INTERNAL POLICIES

Policies can be divided into two categories, those concerning external matters and those dealing with intracompany affairs. Examples of specific policies were given by function earlier in the chapter. However, it is frequently crucial to have a clear understanding of the who, what, how, when, and why of handling matters involving affairs outside the company. Some examples will clarify the point.

External Matters

Government

Controls over business are increasing. The list of agencies, commissions, and departments probing, monitoring, investigating, auditing, and so on business would fill a chapter, and perhaps a book. The Internal Revenue Service would rank at the top of most lists.

Courses of action to cope with the impact of controls on profits and other company goals are being formulated and revised every day of the year. The facts and opinions presented to government, or discretionary absences of response, are critical. This does not imply deception or unethical practices of any kind. It suggests that disclosures about a company's affairs to any segment of the government must be carefully controlled to avoid lost time and money through misinterpretations leading to investigations, hearings, and so on.

In the competition for investor capital and funds from leaders, the firm must grow and earn increasing after-tax profits. One of the greatest challenges to management in the 1970s will be achieving this basic aim in conjunction with complying with government controls. The assistance of a policy framework will be needed to meet this challenge.

Community

Consumerism and social responsibility, and their relationship to company goals, were mentioned in Chapter Two. Methods for implementing programs with the most beneficial effect on these goals were covered in Chapter One. The primary thrust at this point is the critical importance of setting policy on these matters to identify the following:

1. The company's true position on consumerism and social responsibility including the law as one constraint and actual intent as another, rather than platitudes reflecting the net vector of pressure groups.
2. Personnel in the company who are to deal with problems and programs in these two areas affecting the community, either by rank or by function with subsequent identification within the function.

Until recently most companies treated consumerism and social responsibility as a peripheral annoyance that could be handled as occasions arose. This approach has been disastrously expensive for many firms. It is now clear to executive management that plans and strategies for current and future operations must include assessment of the impact on communities affected and suitable courses of action.

The Bank of America, which has suffered boycotts and bombings of its branches, says: "The corporation, by virtue of its own enlightened self-interest, the conscience of its officers, and expectations of the public, has a role to play in solving contemporary ills. Profits are and must continue to be the central concern of any responsible enterprise. . . But in the long pull, nobody can expect to make profits—or have any meaningful use for profits—if our entire society is wracked by tensions."[4] Policies at the Bank of America will guide decision making on allocation of resources to community matters.

Worker Organizations

The most significant point relating to worker organizations is the need for current policies reflecting the most recent developments, not guidelines fashioned by years of tradition. It is true that a fundamental success factor in business is anticipating situations and making decisions that optimize a company's position under those circumstances. However, this is doubly true in dealing with the workforce. Large corporations have staffs charged with the responsibility of counseling top management on policy for organizations representing employees. Medium size and small companies are often caught reacting to labor union strategies without an adequate policy framework.

Foreign Countries and Associations of Countries

Recognition of the responsibility of collective power attained by American business in many countries has been slow to develop. Opportunities have been created for foreign companies because some members of management have been overly aggressive in pursuing profit objectives or have not adopted methods reflecting customs and attitudes within the country. Also, most countries fear the political and military power of the United States and resist what some call the "American tidal wave."

Recognizing these facts and acknowledging attractive foreign markets, it is necessary for executive management to set policy, sometimes prudently restricted to verbal guidelines, in areas such as:

1. Joint ventures, types of partners, and percentage ownership requirements.
2. Economic development and community posture within the host country, including reinvestment of locally generated funds.
3. Personnel contacting government authorities, officially or unofficially, and the preparation expected by executive management in language capacity and knowledge of the national mentality.[5]
4. Definition of the expected composition of nationalities in top management, employment of nationals for management positions, and development of these employees in order for them to advance within the organization.

[4] "Business Week's Manual for Social Action," *Business Week.* May 20, 1974, p. 104.
[5] Excerpt from *The Silent Language*, copyright © 1959 by Edward T. Hall. Used by permission of Doubleday & Company, Inc.

Policies on these matters will provide a framework for operating decisions that have a higher probability of being correct. Companies recognize that the specifics of these guidelines will come, in part, from experience. It could mean learning the hard way and, in part, from investigation and analysis in advance of initiating or expanding multinational operations.

Other Outside Influences

Policies involving competitors, suppliers (for example, reciprocity), lenders, and similar influences on decision making are usually clearly defined or generally understood by employees. What is not clear is the policy toward shareholders needed by professional management.

Shareholders are the owners, and they are theoretically represented by the board of directors. In the majority of today's corporations shareholders are individuals and organizations that regularly change their investment portfolio. They have no special loyalties and could very possibly hold the stock of competitors.

Under these circumstances, executive management must have guidelines on what information can be exposed to shareholders. In addition to Securities and Exchange Commission regulations, a company has an obligation to inform shareholders about factors that could affect their desire to remain owners. Reasons for ownership encompass a wide variety of motivations. Therefore, each company has the difficult task of identifying executive management's position on policies and obtaining approval of the board of directors. Figure 3–6 identifies groups for which external policies are created.

Intracompany Affairs

The most significant thing about internal policy is the changes taking place within most corporations. Professional management is probing the reasons for traditional policy to find better ways. The issues are:

1. A broad view of the corporation's basis of existence, which emphasizes the profit motive, but also places importance on the effect of decisions on the community and consumer.
2. The content of each job to gain optimum individual performance and the organizing of work to achieve maximum collective efficiency while allowing for human needs on and from the job.
3. Any overall life style for employees, particularly managers,

Figure 3-6. External Policies

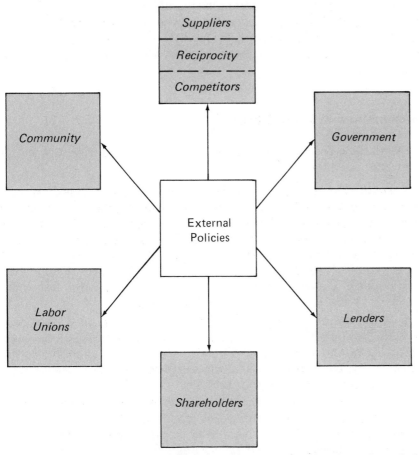

that offers a balance between the demands of work and those of the family in order to attract better personnel.

Behind these issues is a change in attitude by young members of management. The company is a means to an end, not the end to which: (1) you give unanswering loyalty, and (2) your performance is measured not only by competence but by an unquestioning attitude toward company policy. When this development was perceived in the late 1960s, executive management first interpreted it as a rebellion against the demanding life style of business. In the 1970s it has become clear that all three points just given are involved.

Policy, therefore, is being set by professionals who recognize that the company must sustain itself through profits, but it must also be the means through which men and women may lead constructive lives. The acceptance of social responsibility by these executives is tempering decisions because they recognize more and more that they themselves are part of the communities affected by internal policy. These new attitudes by management on the reason for corporate existence are changing guidelines for capital allocation, deployment of personnel, management practices, product lines, and other areas of decision making.

Basic Considerations in Internal Policy

Listed here are the basic considerations involved in setting policy on internal matters.

1. *Legal.* The policies must be within the law. Government investigation and surveillance of business, social programs involving company bookkeeping and payments, and enforcement of regulations on the ecology, minorities, taxation, and so on necessitate a policy framework that assists the company in avoiding litigation, fines and time consuming hearings. Regulations are getting complex and often require special expertise. Management has a responsibility to comply with laws at the local, state, and federal levels.

2. *Philosophies, Principles, and Purpose.* Policies must be consistent with these standards that become almost as binding on management as laws and regulations. Guidelines on ethics, integrity, social responsibility, consumerism, and similar factors involve less management discretion than operating policies.

3. *Operations.* Policies must be up to date and reflect current business conditions. While still being applicable for years instead of months, their longevity is less than those stemming from laws, regulations, philosophies, and principles.

4. *Definition of Terms.* Policies must use terms that mean the same thing to everyone in the organization. Simplicity is important. Most companies have a section at the beginning of the policy manual to clarify the definition of words commonly used in the business.

5. *Authority.* Policies must be set at the proper level in the organization. People taking such actions should not be left to chance. A system must be established to assure that the proper managers are involved, and approvals are being given at the organizational level required.

6. *Monitoring Compliance and Effectiveness.* Policies must have a mechanism to be certain that their purpose as a framework for improving company performance is achieved.

Performance will suffer both if the six considerations are not applied or they are not practical. Prosecution and serious losses can result. Consequently, executive management must establish a continuing means of keeping policies current and in use.

SUMMARY

A policy is a statement, verbal, written, or implied, of those principles and rules that are set by executive leadership as guidelines and constraints for the organization's thought and action. Their purpose is to enable management to relate properly the organization's work to its objectives.

Policy is set by management at various levels in the firm, the importance of the policy depending on the individual's level in the organization. Some involve charting a course for future operations while, at the other extreme, they pertain to routine business. Directives, orders, procedures, and work rules are not policies and refer to matters less important than achieving company objectives.

Business terms such as company philosophy, creed, principles, doctrines, and purpose involve broad statements intended to be applicable under a wide range of conditions over a period of several years. A goal or objective is an end to be achieved, a future condition or result to be accomplished in carrying out an activity. However, they are not policies.

Written policies are usually contained in a manual administered by an officer such as the corporate secretary, and they provide tangible references for decision making. It is essential that these guidelines are made available to members of management through selective distribution. Verbal or implied policies reflect tradition and the degree of leadership by top management. Communicating the guidelines and constraints not contained in the manual could be important to realizing company potential.

External policies concern government, the community, worker organizations, foreign countries, suppliers, and lenders. Professional management defines policy relating to shareholder affairs as carefully as external organizations because of the ease with which an investor can switch allegience.

Policy pertaining to intracompany affairs is going through change. The profit motive is being tempered by concern about the consumer and social responsibility. Also, employees want contentment in work that is challenging, not routine, and are less inclined to follow company orders that affect living a full life. They resist extensive commuting, transfers, business travel, long work weeks, and company entertainment.

Basic considerations in setting policy involve the constraints of laws and regulations, and philosophies, principles, and purpose. Policies affecting operations must reflect business conditions and change more frequently than those covering constraints. Other considerations include definition of terms, clarifying who has the authority to set policy, and monitoring for use and practicality.

DISCUSSION QUESTIONS

1. Who sets policy? Identify organizational levels and reasons for establishing guidelines at various levels. What limits a manager's capacity to make decisions on policies?
2. Why is it so important to use correct terminology in business? Can you think of specific examples where difficulties could arise as a result of carelessness?
3. To what degree do philosophies, policies, goals, plans, and strategies change over time?
4. Give examples of verbal and implied policies. Are they different than written policies? If so, in what way? Are communications problems involved?
5. Should managers be held strictly to existing company policies or should they be given leeway where they see fit? Under what conditions, if any, is it justifiable for a manager to go contrary to company policy?
6. What are the main determinants of external and internal policy? Do you see possibilities for the need to keep policies confidential from portions of the organization, the public or other outside parties?
7. If a company is already in the state of change, is it a good idea to change policies to any great extent?

SUGGESTED READINGS AND BIBLIOGRAPHY

Barton, Richard F. "Reality and Business Policy Decisions," *Academy of Management Journal.* June, 1966.

Baynton, Robert E. "Policies of the Successful Manager," *California Management Review.* Fall, 1970.

Broom, H. N. *Business Policy and Strategic Action; Text, Cases, Management Game.* Prentice-Hall, 1969.

Byrne, Harlan S. "Privately Held Hallmark Regards Philanthropy as Key Company Policy," *The Wall Street Journal*. August 22, 1973, p. 1.

"Freeman: Is Corporate Purpose Fancy Words or Real Direction?" *Industrial Marketing*. July, 1971, pp. 32–33.

Glever, John G. "Management Policy," *Selected Readings in Management*. Richard D. Irwin, 1958.

Higginson, M. Valliant. "Management Policies I — Their Development as Corporate Guides," American Management Association Research Study, 76. 1966.

Jones, Don E. "The Employee Handbook," *Personnel Journal*. February, 1973.

"Policies and Related Documents Defining Common Purposes," *GE Organization and Policy Guide*. April 8, 1959.

Riclefs, Roger. "Young Managers Today Less Eager to Adapt, So Firms Alter Policies," *The Wall Street Journal*. May 16, 1973.

Ulman, Neil. "Giving Employees a Say in Firms' Management Seen Gaining in Europe," *The Wall Street Journal*. February 23, 1973, p. 1.

Urwich, Lyndall F. "The Problem of Management Semantics," *California Management Review*. Spring, 1960.

Ziegler, Raymond J. *Business Policies and Decision Making*. Appleton, 1966.

Case: Trenton Industries, Inc.

The case identifies some of the practical motivations for having formal policies. It also reveals problems that can arise when guidelines are written down. Most important, the Trenton case further clarifies the nature and purpose of policies.

Trenton Industries, Inc., manufactures farm implements with a universal hitch that will adapt to any tractor or other heavy duty vehicle such as a four-wheel drive jeep. The firm's reputation is based on having "just the right equipment for our region." Also, the cutting edges of implements may be harder or the bins oversized. In some cases Trenton implements are identical to those of competition but still outsell the others. Distributor information confirms fewer quality problems with Trenton products.

The business had not grown significantly in recent years until the Wichita expansion in 1974, although profits have been improving with the exception of 1970. In that year Tren-ton carried distributors who were in trouble financially due to slow payments from customers. Prices for its products have been slightly higher than the competition, and they have been adjusted to increased costs approximately every other year. The firm has always been very careful to justify increases and spends time and money to inform distributors and their customers about the reasons. As a result, the Omaha and Wichita plants are considered a prime source of implements for farming operations within a 200-mile radius of each location.

The Trenton family always lived very well from the business, owning 82% of outstanding shares, "but never forgot the people who bought

	$ Million					$ Million
	1975	1974	1973	1972	1971	1970
Sales	5.725	4.355	3.860	3.370	3.675	3.140
Profits after Taxes	.525	.310	.340	.321	.280	.065
Cash or "Liquid" Investments	.155	.430	1.745	1.515	1.350	1.210

their gadgets." The remaining 18% of the shares are owned by important distributors and regional bankers. Other distributors and suppliers have options, but Trenton Industries had been an unattractive investment until the recent expansion. It always paid a low dividend and had not been considered a growth stock. Dividends have not been increased despite steady earnings because of the tax impact on the Trentons and recent concern about meeting repayment obligations on a medium-term loan.

Some company statistics are given above.

EXPANSION OF OPERATIONS

In 1974 the company invested most of what was regarded as excess cash ($1.745 million) accumulated by Trenton over the years. Expansion, acquisition, and merger possibilities were explored by the company in 1972−73. The sharp increase in demand for farm implements in 1973 influenced top management to open a new plant for "Doing more and better what we know best how to do." The specifics of the commitment approved at the Board meeting on September 29, 1973, are given below.

	$Million	
Total Investment	Equity Commitment	Loans*
2.975	1.575	1.400

$ Million 1974		1975		$ Million 1976−78	
Sales	Earnings	Sales	Earnings	Sales−Avg.	Earnings
.345 (Start-up)	(.085) (Start-up)	1.750	.145	3.675	.340

* Loans were arranged in Omaha through two banks that had handled Trenton Industries accounts for decades. The schedule for interest and repayment is as follows:

	Takedown	12/31/75	12/31/76	12/31/77	12/31/78
Principle		$350,000	$350,000	$350,000	$350,000
Interest 9%	May 15, 1974	204,750	94,500	63,000	31,500

The new facility is on the main line of the Atcheson, Topeka, and Santa Fe Railway near Goddard, Kansas on the outskirts of Wichita. The site was chosen because of an ideally suitable building recently abandoned by a small plane manufacturer, which accelerated market entry and saved $555,000 in capital costs.

Performance in the first year of expansion, 1974, was slightly better than predicted. Sales reached $405,000, and contribution to earnings after taxes as a loss of $45,000. The next year was also slightly better than the forecast. In 1975 sales were $1.760 million, but profits reached $165,000.

Executive management and the entire Trenton organization were responding to some important changes in the mid-1970s. The impetus for these changes came from Homer Strausfelder Trenton VI, a recent Stanford University M.B.A. and a veteran of 12 years of summers and vacations at all levels in the business. In fact, Hank Trenton is the first member of the family to work as a laborer on the line since his great grandfather started the Trenton factory.

PERSPECTIVE ON THE PROBLEMS

As a teenager in the early 1960s Hank Trenton sensed that the business was "operating in a daze." He thought that something needed to be done but had no idea about the steps to take. His ideas started to form at the University of Nebraska while majoring in agricultural administration. The most important contributions made by Hank's two years in Palo Alto, California in addition to management techniques were: (1) greater confidence that his business judgment is sound; (2) maturity developed from additional age, exposure to excellent talent, and travel away from Omaha, and (3) technical knowledge resulting from research among agribusiness companies in the Far West and exchanges with experts at the University of California at Davis.

Hank Trenton returned to Omaha in May 1973 after four years of additional experience with International Harvester. He was made vice president of corporate development when joining Trenton Industries at the age of 28.

His initial assignment at Trenton Industries was solving the problems of accumulated cash, no growth, and losses of potentially competent personnel in management. This led to several steps including the elimination of several diversification alternatives and the decision to expand in farm implements. Within a few months other recommendations to the family controlled board indicated that Trenton Industries had a strong leader the family had not provided for decades.

Organizational Changes

The new plant presented an opportunity to redesign the management structure. The organization in Figure 3C—1 was prepared by Hank

Figure 3C–1. Trenton Industries' Organization

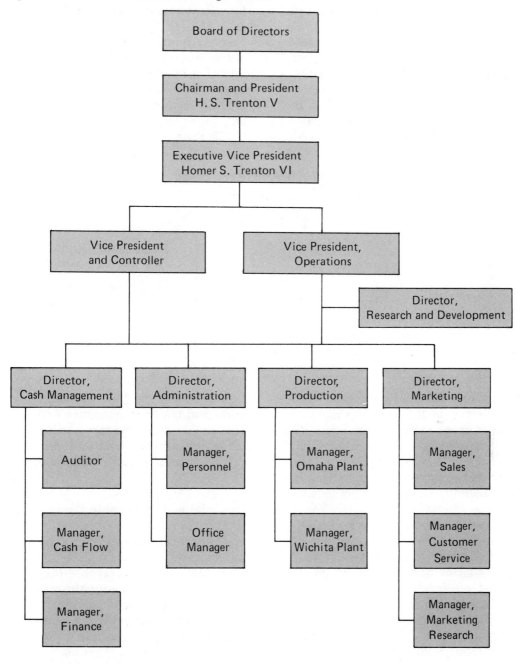

Trenton with the assistance of one of his Stanford professors. H. S.

Trenton V reluctantly agreed to the changes including early retirements of brothers and cousins, terminations, and promotions of younger outsiders.

The concept was to create cost centers at each plant. To avoid competition in marketing Trenton products from two plant locations in overlapping market areas shown in Figure 3C–2, separate sales managers were not created for the two

ton for experience but left because they thought they were "blocked off" from the top by members of the Trenton family. Removal of three older Trenton brothers and termination of a cousin that "visited the office only to collect his paycheck" created excitement amongst middle and lower management.

The new organization retained

Figure 3C–2. Marketing Deployment

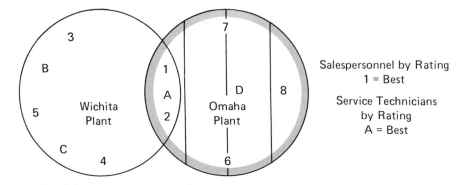

Salespersonnel by Rating
1 = Best

Service Technicians
by Rating
A = Best

territories. The best personnel were transferred to the overlapping market area to minimize the possibility of confusion on orders. Customer-oriented service, which built the Trenton reputation, was increased by establishing a senior position to manage this operation. Previously the field sales representative handled the service calls in the area, but expanded production and realignment of territories necessitated an improved approach.

In addition to greater incentives for efficiency, the new structure created opportunities for young managers with production, marketing, or other talent. Up to the time the changes became effective on July 1, 1974, people with talent joined Tren-

experience in the key functional areas and the chief executive officer. This meant that Trenton was not launching a major expansion without sufficient managerial competence.

Financial and Ownership Development

The Wichita expansion solved the short-term problem of accumulated cash. It is conceivable that addition of a third geographic area in the United States and an idea for Darwin, Australia would consume cash generated in the late 1970s. However, eventually Trenton Industries would be earning a high level of after-tax profits that would need distribution to shareholders. As long as the Trentons controlled 82% of the common stock the board preference would be to avoid dividends.

This complication arose in 1974 when an exchange of shares was discussed with a small, specialized farm implement producer within the existing marketing area. The owner was 66 years old and anxious to sell, but he needed an income from the assets gained from disposing of his company. Also, it was not clear what the actual value of Trenton stock would be if he sold it. Hank Trenton designed an installment payment plan for the 1974–78 period, which provided the needed income plus a note for the remainder, payable in full on June 30, 1979. While this small acquisition was completed, it pointed out the need to restructure ownership.

After consultation with tax experts and discussing the plan with the Internal Revenue Service, Hank Trenton presented the following proposal to the board of directors after obtaining approval from his father:

1. The 820 shares owned by the Trenton family out of 1,000 shares outstanding would be exchanged on a hundred-for-one basis. 82,000 shares of a new issue of 4% voting cumulative preferred stock would be issued to Trenton family members. This permits retention of control, a known income that maximizes tax benefits, and flexibility in paying dividends to other shareholders.
2. A new common stock would be issued. 80,000 shares would be authorized which totals 49% of voting stock (82,000 voting, cumulative preferred shares and 80,000 common shares make up the voting stock).

The dividend on these shares would reflect growth and after-tax profits. It would be possible to pay a substantial dividend to the shareholders and have adequate cash for expansion plans since a lower rate is being distributed to the Trentons.

3. Owners of the 180 shares not within the family would exchange their certificates for the new common stock on the basis of a hundred for one. This would use 18,000 of the 80,000 shares and permit the company to expand through sales of stock to other outside investors or exchanges of shares in acquisitions.

The proposal received unanimous approval by the board[1], and the existing shareholders were delighted with the prospects of sharp increases in both dividends and share value. Also, the actual appreciation would be identified periodically when a transaction with an outside party was completed. Eventual listing on a stock exchange was discussed at the September 27 board meeting.

POLICY AT TRENTON INDUSTRIES

Policy at Trenton had been established through decades of tradition and verbal communications on guide-

[1] The Board of Directors' composition in 1974 was H. S. Trenton V as chairman, three Trenton family members who are successful in other small Omaha businesses, and three industrialists from major grain companies.

lines. Nothing had been written. It had never been necessary, or even desirable. However, in 1974 three situations motivated formalizing policy at Trenton.

1. Discussions with newly appointed managers indicated that they were uncertain about authority to set policy in their new jobs because of the historical practice of a family member making such decisions. This was creating two factions, one taking initiative on the assumption they would be backed by Hank Trenton, and the other taking a laissez-faire position. Friction was building.
2. Hank Trenton wanted clear guidelines on growth objectives, plowback of cash, leverage limits, and distributions to shareholders.
3. Marketing needed policies on service, guarantees and company paid repairs, particularly in the new sales territories where customers had no experience with Trenton and would want formal understanding, on liability in addition to verbalized good will.

It was clear at the close of 1974 that Trenton Industries was at a major turning point and that a policy framework was needed for the company to realize the opportunities foreseen by Hank Trenton. During January 2–4, 1975, he assembled a management team composed of himself as executive vice president, the vice president of administration and controller (a 36 year old, very competent and respected Trenton), and the vice president of operations (a 48 year old outsider who had been promoted from manager of the

Omaha plant). He rented a conference room at the Mid-America Motel in Omaha and secluded the group away from telephones to draft the company's first policy manual.

The objective was to establish a broad framework of policies into which upper management, and others to whom they delegate responsibilities, could add specifics needed to manage efficiently.

Outline of the Manual

Given here is the outline prepared by the team in the first morning as a basis for subsequent discussion and writing.

1. Introduction: Purpose
   Company Philosophy
   Distribution (Two Classes of Manual — First, full disclosure of all policies, called the executive manual, for distribution to top management including directors. Second, limited disclosure for managers reporting to directors or equivalent, and selected employees at lower levels.)
2. Definition of Terms: General Business Terms
   Industry Terms
   Company Terms Important to Common Understanding.
3. Top-Level Policy Component:
   Board of Directors: Compensation Packages, Incentive Programs, and Bonuses for Management
   Disposition of Assets including Acquistions, Sales, and Joint Ventures.
   Dividends to Shareholders
   Loans and Leverage
   Executive Management: Allocation

of Capital Proposals (General
Portions for Plowback, Re-
serves, and Social Issues)
Developmental Programs for
Management Personnel
Goals for Rate of Annual
Growth in After-Tax Profits
Guidelines for Long Range
Planning and Strategy Includ-
ing Time and Expenses
Diverted to Community
Responsibilities
Legal and Taxation Counsel
Sources of Growth (Ac-
quisitions, Diversification,
Internal Development,
Mergers, Foreign
Operations, and Spin-offs)
Unions and Worker Represen-
tation
4. Operations Management Com-
ponent
Marketing: Sales Forecast for
Planning
Pricing Guidelines Including
Discounts
Service and Guarantees (Gen-
eral and/or Specific, such as
Equipment Operating
Manuals)
Distribution Methods
Customer Relations (Entertain-
ment, Paid Plant Visits, and
so on)
Competitor Relations
Advertising and Promotions
Production: Quality Control (Relate
to Service and Guarantee)
Cost control (Unit Cost Relation-
ship to Price)
Production Planning (Relation-
ship to Forecast)
Investment in Facilities and
Maintenance
Purchasing Procedures

Research and Development
Make or Buy
Personnel: Labor Union Negoti-
ations
Personnel Evaluation and Re-
cord Systems
Employee Training Procedures
Employee Promotion and Ter-
mination Procedures
Employee Screening and
Selection
Vacations, Bonuses and
Compensation Ranges,
and Pension Program
Workforce Benefits (Contract
Minimums and Worker
Morale)
Money Management: Interest
Earned on Cash
Interest Paid on Loans
Working Capital Minimums
Financial Condition Standards
Receivables and Bad Debts
Payables (Discount, Full Period
and Approvals)

The three executives worked on
principles and constraints that would
act as guidelines or rules for each
area. Additions and regrouping
changed Hank Trenton's outline. By
noon on Saturday they had a pile of
handwritten policies in the order
agreed after a series of exchanges.
Hank's secretary was ready on Monday morning to work on a finished
draft. She took the precaution of
making only one original, thereby
avoiding carbon copies getting into
the wrong hands. By Wednesday the
last page was typed and photocopies
were made for the two vice
presidents.

The next step was a meeting on
Saturday, January 11, in the same

conference room to polish the rough draft. They were amazed at some of the platitudes and "dribble" they had written in some policy areas. Originally they had thought the morning would be sufficient, but at 5:30 p.m. they were only through two-thirds of the material. The three agreed to recess until Sunday morning and "let their wives handle the church going." The secretary produced another draft by Tuesday, and on Saturday, January 18, agreement was reached on the preliminary draft of a policy manual.

The plan for instituting the policies and distributing the manual was:

1. Approval of the chief executive officer, Hank's father, on the material in the preliminary draft and obtain his agreement on the following steps.
2. Exposure of the content to the next level of management, those with the title of director, to obtain their suggestions and comments.
3. Board of director approval for the policies.
4. Review of the operations management manual with subordinates of the directors to refine the content.
5. Preparation and distribution of the final version to appropriate personnel. The executive version would be placed in gold binders, and green binders would be used for the operations manual.

A Snag in the Plan

The chairman and president, H. S. Trenton, V, was given the original of the manual on January 23, 1975.

The next day, a Friday, he told Hank Trenton that he had no decision. The explanation given for no immediate decision was the magnitude of interrelated points in the policies.

In reality he thought that Hank was moving too fast in reorganizing and expanding, and written policies were a sign that Trenton needed a consolidation period. The senior Trenton had arranged a meeting with the three other Trentons on the board for an informal discussion Saturday morning with the intention of gaining support for the rejection. He had been prepared for prodding by Hank for immediate approval. Instead, Hank's reaction was, "It's important, and I think you should take the weekend to think about specifics. It would be difficult to operate the company without the manual."

The points causing concern at the Saturday meeting, in addition to the speed of changes at Trenton Industries were:

1. Factions and politics developing after the reorganization.
2. Delegation of authority to management to choose the course of future growth in the policy draft proposed for approval.
3. The transfer of power away from H. S. Trenton V to Hank's management team.

However, the three other Trentons agreed that the policies might provide solutions to their problems rather than aggravate them. A compromise was reached at the end of the discussion.

On Monday morning H. S. Trenton V proposed testing the two

manuals throughout 1975 for their practicality and positive impact on the firm. The entire content would be "on trial." Revisions would be made in a year, if the written policies were helping, and that version would go to the board in early 1976.

Furthermore, the annual revision process would continue in future years to assure that policies properly reflected the needs of the company.

Hank Trenton felt his father was stalling, but he had given considerable thought to possible reactions and counteractions over the weekend. Consequently, he asked if they could proceed to obtain the refinements that would result from exposure to the remainder of management stated in Steps 2 and 4 of the plan to implement formal policies. Hank argued there could be no fair "trial" without this type of procedure.

It was agreed that contributions to policy by personnel down to the level of those reporting to directors would take place on schedule. No special printing or manuals would be used. All copies would be marked "draft." Formal assessment would take place in the week between Christmas and New Years Day. Upper management would participate at that time, and they would be expected to have feedback from subordinates. At that time H. S. Trenton V would preside at the meetings.

The three-man management team, which had prepared the draft read by the senior Trenton, met immediately after Hank left his father's office. Plans were formulated for meetings with the directors level of

management and for obtaining refinements from the director's subordinates. While disappointed that their work did not receive immediate endorsement, Hank said they could consider the reevaluation in December as a formality.

STUDENT PROBLEMS

1. Do you agree with the senior Trenton's approach plan for introducing written policy or would you have gone ahead with Hank's proposal?
2. Is it necessary to obtain the reactions of all members of management, or would you restrict the evaluation process to upper management?
3. Would it be feasible to operate an expanding Trenton Industries without written policies contrary to Hank's position? Are the policy areas listed in the outline as the basis of detailed guidelines sufficient? Can you think of possible omissions?
4. Comment on Hank Trenton's approach in seeking approval from his father. How would you improve it? Is reevaluating in December really only a formality?
5. Speculate about the developments behind the other reasons for concern cited by the Trentons, other than Hank moving too fast and the need for consolidation. Is a power-play evolving that would force out H.S. Trenton V?

Organizational Design for Executive Management

Major influences on organizational design are identified including recent business developments. Factors in design are summarized, and the impact of centralization and decentralization is discussed. When changes in the organization are required, methods to optimize under resulting conditions are outlined. The chapter takes the position that the organizational structure of a company must be tuned to fit the personnel in charge and the operating conditions foreseen for the months ahead.

4

The organization of people into formal relationships within a firm and the assignment of specific responsibilities to each position, have the objective of providing structure for conducting business in an orderly and efficient manner. This structure is extremely important to executive management because it can be a source of both problems and solutions in achieving company goals.

Basic configurations of the structure are reviewed briefly in this chapter. However, the primary purpose is to examine fundamentals affecting organizational design and the means of improving employee performance as a result of different designs.

MAJOR INFLUENCES AFFECTING THE DESIGN

The design of organizations is the synergistic sum of four important influences on decision makers conceiving and approving the concepts. *First*, their assigned responsibilities in the company direct thinking toward efficiency and the practical relationships that achieve the best performance. *Second*, their personal needs for power and status affect the direction and organizational value of this thinking. *Third*, decision makers' assessment of talent in the company will influence executive management in the choice of specific designs. *Fourth*, outside parties, particularly those with a financial stake in the business, play a role in choosing the structure.

There is a common characteristic in each of the four influences —*lack of preciseness* possible in the interpretation of responsibilities, personal needs, available talent, and the impact of outside parties by individual executives. Opinions can vary substantially. As a result, competent managers will come to different conclusions from the same facts and opinions.

For example, after considerable discussion and several compromises, top management might design an organization that is the best from their perspective. A consulting firm specializing in such matters might choose an entirely different approach. The optimal design might be a third concept because of limited knowledge of talent in the firm by the consultants and misinterpretation of outside influences, such as major shareholders and competitors, by management.

It can be seen that the intangible nature of the four influences leads to difficulties in judging which design is best. Figure 4–1 illustrates the need to have the net vector of these influences directed toward the optimal structure for the company rather than the one best suited to executives or outside groups with special interests.

Figure 4–1. The Net Vector of Organizational Design

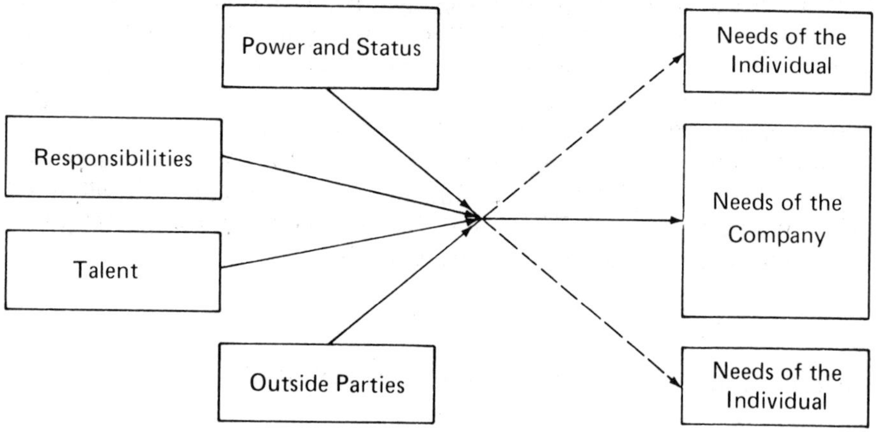

Major Developments

Expanded use of the *computer* is slowly changing the work of some components in the organization and the names of some departments. The revolution expected in the 1960s as a result of computer developments did not occur. However, the pace of change is quickening because of global competition in most industries and the critical need for efficiency.

The *multinational corporation*, with operations in several countries, has led to new concepts of how to link divisions, subsidiaries, and joint ventures separated by long distances. Improved capability to communicate by telephone, telex, and personal visits as a result of technological advances has motivated top management to reconsider the organizational designs used in the past which emphasized geographic configurations.

Diversification has had an impact similar to the multinational corporation. Aggressive growth programs pressured organizations to the point where doing more of what was done in the past was not adequate. Decentralization of responsibilities to groups that have several divisions and wholly or partly owned subsidiaries have created, for example, an executive management layer with enormous power beneath the traditional executive management at the top.

Technological advances, rises in the cost of energy, problems of shortages and inflation in the 1970s, and intensive competition, have acted as stimuli for probing existing organizational designs for efficiency producing changes. Even the concept of a design intended to last several years is being dropped in many major firms in favor of an evolving structure of relationships that best fits plans and strategies for specific future periods.

REVIEW OF TERMS AND CONCEPTS

Before discussing specifics, let us define terms and concepts that apply to organizational design.

ALIGNMENT OF THE STRUCTURE Departments divided by type of customer (consumer, government, industrial, et cetera), functions (see definition), geography (western region, European operations, et cetera), process (heat treatment, glazing, et cetera), or products (plastics, fibers, et cetera). Normally a company uses more than one of the possibilities in combination such as a marketing department divided into geographic regions, and regions divided into types of customers.

CHAIN OF COMMAND The formal series of reporting relationships between an executive and a specific position in the organization such as an accountant, sales representative or supervisor. This normally assumes that an individual reports to only one person.

DEPARTMENTALIZATION The division of work in a company into separate areas of authority and responsibility with the objective of improving performance through well-defined, reasonable assignments and more efficient supervision. This division creates the structure of the organization, and is interrelated with span of control and specialization.

FAYOL'S BRIDGE The authorization of a subordinate to contact peers in other departments on a regular basis without obtaining approval from a superior each time a need arises.

FUNCTIONS The basic departments in a business carrying out responsibilities in accounting, finance, marketing, production, and personnel.

LINE Positions directly involved in the making and selling of goods or services. This book includes cash management as a line position. Executive management charged with the responsibility for performance of the company or divisions and subsidiaries are line personnel.

SPAN OF CONTROL The amount of work assigned to a single supervisor usually stated in numbers of employees. This allocation of work is interrelated with departmentalization, and decides the layers in the organizational design.

SPECIALIZATION OF WORK The division of work into jobs with specific functions which could subsequently be grouped into departments. This basic concept is interrelated with departmentalization and span of control in designing the structure.

STAFF Positions that develop employees, good will, ideas, information, new products, and recommendations to support line operations.

THEORY X Douglas McGregor's impressions of employee attitude and characteristics which strongly influenced classical organizational theory; (1) Employees dislike their jobs and will resort to secretive and disruptive practices to avoid work. (2) To achieve company goals, most employees must be coerced, controlled, and threatened. (3) Most employees desire a formal supervisor and will avoid assuming responsibility whenever possible. (4) Job security is the primary factor motivating employees.

THEORY Y Behavioralists' impressions of employee attitude and characteristics which influence current organizational theory: (1) Employees do not inherently dislike work and welcome job challenges. (2) Employees do not wish to be rigidly controlled, and will exercise self-control in carrying out well defined assignments. (3) Under most conditions employees will accept responsibility, and many will seek greater responsibility as a means of advancing within the organization. (4) Security is important but social needs, esteem of others, and the desire to fulfill one's potential are also important.

PRIMARY FACTORS IN ORGANIZATIONAL DESIGN

The general objective of a formal organization has been stated as providing a structure for conducting business in an orderly and efficient manner. More specifically, fulfilling assigned responsibilities in the vast majority of American companies depends on the division of manageable amounts of work into departments and jobs. This logical and simple fact is one aspect of Figure 4−2, which schematically illustrates the necessity of delegating authority to others in order to cope effectively with a complex business environment.

Factors in organizational design are discussed here and include: (1) degrees of structure; (2) committees; (3) profit and cost centers; (4) staff departments; (5) job satisfaction, and (6) size and complexity. The primary emphasis in these sections is on communications and flow of information in order to make good decisions.

Figure 4−2. Communications within the Dimensions of Complexity and Delegation of Authority

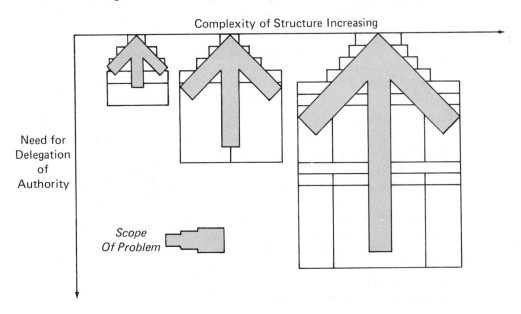

Degrees of Structure

As companies grow in size and complexity, a chain of command develops. This means an increasing number of layers in the organization separating executive management from line personnel directly making and selling the products or services and managing cash. It is essential to be informed about day-to-day business in order to make decisions about the future of these operations. This requires two-way flow (up and down). In a course on the principles of management you learn generalities about the communication characteristics of tall highly structured designs with narrow spans of control (few employees reporting to a supervisor) as compared to progressively shorter, wider designs with greater numbers of employees reporting to a supervisor. These characteristics are summarized in Table 4–1 and graphically portrayed by the arrows in Figure 4–2.

Table 4–1. Characteristics of Typical Organizational Designs

Tall	*Flatter*	*Flat*
1. Many organizational layers between top and lower management 2. Centralized authority 3. Vertical communication a potential problem 4. Narrow spans of control 5. Traditional status symbols and formality	1. Fewer organizational layers between top and lower management 2. More middle management decision making 3. Communication channels less extended 4. Moderate spans of control 5. Fewer entrenched status symbols and greater informality	1. Minimal organizational layers 2. Decentralized authority 3. Horizontal communication a potential problem 4. Broad spans of control 5. Informality and greater individual job satisfaction

Let us examine two extremes for their impact on communications. Most companies lie between the extremes shown in Figure 4–3.

A highly structured organization with neomilitaristic reporting relationships depends of formal channels for flow of information and intelligence. This approach places a fine mesh filter on ideas, "hunches," and suggestions. Fear of impact on one's career discourages individuals from making qualitative contributions to superiors. This rigid framework maintains operational control under conditions that are unchanging. However, in today's dynamic environment use of this design is dangerous because it tends to block communication of important facts and opinions that could seriously

Figure 4-3. Two Extremes of Structure

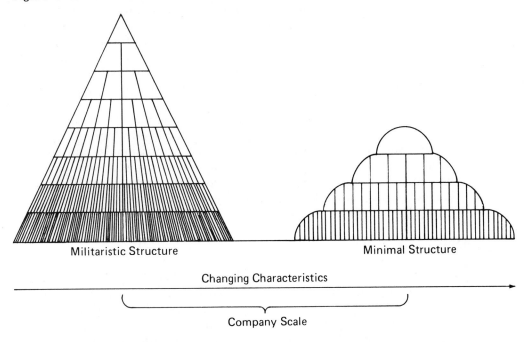

Militaristic Structure   Minimal Structure

Changing Characteristics

Company Scale

affect performance. Usually this approach is (1) a holdover from a design selected by an entrepreneur in past decades, and (2) an indication of stagnancy.

Businesses employing personnel with a high percentage of medium to low skills usually are task-oriented and have the need for comparatively tight control of operations. Communications critical to performance tend to come from the top down. Bottom-up reports are normally statistical and contain little qualitative input that could affect decision making on major items. Under these conditions control is essential rather than free flow of communications, and a highly structured organization is advisable. However, even when employing personnel with a lower level of skills successful management will try to avoid a militaristic atmosphere. They will strive for an environment in which everybody feels they are an important part of the company.

A completely different approach would be an organization with a minimum of layers between top management and the lowest ranked job in the company. Let us assume reporting relationships exist and responsibilities have been defined. Otherwise, there would be chaos, and no formal organization would exist. In this concept an employee is not restricted to obtaining a superior's approval to talk with personnel in other departments and managers with higher rank. An informal atmosphere is created where the free exchange of ideas occurs without concern about impact on careers. In selecting this design, executive management eliminates many status symbols and closed doors. There is a higher probability of employees at all levels feeling that they are contributing to company performance. On the other hand, serious problems can arise in horizontal communications. Executives in upper levels of the structure have increased responsibilities in being certain all of their subordinates are adequately informed.

When a firm is composed of highly skilled professionals, a minimum of layers and an informal structure is advisable. Personnel with lesser skills are administered by the professionals, and control is not as important. Communications flow freely, and individuals can be expected to initiate ideas and information for decisions. Examples are law firms, consulting engineers, and high-technology businesses.

Committees

The old joke about a camel being a horse designed by a *committee* summarizes one view of this entity within a company. On the other hand, a committee is sometimes the only means of assembling talents from different components of the organization. In addition, it can act as a catalyst to induce communications between departments. A paragraph in Cyril O'Donnell's article, "Ground Rules for Using Committees" in the October, 1961 issue of *Management Review* summarizes possible applications.

"Committees can be created within any type of organization to facilitate group communication, to secure group interaction, or to deal with specific problems. They may be used to plan, coordinate, or control the performance of various functions within the organization."

The primary consideration in use of committees is creating sufficient authority to carry out their conclusions and recommendations. Knowledge and expertise is accumulated, but too often the results are turned over to a part of the company with permanent responsibility for the business involved and this component has the authority to ignore the committee. In these situations time and money are wasted.

Another consideration is leadership within the committee. A chairman who is not afraid to take charge is needed for a group of managers in order to establish objectives, assign responsibilities and deadlines, and reach reasonable conclusions. The purpose for creating the committee is undermined when management selects an individual who cannot command the complete respect of the members and who will not initiate action to accomplish specific objectives.

A *task force* is a type of committee formed for a given period to accomplish a specific assignment. Because it is not a standing committee with permanent relationships, executive management has greater flexibility in appointing members. Talents needed for the assignment can be added regardless of position in the company without offending managers at a higher level in the firm. Some personnel try to avoid being placed on a task force because it takes them away from their permanent jobs and could affect their progress within the organization. On the other hand, a unique assignment, which has exposed a young executive to top management, has been the "springboard" for some careers.

Profit and Cost Centers

When authority is delegated to a portion of the organization, executive management must establish a measure for performance. A fully integrated, short-range operating plan is one means of accomplishing this objective. Each component of the organization has a budget to control expenses. The budget for divisions, departments, and other company components become *cost* centers, and these centers become a means of knowing whether organizational components are adhering to the plan.

Profit centers are superior to cost centers in judging performance because conservation of money does not necessarily confirm greater efficiency and profits. Too, there is a detailed sales forecast to identify expectations for cash inflow and money management. The concept is illustrated in Figure 4–4, and the NEM case at the end of this

Figure 4–4. Possible Differences between Profit and Cost Centers

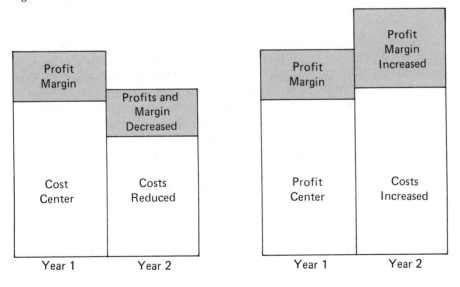

chapter further clarifies some of the advantages in establishing multiple profit centers in a firm.

It can be seen that a company with two or more product lines can design an organization that pinpoints the profitability of each product line. Profit centers can also be created for geographic and customer alignments, as well as combinations of the three. For example, the parent company could set up regional profit centers, and managers within the regions could create profit centers for consumer products and industrial materials.

Sometimes the cost of the design required for profit centers prevents their use. Duplicated departments, diseconomies of a smaller scale, and parallel facilities can undermine the purpose for creating profit centers. However, many companies have avoided this problem by coordinated use of the same departments and facilities through the use of centralized purchasing, production, transportation, and warehousing.

Staff Departments

Consideration must be given to the reporting relationships given to the following departments:

1. Computer administration, program design and analysis, and liaison with other parts of the company.
2. Information systems and linkage with users of the systems.
3. Planning, corporate development, acquisitions, and similar growth-oriented departments.
4. Special functions such as legal, public and shareholder relations, environmental affairs, and property administration.

The purpose of staff departments, as defined in this chapter, is to develop employees, good will, ideas, information, new products, and recommendations to support decision making by personnel in line positions. Company money and time are wasted if employees with these responsibilities are organizationally blocked from carrying out the work. Some examples will illustrate the potential problem.

The manager of the computer department reports to the controller. The manager's primary function is getting out the payroll, invoices, and reports on the status of receivables. A current assignment is to design a program that moniters payables and maximizes use of cash by not paying early and obtaining full discounts if justified by alternative uses of cash. Parallel to this situation, the company's information system is antiquated. No use is made of microfilm or other methods of storing facts and opinions that could utilize the computer.

Modern concepts for computerized applications in operational control and strategic decision making are not even considered. As long as computer operations are in the controller's office, it is probable that use of the computer will be limited to aspects of cash management rather than expansion into assisting executive management and other company functions.

Consider the environmental relations department and progress toward a comprehensive program to achieve the optimum balance between profits and social responsibility. It is feasible to "bury" the effort so that output focuses on public relations instead of truly assisting operations toward the best short- and long-range plans. This could mean reporting to the head of public relations. If executive management actually recognizes the problems in social responsibility and the potential contributions to performance from environmental relations, the reporting relationship will be at a senior level such as the executive vice president.

In organizational design, an examination should be made of comparisons between: (1) actual and potential use of existing staff departments; (2) existing, normal, and optimum reporting relationships in the specific company, and (3) costs and benefits of the departments in order to estimate the net payout of the support rendered to operations.

Job Satisfaction

While the results of good morale are usually intangible, satisfaction resulting from people accomplishing important tasks is an integral objective of organizational design. Authorities generally agree that better profit performance will result from a management team motivated by clearly defined jobs and responsibilities that are properly placed in the structure. Sometimes management has difficulty in knowing which factors have a positive effect on employee attitude. Isolating the impact of organizational design from other variables such as interesting product lines, managerial competence, the compensation package, pleasant environment, and other contributors to above average morale is a problem.

The starting point of maximizing job satisfaction is establishing the necessary structured relationships in the company. Some require an organizational framework nearer to the militaristic structure in Figure 4—3. Others can shift towards the minimal structure portion of the scale. There is usually a direct relationship between good internal communications, discussed previously, and job satisfaction. It relates to wanting to feel important and being placed in a position within the structure of the firm, which indicates that the individuals and their contributions are important.

The next factor that relates to job satisfaction is status. This involves a person's title, the physical surroundings one works in, privileges available to one person and not another, and miscellaneous points such as dress, travel, location, and so on. The status symbols of each company are different in some respects. Executive management must consider what is important within the firm in order to be sensitive to status in selecting a design.

The third factor involves organizational design and executive management's assessment of talent available in the company. Structures particularly applicable to a group of employees can induce job satisfaction. For example, a design with a minimum number of reporting levels and wide spans of control is often a good choice if middle management is strong. They respond to important responsibilities and frequent contact with top executives. Consequently, it is essential to conduct more than occasional evaluations based on the impressions of a supervisor. A formal system should exist based on multiple appraisal factors and ratings for each factor according to potential and actual performance. These ratings, if updated regularly, provide the means of judging the extent to which flatter structures and decentralized authority can be included in the structure.

Management can use several methods other than organizational design to improve morale and job satisfaction. However, these are covered in other courses.

Size and Complexity

Practical considerations in organizational design are created by both the size of company and complexity of operation. The key variables include:

1. Number of employees often divided into categories of 0−500, 501−5000, and over 5000.
2. Number of product lines, customer categories, and manufacturing processes.
3. Geographic scope of operations, particularly multinational operations.
4. Degree of technology.

It is extremely important for executive management to perceive the impact of the four variables on the design within a particular company. The spectrum of assessment is involved again, and different managers will react differently to the same facts.

Perception of size is easier than assessing complexity. In most companies the people making the decisions about organizational design are not involved in day-to-day line operations. They make judgments on the basis of:

1. Knowledge of how it was (if they have had such experience).
2. Information filtered by levels in the existing structure.
3. Observations on what other similar companies are doing.

Consultants are often asked to break through the "haze" that might be created by impressions gathered only from these sources. With fresh perspective and expertise developed from working with many companies, a management consulting firm can make valuable suggestions on structure and reporting relationships in large and complex companies.

Research and development (R and D) is an example of a department that needs special considerations to produce a flow of ideas usable in the business. Traditional structures have tended to keep the optimal combination of talent from being assigned to projects and have slowed communications on discoveries. Once an organizational problem is perceived, design concepts can be applied, such as the project management and matrix approaches discussed later in this chapter.

Another department or division that has organizational problems is international operations. Headquarters personnel in the U.S. usually do not have an accurate perspective on the situation in a foreign country to make good operating decisions. However, the needed expertise may not be justified by the scope of business in a country. International Telephone and Telegraph is using a decentralized regional approach with wholly owned subsidiaries such as ITT Europe and ITT Latin America. Executive management of these companies are aware of local conditions, speak the languages, and retain the best expertise available. Under this structure there are at least three tiers of profit centers: (1) headquarters, New York; (2) regional headquarters, for example, Brussels, and (3) operations in country Z which might have its own division of profit centers. Accountability is critical when relationships with top management become remote through decentralization.

CENTRALIZED AND DECENTRALIZED AUTHORITY

A fundamental consideration in design is the degree to which executive management will delegate authority to lower levels of the organization. Figure 4–5 illustrates the two extremes of: (1) authority centralized at the top and (2) authority decentralized to divisions, regions, and similar components of the structure.

Figure 4–5. Degrees of Delegation of Authority

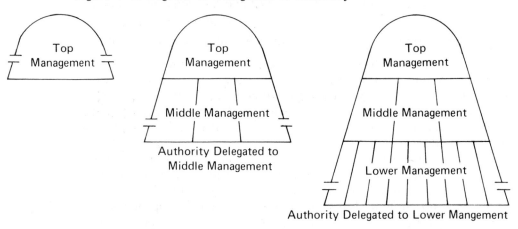

Motivations in the Degree of Delegation

Operational requirements necessitate decisions on the matter of centralization or decentralization. The basic question asked by top management is, "To what degree must we delegate authority to first-line management in order to be sensitive to and take effective action on developments in operations?" This consideration is the foundation for executives to determine the degree of delegation that is practical in their company. It applies through tiers and tiers.

The *entrepreneurial* instinct leads many top executives to retain the right to make key decisions. They have the responsibility for company performance and are reluctant to rely on subordinates. These executives want to minimize the probability of poor decisions that could adversely affect the business. The result is the existence of very few, if any, general managers of divisions or functions. With authority centralized, the quality of executives at the top has an immense impact on performance.

The opposite attitude motivates decentralization. *Confidence* in the capability of subordinates usually leads to delegation of authority to them. A management team can develop to make lesser decisions individually and important decisions collectively. The opportunity for individuals to make poor or good decisions that seriously affect the business is small because their areas of authority are small and segmented. It is true that delegation of responsibility assists in developing managers. However, inferior decisions on a broad scale have led several firms to shift back toward centralized authority.

In addition to the psychological implications, assessment of *talent* again plays a role. You cannot give authority and responsibility to lower levels in the organization, generally or specifically, if an evaluation of competence and leadership indicates that decision making on major issues would be poor. Mixed performance of employees at the managerial level should be anticipated so that, once a commitment to decentralization is made, potential problem areas can be monitored for necessary changes.

Examples of Centralization and Decentralization

Ampex Corporation decentralized in the late 1960s under William E. Roberts after serious financial problems. He delegated authority to line managers who headed operations that had been diversified from the company's line of electronic products. Some of the decisions at lower levels were disastrous. The company came to the brink of bankruptcy, losing $12 million in 1971 and $90 million in 1972. Observers felt that, considering Ampex's financial condition, it was poor timing to permit autonomous units to make major capital commitments without careful coordination at the top.

In 1973 the board of directors stepped in to save the company. They appointed Arthur H. Hausman as president and chief executive officer. Authority for spending and plotting the future course of the company was shifted back to headquarters. Mr. Hausman eliminated some of the operations that were losing money or did not fit Ampex's survival plan. Investigations by the new management team led to these quotes, which give emphasis to the importance or organizational design. "We rushed to the market before the engineering was proven." "What I found was a multimillion dollar business run like a candy store."[1]

Ampex is back under control, and sufficient cash is being earned to service a heavy debt burden. This situation exemplifies the fears entrepreneurial executives have in delegating authority to lower levels of the organization.

Kaiser Aluminum and Chemical Corporation had a classical pyramid with highly structured reporting relationships until 1973. One executive felt uncomfortable talking to top management about anything. Another said decision making was mysterious, "Things just happened." President Cornell C. Maier has changed this to a flat design with 10 operating managers and 9 staff specialists reporting directly to him. He depends on the 19 people to be competent and carry out their responsibilities independent of his direct supervision.

The reorganization involved the pruning of 10 jobs at the level of

[1] *Business Week*, June 16, 1973, p. 70—72.

vice president and above. People wedded to the classical approach either adjusted or left. Communications have improved sharply. However, some executives are now concerned about keeping and motivating a large number of self-sufficient managers. There are fewer promotion opportunities, and studies[2] indicate the flatter structure works better in smaller companies than in those the size of Kaiser.

If C.C. Maier can retain the executives he needs under a decentralized approach, Kaiser will probably benefit from the change in design. Profit margins have narrowed in the industries this company serves. The 10 profit centers created at the operating manager level reporting to the president is a means of monitoring progress.

Allied Stores Corporation has been reorganized by Thomas M. Macioce. He has brought his 3 group vice presidents who supervise the 18 store division managers into New York, "Where we can get at them." Each reports to the executive vice president. A general management committee consisting of 23 people has been formed to improve communications and coordination. Two other committees involving lower levels of the company, the divisional merchandise manager's committee and buyers steering committee, have the same purpose.

President T.M. Macioce "Wants to know everything—and I mean everything—that goes on."[3] This autocratic approach to management is facilitated by Allied's MOPP, the management operating profit plan. This is a one-year statement on performance by each of the 18 store divisions. Every number is reviewed by the president and his staff experts.

It is possible that talent in the divisions may not like the highly centralized approach by T.M. Macioce. However, performance of Allied Stores at its nationwide locations improved significantly in the early 1970s.

Forms of Organization

Some new terms are being used to describe structures developed to meet needs created by the complexities of multinational corporations, conglomerates, technology based companies, and other diversified operations. The classical pyramid and the flat design in Figure 4—3 were covered previously and are excluded from this discussion.

BEEHIVE The structure is three-dimensional. Picture tubes set in beehive fashion on top of each other. The chief executive officer and

[2] *Business Week*, February 24, 1973, p. 81—84.
[3] *Business Week*, November 17, 1973, p. 55—62.

executive vice presidents are in the tube at the top of the structure, the vice presidents in the next layer, plant managers in another layer, and so on. The lower layers report to an upper layer rather than individuals reporting to individuals. For example, a plant manager would report to the operations vice president about production, to the controller about budgets, to the personnel vice president about labor relations, and so on. This design variation is intended to improve personal relations and communications by having a head in each tube (a queen bee) who coordinates that responsibility and acts as a focal point for communication between tubes above, below, and on the same level.

BOTTOM-UP MANAGEMENT   This design was originated by William Given, formerly President of Apex Corporation, and pushes the decision-making authority to the lowest possible level. This is an extreme of decentralization that gives managers unusual latitude to initiate action.

COLLEGIAL MANAGEMENT   Common in Europe, this approach involves having more than one chief executive. Terms such as "office of the president" or "executive management committee" describe approaches having two to four people sharing the responsibility delegated to management by the board of directors. The organization of Powerite Tools, Inc. is an example.

DOUGHNUT   The design is similar to the beehive in concept; however, it is two-dimensional. Picture concentric circles. The inner circle is for executive management. The next ring is for staff specialists such as personnel, finance, and legal who do not report to any particular officer. They provide services for both executive management. The third ring which has operating managers of divisions who also do not report to a specific individual. The divisions could have conventional organizations or more doughnuts. A high degree of team work and communications has resulted at C.I.T. Financial Corporation using this design, and it is said to be suited for some conglomerates.

LADDER   This applies to staff departments in large companies. General Electric has recently adopted this design. Instead of clustering these departments between top management and the operating divisions, they are strung out to the side of the structure like a ladder for easier access by line personnel.

MATRIX   The concept was conceived to manage complex situations having product systems. Managers are appointed to be responsible for the system. For example, one manager's responsibility might be the assembly and sale of an information system made up of several products sold by divisions. In carrying out this responsibility,

Figure 4–6. Variations in Organizational Design

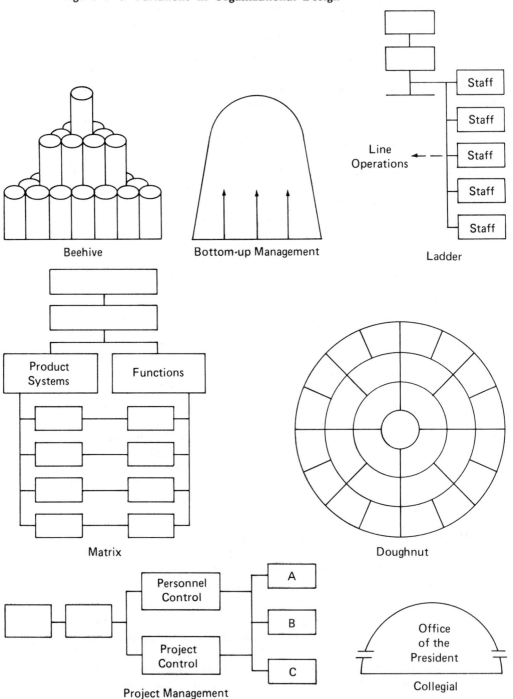

Beehive

Bottom-up Management

Ladder

Line Operations

Staff

Matrix

Product Systems

Functions

Doughnut

Project Management

Personnel Control

Project Control

A

B

C

Office of the President

Collegial

the manager would use employees and facilities of other components of the company and would be charged for the service.

PROJECT MANAGEMENT People are assigned to projects with specific goals. When the project is completed, the individuals are returned to a holding position in the organization until they are reassigned. This approach, instead of a structure with fixed reporting relationships, has become the preferred approach for technical research. In fact, companies with the traditional pyramid have adopted this design for R and D.

Figure 4—6 illustrates the elements in each of the seven design variations. Companies alter these fundamentals to suit their individual needs.

CHANGES IN THE ORGANIZATION

In a reorganization it is essential for the people involved to have the maximum amount of objectivity rather than being influenced by personalities in the structure being changed. This can be accomplished by the following steps given here:

1. Establish a list of all functions and activities in the division or company numbering each one.
2. Interrelate them by placing the number of a function or activity next to every other function or activity on the list to which it has some relationship.
3. Diagram the relationships in a way that acknowledges the functions or activities most related to each other.
4. Identify clusters that logically fit together as a basis for considering design possibilities.
5. Experiment with designs, discussing the ideas with key personnel in order to reflect factors previously discussed in the chapter.
6. Finalize the design.

Some top executives start with a preconceived idea of the design without using this method. They have a style of management that requires varying degrees of structure from autocratic, at one extreme, to highly decentralized at the other. From a company overview, the systematic method is superior. However, dynamic leaders can produce exceptional results, and they should have the prerogative to use the methods that suit them. Performance is critical under these circumstances. The structure must be successful.

Some Psychological Implications of Change

A major organizational change in a company is an uncomfortable experience for even the most secure individual. Times of uncertainty are times of pressure and unpredictable alliances. Absurd rumors permeate the company, and minor decisions are given exaggerated importance. It is a tense period in an organization. Members of executive management who are insensitive to the feelings of lower levels of the organization could create problems of morale and job satisfaction that are difficult to correct.

Communicating Change

Usually a company's best talent, and therefore the people executive management would most like to retain, are the most mobile. They are also attractive to other firms. The remainder of employees are less mobile and more likely to stick with the firm during difficult periods. So, there is a danger of losing good managers and keeping poorer performers if a change in organization is not handled correctly.

Some executives will claim that "birds that will flush with a little rustling in the woods" are not the kind of people they wish to retain. This point of view is partially defensible, but usually it is offered as an excuse for losing managers with above average potential during a reorganization.

Communications between those deciding on the changes and those affected by them are critically important during the period when it is known that the organizational design is being modified. There are three stages.

1. *Exchanges of Ideas on the Changes.* Top executives will normally discuss the alternatives (Step 5, see p. 103), and it is expected that these exchanges would remain confidential. However, rumors can start at this stage through leaks originating with secretaries and staff personnel. It is essential to handle these rumors competently and without emotion. Ignoring them is occasionally the correct answer, but positive action is more likely the answer.

2. *Announcements to Those Affected.* It is good to make the decisions known at one specific time, but this is not always possible. In the case of phased disclosures, portions of the new structure will be known and speculation on the remainder will be initiated. At this stage, managers, whom the company wishes to retain and are not yet informed of their new position, could accept jobs with other firms. From their viewpoint, they have been passed over because they were not informed at the time of the first disclosure and their self-image resists being in the second wave of announcements. However, careful wording of early disclosures can avoid this difficulty.

3. *Companywide Announcements.* The objectives of the change is improved performance. Part of the improvement will come from the operating results originating with the structure, and another part from employee reaction to new reporting relationships. Attitude can be positive if employees feel informed about motivations for change and the goals of the new design.

Executive management can become absorbed in designing the organization and forget about the very important aspect of employee interpretation of the changes. Therefore, add Step 7 to the six just described for reorganizing all or part of a company to cover these psychological factors.

Early Stage of Change

It takes time to realize the improvements sought by change. Some individuals respond more slowly than others. The time period between the initial announcements and final reorganization is utilized by people to adjust to new jobs and new superiors, peers, and subordinates. The resulting delay often causes executive management anxieties because they want the organization to function at optimum performance as rapidly as possible.

Some ideas for accelerating adjustment are:

1. Clearly stated job descriptions.
2. Objectives for components of the organization to provide direction for groups of individuals.
3. Meetings of individuals in each component and clusters of components to achieve management efficiency and accelerate adjustment.
4. Sessions with executive management on expectations.

These methods are supplementary to the fundamentals of a short-range operating plan. By requiring operating goals, budgets, and forecasts of cash inflow, components of the company are compelled to define performance for months and quarters in the coming year. This process pulls together the "loose ends" created in the reorganization.

The Time for Change

One frequent motivation for redesigning an organization is serious problems within a company, division, or another type of profit center. New executives are appointed to rectify the situation. They analyze operations and the present structure, and make judgments on the design for compatibility with their management philosophy and perception of the problems.

Less frequently, executive management will anticipate difficulties and initiate changes before the circumstances seriously deteriorate. Also, new managers are appointed for reasons other than serious problems, such as new product lines, acquisitions, resignations, and expansion. Assuming that authority to reorganize is delegated to these managers, they must move quickly to organize and get the operation moving.

Large corporations are involved in constant organizational change through growth, product obsolescence, response to market situations, new technology, and other corporate developments. Programs to prepare managers for promotion under these dynamic circumstances have been mentioned in Chapter Two. In some companies, a new structures is designed with each revision of strategies or long-range plans to meet the needs of changing operations.

The reasons for a company's organizational structure must be reviewed periodically by executive management to compare current operations with those at the time of the decision. Also, a conscious effort is required to be certain that the purpose behind the structure has actually been implemented at lower levels in the company. Sometimes titles and reporting relationships can be changed, but the problems motivating the changes, particularly the need for improved communications, are not corrected. Upper levels of management monitor such developments to have good perspective on organizational requirements at the time of redesign.

SUMMARY

The objective for organization of people into formal relationships is to provide a structure for conducting business in an orderly and efficient manner. The design is influenced by the responsibilities assigned to decision makers, their need for power and status, assessments of talent, and outside influences. Also, developments in computers, multinational corporations, diversification, and technological advances have an impact on corporate structure.

The primary factors in organizational design are:

1. *Degrees of Structure and Committees.* Managers must have adequate facts and opinions to make good decisions. Two-way flow is affected by the organizational structure of the company and by proper use of committees as well as directives and leadership by management, conscious efforts to develop formal and informal communications, and other nondesign factors.

2. *Profit and Cost Centers.* Accountability of performance in

fulfilling responsibilities needs measures that are clearly defined. The use of multiple profit centers for this purpose is a method that supplements cost centers in identifying the performance of managers.

3. *Staff Departments.* Reporting relationships can assist or prevent staff departments from making significant contributions to profits. Continuing existence of a staff department is dependent on these contributions. A cost benefit analysis at the time of an organizational redesign will assist in identifying the best relationship.

4. *Job Satisfaction.* People perform more efficiently if they like their work and feel it is important. The structure of a company plays a major role in creating good morale as do status symbols and generating an employee attitude that recognizes the needs of the company in addition to their own.

5. *Size and Complexity.* Executive management perception of the impact on organizational design created by number of employees, product lines, customer categories, manufacturing processes, geographic breakdowns, and technologies is critical to deciding on the optimal structure.

Companies shift from centralized to decentralized authority depending on operational requirements, entrepreneurial attitude of top management, confidence in the competence of subordinates, and actual performance of middle management. Also, conditions change and it is necessary to adjust the organization to be compatible with current needs.

Forms of structure are changing from the traditional pyramid and flattened modifications called the pancake, bell-shape, and so on. Possible configurations now include doughnuts, beehives, and ladders, as well as variations such as two to four chief executive officers instead of only one.

Changes in the organization, if needed, should be made after the six steps are completed to gain maximum objectivity. The psychological implications of change can reverse the benefits expected from reorganization, and careful consideration must be given to communicating the decisions. As a result, a seventh step is added to the six dealing with these communications and the crucial period immediately after implementation.

DISCUSSION QUESTIONS

1. Relate communications to degree of structure and size and complexity. How do you assure good communications in a reorganization?

2. How do you make committees work effectively?
3. What elements in redesign affect job satisfaction?
4. Contrast profit and cost centers. Why was a cost center selected for the reorganization of Trenton Industries in the Chapter Three case?
5. What motivates a top executive to select a structure with centralized authority?
6. What are the causes of losing good managers during a change in organization? How can you avoid this problem?
7. Select two local companies. Determine their organizational structure. Contrast the two by applying the principles of the chapter.

SUGGESTED READINGS AND BIBLIOGRAPHY

Erhle, R.A. "Management Decentralization: Antidote to Bureaucracy," *Personnel Journal.* May, 1970.

Gibson, James L., Ivancevich, John M., and Donnelly, James H. *Organizations.* Business Publications, Inc., Dallas, Texas, 1973.

Halme, R.D. and Maydew, J.C. "A View from the Top—Study of Collective Management Organization," *Business Horizons.* October, 1972, pp. 19-30.

Hanan, M. "Make Way for the New Organization," *Harvard Business Review.* July—August, 1971, pp. 128—138.

Higgins, R.B. "Managerial Behavior in Upwardly Oriented Organizations," *California Management Review.* Spring, 1972, pp. 49-59.

Kast, Fremont E. and Rosenzweig, James E. *Organization and Management—A Systems Approach.* McGraw-Hill, 1974.

Mockler, R.J. "Situational Theory of Management," *Harvard Business Review.* May—June, 1971, pp. 146—154.

Muther, R. and DeMoor, R.J. "Planning An Organization Structure," *S.A.M. Advanced Management Journal.* January, 1973.

Odiorne, G.D. "Up the Pyramid ... er ... Doughnut ... er Beehive," *Nations Business.* January, 1972, pp. 62—64.

O'Donnell, Cyril. "Ground Rules for Using Committees," *Management Review.* October 1961. "Organizing for Fast Change," *Industry Week.* December 11, 1972, pp. 41—42.

"Remodeling Management Structures," *Nations Business.* November 1970, p. 46.

"Room at the Top Getting Scarcer," *Business Week.* December 15, 1973.

Shinn, J. "Who Is Running the Company," *International Management.* December, 1970.

"Teamwork Through Conflict," *Business Week.* March 20, 1971, pp. 44—45.

"Telltale Signs of Weakness in a Company," *Nations Business.* January, 1973, pp. 70—71.

Uyterhoeven, H.E.R. "General Managers in the Middle," *Harvard Business Review.* March—April, 1972, pp. 75—85.

Case: Organizational Changes at NEM, Inc.

The situation, based on a real business situation with names and statistics changed to avoid identification, required a major organizational overhaul and a change in design in 1969. While achieving most of the financial objectives, the new design illustrates aspects of "fine tuning." Fundamentals discussed in the chapter are further developed by problems at NEM, Inc.

New England Manufacturing (NEM) was founded in 1889 by the Bonner family and is headquartered in Waterford, Connecticut. The company grew under their sole leadership until, in 1952, they issued 872,515 shares of stock to be sold on the American Exchange.[1] By 1954, net sales had reached $29,703,938, and net earnings were $1,863,061. On June 25, 1956, Gordon R. Bonner died after serving as president of NEM since 1922 and spending a total of 49 years in the paper and plastics industry.

James Schmidt became president in 1956 and served in that capacity until December 31, 1970. He considered himself a professional manager and was not related to the

family. Figure 4C−1 shows the organization when he took over. One of his first moves was to acquire Brittingham Brothers, Inc. through an exchange of shares. The paper company was located in Framingham, Massachusetts and had been selling its entire output to NEM since 1935.

Product lines in the 1960s consisted of high-grade paper, laminated plastics, containers, and fabricated metal products. NEM, besides developing domestic markets, established two plants in Belgium, Antwerp and Liege, and one in Hamilton, Ontario, Canada.

THE GORMAN TAKEOVER

In 1968 Joseph Gorman began buy-

[1] Total shares outstanding in 1975 are 976,000, of which 898,000 are not held by descendents of the Bonner family.

110

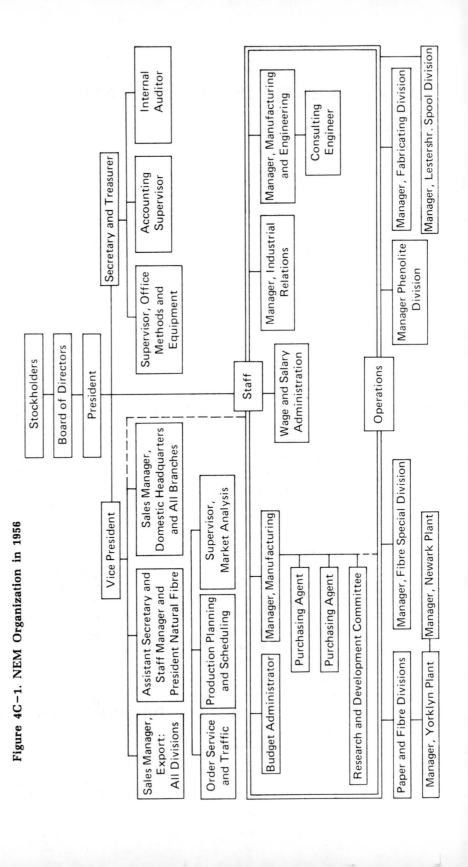

Figure 4C-1. NEM Organization in 1956

Figure 4C–2. NEM Organization in 1967

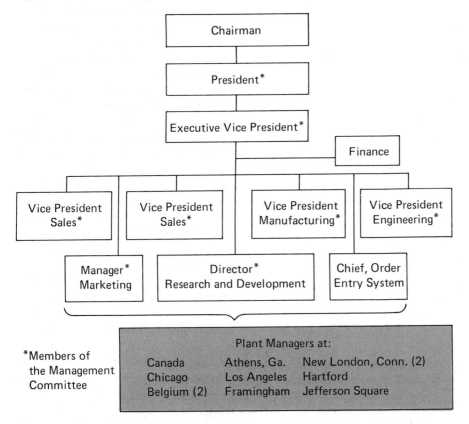

```
                        ┌──────────────┐
                        │   Chairman   │
                        └──────────────┘
                                │
                        ┌──────────────┐
                        │  President*  │
                        └──────────────┘
                                │
                ┌──────────────────────────┐
                │ Executive Vice President* │────────┐
                └──────────────────────────┘    ┌─────────┐
                                │                │ Finance │
                                │                └─────────┘
   ┌───────────┬────────────┬────────────┬─────────────┐
┌─────────┐ ┌─────────┐ ┌────────────┐ ┌────────────┐
│  Vice   │ │  Vice   │ │   Vice     │ │   Vice     │
│President│ │President│ │ President  │ │ President  │
│ Sales*  │ │ Sales*  │ │Manufactur-*│ │Engineering*│
└─────────┘ └─────────┘ └────────────┘ └────────────┘
    ┌────────────┬──────────────────┬──────────────┐
 ┌─────────┐ ┌──────────────────┐ ┌────────────┐
 │Manager* │ │    Director*     │ │Chief, Order│
 │Marketing│ │Research and      │ │Entry System│
 │         │ │Development       │ │            │
 └─────────┘ └──────────────────┘ └────────────┘
```

*Members of the Management Committee

Plant Managers at:

Canada	Athens, Ga.	New London, Conn. (2)
Chicago	Los Angeles	Hartford
Belgium (2)	Framingham	Jefferson Square

ing stock in NEM as an investment. By the end of the year he had sufficient ownership, roughly 350,000 shares, to obtain three places on a nine-man board of directors. The next year sales of the company grew to a record of $60.64 million. Profits, however, were $378,624, 20% of 1954, and only $108,086 before extraordinary items. NEM went into the "red" in early 1970, and the need for a change in management became urgent.

When the situation became clear in 1969, Mr. Gorman increased his ownership to 655,000 shares and increased board membership to six of nine. He was then elected chairman of the board. In April, 1970 Scott M. Walters was employed by Mr. Gorman for the position of executive vice president.[2] As indicated in Figure 4C–2, there was an executive vice president before his arrival and he was fired with 30 days termination pay plus accumulated vacation. Mr. Walters was given the full authority to carry out the reorganization

[2] Scott M. Walters was President of Nolo Manufacturing in Pittsburgh until March, 1970. Sales of Nolo were $10.8 million and the company had $875,000 in after-tax profits. He took early retirement and accepted the NEM position the next month.

of the company without involving James Schmidt, and received the title of president as of January 1, 1971, after his predecessor took early retirement at the end of the year.

The Organization at the Time of Walters' Arrival

NEM had a committee as its primary source of leadership in 1969. In fact, area colleges have prepared cases on the effectiveness of administration by committee at NEM as early as 1954. When Gorman and Walters began to redesign the organization in 1970 they found seven members of an executive committee plus the president as its chairman. In addition to this unusual approach to top-level decision making, other features of the organization included the following.

1. Plant managers had no specific reporting relationship. Nearly all members of executive management were in charge of a portion of the production plants through their functional responsibilities. Control was uncoordinated and frustrated by contradictory orders.
2. NEM had a long-range plan but no short-range operating plan. The vice president of engineering had a large staff thinking about the future. Consequently, the company was then incurring an expense of $47,800 per month in computers, largely because of engineering. However, there were no means for managers to account for current decisions and no formal way of phasing in programs and projects needed to accomplish long-range objectives.

3. An order entry and processing department had been established with consulting assistance costing $500,000± per year. It created a bureaucracy that actually slowed receipt of products by the customer.
4. All reporting of performance by managers was in units with no accompanying dollar amounts. The controller and plant managers had no means of developing standard costs or profit margins by product. The organization seemed to be based on avoiding accountability and any possibility of embarrassing one of the executives.
5. There was major duplication of jobs. Also, nearly identical reports would be prepared and submitted on the same subject. Neither member of management knew about the other's work.
6. Some personal expense accounts appeared excessive for the type of business conducted on the trips or when entertaining. This led Mr. Gorman to conclude that the organizational structure placed no constraints on employee behavior, and the shareholders were being abused by the absence of managerial control.

Serious cost control trouble at NEM became evident in early 1968. Even under boom conditions it had begun losing money. With a recession on the horizon, Mr. Gorman's investments could have evaporated without quick action.

Organization Redesign

Mr. Gorman had one primary goal for the redesign of the NEM organization: improved operational efficiency through cost control to increase profits. Figure 4C–3 identifies the NEM organizational concept to be realized at the close of the first stage of changes.

The following four profit centers were created to monitor performance more closely.

The Paper Division

High-grade paper for stocks, bonds, diplomas, travelers cheques, and watermark paper. (For example, the Jutland Government bought half million dollars worth of this paper to print their currency.) Two plants near New London and one in Hartford.

Technical Plastics Division

Laminated phenolic, melamine, epoxy, polyester and silicone sheets, tubes and rods serving electrical, electronic, textile, and automotive industries. Typical applications include gears, printed circuit materials, fuses, bobbins, and so on. Lamiclad polyester glass plywood sheets have major application in truck and trailer industry. Raw material plant at Willow Forest, Pennsylvania. Fabricating plants at Waterford, Connecticut; Chicago, Illinois; and Los Angles, California.

Container Division

Durable containers for shipping and storing products; plastic cases to store drinks in airplanes; waste baskets, and so on. Plants at Jefferson Square, New Jersey and Athens, Georgia.

International Division

Belgium: Antwerp, technical plastic products and Liege, containers. Hamilton, Ontario, Canada: tech-

Figure 4C–3. Transitional Organization at NEM

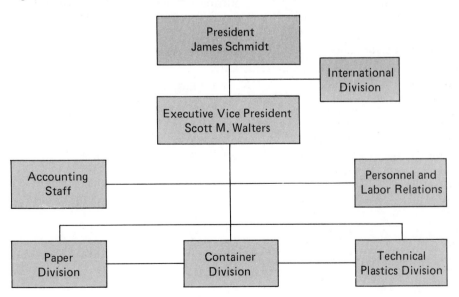

nical plastic products, warehousing and marketing paper products.

After creating Mr. Gorman's basic design, Mr. Walters met individually with each existing vice president and high ranking executive and asked, "What do you do at or for this company?" "How do you relate to others in the company?" "What changes would you make in the organization?"

Within a month after hearing the responses he had dismissed three vice presidents and four plant managers. Several others in lower and middle management left of their own choice during this period of time. During this transition phase and careful analysis of personnel, Mr. Walters appointed men to fill his organization. Within the year, headquarters personnel dropped from 151 to 48. All of those remaining were able to move into the renovated office building vacated by the dismantled engineering department. The cost of computer services for NEM were reduced to $5,700 per month through a timesharing arrangement with a nearby insurance company.

The goal of achieving operating efficiency can be measured by the profit performance shown in Table 4C–1. Employees who had meaningless titles and/or little to offer the company were dismissed. Although salaried employees were released during the transition phase, the company is achieving and maintaining peak profits and production.

The delegation of authority to the four division general managers played a major role in the success. Previously it was possible to "duck" being identified as the individual(s) contributing to operating problems. Afterwards, the profit centers concept influenced more careful evaluation of capital spending and a general reduction in outlays. Although short-range planning did not achieve a major degree of sophistication, accountability became important at NEM.

Much of the equipment and facilities existing in 1970 were not operating at full capacity. Therefore, in

Table 4C–1. NEM Performance

Year	Net Sales	Net Earnings	Salaried Employees
1945	20,411,395	1,273,455	269
1954	29,703,938	1,863,061	321
1960	34,102,711	1,764,278	523
1963	40,218,753	1,899,119	642
1966	51,606,021	1,975,334	887
1969	60,541,231	108,086*	948
1970	60,897,100	1,710,444	607
1971	72,701,234	3,312,659	604
1972	81,002,728	5,117,431	612
1973	84,537,969	5,821,122	615
1974	86,078,117	5,999,076	621

* Before extraordinary items.

addition to cost control, Mr. Walters instructed the division general managers to have their marketing departments attract additional sales by passing on all cost savings realized in large orders. The plants could then run at near capacity and improve operating efficiencies.

During the 1970–74 period production costs were cut 35% and earnings from operations rose 250%. The elaborate order entry system and computer center were abandoned. At the end of the period the operating rate was at full capacity, and the company was in a strong competitive position. NEM could offer its products to the customer at lower prices than in 1970, despite inflation during this period.

Mr. Gorman thought much of the change in performance was attributable to the organizational redesign and a shift from the confused reporting relationships existing in 1969 as a result of committee leadership. Except for Mr. Walters, a controller and two specialists, only NEM employees filled the new positions.

In December of 1970, Mr. Walters was elected to the board of directors and President of Technology, Inc., another of Mr. Gorman's acquisitions.[3] At the same time, Lester Russell was elected executive vice president of NEM. He had been one of the two vice presidents of sales when Scott Walters

[3] Technology, Inc. of Red Bank, New Jersey manufactures solid-state electronic gear for racing sailboats, such as wind direction finders, depth sounders, knotometer, distance logs, and similar items. While technologically advanced, managers could not control costs. The founding partners agreed rarely and all four "wanted out." Sales in 1970 were $17.4 million and the loss was $48.175.

took over. This enabled Mr. Walters to reorganize Technology, Inc. while Mr. Russell made the day-to-day decisions at NEM under an increasingly detailed operating plan. These moves completed the first phase of streamlining the company.

Second Stage of Redesign

Although the company is operating at peak production and profits, some problems related to the 1970 reorganization began to surface in 1975.

First, very little emphasis had been placed on long-range planning, largely because division general managers had been under intensive pressure to show improved performance during the immediate future. Long-range plans in which the profit centers participate were regarded as a possibility in the late 1970s to permit orderly expansion. However, for the present, only the four top executives (Gorman, Walters, Russell and a new executive to be discussed) consider future possibilities.

Marketing management in all four divisions feel sales were lost in 1974 because the company had not expanded to meet demand, and that long-range planning in 1972-73 might have prevented this. Top NEM officials cite the excellent sales and profit performance in that year, and claim expansion beyond capacity at that time would not have been the best application of capital.

Second, lower and middle management were complaining that their general managers waited too long for top-level decisions. In their opinion, Mr. Russell did not have sufficient authority; Mr. Walters had "at least one other full-time position"; and Mr. Gorman lives in Palm Springs, California. There was a feeling of absentee management. While acknowledging the positive steps taken by the Gorman team, many felt the momentum was slipping away.

Third, some executives were insecure and avoided making the decisions necessary for a profit center to function at full efficiency. While some insecurity had led to greater productivity efficiency, it also resulted in delays in handling key proposals and obstructions to channels of communication outside the formal chain of command. Information was passed horizontally rather than upwards in a vertical or circular pattern. A contributing factor to this situation was the great number of dismissals in 1970 which made executives in their 50s nervous about taking chances.

Fourth, clear definitions of authority and responsibility were not established at lower levels within the profit centers. The general managers delegated little authority to subordinates and were overworked. Consequently, some decisions were not made because a manager was not certain that it was within the scope of his job.

Fifth, communications barriers at NEM were beginning to interfere with efficient management. Employees seemed very concerned about top executives not responding to suggestions based on field experiences at the same time that Gorman, Walters and Russell were working on

ideas and solutions to problems resulting from the suggestions. The decisions would benefit, however, from more feedback from line personnel involved with those aspects of the business.

Finally, a companywide, short-range plan exists, but it is severely criticized by middle management. Most claim reliability of the plan is lost in number "bending" to make monthly performance look satisfactory to executives. Some cite the transfer of products from one warehouse to another to increase the totals for shipments. As a result, NEM probably does not have the basis for operational decisions.

Current Organizational Changes

Scott Walters became President of NEM when the previous President took early retirement in 1970. Nevertheless, he continued in his capacity as chief operating officer of Technology, Inc. and lived in New Jersey rather than near corporate headquarters in Connecticut. Consequently, only a few structural changes were made in the organization during the 1971–74 period at the close of which he moved back to Waterford. Recently, some needed adjustments have been made.

Figure 4C–4 shows the addition of J.A. White as *vice president of technology*. Jack White was with Hercules Chemicals as technical director, but felt blocked from future promotions at 48 years old. This new position acknowledges the need for planning to avoid technological obsolescence and the strengthening of this input in operating strategy.

Centralized purchasing has been established as a staff function at headquarters to overcome persistent shortages of materials. NEM will be better able to control inventories, and economies will result from volume purchases at discounts. Also, a *cost analyst* has been employed to advise executive management on developments that could affect short-range plans (which now include a look at one year beyond the most current 12 months effective January 1, 1975). This includes material substitution and greater commitments to safety stocks as well as improving standard costs.

Figure 4C–4. NEM Organization in Early 1974

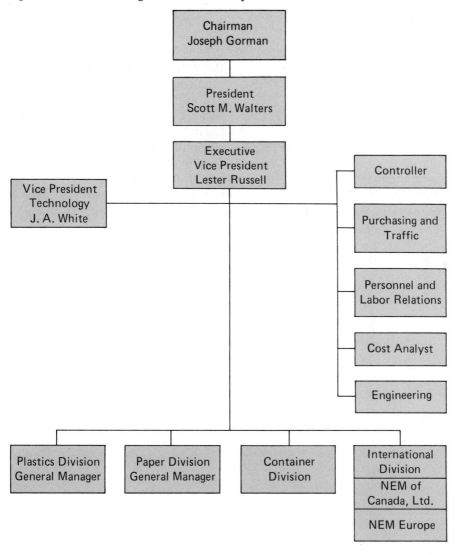

Engineering at the corporate staff level has been reestablished after dispersion of many engineers to the profit centers and termination of others in 1970. A skeleton group has begun work on programs and projects conceived by executive management.

STUDENT PROBLEMS

The initial redesign of the organization by Mr. Gorman and implemented by Scott Walters corrected many of the problems affecting profit performance at NEM. Profit centers related to product groupings created points in the company at which management effectiveness could be measured. In addition, divisions theoretically could take better advantage of market opportunities through better and more rapid decision making.

There was a positive impact from the changes in 1970–71. Now new organizational decisions are required. Identify:

1. The steps you must take as president to refine the NEM organization based on facts presented in the case. How will you handle your relationship with Mr. Gorman and the assignment at Technology, Inc.?
2. What changes would you make in the original steps taken by NEM management? Include in your evaluation an appraisal of the techniques used in the 1970–71 period during which Mr. Walters streamlined the organization.
3. Give your opinion on what occured at NEM in the period between the death of the last Bonner and the takeover by Joseph Gorman.

Case: Liberty Gas Co.

A proposed reorganization effective September 15, 1974 is involved. It attempts to resolve a serious conflict between the two top executives in the company. The period covers June 1, 1973 to August 31, 1974.

Liberty Gas Co.[4] is a large independent propane gas distributor in southeastern Pennsylvania. Company headquarters is in Lancaster. Customers are primarily in southeastern Pennsylvania excluding Philadelphia. However, the firm also uses its fleet of tank trucks to service industrial customers in several neighboring states.

Propane gas is purchased from three oil companies in the Philadelphia–New Jersey refinery complex. Liberty has dealers in some parts of its market area and serves customers directly in others. Uses of propane range from home heating and appliances to grain drying. A critically important customer is the greenhouse industry.

Storage of gas by the company is mainly in large 30,000-gallon cylinders, but everything that will hold gas is used during the off season buildup of inventories in summer when prices are historically lower. This includes tanks owned by customers because they are normally invoiced for metered usage rather than at the time of delivery.

Billings are approximately $5 million per year. Cash inflow is heavily concentrated in the December–April period. The company is usually forced to use its line of credit in the August–November period to

---

[4] The names and places are fictitious. The case is a synthesis of two actual situations blended in order to emphasize principles in the chapter.

permit gas purchases from the oil companies that are on a 10-day credit basis. In 1973 sales to industrial customers during this low cash period created sufficient receipts to avoid borrowing.

TRANSFER OF OWNERSHIP

Until May 31, 1973, the firm was solely owned by Bill Rollins, the company founder. In recent years

Figure 4C – 5. Organization before the 1973 Sale

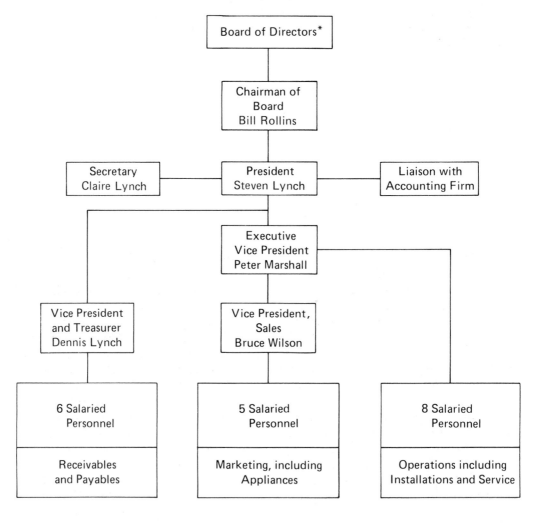

Liberty Gas Co.

* Board membership included B. Rollins, Chairman, and S. Lynch, P. Marshall, D. Lynch, and B. Wilson.

Mr. Rollins resided in Florida and depended on management whom he had known for decades. Organization in early 1973 is shown in Figure 4C—5.

The decision to sell was made in early 1973 by Bill Rollins after years of considering alternative approaches. He selected Peter Marshall, the executive vice-president, and his 31 year old nephew, Joseph Rollins, as the people to whom he wished to transfer ownership on a 50-50 basis. Details of the arrangement are confidential, but they involve a very low equity commitment by the new owners and a long-term loan agreement. Interest installments provide an adequate retirement income for Mr. Rollins, and repayment of principal builds his estate.

The Lynch family (Steven—president, Dennis—vice-president, Claire—secretary, and relations) was not given the opportunity to participate, nor was Bruce Wilson, vice-president of marketing. Steven Lynch, the president, currently receives a substantial annual "consulting fee" for resigning immediately. The remaining Lynches left individually during the summer of 1973. Mr. Wilson remained with the firm.

Transition

During June, 1973 the Marshall/Rollins partnership made several operating changes to improve efficiency and correct situations which had developed over the years under Steven Lynch. Joe Rollins had been with the firm for only a few months in a junior position before the sale, but Peter Marshall had had over 20 years to accumulate ideas on how to increase earnings.

Regarding personnel resources Peter Marshall initially identified seven levels of job seniority in the organization without attempting to attach titles. As people were placed in each category, additional information on work experience, personal characteristics and compensation was noted on the guide. This enabled the new partners to put together the organization given in Figure 4C—6 effective July 1, 1973.

Problems at the Top

An equal division of authority and responsibilities between Peter Marshall and Joe Rollins was attempted because each owned 50% of the business. Problems based on the differences in their backgrounds and business experience arose every day. Each could have been resolved if a serious personality conflict, which was not fully recognized when the partnership was proposed, had not distorted communications and complicated decision making. A brief background summary of the two executives in Table 4C—2 gives some insight on the situation (see p. 123).

The relationships at the top in 1973 were further complicated by Peter Marshall's 24 year old son and only offspring. Rick Marshall joined Liberty Gas Co. after graduation from Drexel University in June, 1972. He performed miscellaneous assignments at the same level as Joe Rollins until the acquisition by his

Figure 4C–6. Organization Effective July 1, 1973

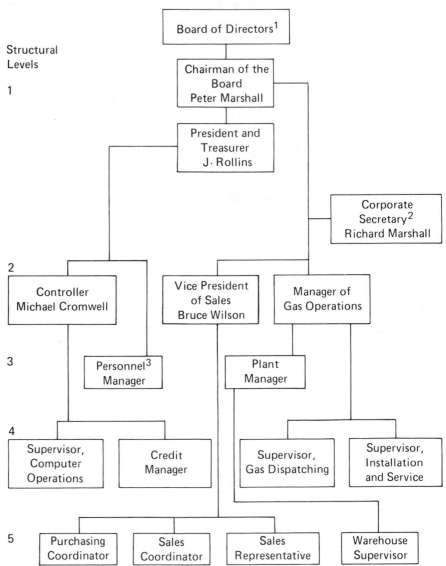

Structural
Levels

1

2

3

4

5

Notes:

1. The Board of Directors is composed of P. Marshall, J. Rollins, and H. T. Maner.

2. Two positions are involved for R. Marshall: (a) Corporate Secretary, and (b) Director, Corporate Development. The latter involves. (i) Completion of studies on profit improvement for existing operations and development of diversification opportunities, and (ii) Special assignments from the chairman. The Board will establish priorities for studies and venture analysis. R. Marshall will also be familiar with the Controller's job.

3. This position can be filled indefinitely by J. Rollins.

father when he became corporate secretary. In the transition phase he handled: (1) conversion of invoicing and payrolls to an IBM System 3; (2) supervision of all duties and responsibilities of the future controller's job, and (3) miscellaneous assignments from his father.

When Michael Cromwell was hired as controller in September, 1973, Rick Marshall retained only the miscellaneous assignments role. It was then decided to add the responsibilities of director of corporate development to his position in order to look for profit opportunities in business not associated with propane gas. This uncovered a major difference in attitude about future allocation of company resources. The Marshalls saw the objective as identifying small local opportunities that offered income counterseasonal to propane and could be covered from working capital or short-term loans within the limit of the line of credit.

Joe Rollins saw any acquisitions as a means of large-scale diversification and a possibility of escaping Lancaster for Philadelphia. Rather than looking for small businesses, he preferred to accumulate cash reserves for a major investment. Both owner/executives avoided challenging each other on this point in the 1973—74 operating season. The consequence was the elimination of any meaningful work in this area by Rick Marshall.

The relationship deteriorated badly during the first year. Joe Rollins portrayed his feelings in the following comments made during 1974:

"I am outgunned by Peter Marshall."
"My long-term role when compared to a better trained Rick Marshall is not very certain."
"I have suspicions about the Marshalls' using company resources for personal investments. This reduces my possibility of running a subsidiary not dominated by Peter Marshall."

Table 4C–2.

Peter Marshall, Chairman of the Board—51 years old; lifetime resident of Lancaster County; outstanding entrepreneurial instincts; collector of antiques; board of director member of several local firms; respected executive in the propane industry with valuable contacts for supplies, trade-offs on inventories, industrial customers, etc. Attitude shaped by drive for improvement in current personal income and use of the Liberty opportunity to increase personal wealth through peripheral investments such as real estate. Respect of employees gained from competence in day-to-day decision making and fairness rather than through personal friendship or magnanimous gestures in salaries, bonuses or benefits.

Joseph Rollins, President and Treasurer—31 years old; resident of Harrisburg and other urban areas including New York City until his recent relocation in Lancaster; master's degree in music at Cornell University and strong culture orientation; limited business experience confined to the music field; father a minister. Attitude shaped by a high degree of social consciousness; has considerable confidence in theories presented in text books; not strongly motivated by wealth or personal income. Awkward employee relationships following elevation to position of President after many months at a low level in the organization.

These remarks did not mean he lacked confidence about learning enough to survive eventually. However, the current personality differences intensified anxieties, closed doors, and cut off communications. Both worried about the actions of the other, but rarely informed the other unless he was directly involved. Consequently, Joe Rollins made some very poor decisions such as destroying some records needed for the Internal Revenue Service. During the same period he refused to fire a person guilty of gross negligence and failed to back a subordinate who had disciplined a worker.

The Monday morning executive management committee, set up to improve communications and to increase the contributions of Bruce Wilson, was not convened after the first few weeks. Peter Marshall was annoyed with Joe Rollin's attitude, but more important, he was genuinely concerned about the future of the business.

DEVELOPMENTS IN 1973-74

The results of organizational changes during the winter are given in Figure 4C–7 and are summarized in the following paragraphs.

1. Peter Marshall wanted to make greater use of some talents in the company. Minor reorganizations would also provide a test of his power. He also wanted to use promotions as a basis of increasing loyalty during his first year at the top of the company.

2. Central purchasing was given to Bruce Wilson. Control of unnecessary purchases, overaccumulation of inventories, and discounts from consolidated orders were the objectives. The system resulting from changes instituted by Mr. Wilson was a minor disaster. This responsibility remained under his direction, but revisions instituted by Rick Marshall and Michael Cromwell were required to begin rectifying the mistakes.

3. Improved flow of accounting data permitted the creation of profit and budget centers. It showed that the applicance business, established to enable customers to get appliances needed to use propane, was losing considerable sums of money. High overhead, (which included most of Mr. Wilson's salary), low volume, inventory charges, poor planning, and a low level of advertising and promotion were the causes. Consequently, Bruce Wilson was given until Spring of 1974 to develop and implement a plan for improving performance. Very little resulted from Mr. Wilson, largely because his successful local real estate firm and profitable greenhouse business left him with little motivation to "hustle" for the new owners.

4. Michael Cromwell, the controller, realigned his staff. Up until the time of the sale no internal accounting had been undertaken. At Bill Rollins' request, all financial information was turned over to a local public accounting firm. The company's officers received late and inadequate data on the business. This situation had served to

Figure 4C-7. Organization Effective January 1, 1974

Liberty Gas Co.

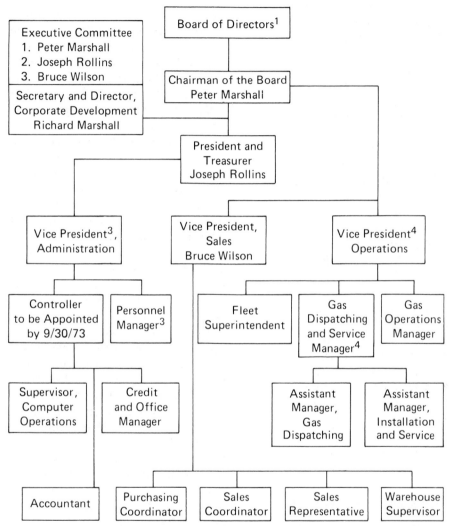

1. The Board of Directors will be composed of P. Marshall, and J. Rollins, plus one other person whom both can trust as an arbitrator.

2. Two positions are involved for R. Marshall: (a) Corporate Secretary, and (b) Director, Corporate Development. The latter involves: (i) Drawing-up an agenda for the Monday, 9 a.m. meetings, (ii) Completion of studies on profit improvement for existing operations, and (iii) Development of diversification opportunities. The Executive Committee will establish priorities for studies and venture analysis. R. Marshall will also be familiar with the Controller's job.

3. These positions can be filled indefinitely by J. Rollins.

4. These positions can be filled by P. Marshall, but a full-time Gas Dispatching and Service Manager should be employed next year.

125

encourage a "don't rock the boat with organizational changes" environment. Rick Marshall initiated analyses of where the company stood in Summer, 1973. However, Michael Cromwell established fundamental practices within Liberty Gas to give financial details promptly and regularly through the IBM System 3, and retained J.K. Lasser and Co. for audits and advice.

5. The "management board" is not shown on Figure 4C−7, but it consists of all salaried personnel who are not clerical. The board has become important to improved top/down communications and to shaping employee attitude on key issues. Peter Marshall, Joe Rollins, and Rick Marshall attend monthly meetings to answer questions and receive suggestions and proposals, but are not officers of the organization. One example of benefits to top management was an agenda item in March, 1974 on handling union organizers when neither Marshall nor Rollins were aware of the Teamster's attempt to unionize the company's workers. Early knowledge enabled the firm to resist the attempt successfully.

Operating Performance in 1973−74

Peter Marshall's long time relationships with the three suppliers helped to maintain a flow of propane from the refineries during the energy crisis. Optimizing logistics of the flow was assisted by Marshall's intuitive capacity to reduce the times and distance a truck traveled empty.

During the year actual cash flow was never near the forecasts made in the summer of 1973 and revised in October. The primary reasons were:

1. The average time for outstanding receivables was steadily shortened from about 60 days to 28 days during 1974. The customers seemed to be afraid that any delays in payment could lead to being cut off in a severe propane shortage.

2. Propane prices more than tripled during the year, the average price going from 8¢ per gallon in September, 1973 to 25¢ in February, 1974, after which it eased slightly. Purchases of propane are payable in 10 days, but there is a lag of 30 days in passing on the increase to the customer and receiving the cash. Marshall partly offset the problem by blending cheaper gas purchased earlier in the season with the more expensive gas, but there was an impact on cash flow.

3. Industrial sales, never previously considered by management, began in mid-summer of 1973. Liberty could obtain extra propane from the refineries through most of October to supply these new customers. Firms such as textile manufacturers and chemical producers, usually outside the company's marketing area, wanted all they could hold because of a potential shortage period.

The result of these developments was an abnormal cashflow curve in 1973−74, which flattened the seasonal impact and avoided any borrowing throughout the year. Summarizing, profit performance was significantly better than in previous years, despite:

1. the unusual operating circumstances in the first year under new ownership.
2. temporarily increased tax liability during 1973-74 from establishing a new fiscal year to better coincide with the seasonal nature of the business.
3. increasing tension between Peter Marshall and Joe Rollins.

The company would have cash to strengthen its present business and/or diversify.

Resolving the Problem at the Top

In May, 1974 a consultant from Rutgers University was asked to conceive a solution to the conflict between the two owners. Several incidents of mismanagement by Joe Rollins and problems stemming from poor communications had occurred during the first year. Peter Marshall feared that, if 1974—75 was a year of confusion and indecisive management, the future of the company might be jeopardized.

The proposal by the consultant shown in Figure 4C—8 evolved from a series of meetings with either Marshall or Rollins but not both at one time. It was discussed jointly in June, 1974, and there was general agreement that normally it was a workable solution. However, Peter Marshall did not have confidence in the judgment Joe Rollins might exercise in selecting investment alternatives. Also, Marshall freely admitted that he wanted the location of new businesses where "I can watch them every day."

Parallel to this development, Joe Rollins became unsure about being ready for the responsibilities given him in Figure 4C—8. It was apparent that he had not taken full advantage of the situation to gain needed experience in 1973—74, and the probability of failure was quite high. Rollins felt it would be better if he learned more about management before accepting the proposed position. Figure 4C—8 is found on pp. 128—129.

STUDENT PROBLEMS

1. Assume the role of Peter Marshall in August, 1974 and propose a solution to the problem which can be announced at the September 9 management board meeting. Describe how you plan to implement the solution in the organization by creating a Figure 4C—5 and a job description for both Peter Marshall and Joe Rollins.
2. Should either partner offer to buy the other partner's share? What would be an equitable settlement from Joe Rollins' point of view? From Peter Marshall's point of view? From Bill Rollins' point of view?
3. How could the existing problems have been averted by Bill Rollins when he sold the company to his nephew and Peter Marshall?

Figure 4C-8. Organizational Realignment Proposed by the Consultant

1. The following diagram summarizes the reorganization. It requires the formation of a new corporation in Summer, 1974 called the Liberty Development Corporation (hereafter called LDC). The titles of P. Marshall and J. Rollins will change accordingly in the subsidiary companies. Otherwise, officers and board members will remain the same.

Liberty Services, Inc.

Liberty Gas, Inc.
(Gas Operations)

Peter Marshall,
Chairman and President

Full Authority for Organizational and Operational Decisions

Full Authority to Buy Capital Items up to the Amount in the Annual Capital Budget

Full Authority to Commit to Projects Related to or Utilizing the Assets of the Existing Business up to $100,000/ Year Investment

Liberty Development Corp.
(LDC)

Joe Rollins,
Chairman and President

Full Authority to Set up Company Operations on a Budget of $1,500/Month

Full Authority to Investigate Acquisition Candidates, Identify Acceptable Terms, and Negotiate within Board Approved Terms on a Budget of $25,000 per Year

Full Authority to Guide Acquired Firms within Terms Set by the Board

2. Additional details of the reorganization affecting P. Marshall:
 * He will manage the gas business in a manner which maximizes net cash flow from operations. This includes full authority to make the decisions necessary to achieve this objective.
 * He is authorized to commit to capital items up to the amount established in the annual capital budget.
 * He is authorized to commit up to $100,000 per year in investments which: (a) are needed for gas operations separate from the capital budget; (b) improve earnings from appliances; (c) provide counterseasonal opportunities through greater utilization of personnel and facilities of the existing business; and (d) become essential for the growth of gas operations. Other types of investments will be handled by LDC.
 * He agrees to support LDC through the services of the Controller, the outside accounting firm and other gas company resources to assure LDC is complying completely with state and federal regulations. This would include LDC employees in personnel benefit packages, assistance from central purchasing, etc.
 * He will report to the Board of Directors on the profit performance of gas operations.

3. Additional details of the reorganization affecting J. Rollins:
 * He will investigate (within established budgets), negotiate (within Board approved limits), and acquire (contingent on Board approval) a going concern which conforms to the acquisition criteria and offers diversification to Liberty Services, Inc.

* He will set up a Philadelphia office which is ready to function on January 1, 1975 within established budgets.
* He will confine his interest and activity in gas operations to concern about profit and cash performance as a board member, 50% owner in the overall organization, and someone who may need cash equity to acquire a superior opportunity.
* He will receive headquarters administrative support for LDC, expenses to increase his knowledge in the field of acquisitions and mergers during the June–December, 1974 transition period, and full moving expenses.
* He will concentrate LDC activities, in the 2–3 year period following the first acquisition, to development of the new company rather than seeking new acquisitions in different fields.
* He will report to the board on LDC performance.

4. Reporting by the chief executive officers of the gas operations and LDC:

   Gas—Internal reporting will continue to evolve and improve in 1974–75. Monday financial summaries, monthly reports, 12 month operational plans, and other reports including budgets will be mailed to J. Rollins at the LDC office. Also, an updated organizational chart will be available at the LDC office at all times.

   Development—Budgets established for operations will be analyzed each month, the first report to be mailed to P. Marshall in the first week of February, 1975. This report will detail payments made for consulting and auditing services, and compare expenditures to budgets. In addition, J. Rollins will summarize progress toward an acquisition each month. The format for this report will contain analyses of candidates including market position, financial information, management/personnel appraisal, and a statement on operations, condition of plant and equipment, etc.

   Board of Director Meetings—A formal meeting will be held once per month, the location being determined a week in advance. Agenda items will be accepted by the Corporate Secretary up to that time although new business can always be introduced if necessary. Each meeting will include verbal reports on operations by P. Marshall and J. Rollins. It is agreed that the time between meetings should not exceed six weeks.

5. The time schedule for important events to implement the reorganization:

June, 1974	Board approval of the reorganization
Summer, 1974	Formation of LDC
June–December, 1974	Transition period. J. Rollins is located in Lancaster but spends full time on development and organizing the move to Philadelphia
January, 1975	Begin search
May, 1975	2–3 realistic acquisition candidates for Board guidance on priorities
June, 1975	Negotiating parameters for the prime alternative determined by the board
Summer, 1975	First acquisition completed

6. The criteria for the first acquisition is as follows:

   * LDC has majority ownership with full decision making authority (or Liberty Services, Inc., whichever is the appropriate entity).
   * Management is adequate to superior so that day-to-day operations need not require the input of P. Marshall and J. Rollins.
   * Debt portions of the financial package can be serviced by the cash flow of the acquired company.
   * Equity, if required, can be paid in installments, through an exchange of shares, notes, or other means which minimize the drain on cash from gas operations if a concern about availability of cash develops.
   * Scope of the acquisition exceeds $1 million in sales, and after-tax earnings plus depreciation is better than 15% DCF (discounted cash flow) rate of return.
   * A detailed takeover plan is to be prepared in advance of the acquisition to minimize the probability of a post-acquisition decline in profit performance.
   * J. Rollins must be able to communicate with no friction and establish good rapport with the general manager of the acquired firm.

129

Management Information Systems
for Executives

The importance of an information system to company performance is emphasized. Common personal systems of managers and those provided by the company are summarized including developments involving the computer and peripheral equipment. Principles for managing special studies to gain needed information not readily available are included as well as comparative systems. This chapter completes Part 1 which provides a foundation for learning about techniques in planning and strategy formulation in the next part. The student should know the basic points about responsibilities, policies, organization design, and information systems before proceeding to planning and strategy.

Information gathering is the next step in the decision-making process after definition of the objective or problem. Its purpose is to have as many relevant facts and opinions as possible prior to making the decision in order to increase the probability of taking the correct course of action. Management is often involved in complex situations, and so the information gathering step is complicated. Also, in few cases does management have sufficient time to obtain everything needed. As a result, managers often are forced to make decisions without all the relevant facts and opinions that exist on a given subject. Confidence in information sources available to the manager is critical in these situations.

5

Visualize a spectrum ranging from no information to complete information. Each time an executive makes a decision, the individual must ask, "How much information is available on this situation and what portion is required to make a good decision?"

Developing a system to provide management with adequate, reliable information is becoming a science. Careful design of the flow and volume of facts and opinions in companies is being motivated partly by the tremendous output of the computer, partly because of intense competition in most industries, and partly because many more decisions must be made quickly.

Figure 5–1. Information Scale for a Decision

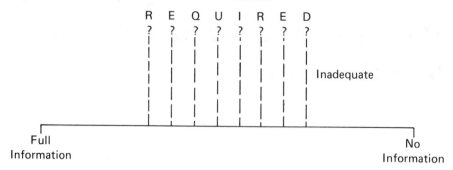

COMPANYWIDE INFORMATION SYSTEM

Most information gathering in a company is for use by all personnel. If an employee has a job in which he or she makes decisions, the person is usually a member of management and needs information in a particular field to perform adequately. This is the derivation of the term *management information* system and the shortened form, MIS.

MIS, it should be emphasized, is not only data from a computer. An information system must provide both qualitative and quantitative inputs for a decision. *The objective of a complete MIS is to supply the proper amount of accurate information to the correct user at the optimum time.*

Consider the following categories of information that pertain to decisions being made by executives and that make up the next four sections of this chapter.

1. *Executive Accumulated Information.* Astute managers are able to retain relevant information in their minds and establish files on a broad range of subjects relating to their responsibilities and those of others in top management, which might affect their performance. This knowledge is immediately available when they are asked to decide on a matter with no warning. Information is partially analyzed by executives as it is accumulated.

2. *Company Accumulated Information.* The library, interlibrary relationships, computer storage banks, data banks available on timeshare, and microfilm systems provide information on a regular basis to management (part of which might also be accumulated by the executive). This service may be limited to departmental scope, support divisions and subsidiaries, or may cover the whole company. A well-designed system provides the knowledge needed for a decision in a short period of time.

These two categories can represent: (1) a very small percentage of what is required for a good decision on an investment in a new geographic area, or (2) all of what is needed for a routine operating decision. For major decisions by executive management, the two sources of information typically provide up to half of the total information.

3. *Special Studies*. Frequently, studies are authorized to provide more information on a specific subject. This means gathering existing facts and developing new information not available in the MIS. The step is common for both minor problems and serious situations such as estimating important strategic variables (see Chapter Seven), determining company image, conducting feasibility studies, and undertaking technical research.

The third category might allow us to have most of the relevant information on a given subject. Very rarely do studies uncover 100%, and often when it occurs, the report does not disclose everything developed. Special studies usually represent the final effort to find facts and opinions for a company decision.

4. *The Unknown*. This is the category that makes most executives uneasy about important decisions. The question is, "Are there unknown facts that would provide other alternatives or change the conclusions reached on known alternatives?"

It is critically important for executive management to distinguish between:

Direct information that pertains to the subject only and issues of the subject for which facts and opinions are being developed.

Peripheral information that pertains to matters that could affect, but are not part of, the subject.

The combination of direct and peripheral makes up total relevant information on a subject. As mentioned previously, it is extremely uncommon to have total information pertaining to a decision. Frequently, there is a dominance of peripheral information. Executives must guard against this situation and consciously build a flow of direct information that will contribute to making them effective in decision making.

For example, the general manager of Division Z is evaluating a forecast of sales by a product manager. The manager must either approve or revise the forecast. If the forecast is revised, there must be sufficient grounds to overrule the person to whom responsibility for the product has been delegated. Direct information would include: (1) economic and relevant industry forecasts; (2) accuracy of the manager's previous forecasts; (3) strategies, factors and assumptions about competitors in the forecast, and (4) specific constraints such as production, warehousing, and so on.

Peripheral information in this case would be: (1) the forecasts of other product managers for the same time periods; (2) attitudes of top management on the general outlook for next year; (3) the job market for technical sales representatives if new personnel are required to achieve the forecast, and (4) the impact of expense accounts on the budget in years with a similar forecast.

Both direct and peripheral information are related to the decision. Each type is relevant because the general manager has overall responsibility for Division Z. However, direct information is usually more significant in a decision. Portions of peripheral information are important because of company interrelationships and the potential impact on other components of the division. For example, it might be necessary to ask the product manager for a revision to balance the forecast with other product managers, or to request an upward revision to use as a focal point in generating optimism for the coming year.

INFORMATION ACCUMULATED BY AN EXECUTIVE

The decision-making process reviewed in Chapter One is briefly as follows: (1) definition; (2) information gathering; (3) analysis and formulation of alternatives; (4) selection of the best alternative, and (5) evaluation of results and adjustments. The foundation of this process after definition of the decision parameters is the information gathering stage. Consequently, executives regard being informed as the basis for their managerial performance and career development.

Most positions in top management necessitate quick decisions and fast, competent opinions. The atmosphere is dynamic. Therefore, in order to be prepared, an executive should strive for the following objectives:

1. Establish a filtering process with the objective of segregating information into five types: (a) direct and important; (b) direct, but less important; (c) peripheral and important; (d) peripheral, but less important, and (e) not relevant. This task is carried out by instructions to the companywide information system, secretaries, and staff assistants. It is important that executives monitor the screening mesh to be certain it is neither too coarse nor fine. They must avoid the extremes of either inundation by paper or not having enough key information for their responsibilities.

2. Absorb the relevant information to have immediately avail-

able for decisions and rendering opinions. This involves reading vast amounts of material with above average comprehension and memorizing important statistics, innovative ideas, and operating details. Speed reading (at least three times the national average of 300 words per minute) is an essential management tool for executives.

3. Set up a filing system for information pertaining to normal decisions, projects affecting assigned responsibilities, and situations that could have impact on a manager's career such as information on a position to which he could be promoted. A modern system would involve microfilm, microfisch[1], and display screens with the accessory to make hard copies. However, this is quite elaborate for most executive positions in the 1970s.

With this system, a member of top management has a high probability of making good decisions. This assumes the person uses the company MIS to the maximum degree practical within a personal system in order to be prepared for quick decisions and opinions.

MIS ranges from a simple set of files in small companies to elaborate support systems in large corporations. Top management is expected to use this information and takes preference in situations when there is demand for the same item by lower levels in the organization.

Foundations of MIS

Study Figure 5—2. This diagram on how information is handled within a company is taken from *Computers and Management* by Donald H. Sanders, published by McGraw-Hill in 1970. The diagram is expanded by showing the types of detail that enter the system and the methods of handling qualitative information (see p. 136).

The process of gathering information from hundreds of sources is important and complicated. However, this work is useless if the people who need it do not know it exists or cannot obtain photocopies. The data, publications, documents, reports, memorandums, and so on are held in the following possible locations within the company.

1. *Library.* If one exists, the director establishes a standard system of cross-referencing in a card file. The material is either readily available on shelves or must be called from archives upon request.

---

[1] Microfisch is stiffer than microfilm and is stored in flat segments of a few inches rather than coils. Magazines and journals can be purchased in this form, and it is a convenient means of keeping reports and plans prepared for management.

Figure 5–2. Handling Information

Ideas → Quantitative Facts → Quantitative Estimates and Forecasts → Qualitative Facts → Qualitative Opinion → Ideas → Quantitative Facts

Steps in the Data-Processing Operation

Processing Methods	Originating—Recording	Classifying	Sorting	Calculating	Summerization	Storing	Retrieving	Reproducing	Communicating
Manual methods	Human observation; hand-written records; pegboards	Hand posting; pegboards	Hand posting; pegboards; edge-notched cards	Human brain	Pegboards; Hand calculations	Paper in files, journals, ledgers, etc.	File clerk; bookkeeper	Clerical; carbon paper	Written reports; hand-carried messages
Manual with machine assistance	Typewriter; cash register	Cash register; bookkeeping machine	Mechanical collators	Adding machines; calculators; cash registers	Accounting machines; adding machines; cash registers	Motorized rotary files; microfilm		Xerox machines; duplicators; addressing machines	Documents prepared by machines; message conveyors
Electro-mechanical punched card method	Prepunched cards; Keypunched cards; mark-sensed cards	Determined by card field design; sorter; collator	Card sorter	Accounting machines (tabulators) calculating punch		Trays of cards	Manual tray movement	Reproducing punch	Printed documents
Electronic methods	Magnetic tape encoder; magnetic and optical character readers; card and tape punches; on-line terminals	Determined by systems design; computer	Office card corter; computer sorting	Computer		Magnetizable media and devices; punched media; computer	Online inquiry with direct access devices; manual movement of storage media to computer	Multiple copies from printers	Online data transmission; printed output; visual display; voice output

2. *Computer Center.* If one exists, the director establishes a card file system similar to the standard library system. The information is sometimes stored directly in the computer memory bank, but most often storage is in trays of cards, magnetized media, and punched media.

3. *Departmental Files.* Some information retained by segments of the organization are required for carrying out particular responsibilities. This may include a small library for specialized purposes such as law.

4. *Personal Files.* The distinction between personal and departmental files is who has access to them. An executive and personal staff can be expected to accumulate information directly from bankers, consultants, customers, government, and miscellaneous outside sources. Some of this material is filed for counterproductive purposes such as company politics and power struggles for funds.

It can be seen that important information, which could significantly clarify alternatives in the decision-making process, is occasionally filed without reaching the appropriate person. To avoid this, some companies are appointing a director for MIS who coordinates the accumulation of information and consolidates this material through a reference system. This position is new to many firms and is often an expansion of the duties given to the director of either the library or computer center.

One reason for initiating organizational changes to improve flow of information is the technical advances that have occurred in the past few years. These include:

1. *Microfilm and Microfisch Display Systems.* These necessitate reducing pertinent information onto film and slides for both compact storage purposes for ready display with the assistance of the computer. Using call numbers similar to a library system, a terminal will retrieve the desired information and show it on a viewer. If a copy is needed, a hard copy printer can produce a photocopy as part of the system.

2. *Timeshare Data Banks.* Links with detailed data offered to the company on a fee basis have been made possible by using telephone line connections with a computer being shared by other companies. An example would be financial information for the Fortune 500 and Second 500 companies. Users often design subprograms to capsulize the volumes of data for specific purposes. The economics from multi-users has resulted in charges of only $20−25 per hour.

3. *Computer Speed and Capacities.* The objective of an integrated MIS for the whole company has become a real possibility by computer memories of 100 million± bits at low cost. Also, ac-

complishment has been accelerated by the capacity to handle this scope of information at great speed.

Examples of some of this equipment randomly selected from several alternatives are shown in Figure 5–3.

One reason for advanced equipment being desirable for MIS is the diverse demands on the system. It services accounting, engineering, finance, industrial design, law, personnel, productions, research, and other departments. Many of the uses cross organizational lines, and there is a need for ideas, not just data. Interfunctional committees may need the same information as three to four departments. The stress on a MIS can be understood by adding one additional complication—divisions and subsidiaries with completely different product lines.

The design of MIS for a complex organization is taking two broad directions:

Centralized. This approach involves gathering information under a master control center from all organizational entities and supplying reports and servicing special requests from headquarters and other branch locations. Operation of the MIS and authorization for access to information in the system is under the control center.

Decentralized. Divisions, subsidiaries, and major functional entities build their own MIS. Companywide coordination takes various degrees of formality ranging from a headquarters listing of the information retained at the other locations under a simplified control center to only top executives reporting on the operation to executive management.

It is a responsibility of executive management to make sure that the system selected for the company actually functions. The probability of making creative, workable plans at the top level is jeopardized by a poor MIS. Also, performance at all levels will decline if people have inadequate information on which to make decisions.

Summarizing, information that has been kept in several places within the firm can now be centralized so that all levels of management can have access to what they need to meet their responsibilities. The motivation to establish an effective companywide MIS has developed from: (1) avoiding information being available within the firm but not being used to make decisions because it was not known to be there, and (2) introduction of technical advances in equipment which make a companywide system economically and physically feasible.

It should be emphasized that while an integrated or companywide MIS is feasible, many years of evolution are necessary for firms to realize the full potential while actively trying to establish such a system. This means creating a position that effectively acts as the

Figure 5–3. Random Examples of MIS Equipment

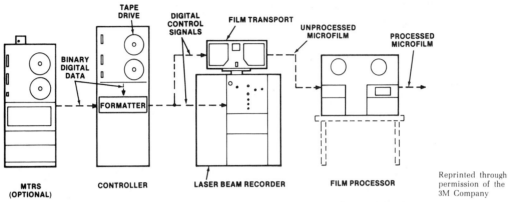

MTRS (OPTIONAL) — CONTROLLER — LASER BEAM RECORDER — FILM PROCESSOR

The diagram shows how information is routed in a system using 3M's new Laser Beam Recorder (LBR). A mini-computer (left) is optional—if not used, a computer tape may be mounted on the tape drive of a controller.

1. Kodak Miracode II Encoder. The input unit is a compact tabletop electronic device which controls the code and document functions of the microfilmer.

2. Kodak Miracode II Controller, Mod 12. The Mod 12 is a small tabletop electronic control unit designed primarily for those applications in which the document coding requires standard search logic and a retrieval handle up to 12 digits.

3. Kodak Miracode II Controller, Mod 18. For more complex applications, the Mod 18 is used where greater depth of retrieval search and expanded logic capabilities are needed.

4. Kodak Miracode II Retrieval Terminal. Linked to either the Mod 12 or Mod 18, the retrieval terminal allows the operator to locate and display any coded document.

focal point for consolidation of information, delegating sufficient authority to that position to obtain and centralize data and files throughout the firm, and gaining executive management support for companywide MIS.

Problem Areas

Some problems are shared by simple and complex systems.

Management Routine

An executive develops a routine for acquiring and storing information. If it has worked for the individual over the years, he or she is reluctant to change. While it seems logical to make full use of new systems, many of these innovative concepts have failed the manager in the past. The worst aspect of top management adhering to an outdated system is that others in the organization follow this attitude and do not give full support to a comprehensive MIS. Usage under these circumstances may not justify the expenditures needed to make it work. Lack of confidence in the system, particularly occasional failures to obtain qualitative information needed for judgments, contributes to reluctance about endorsing companywide MIS.

Organizational Changes

MIS needs a manager with sufficient authority and budget to plan and implement the steps toward a successful companywide system. Without full commitment through required organizational changes, the company will usually get an inadequate system. Corporate politics and power struggles sometimes play a role in giving authority to the MIS manager.

Changes in Reports and Other Systems

The need for authority becomes more evident when it is necessary to alter, for example, the layout of accounting reports or budget forms to be compatible with the MIS being introduced. Report timing and content may have to be changed. The controller, manager of administration, and the heads of finance, marketing production, and so on must be willing to cooperate. While success is partly dependent on personality and approach, authority will play an important role in obtaining the cooperation.

Uprooting the Existing MIS

Management wants a demonstrable return on money invested in

new equipment and the expense of changing to new systems. Executives hear many optimistic forecasts of results from proposals such as modern MIS, and have been disappointed by actual performance. As a result, some executive cynicism about return on investment is common. To obtain support, the cost/benefit analysis must be thorough yet conservative in predicting the return a company will gain from this installation.

MIS on a modern scale is not economically feasible for every company. However, developments in the 1970s have greatly increased the number of firms that can benefit from a good information base for decision making. New concepts in low-cost storage, immense high-speed computers, reasonably priced microfilm systems, and nearly total automation makes viewing and hard copies relatively inexpensive for large companies. The growing complexity of business justifies installation in more and more instances. However, actual realization of the potential of MIS will depend on the success with which the four problems are overcome.

Comments on Executive Management Information Systems

The concept of MIS is *statistics* for many people, including some experts. However, MIS is a broader concept than this. It includes subjective opinions, written reports, memorandums, ideas from periodicals, pictures of new equipment, and other nonquantitative information. This scope results in complications for executive management.

Confidential Information

Top management must have the option of keeping reports confidential. The computer permits security, but a companywide MIS presents problems for restricting access to key documents.

One solution is use of timeshare, telephone lines, and computers used by several other clients but carefully guarded against leaks. Programs designed for executive needs, such as personnel evaluation systems, can be obtained only by certain members of executive management through restricted computer terminals, a password and dial codes. This portion of MIS could be seperate from the companywide system.

Another solution is the Strategic Decision Center discussed in Chapter Nine. Several decision-making aids are concentrated in one large room with peripheral equipment in a limited number of offices. This method permits use of security precautions less feasible when individual executives at all organizational levels are using MIS.

Summaries

Time is a precious resource for top management. To get needed information without exploring several possibilities for each item there are four alternatives.

1. The executive's staff does the hunting and summarizes the detail for efficient use.
2. The MIS format requires an "executive summary" for each report exceeding a specified length. A hard copy from the microfilm gives a synopsis of the originator's version of the information.
3. The MIS staff prepares a summary of developments in areas of interest to various members of executive management. These can takes the form of regular reports and alert bulletins.
4. Outside services provide concise summaries such as foreign reports for the manager of international operations.

All four methods are probably necessary for executive management to achieve a high level of performance. While many executives are still casual about information flow and do not make good use of advanced MIS's, the scarcity of time, increasing competition, complexities from social responsibilities, government involvement, and so on necessitate more highly informed executives.

Selection of Information to Be Received

It is important to stress that these comments are from the perspective of executive management. Less precise methods might be acceptable for lower levels of the organization.

View the information gathering process from the position of an executive in top management. The individual has the multiple channels of information shown in Figure 5—4.

Some examples will clarify specifics about the channels. The MIS provided by the company is formal and internal. An executive's contacts outside the company provide facts, opinions, and rumors, which are informal and external. Consultants retained by the firm are formal and external. Contacts inside the company, which include verbal reports gathered by the executive and personal staff, are informal and internal. It is essential to realize that an executive has these multiple channels. The staff must design systems to utilize fully these critical sources.

Regarding the company MIS, convincing executives that they must avail themselves of all this information is sometimes stated as a responsibility of those directing the system. This is nonsense. Top management is normally a sponge for details that will help them perform more effectively. While the manager of MIS has the

Figure 5-4. Channels of Information

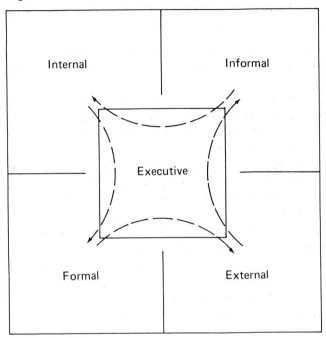

responsibility to communicate what is available, there is a parallel responsibility at the top to locate what is needed.

Adjusting the Flow

After examination of the total system, a formal 60–90 day trial period should be established. If it is not formal, there will be little motivation to review carefully the flow and determine if it is what is required. Adjustments will lead to a second stage of an equal period to decide on the type, frequency, and detail the executive desires. The third stage stabilizes the flow until revisions are made.

The executive and staff can regard the flow casually or treat it as a resource that can be adjusted as one would adjust a valve in a refinery to get the right mixture. Because this source will probably produce a great volume of information, and consequently needs most to be controlled, it is logical to monitor inflow and modify the number and type of sources for this information.

SPECIAL STUDIES

In large companies there are special studies being conducted regularly. The purpose is to: (1) gather information from sources inside and outside the firm; (2) analyze the results of this research; (3) reach conclusions, and (4) make recommendations. The subjects for studies, concerning executive management are:

1. Feasibility studies on expansion programs, acquisitions, mergers, divestitures, and other major applications of the company's capital.
2. Analyses of competitive position including new product developments, marketing strategies, sales forecasts, cost reduction breakthroughs, and similar areas to assess the company's present and future positions.
3. Shareholder problems such as dividend policies, company image in the stock market, possible discontent with management decisions, and other matters that might be suggested by the board of directors.
4. Probes for future opportunities ranging from market studies to research projects for internal product development.
5. Sources of capital for future investments including creative terms for loans, new issues of shares, potential partners, and unusual means of obtaining funding.
6. Miscellaneous subjects including: back-up information for government investigations, suits against/by competitors, union negotiations, and so on; strategies on sources of raw materials, energy, key executives, and so on; reorganization analyses, and similar areas.

Special studies are sometimes part of company politics and power struggles. Decisions can be delayed by study after study until the project or issue dies. Careful planning is needed to avoid this tactic by opposition within the firm or at the board of director level. While valid concern about important points in a proposal is the usual motivation leading to a study, maneuvers to avoid unpopular decisions or those obstructing career plans are common.

Managing Special Studies

Executive management is rarely involved in directing studies. This occurs only when the situation is extremely important to the company in achieving either its short-range operational plans or long-range goals. More often, key executives limit their involvement to the following:

1. Defining the objectives and scope of the study including guidelines for expenses to be incurred.
2. Selecting the manager of the study who will have direct responsibility for results.

3. Analyzing the research approach designed by the project manager for creativity, thoroughness, and compatibility with objectives and budgets.
4. Approving personnel and consultants selected to participate in the study.
5. Monitoring progress at important checkpoints in the study and making suggestions on adjustments to the research approach.
6. Reviewing and criticizing drafts of the results to be certain conclusions and recommendations relate to objectives of the study.

Because of the need to allocate time to several responsibilities, the executive must resist the temptation of doing someone else's job and overmanaging the study. On the other hand, many decisions might be waiting for specific results, and the project manager may have no knowledge of important strategies dependent on the work. This means more involvement for a top executive than waiting for a bound report to appear on the desk.

Guidelines on Cost and Performance

Table 5−1 gives estimates for an average study. Total cost can vary immensely depending on scope, management of the project, need for special experiments such as core drillings or computer simulation, use of consultants, travel and type of report required.

The table shows that conclusions and recommendations will be

Table 5−1. Cumulative Percentage of Completion in an Average Study

Stage of Study	Information Gathered	Analysis Completed	Costs Incurred
Design, Orientation, and Preliminary Information Search	33−50%	10%	10−15%
Field Work, and Experiments, and Other Research	75−80%	50−60%	75−80%
Report Drafts, Study Completion and Presentations	80−85%	100%	100%

based on less than total information. It is unlikely that something of major importance will be included in the missing information. However, this occurs and is more probable when a study has been poorly managed or some participants have not performed effectively. Total information developed might be only 60–75%, and key items could be missing.

An executive cannot be certain whether a study has been thorough. An estimate will be more accurate if the individual has completed the six points given under "Managing Special Studies." Developing more information is expensive. Direct experience indicates that each 5% added after completion of an average study will cost about 25% of the original budget. For example, a $20,000 analysis of a potential acquisition is completed, but executive management has the feeling it should conduct an audit of executive salaries, expense accounts, loans to/from the company, and other details of their compensation arrangements. This analysis would cost about $5,000 or 25% of $20,000.

It takes judgment gained from several years of business experience to gauge whether the decisions depending on the study are sufficiently important to justify the overall cost, and if additional information is needed at the conclusion of the study to make a good decision. Recommendations in the report will give some indication, but executive judgement is more often the basis for authorizing additional work.

Guidelines on Study Design and Implementation

The following are fundamental points for an executive with the goal of completing a successful study within budgets.

1. Definition of the objective must include the detail required for a decision. For example, it should be known whether cost data must be as detailed as possible ($5.98) or estimates based on available information ($6±).

2. The total budget should be composed of details on expenditures, not just rough estimates for major categories such as personnel, travel, consultants, special experiments, and so on. It is rare that studies are completed in less than the budgeted expense. Management should recognize this and allow for contingencies in their planning.

3. Contracts with consultants should be carefully reviewed to be certain that: (a) talent within the consulting firm is actually being applied to the study in amounts of time specified and not junior inexperienced people. (b) all costs are identified. (c) timing is stated and incentives to meet timing obligations are included such as penalty clauses for late submission of reports.

4. Time to orient personnel participating in the study is usually an advisable investment. They should receive a job description; clarification of the timing required, leads on necessary information if known, and any special instructions such as confidential treatment of their work. The project manager should stress the free flow of communications between study team members.

5. The study design should include checkpoints at two to three times during the work to evaluate what was expected to have been accomplished and what has actually been done. This identifies problem areas, permits adjustments to be made, and increases the probability of meeting deadlines.

6. The project manager should obtain a synopsis of findings by each study team member either at the completion of field work but while still in the area, or at the beginning of writing draft reports. This gives an early indication of results, and isolates any missing pieces of information needed before drawing conclusions.

7. The project manager should know the quality of report expected (printing, professional graphics, and so on) and whether presentations to committees and groups of executives are anticipated.

Attention to the seven points results in improved quantity and quality of information. The process of thorough design, efficient preparation, well-supervised research, and free flow of communications will lead to good conclusions and recommendations.

Computerized Control

An important development in project management is the use of computerized network models. Commercial programs and those designed by individual companies give details on timing, costs of early completion, and the usual information expected from PERT, CPM, (or combinations of these network models), simulation, and linear programming. Examples include CPM (based on the Rand Corporation's Ford—Fulkerson Algorithum), MRPL (Maximum Remaining Path Length), PERTSIM (Monte Carlo simulation of a PERT), and PERT 6 (standard PERT solution). Hours of executive time can be saved both in study design and later in supervising the study.

Use of the Studies

Executive management is rarely unanimous in their evaluation of a study. Disregarding company politics, which is not easy to eliminate from executive opinions on a matter, different perspectives yield different opinions on the conclusions and whether recommendations are valid. Recognizing this point, the person authorizing the study usually takes the following steps:

1. Results are compared with the objective to determine the position on the business situation. If the individual concludes that the study supports the contentions supposed before it was undertaken, the person will decide on how to use it in persuading other members of executive management to accept this point of view. If the study is contrary to the original assumption, the next step will be either to modify the position or contest the results for justifiable reasons.

2. The executive must then develop strategies that will make maximum use of the study and other information on the decision to be made. The purposes of this step are to develop the backing of key members of executive management, and avoid maneuvering by the opposition that damages his position. For example, the individual might arrange a series of breakfast meetings to give him an opportunity to persuade other executives without interruption.

3. Constructive ideas and suggestions come up in the discussions, and modifications are needed to refine the approach and secure the support of other executives. Ultimately, the executive defines the position of others in executive management and whether they will give overall approval.

The investment in time and money for a study can be justified both by offering additional evidence that the proposition is good, or that it is bad and should be dropped. An inconclusive study makes a decision difficult. However, if it has been well managed, even no conclusions and recommendations can lead to postponing a decision that should not be made.

UNKNOWN INFORMATION

Despite a conscious effort to be informed on subjects related to responsibilities and specific decisions, portions of total information remain undiscovered.

Most of the time decisions would be unaffected by the unknown information even if it had been retrieved by one of the systems. However, each day the *Wall Street Journal* reports business mistakes that rational executives would not have committed if they had been fully informed. Consequently, top management is cautious about the information base on which major decisions are made. Quoting Robert Townsend in *Up The Organization*, "Decisions are of two kinds, those which are expensive to correct and those which are not." The objective of the information sources described in this chapter is to make decisions that either do not have to be corrected or are inexpensive to rectify.

Figure 5-5. Executive Management Information System

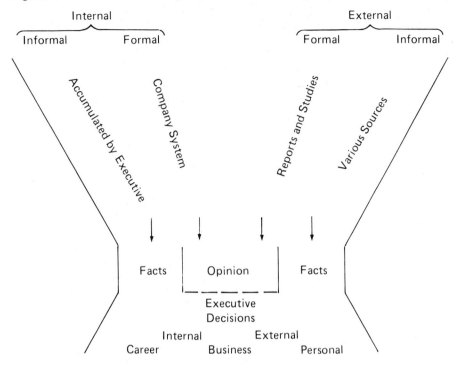

Figure 5-5 illustrates an example of an executive management information system.

COMPARATIVE COMPUTERIZED INFORMATION SYSTEMS

Three relative levels of system sophistication describe business use of the computer in processing information: (1) repetitive data processing; (2) management control information, and (3) strategic decision-making information. A fourth situation occurs when companies have strong engineering and research components in the organization and require access to a wide variety of sources for solutions and ideas. This section, however, emphasizes the third level, strategic decision-making information systems.

This system level is designed to improve the probability of major decisions being correct and to shorten the time needed to take appropriate action. This is accomplished by utilizing: simulation; mathematical models for forecasting; programs for common quantitative methods; high-speed executive summary printouts of present position; comparisons with historical performance and relationship with plans, and specially designed programs such as personnel evaluation and capital allocation. Experimentation with variables is feasible, and this enables executives to avoid costly mistakes. Also, excellent display screens are linked with the data base and computer to communicate the information graphically rather than just in print-outs. Figure 5–6 illustrates the flow of such a system.

Stages of development for strategic decision-making information systems at three companies are described briefly to clarify the range of possibilities.

Figure 5–6. A Schematic of Information Flow Assisted by a Computer

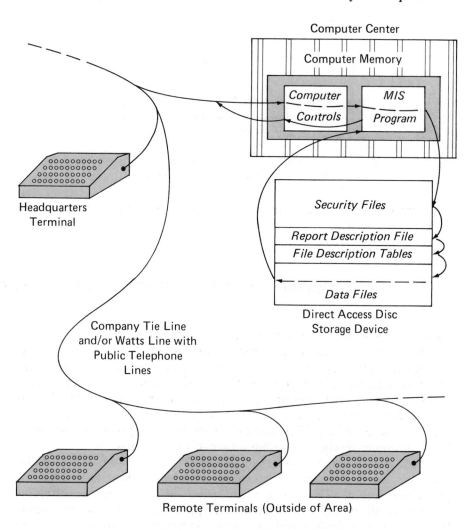

Armstrong Cork Company

Armstrong Cork was established in 1860 and currently manufactures and markets a comprehensive range of interior furnishings including resilient flooring and carpets, ceiling systems, and furniture. It also handles a variety of specialty products for the building, automotive, textile, and other industries. Sales for 1974 totaled more than $889 million and earnings over $37 million after taxes. Armstrong has assets of $734 million, more than 50 plants around the globe, and employs 24,000 people.

At the present time, Armstrong's MIS is used mainly for repetitive data processing and management control information, rather than for strategic decision making. However, the company is building a more sophisticated system to contain strategic planning information utilizing operating results and employee data bases. Eventually, cathode ray tubes will be installed for information retrieval. Initial access to the data base is through the use of proprietary file management and an inquiry software system called Mark IV. In most cases, the inquiry is made by an intermediary person for use by management.

E. I. duPont de Nemours and Company

The duPont Company was originally established in 1802 to manufacture explosives. Since then it has become one of the world's largest and most diversified manufacturing enterprises. Included in its product line are fibers, such as Dacron, Nylon, Orlon, Quiana, and Kevlar; plastic materials, such as Polyethylene and Teflon; and film. Sales for 1974 totaled more than $6.9 billion, and after-tax earnings were $404 million. DuPont has more than 4.8 billion dollars in net assets and employs more than 118,000 men and women in its total operations.

The Information Systems Department (ISD), which is located in Wilmington, Delaware, operates an impressive central computer facility and offers programming to all departments. When a manager has a need for potentially strategic information that is in storage in the computer, the individual contacts ISD. Computer hardware for information is under this department's control. An exception to this would be some research engineers and chemists who operate a timesharing terminal for their own project information and calculations.

DuPont makes significant use of computer output, and microfilm techniques that (1) increase the availability of data; (2) reduce the use of paper and (3) save storage space. Sales data, sales forecasts, and financial data are examples of information readily available to managers. Detailed comparisons between historical, present, and projected performance facilitate decision making by managers at all levels in the organization.

DuPont's total company information system is extremely sophisticated and aids executive management in major company decisions. Consequently, duPont is considered to have a start toward a strategic decision-making information system. However, line and staff management are not permitted to have direct access to hardware.

General Electric

The General Electric Company was formed in 1892 with the merger of the Edison Company and the Thomson—Houston Electric Company. In 1974 General Electric sales and after-tax earnings were $13.4 billion and $608 million, respectively. That makes General Electric the fifth largest industrial company in the world. Growth for GE has come in chemicals and plastics springing from the search for better insulating materials; Man-Made™ industrial diamonds and special metals; services such as computer timesharing and entertainment; and space equipment such as the Earth Resources Technology Satellite.

GE, through its worldwide Mark III information service computer network, is the world's largest network computer services supplier. GE operates two computer "super centers," one located near Cleveland, Ohio and one in suburban Washington, D.C. Even though the two centers are more than 300 miles apart, they are totally integrated, through the use of high-speed communication links, and can operate as if they were under the same roof.

These super centers coupled with several regional centers and locally operated computers provide the basis for a very high level of strategic decision making. GE uses the "utility concept" which is computer power, like electrical power, delivered to a user who decides how it will be used and what type of equipment will be plugged in for usage.

The level of systems sophistication varies widely within GE despite access to super center facilities. In some locations historical data, mathematical models for forecasting, and simulation techniques are available to managers on cathode ray tubes or other high-speed terminals to facilitate manipulation of variables. In other locations, however, systems are limited to repetitive data processing. As a result, no single level of system sophistication can be said to exist within GE.

Figure 5—5, found on page 149, summarizes the concepts in this chapter.

Four categories of information confront an executive making a decision: (1) accumulation in personal files for immediate reference; (2) companywide information retrieval systems; (3) special studies that gather facts and opinions from outside sources as well as internal information systems, and (4) the unknown which could affect the decision. The equation here is important in evaluating applicable information.

Direct + Peripheral + Unknown = Total information for a decision

Top managers usually have personal systems that include: (1) filtering information flow to establish files which are quickly retrievable; (2) a conscious effort to retain key information in mind, and (3) a career plan with diary notations on important points. The executive will achieve such a system most efficiently with contributions by competent staff assistants who understand the value of the system.

Companywide systems involve cross-referencing and a method for retrieving information in company libraries, the computer center, departmental files, and personal files. Although complex, the development of microfilm display systems that are computer controlled, timeshare data banks and much greater computer speed and storage capacity make these systems feasible. Executive management must strive toward having all possible information available for decisions and avoid having important details buried in files. However, five problem areas are cited that limit progress toward a fully efficient system.

Executive management must participate in the design of an MIS because of concern about restricting access to confidential information. Also, executives will wish to receive summaries to conserve time, and guidelines must be given on content and layout. Finally, they must continually refine the information flowing from the MIS in an effort to be current and reflect changing responsibilities.

Six categories of special studies involving executive management are given. Quality of results will depend on: (1) defining study objectives; (2) selecting the project manager; (3) analyzing the study design; (4) approving personnel and consultants; (5) monitoring progress, and (6) criticizing drafts. Review Table 5-1 for guidelines on costs and performance and the seven points that are fundamental in achieving a successful study.

DISCUSSION QUESTIONS

1. The rate of growth of American business has increased at a very rapid pace in the 1960s and 1970s. How much of this growth can be attributed to the emergence of MIS and computerized information control?
2. What is behind management reluctance to utilize MIS to its fullest potential?
3. What are some of the cost benefit aspects of MIS in a small company as compared to duPont or General Electric?
4. What are the dangers of making decisions with the knowledge that some information is not known?
5. Explain the difference between direct and peripheral information.
6. Why would some successful companies centralize MIS while others decentralize? Is there a relationship to organizational concepts given in Chapter Five?
7. Will MIS overcome the problem of having information within a company and important to a decision, and executives not knowing it is available?
8. Give additional examples of internal, external, formal, and informal channels of information.

SUGGESTED READINGS AND BIBLIOGRAPHY

"A Decision Oriented Information System," *Journal of Systems Management.* October, 1972.

"A.A.I.M.S. American Airlines Answers the What Ifs," *Infosystems.* February, 1973, pp. 40–41.

"Beyond MIS: A Practical Total Informations System," *Data Processing Magazine.* Winter, 1973.

Brown, R.G. "Questions Users Should Ask About Information Systems," *Management Review.* April, 1972, pp. 59–60.

"Communication Needs of MIS," *Journal of Systems Management.* December, 1972.

"Decision and Information Systems for Strategic Planning," *Business Horizons.* April, 1973.

Fisher. "Management and the Information Revolution," *Datamation.* June, 1969, pp. 53–57.

"Giving the Newly Annointed Some Help," *Infosystems.* September, 1972, pp. 26–28.

Gerry, G.A. and Morton, M.S.S. "Framework for Management Information Systems," *Sloan Management Review.* Fall, 1971.

Head, R.V. "New Breed," *Journal of Systems Management.* May, 1969.

Joseph. "Coming Age of MIS," *Finance Executive*. August, 1969, pp. 45−46.

"MIS Concept or Misconception," *Journal of Systems Management*. December, 1972.

Murdick, R.G. and Ross, J.E. "Future Management Information Systems," *Journal of System Management*. April, 1972, pp. 22−25.

"No, a Management System Isn't Possible," *Industry Week*. January 8, 1973.

"Problems in Planning the Information System," *Harvard Business Review*. March, 1971, pp. 75−89.

"Selling the System (MIS)," *Journal of Systems Management*. October, 1972.

Spiro, B.E. "What's a M.I.S.?" *Data Management*. September, 1971, pp. 48−51.

"The Concept of Management Information Systems for Managers," *Management International Review*. 1972, pp. 25−29.

Comprehensive Case: Control Data Corporation

Developments at Control Data Corporation (CDC) provide a unique opportunity to reinforce the fundamentals learned in Part 1 and to prepare for Part 2 on techniques. The company experienced a very difficult period between 1968 and early 1973, and Section 1 concentrates on these events. Section 2 uses the CDC Systems and Services Co. as a means of giving insight on both the material in the first five chapters and information systems.

SECTION 1: BACKGROUND ON THE COMPANY

When William C. Norris, chairman of Control Data Corporation in Minneapolis, settled his company's private antitrust suit against International Business Machines Corporation in January, 1973, he called his 1968 move to go to court the "best business decision" he had ever made. The settlement is given in Table C–1.

Mr. Norris, 64 in 1975, is the only technical pioneer to end up operating a major company in the computer field. In 1957, after five years as general manager of Sperry Rand's Univac Division, Norris gathered a group of engineers who founded

Control Data. Working out of an old warehouse, CDC produced a successful line of solid-state computers designed primarily for engineering and scientific use. This led to larger and larger machines, and the company won significant contracts from the Navy and the Atomic Energy Commission. Mr. Norris had to run a tight, low-overhead operation that gave him a reputation for being a dour and blunt manager.

The recession in the computer industry in 1969–71 hit CDC particularly hard. The company was overdependent on the volatile government markets for engineering type computers. In 1970 the company had the operating loss, shown in Table C–2, and a sales decrease of $45 million from the previous year.

Table C-1. Settlement with IBM

On January 15, 1973, Control Data and IBM announced a settlement of the 1968 antitrust suit against IBM:

* Sale by IBM to Control Data of Service Bureau Corporation (SBC), a wholly owned subsidiary of IBM, including an agreement by IBM not to engage in the data services business in the United States for six years.

* Award by IBM to Control Data of four five-year research and development contracts expected to gross about $6 million per year over the next five years.

* Extension of a worldwide patent cross-licensing agreement between Control Data and IBM until June 30, 1978.

* Reimbursement to Control Data by IBM for costs and expenses including legal fees, in the amount of $15 million.

SBC was purchased for approximately $16 million. IBM has agreed to leave its equipment installed with SBC for six months without rental charges. It has about 40 offices throughout the United States engaged in data processing operations. In 1972 SBC earned $1.5 million after taxes on revenues of $63 million.

IBM has contracted for the continuing use of data processing services from SBC and minimum services and availability charges are expected to be in the range of $5 million per year for the next five years.

IBM has provided for reimbursement of $2.6 million per year for ten years to SBC for future retirement and other fringe benefits of current employees.

Table C-2. Financial Details

	$Million					
	1974	1973	1972	1971	1970	1969
Net Sales	556.1	506.4	386.9	347.8	353.7	398.4
Rentals and Service	544.9	441.8	276.8	223.4	185.8	172.3
Total Revenue — CDC	1101.0	948.2	663.7	571.2	539.5	570.7
Net Earnings — CDC	(30.7)	17.2	10.3	(9.9)	(36.1)	18.5
Net Earnings — CCC*	34.4	43.7	55.6	50.3	38.2	34.8
Other Affiliated Companies	—	—	(3.5)	(4.6)	(5.3)	(1.6)
Total Corporate earnings	3.7	60.9	62.4	35.8	(3.2)	51.7

* Commercial Credit Company is a large financing firm acquired in 1969 by CDC to support the sales and rentals of its equipment. It is, however, an independent operation not related to the computer business.

At the same time CDC was tooling up to make its newest supercomputer, the 7600. This was by far the largest and most costly engineering and production effort that the company had ever undertaken. And at the same time, it was developing two other supercomputers.

Morale plummeted as the company laid off employees, trimmed budgets, and cut costs by asking its workers to take an extra two-week unpaid vacation. The market value of CDC stock dropped to a low of $29 per share from its 1967 peak of $166. Security analysts criticized its single-minded pursuit of supercomputers under its reclusive computer design genius, Seymour Cray, and its unpopular attack on giant IBM.

Cray who had been responsible for designing all the company's supercomputers, resigned in the middle of the development of the 8600 computer, another superscale machine four to eight times as powerful as the 7600 and considered by many to be the company's future hope. Perhaps even worse, the development work on another supercomputer, the Star, ran into prolonged programming delays under the direction of James Thornton, a colleague of Cray and the company's alternate technical hope. Later Thornton, then vice president for technology, went on indefinite leave and now has only a consulting relationship.

One critically important decision in the late 1960s, in addition to the Commercial Credit merger in 1969, which provided financial strength and profits for plowback into computers, was concentrating sales of computer peripherals to original equipment manufacturers (OEM). Because none of IBM's competitors had as much as 10% of IBM's volume, it was almost impossible for CDC and others to compete across the board in all computer products. Without high-volume production, the manufacturing costs of precision products such as line printers, disk files, and sometimes even computers themselves exceeded the going market prices. To get production volume up, CDC concentrated on selling its peripherals to other manufacturers.

CDC's biggest success was in tape transports, printers, and disk files. Thomas Kamp, who now heads CDC Peripheral Products Co., recalls a number of times that other mainframe manufacturers decided to make their own disk files, only to find their actual costs were higher than CDC's prices, so they kept CDC as supplier. The operation was a steady profitmaker, and executives feel the company would never have survived without the OEM policy.

In 1971 these sales, rentals, and income from services, substantially lessened losses. The major problems with supercomputers were worked out and the company was ready for the upturn in the economy which occurred in 1972.

Reorganization after the IBM Settlement

After the January, 1973 settlement, the company resumed the growth experienced before the 1969–71 recession.

To keep the momentum, Chairman Norris has: (1) changed his management organization to put more emphasis on service and marketing, and (2) has initiated an acquisition program.

In April, 1973 the company announced a major reorganization of top management. The design switched from two entities, CDC and Commercial Credit, to an arrangement of four major groups, which are called companies. Each company is semiautonomous, has a defined mission, and a president who acts as chief executive. Norris spends more time on long-range problems and matters including the antitrust environment, cooperative ventures, and acquisitions.

CDC's internal reorganization has caused a noticeable improvement in the degree of enthusiasm in top and middle management offices at the company's new gold glass-sheeted headquarters in suburban Minneapolis. The reorganization left Commercial Credit Co. virtually unaffected, although Donald S. Jones, chairman of Commercial Credit, joined CDC executives Norris, executive vice president, William R. Keye, who heads the corporate budget and plans committee, and senior vice president Robert D. Schmidt, who heads international development, in the company's four-person corporate office. In the corporate hierarchy, Commercial Credit becomes one of four operating companies. The others are:

CDC Marketing Co., headed by Paul G. Miller, handles both domestic and international sales, except sales to original equipment manufacturers (OEM).

CDC Systems and Services Co., under Robert M. Price, handles hardware and software development and manufacture. He also manages the operations of the computer network services and specialized product and programming development groups. This operation tailors data-processing and computing systems for 14 different industry groups, ranging from atomic energy to education.

CDC Peripheral Products Co., headed by Thomas G. Kamp, includes the joint venture with NCR, Computer Peripherals (see below), plus the company's manufacturing operation in terminals, memory products, and business forms. Kamp's company also handles sales of peripheral equipment to other manufacturers and is the largest OEM supplier in the computer industry.

The change at CDC brings the company into line with similar management organizations at other mainframe computer companies, all of which have more or less autonomous marketing divisions separate from manufacturing—a pattern that IBM set in 1956. At CDC, the shift has been accompanied by a corporatewide program emphasizing a full range of customer service.

The change at CDC was overdue. By the end of the IBM antitrust action, CDC's business was in desperate need of management attention. The court fight had drained $15 million from operations at a time the company could least afford it, and it distracted the company's thin layer of top management as its lawyers and those of IBM examined every file of records in almost every office.

In 1974 CDC had an improved organization and a full range of computers from small to superscale. Mr. Norris' determination to build a total service company is already reflected by a sharp increase in marketing expenditures, which were nearly double those of 1973. But to stay competitive, CDC will have to start on a new generation of equipment as well. For that objective the Norris strategy is to team up with other producers to share costs and talents.

Cooperation with NCR

National Cash Register Co. (NCR) and CDC have had a close association since the middle 1960s, primarily as customers for each other's products. But three moves in 1972 aroused industry financial analysts.

1. Formation of jointly owned Computer Peripherals, Inc., which develops and manufactures high-speed computer printers, magnetic tape systems, and punchcard equipment. The new company's products are marketed by NCR and CDC under their own labels. The two companies contributed $30 million each to CPI, and the operation produced $100 million worth of products in 1974.
2. Transfer of NCR's disk-memory manufacturing operations in Hawthorne, Calif., to CDC for $20 million. Under a 20-year contract, CDC will fill NCR's disk requirements and CDC will purchase NCR's low- to medium-speed serial printers for use in terminals and computer consoles.
3. Cooperation in a joint advanced research and development program for new generation computers. The two companies originally planned only to build a computer that would run either NCR or CDC programs, but the joint effort has expanded to include a complete line of new generation computers. On September 1, 1973 they blended their efforts in a joint Advanced Systems Laboratory to work on both hardware and programming plans for the new series.

The cooperative strategy is based on claims that it costs around $750 million to develop a full computer line. Moreover, technological improvements have cut the hardware costs, so that software, which includes systems control programs and programming languages, now represents a higher proportion of costs. "We are going through a profound change," says Mr. Norris. "The key to the future is software, but at IBM software is included in the machine price; there is no viable software market yet."[1] CDC would like to see hardware and software prices separated.

For many years the idea of close cooperation with another company was controversial at NCR. The company dominated the mechanical cash register market. Management was certain that it could easily afford to enter the computer market through its base in accounting machines. However, the combination of industry recession, conversion from

[1] *Business Week*, November 10, 1973. "Control Data's Comeback: Why Bill Norris is Smiling."

mechanical to electronic products, and the constant R and D costs involved in electronic data-processing systems drained NCR's resources until, in 1972, it was forced to take a $107 million nonoperating loss. For the first time in decades, NCR, instead of ending a year in the black, showed a $60 million deficit. The turnaround in 1973, when the company announced $71.9 million in net earnings, can be partly attributed to cooperation with CDC.

Although both CDC and NCR are intent on remaining full-line computer makers and are expanding in data services as well, their sales forces seldom cross paths. Most of CDC's market is in large and medium systems, while NCR's strength is in the small to medium category, growing out of its strong foundations in accounting and bookkeeping equipment. Consequently, a customer might well buy CDC equipment for its engineering or process control needs and NCR equipment for its administrative and accounting purposes without ever considering the two companies as competitors.

However, the basic trend in computer development is toward more general purpose, central computers that are tailored to their jobs by programming. The industry calls them *soft* machines. Special purpose terminals, ranging from bank teller stations to consoles for use in engineering design, are required. CDC wants to joint venture in building general purpose equipment, but continue independently when it comes to tailored applications, programs, and customer service.

The combination of swap, joint venture, and this technical cooperation with NCR has generated merger rumors. One competitor refers to CDC and NCR as "the Odd Couple." However, both Mr. Norris and William S. Anderson, president and chief executive of NCR, deny any present intention to merge.

With its big computers put to work in services, particularly the Stars, each able to handle as many as 10,000 terminals, CDC has a substantial position in the market. NCR with its terminal-based systems and widespread marketing force at the customer level, is stronger than it has been in years from a marketing standpoint. Together, the two companies are still only one-fourth the size of IBM, but that is bigger than others except Xerox in the office equipment and data-processing industry.

Expanding Data Processing Service

Control Data's acquisition of Service Bureau Corp. as part of the IBM settlement lifted CDC into the top rank of data-processing service companies, with revenues of more than $100 million from services. Soon afterward, Mr. Norris accelerated CDC's acquisition program in the services area.

In March, 1973, CDC acquired ITT's Data Service Division in Britain, the Brazil segment of that operation in June, and ITT's domestic Data Service Division in September. In May, 1973 Systems Resources, Inc. of Dallas, a relatively small company specializing in data service and computer facilities management in the health insurance and utilities fields was acquired. In June, he acquired Greenwich Data Systems, Inc., an American programming and software house with wide experience in large, complex teleprocessing systems. In October, CDC picked up Comma Corp., one of the major independent field maintenance companies for computers.

During 1973 the company also bought up the 50% outside stock of Ticketron, Inc., increasing CDC's holdings of that operation to 99%, and bought out General Telephone and Electronics' 50% share of Brokerage Transaction Service, Inc., a joint venture of CDC and GTE that specializes in teleprocessing services for brokerage firms.

International Operations

In addition to these acquisitions and consolidations, CDC signed a 10-year pact with the Soviet Union that is a complex horsetrade involving the swap of CDC's skills in computer making for Russian research and development in computer programming. The deal could amount to as much as $500 million over the life of the contract, according to Russian sources.

The Soviet agreement is not CDC's first venture with Eastern-bloc nations. The company also has a joint project in Poland to make disk files, and last summer it came to terms with the Rumanian government to build a jointly owned factory to make printers, tape units and card equipment.

CDC also has a joint venture in Japan and a couple of smaller

partnerships in Israel. In Britain and the continent, CDC's Senior Vice President Robert D. Schmidt has completed cooperative deals with Germany's Nixdorf, France's CII, and Britain's ICL. CII and ICL are both favored by their governments as computer suppliers. CDC also has its own operations in Europe and has been negotiating for a role in Interdata, a consortium of Germany's Siemens, France's CII, and Holland's Philips.

To promote industrywide international standards that would permit interchange of programs between computers of different manufacturers, CDC in 1971 organized a joint study company called Multinational Data, with ICL and CII. NCR, which is a powerful marketing and manufacturing presence in Europe, joined the group in 1973.

The lack of adequate standards in the data-processing industry allows IBM to go its own way and create de facto industry practices that others are forced to follow according to CDC. Multinational Data has concentrated on standards for programming language, but it is now also investigating some approaches to standardization of hardware.

SECTION 2: CONTROL DATA'S INFORMATION SYSTEMS

Section 2 gives detail on CDC's information systems to clarify the scope and flexibility users might receive from buying time instead of buying or leasing equipment. CDC Systems and Services Co., under Robert M.

Price, offers data processing to thousands of customers including CDC corporate staff and the three other companies resulting from the reorganization.

The S2000 System Offered by CDC

System 2000 provides users with extensive logical, computational, and analytical powers. It is a flexible, comprehensive, data management system effectively bridging the gaps between the user, raw data, and useful information. Now operational on CDC 6000 series computers in Control Data's CYBERNET[2] network, System 2000 uses CDC MARC Terminals. A client can gain access to the data and needed output in seconds. A permanent record of a report or detail on a given subject is obtained on a high-speed line printer or on CDC's MARC-1 Teletypewriter terminal.

System 2000 provides users with access to one or more data bases, simultaneously and immediately, from locations anywhere in the country. Data bases are structured by a storage technique that makes total searches unnecessary. Retrieval and updating operations occur in seconds.

Users develop their data bases without restriction as to size or number of users. Any type of computer input device can be used to load and update the data bases: punched cards, paper tape, magnetic tape, optical character readers,

[2] Cybernet is a system of interlinking computer facilities which permits a user to tap a nationwide network in the U.S.

cathode ray tube display kayboards, or teletypewriter equipment.

System 2000 is designed to eliminate the possibility of disclosing any privileged information to unauthorized personnel. A company is protected at every level, beginning with access to the system itself. Each user can be assigned a code that will provide a specific degree of access, allowing him to "look in and update" and "look in only" for specified data bases.

Applications

System 2000 is a general purpose data management system that means that users can apply the full potential of this system to an exceptionally broad range of problems. Examples include:

1. General corporate MIS.
2. Inventory control.
3. General accounting.
4. Sales volume analysis.
5. Market analysis.
6. Personnel records.
7. Portfolio management for stocks and bonds.

1974 Plan for Data Services

In addition to S2000, CDC has several special purpose services such as Ticketron Airlines Systems Center and Brokerage Transaction Services. The entire complex is administered by the Systems and Services Co. Given in the following paragraphs is the 1974 plan for the services portion of operations and the basis for various information systems.

Mission

Plan, develop, implement, manage, and operate a highly reliable, efficient computer and communications network including the Cybernet Centers at the lowest cost consistent with user requirements.

Scope

The scope of this mission will include the ownership and operation of all computers and all communications networks used by CDC and its subsidiaries except those computer systems used for equipment testing or controlling automated manufacturing processes.

Objectives

1. Provide a network of advanced computers and telecommunications for all users.
2. Reduce cost per unit of services provided.
3. Increase availability, reliability, and responsiveness.
4. Communicate products, plans, rates, and charges to users.

Policies to Meet Objectives

1. Data Center Operations
   a. Optimize resource utilization and reliability by consolidating facilities.
   b. Establish multimainframe data centers where required and economically feasible.
   c. Plan and establish networks that allow for maximum utilization of all data centers.
   d. Implement new standards for site and data security at all data centers.
   e. Plan for power reliability at all data centers.
   f. Minimize leasehold expenses through long-range planning.
2. Software
   a. Utilize corporate standard software.
   b. Promote standard software that is more "forgiving" of hardware failures.
   c. Develop and expand software capabilities to include multi-mainframe and compatible data base files. Provide automatic backup when feasible.
3. Data Communications
   a. Develop plans and goals to provide a reliable network that insures maximum efficiencies in telecommunications, including effective use of existing corporate networks. Plan for new communications media that may be more attractive economically and technically, now and in the future.
   b. Develop the ability to include intelligent communications in the existing and expanded networks.
4. Procedures
   a. Develop and implement procedures and protocol that are standard at all data centers.
   b. Improve and reduce operational housekeeping.
   c. Revise operational policies to optimize resource utilization.
   d. Solicit planning inputs from users and communicate plans and policies to users.
   e. Be responsive to user requirement for services.
5. Accounting
   a. Develop fair and consistent

rates for data services and communicate these to users in a timely fashion for their planning purposes.

b. Provide accurate and timely charging for computing services consumed.

Division Operating Objectives and Supportive Policies

RELIABILITY Service interruption must be minimized through improved hardware and software reliability. A close working relationship with customer engineering (a maintenance department to service customer facilities) is essential to assure that each system has the benefit of the best possible maintenance practice.

Data Services can improve Control Data's overall computer reliability by providing a test bed for hardware and software development. New devices, software features, and other product improvements can be tested in a controlled production environment to thoroughly qualify the product before distribution to customers. Feedback of operational experiences to the development activities will produce further enhancements. These systems can also provide an operational system for instrumentation to measure performance and utilization.

The highest degree of reliability can be achieved by backing up an entire system, or, if that is not practical, by backing up selected components on that system. Cluster centers will contain multiple systems each capable of backing up or being backed up by another system or systems.

Another method improving reliability is to have stricter security procedures implemented through data services. All new centers are being designed for much tighter security, and existing centers are implementing all practical controls.

Alternate sources for power and cooling must be installed in all cluster centers. Automatic switching between power sources buffered by 60-cycle to 60-cycle motor generators will reduce unscheduled power interruptions as well as provide a much "cleaner" power supply. Both of these features will materially improve system reliability.

DATA SERVICES CAPACITY Data Services must provide the computing capacity for Control Data's production requirements. Systems with stable hardware and software, staffed by full-time professional operators are required in large numbers. These production systems are used for all of Control Data's internal data processing requirements and are the resource which provides the computing power for Data Services operations. A variety of hardware and software systems, each stable within its own environment, is available to satisfy these needs.

Closed-shop computer operations are those in which physical operation of the system is denied to the ultimate user. These systems are operated by professional operators where work is submitted at the counter or over data communication lines, processed on the system, and then returned to the counter or directly to the user over the communication lines. Most of these centers operate around the clock, seven days a week. Many of these closed-shop systems are connected directly to the user by remote batch terminals and in some cases, conversational terminals.

There are currently 30 large-scale, closed-shop production systems within Data Services.

Job scheduling ranges from pure competition, with and without priorities, to preschedule processing or dedicated time. Changing requirements and limited availability of the systems make this a demanding task. Priorities are resolved by Data Services management.

On-line interactive systems such as Ticketron and Airlines Reservation Systems have transaction-oriented terminals connected directly into an on-line system. This workload will shift toward the Data Services cluster centers because of their transaction-oriented system.

Open-shop computer operation satisfies the need for a user to physically have his or her hands on the hardware in order to accomplish the specified task.

Twenty operational large-scale, open-shop systems with stable hardware are operated by Data Services. By providing more on-line programming capabilities, this workload will partially shift to the closed-shop system where potential utilization is much higher. Data Services activity promotes on-line programming.

The geographical dispersion of Control Data's computing requirements is worldwide. Systems can occur in clusters such as in the Twin Cities and Sunnyvale areas, or they can be installed as stand-along systems in various cities throughout the United States, as well as the rest of the world. Today Data Services is responsible for major systems at 27 different locations in the United States.

The computing network will consist of three cluster centers located to satisfy geographical distribution: Washington, D.C., Twin Cities, and the West Coast.

The cluster centers will be linked in a ring by high-speed (for example, 250 KHz.) communications lines for message traffic and back-up copies of data files. The cluster centers would be dual timesharing and remote batch processing systems with shared files and common queues. The balance of the network is the satellite centers, consisting of smaller scale timesharing and remote batch processing systems. The satellite centers will be placed in separate locations to satisfy high concentrations of local activity. The satellite centers would link to the ring of cluster centers by high-speed communications channels (for example, 50 KHz.). All nationally-oriented data base work and overflow will be forwarded to the cluster centers.

Local areas with substantially greater than one system's capacity can be served by a multiple system satellite center when special conditions warrant:

1. Local workload requires significant amounts of on-site data, for example, customer tapes.
2. Significant communications costs can be saved.

3. Dedicated special purposes systems serve a local requirement.

For example, Los Angeles banking illustrates the local file processing requirement and Houston illustrates reducing communications costs by local processing. The challenge will be to minimize the number of satellite centers in order to realize the benefits of the cluster center network.

Measuring utilization is essential to balance capacity with demand. Improving utilization by reducing abusive practices is very important. Often a multiprocessing/multiprogramming 6000 system is used in a serial hands-on mode of operation which, in effect, slows the system down to the speed of the slowest component—the operator. Also, the balanced use of a system can improve the utilization dramatically. System users are encouraged to balance reasonable core usage with computing and input/output that improves a system's utilization significantly.

Other ways to improve utilization consist of performance improvement. By reducing the housekeeping required for such things as dumping and reloading permanent files, more time can be made available for production. Reductions in preventive and emergency maintenance time while sustaining high-performance standards will also improve system availability.

A larger system may be capable of providing a computing resource to a much broader base of users, thereby increasing the potential for higher utilization. This may also reduce the need for frequent reconfiguring of specific systems. It is the responsibility of Data Services to identify such situations and to take advantage of the potential.

Certainly utilization of systems can be improved through the promotion of closed-shop environments. Conversational systems for software development will dramatically reduce the need for hands-on systems.

There is definite opportunity for increasing utilization on a large number of systems by expanding their use in business data processing. Many systems are used heavily in the prime shift for quick turnaround batch processing. Where these systems can be used on the second, third and fourth shifts, for the daily and weekly type productive batch processing, substantial economies can be achieved.

A major objective is to improve Control Data's 6000/CYBER 70 *business data processing capability*. Data Services proposes to achieve that objective by using standard systems in the BDP environment and then by feeding back the operational experiences to our development activities. In this way, we can assure that our designers continue to address the numerous problems that plague all business data processing systems.

Equipment control is the next objective. This includes forecasting future computing requirements, and returns to inventory as well as coordinating the movement of and accounting for Data Services equipment throughout the company. This function also involves the procedures for capitalizing computing equipment that will be used within the corporation.

SOFTWARE   Utilization of standard Control Data software is the next major objective for Data Services. Organizations within the company must be discouraged from using their own software systems, or highly modified versions of CDC released software.

Data Services recognizes that users do have unique requirements that must be satisfied by standard releases. By providing a stable operating system, plus new features as they are proven, we can promote and evolve to the use of a much closer version of the Corporate standard software. In conjunction with the Software Systems Division, Data Services Division is enhancing the standard software releases in order to satisfy more users.

DATA COMMUNICATIONS   The future will increasingly depend upon our ability to utilize telecommunications effectively. Effective use of data communications can provide a substantial competitive advantage and can open the door to many new service opportunities. Without a reliable telecommunications network, there is little need for the terminals or many of the central processors.

Control Data telecommunications networks exist to serve a variety of purposes. They encompass all transfers of information both internal and external, by electromagnetic means, including telephone, data, telegraph, facsimile, and so on. In data communications, for example, there is the necessity to bring in work from remote terminals and to provide the ability to transfer that work between systems for optimum efficiencies. Data communications are also used extensively in the transactions oriented, on-line systems such as Ticketron, Airline Systems Division, BTSI, and soon CYBERLOAN. Many of these systems require telecommunications capabilities that quickly become a major, and sometimes prohibitive, expense.

The responsibility then is to provide a reliable network and to insure that Control Data achieves maximum efficiencies in telecommunications. All users should be able to expect state-of-the-art telecommunications service at a relatively stable cost rate.

An obvious requirement is to exercise a much greater control over cost than has been done in the past. Services must be thoroughly audited to eliminate expensive, inadequate or overly adequate service where better alternatives are available for less money. The purchased services required to build the telecommunication networks for conducting Control Data business must be combined and optimized. Control Data cannot afford the luxury of dedicated telecommunications facilities for every single application. Another major requirement is to improve the reliability and technology. A competent network operations staff is mandatory. The possible use of wideband multiplexors, remote communications concentrators, message switching, network optimization programs, specialized common carriers, cable television systems, communications satellites, and many other systems must be explored and implemented.

And finally under telecommunications, there is a continual need to evaluate Control Data's current and future needs in terminals. Enhancements to standard terminal offerings must be communicated to the proper organizations for inclusion in future product lines. Remote terminals must be matched to the offerings of the public utilities as well as commercially available services in order to optimize the network and minimize costs.

ADMINISTRATION Communication of ideas between organizations produces results in two primary areas. First, by the exchange of information regarding available machine time, a system to satisfy an overload or back-up requirement can be located and time made available. Secondly, communication between operational organizations is also very important for the exchange of people or information regarding operating techniques, mutual goals, and problems.

Another major objective is to provide growth and development for those responsible for operating Control Data's computers. Data Services will assure that proper training is provided to all its employees. Data Services offers a career path within computer operations for advancement to much higher levels than is possible in any individual using division. And finally, Data Services is in a better position to develop performance measurement criteria and to validate these measurement tools over a very large base.

ACCOUNTING There must be accurate computer and data communications accounting records. First, all costs must be identified. Then there is the need for cost distribution according to the resources consumed. Data Services Division is a regulated P and L operation and as such must recover all costs associated with operating systems and data communications. All users must be charged according to their usage. A variety of cost pools are used to achieve this objective. Where it is possible, similar systems are pooled, if impractical, a separate cost pool is established for a single system or group of systems. Data Services has an objective of a uniform computer rate by 1974 for all users with Control Data.

Data Services is responsible for setting rates and doing the accounting for time consumed on all computer systems and for all data communications used internally. An objective is to provide a uniform set of computer rates across the company to eliminate internal price competition and encourage the workload to migrate towards systems availability.

PLANNING Data Services will regularly solicit planning inputs from all user organizations. Users will be asked to forecast computer usage for continuing programs, program enhancements, and development activity. Computer time and on-line storage plus communications requirements should be forecasted.

These plans will be communicated to the users in a timely fashion in order for them to budget accordingly.

INTERNATIONAL Data Services provides staff support in the areas of hardware, software, communications, and management systems to all of the international centers.

STUDENT PROBLEM

Considering the description of advance information systems for strategic decision making in Chapter Five, and the requirements necessary for an effective MIS, design a system that could be used by Norris, Jones, Keye, and Schmidt in their new roles in acquisitions, cooperative ventures, long-range planning, and corporate strategies.

In addition, discuss the advantages and disadvantages from the viewpoint of the management of NEM, Inc. of using Data Services Division and the Cybernet network.

Fundamental Techniques in Planning and Strategy Formulation

The five chapters describe techniques needed by executive management to achieve growth in profits and other company goals. Cases involve situations that illustrate some of the steps to take and modifications to make in the process of realizing actual success from application of the techniques.

PART

TWO

Short-Range Operational Planning

The fundamentals of short-range operational plans are explained. Theories on contingency planning, who should do the planning, and the structure of the format are outlined. Also, the role of executive management in short-range planning is clarified. The chapter is the first which is wholly "techniques"-oriented and therefore, includes some basic points that apply to planning in any time frame.

Two fundamental ideas motivate executives to prepare short-range plans: (1) increased probability of superior profit performance is gained from day-to-day decisions guided by specific objectives, and (2) decisions affecting long-range growth of the company must be implemented in the present to become reality. This takes place through programs and projects that are part of the short-range plan.

6

Middle and lower levels of management usually perform more efficiently within a framework of plans. This framework assures them that decisions in one part of the organization will not contradict those in another part, yet allows them the latitude to use their ingenuity for problem solving. Top management requires this framework because much of its time is spent on planning the future of the business. Specific operating objectives and budgets give personnel direction with minimum supervision. Also, programs and projects that are part of realizing long-range plans go into action with an improved probability for accomplishing necessities on timing, quantities, composition, and so on.

In addition, the individuals within the organization gain an understanding of what is expected from them or their departments now and in the future. These individuals also know more about how their work affects others in the company. The net result is usually better morale and improved job satisfaction as compared to firms without formal plans. Experience indicates that a company using short-range operational planning (SROP) gains improved profit performance, increased productivity, and greater adherence to budgets.

Despite the advantages, there are firms that do not plan or do the minimal job of forecasting sales and adjusting production accordingly. These firms are constantly reacting to company and industry developments instead of anticipating them and making the most out of each situation. The reasons cited most frequently by consultants hired to solve the problems of these companies include:

1. Many managers do not like to be pinned down to specific performance standards. Accomplishing goals is often taken for granted by upper management. Failure to achieve the goals exposes them to criticism.

2. Managers who are otherwise adequate in their jobs sometimes do not have the training or experience to undertake planning that involves other people and departments on a division or companywide basis.

3. Portions of top management do not participate in or support planning concepts employed by the company. This discourages lower levels of management in their attempts to achieve comprehensive plans.

4. The cyclical or seasonal character of some businesses, or dependency on widely fluctuating outside sources such as the price of raw materials, makes it very difficult to plan. In combination with any of the first three points, poor planning, which hurts instead of helps efficiency, is a high probability.

It is a fundamental fact that in spite of the four reasons for the absence of effective planning, a company's profit performance improves with the presence of a framework for decision making and objectives for day-to-day work.

DEFINITION OF SHORT-RANGE OPERATIONAL PLANNING

Short-range operational planning (SROP) means:

1. A time span of no more than one year into the future.
2. Forecasts of operating variables for each major organizational component defined in both words and numbers (dollars, units, workers, strategies, and so on).
3. Assignments within these organizational components to iden-

tify specific responsibilities for both planning and accomplishing the plan.

4. Policies on degree of detail in SROP and those required to communicate the correct amount of information to users.

It is clear from this definition that SROP is a division or companywide system with many interdependent parts. These parts are the subsystems such as marketing, production, cash control, or personnel. Each of these subsystems are sufficiently important to be systems with subsystems. Within marketing, for example, sales, sales administration, market research, market development, advertising and promotion, and distribution of goods are interdependent parts. Each of these will have subsystems until the lowest level in the organization is reached. Figure 6−1 illustrates the integrative concept of SROP.

Figure 6−1. SROP Integration

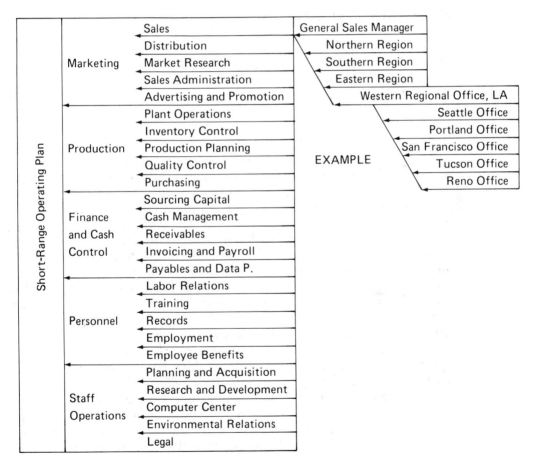

Let us recognize that smart managers realize that their performance will be better if they anticipate, plan, and adjust individually in the absence of a formal SROP. The purpose of this chapter is not to review this type of planning, but to discuss integrated plans that involve divisions as subsystems within the company, the company within an industry, and the industry within an economy.

Finally, SROP must be a practical asset to management. Its main purpose is improved earnings performance. If the SROP is not practical and executive management is spending excessive time on presentations and revisions, then SROP is poorly designed. A paperwork nightmare can be created, and this leads to organizational empires for ambitious managers. The other extreme, too infrequent revisions of SROP, is usually a symptom of an excessively complicated design.

DETAILS ON DEFINITIONAL COMPONENTS OF SROP

It will be helpful in designing SROP to develop some details within each of the four parts of its definition.

Time Span

The typical time span for SROP is one year. However, there are usually separate forecasts of operating variables for each of four quarters, or for each of the 12 months or another combination of subdivisions. Basic guidelines are included in all periods of the plan, but more detailed information is available for the beginning periods.

Let us use quarterly breakdowns as an example. Prices of the company's products, costs including materials, interest rates, and so on, can be predicted with greater accuracy 3 months into the future than 9 to 12 months. In some cases conditions may be sufficiently stable for reasonably accurate forecasts in the second quarter. This situation allows similar detail in both quarters of the first half and less in the remaining two quarters of the year.

The first draft of a detailed operational plan for the approaching quarter is usually completed 30 to 60 days before going into operation. This provides time for adjustments and communications between components of the organization to identify and clarify responsibilities for achieving specific goals, budgets, and so on. The draft is often an updated version of the plan for second quarter of the previous SROP and revisions reflect mistakes and new developments in the quarter just terminating. The process normally involves adding a fourth quarter to replace the one completed so that there is always a one year probe into the future of the firm. However, many companies with formal planning systems only update the current quarter and revise SROP once a year, usually late in the calendar year to enable the new plan to begin January 1.

Figure 6−2 illustrates a typical 12-month planning cycle. The planning method that drops one time period and extends the plan an equal time period into the future is called a *rolling SROP*. However, every firm has special considerations that could influence management to select different timing. A highly seasonal business could force all planning to be completed during the slack period. Fluctuating prices for materials could necessitate monthly plans with less detail than the usual situation to minimize paperwork. Lack of support for SROP could force a compromise in which planning occurs irregularly every few months.

Figure 6−2. Rolling SROP

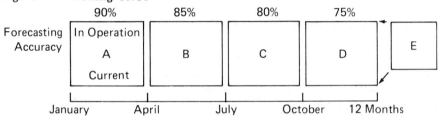

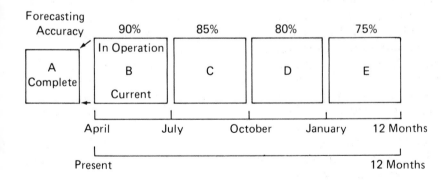

Variables by Major Organizational Component

Operating variables in this usage are those business variables over which a company has some control such as pricing or salaries. Within SROP these variables are finalized as the basis for preparing: (1) strategies that are part of the plan; (2) objectives that can best be stated in words; (3) numerical forecasts of sales in dollars and units, costs in the form of budgets, interest paid and received, factors in computing taxes, and organizational requirements to carry out SROP, and (4) critical factors and assumptions upon which key elements in the plan are dependent.

The decisions in preparing SROP will be greatly influenced by forecasts for *strategic variables*. These are variables beyond the control of a company such as fiscal policy by the U.S. government or strategies of competitors. Usually in a large corporation, staff experts predict the outlook for the economy and the most probable developments in government, competing firms, labor unions and other outside influences. These experts might be part of the central planning staff or assigned to organizational components requiring special information. For example, an analyst for currencies would predict the value of money in various countries affecting the company. The treasurer would use this forecast to manage the firm's cash during the period covered by SROP.

Assignments: The Personnel Who Participate in Planning

One theory concerning who should participate in the planning process is based on the concept that individuals will work harder to achieve goals in the plan if they themselves have set the goals rather than top management. On the other hand, personnel in lower levels of the organization may either set goals that are too easy to achieve or that are headed in the wrong direction because the individuals lack perspective on developments in the business.

Another theory assumes that top management knows more about the company's operations and the probable impact of outside influences than other people in the organization. As a result, plans are developed only by these executives and passed on to subordinates as assignments to accomplish. While the employees do not contribute to the forecasts, advocates claim that planning is accomplished quickly and efficiently with few possibilities of empire building in the process. Critics point out that top executives are often removed from the day-to-day business and are not as informed about current developments as they should be.

Figure 6–3 illustrates the two theories. Details of the theories and a more optimal solution are given in subsequent sections.

Bottom-Up Planning

The "bottom" in the case of bottom-up planning refers to subordinates in the lowest levels of the organization who forecast what will be accomplished at what cost in SROP. The accumulation of

Figure 6-3. Two Extremes in Planning Participation

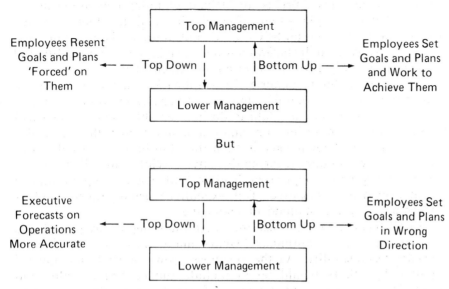

these contributions make up the plan. In pure bottom-up planning with limited supervision on acceptable standards of performance, there are discrepancies between departments. A simple example would be an enthusiastic sales force that requires much more production than the first draft of a plan by operations indicates will be produced. Coordination is needed to achieve a balance, and management works out a compromise.

Pure bottom-up planning is rare because excessive time is lost in reconciling unrealistic forecasts. Inefficiencies and possibilities for interdepartmental conflict cause discontent, possibly more than the concept provides in compensating benefits. The exception is an organization with a high proportion of well-trained, job-motivated personnel. In other companies executive management can achieve the objectives of bottom-up planning by increased supervision and by encouraging subordinates to develop and experiment with models that integrate plans of departments. This results in employees setting standards of performance acceptable to themselves, their bosses, their boss' boss, and so on.

Top-Down Planning

Dynamic authoritative personalities are often behind top-down planning. Entrepreneurs in large and small companies adopt this approach to be certain their decisions are carried out. The approach involves a few key people in top management who decide what has to be done. The tasks of accomplishing specific components of SROP are delegated to personnel who have contributed little or nothing to the plan. Sometimes there is an official planning committee of executives developing plans that reflect the ideas of the chief executive officer, and they make up SROP on a continuing basis. In other companies the work is undertaken on a less formal basis and quality and practicality usually reflect the attention given to it.

The overwhelming majority of employees react to a top-down plan in the same way that people carry out orders in military service. Most will do what they are told to do but very little more. Some will resent being given orders on matters about which they consider themselves more knowledgeable than the "top brass" and will do as they have always done, ignoring directives. While few will refuse to comply, the spirit of cooperation is almost nil. The consequent impact on performance is negative. Top executives usually hurt earnings performance by this method of managing.

Small businesses often use top-down planning, if any planning is done at all. An entrepreneur "wears many hats" and is slow to delegate responsibility. As the business grows, a first step toward planning by others would be to include the controller, sales and production managers, and the head of any key department such as engineering in the process of planning. Sometimes this leads to inclusion of lower levels of the organization for information and opinion, and with this step you shift from top-down planning.

Full-Resource Planning

Top management is a major resource of the company. The executives are responsible for performance in meeting earning goals and other objectives. These individuals have proven talent, and they know the broad directions in which the company must go to achieve required performance.

Other portions of the organization are also important resources. Their talents are oriented to more specific operations within the firm. Sales representatives and their managers know the customers and are aware of changes in buying patterns. Supervisors know about stoppages on machines and expenditures that would rectify the problems. These and other personnel have important information that can lead to a plan maintaining "touch" with the business.

It is necessary to get the inputs of as many resources in a company as practical. Ideally, this means:

1. A lean, well-designed plan, preferably computerized, which provides the correct amount of information with the optimum degree of reliability.

2. Two or three stages of revisions that alternately reflect the in-

put of bottom-up planning, top-down ideas and direction, and experimentation of results on the computer.

3. Incentives based on performance in the various forms of promotion, increased income, censure for inaccuracy, and so on so that both plans and actual results are important, not just pages in bound books.

Figure 6−4 conceptualizes full-resource planning. This approach improves the probability of optimum efficiency not occurring. Important ideas and market intelligence are less likely to be lost in communications up and down the organization. It is true that varying degrees of competence hurt the quality of imput. Lack of confidence in the forecast for the economic framework might affect judgments on allocating company resources. Nevertheless, full-resource planning can improve operating performance even in lower degrees of planning efficiency.

Figure 6−4. Full-Resource Planning

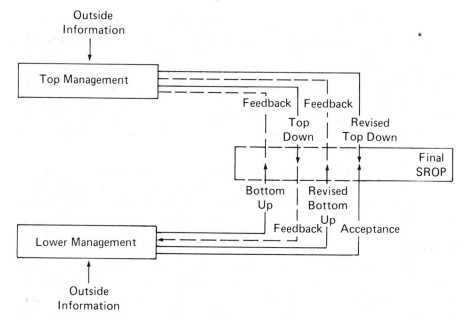

Organizational Assignments

A crucial factor that determines whether planning accomplishes or fails the transition from an array of facts and opinions to a practical management guideline is the assignment of people to specific responsibilities in SROP. The critical areas are:

INSTRUCTIONS AND GUIDANCE Management at the top of an organizational component must understand the purpose and procedures for SROP. If these executives do not, their subordinates will certainly be lost. However, assuming that needed knowledge exists, it is important for them not only to clarify what is happening but to also be available for guidance as complications arise. Regular meetings with each person heading a group contributing to SROP is one method of providing (a) counsel; (b) quality control; (c) coordination, and (d) timing according to a prescribed schedule.

MATCHING COMPETENCE WITH ASSIGNMENT Planning is a full-time job for few people in the firm. Most managers are the decision makers who carry out SROP in specific fields. They are asked to develop planning information and, because the assignment is related to the performance of their job and the instructions are clear, the majority have no problems. A few are not capable of handling the planning, the position, or both. Management must be alert to these situations. Otherwise inadequate, unreliable information will become part of SROP.

DEGREE OF COOPERATION It is a fact that many managers resist establishing a standard by which they can be measured. This applies to good performers who are not naturally competitive as well as marginal managers who fear failure. Another factor is corporate politics. It is not always convenient for departments or individuals to cooperate. SROP tends to force exchange of information in many cases; however, quality of content can suffer from the resistance to standards, politics, and personality conflicts that exist in most companies.

Executive management must remain alert to problem areas in planning assignments. After being certain each employee knows what is expected, supervisors must observe planning performance. Because SROP is a repetitive process, there is an opportunity to compare actual results with forecasts and identify personnel who need extra guidance.

If SROP is new, or an individual is being given a more complicated assignment, or computerized models are being introduced, some personnel give the appearance of being disturbed and not comprehending the new assignment. However, after an adjustment period, most employees adapt to the new system and react positively. Management should be slow to judge personnel who initially resist change during the transition period.

Responsibility for administration of SROP differs by company. Some examples are given in Figure 6−5 to illustrate various reporting relationships in the organization, titles, and source of authority.

Figure 6-5. Levels of Reporting Responsibility in SROP

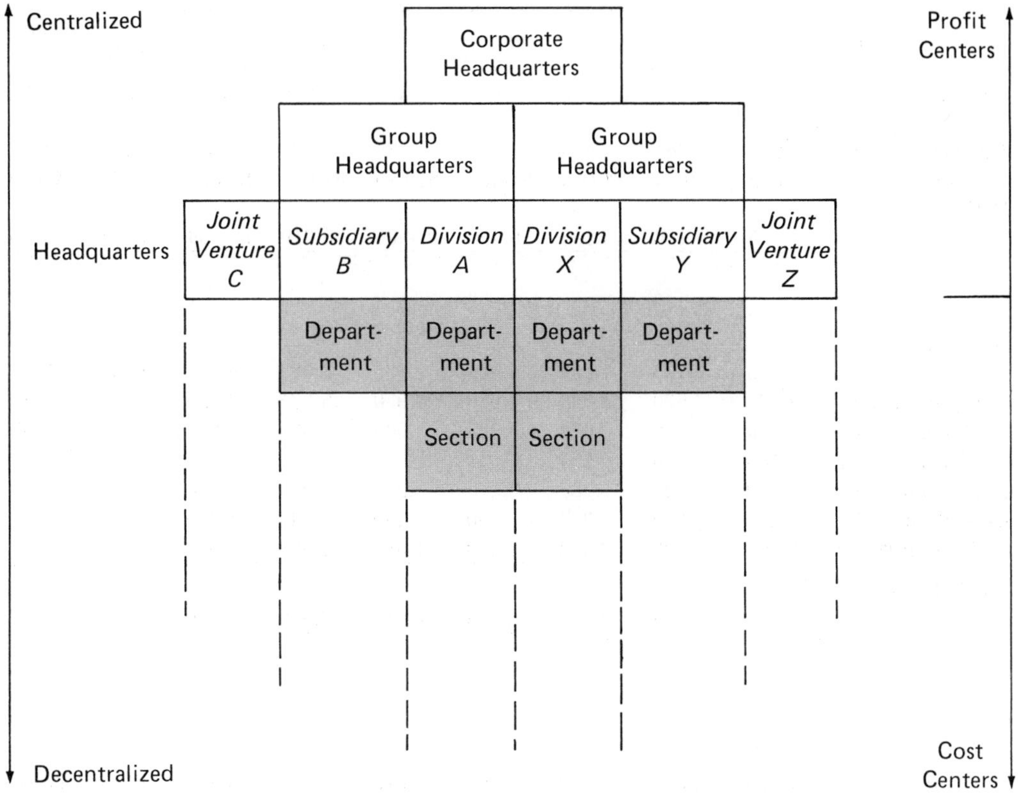

Policies on Degree of Detail in SROP

Hundreds of decisions will make up the basis for policies on degree of detail if a substantial portion of the organization participates in the plan. Comparatively few decisions are involved if top management dictates the content of the plan. Optimal detail might result from either situation.

The best guide is to analyze a summary such as the one given in Table 6-1. What support information is required for these numbers to be reliable? What additional numbers and other details are needed for lower levels of management to carry out their jobs? Also, how important are the assumptions for strategic variables on which industry and company performance are based?

Each major component of the organization should view its portion of SROP as information that contributes to the following.

Table 6-1. Executive Summary — SROP

Zeus Cement Division	Mo. 1	Mo. 2	Mo. 3	Mo. 4	Mo. 5	Mo. 6	Qtr. 3	Qtr. 4	12 Mos.
Operating Rate	60%	80%	82½%	85%	85%	90%	90%	90%	86%
Tons Sold (000)	660	785	810	835	835	880	2.640	2.60	10.085
Price Per Ton	$18.75	$19.25	$19.25	$19.25	$19.75	$19.10	$19.00	$19.00	$19.20
CASH INFLOW ($ Million)	12.375	15.110	15.595	16.490	16.4900	16.810	50.160	50.160	193.190
Fixed Costs (incl. Salaries)	2.155	2.105	2.025	2.085	2.085	2.085	6.255	6.255	25.050
Variable Oper. Costs	3.930	4.670	4.820	4.970	4.970	5.235	15.720	15.725	60.040
Variable Distr. Costs	.070	.080	.080	.085	.085	.090	.270	.270	1.030
Advertising Campaign	.585	.330	.165	—	—	—	—	—	1.080
Admin. (exc. Salaries)	.210	.220	.230	.245	.260	.260	.780	.780	2.985
Sales (excl. Salaries)	.250	.300	.315	.330	.330	.345	1.050	1.050	3.970
Int. and Financing Fees	3.260	2.830	2.450	2.070	1.685	1.305	1.635	—	15.235
CASH OUTFLOW ($Million)	10.460	10.535	10.085	9.785	9.415	9.320	25.710	24.080	109.390
Cash (Before Deprec.) for Taxes, Loans and Dividends	1.915	4.575	5.510	6.705	7.075	7.490	24.450	26.080	83.800
Depreciation	4.120	4.150	4.190	2.230	2.270	2.310	4.250	4.250	27.770
Profit Before Taxes	(2.205)	.425	1.320	4.475	4.805	5.180	20.200	21.830	56.030
Loss Carry-Forward	—	(2.205)	(1.780)	(.460)	—	—	—	—	(4.445)
Taxes @50%±	—	—	—	2.010	2.405	2.590	10.100	10.915	27.020
PROFIT AFTER TAXES	(2.205)	(1.780)	(.460)	2.005	2.400	2.590	10.100	10.915	23.565
Cash for Loan Repayment	1.915	4.575	5.510	4.695	4.670	4.900	14.350	15.165	55.780
Loan Payments	2.135	4.620	3.620	3.620	3.620	3.480	9.600	—	30.695
Subtotal for Cash	(.220)	(.045)	1.890	1.075	1.050	1.420	4.750	15.165	25.085
Provision from Capital to Repay Loans	.220	.045	—	—	—	—	—	—	.265
NET CASH ($Million)	—	—	1.890	1.075	1.050	1.420	4.750	15.165	25.350

1. Top-management decisions affecting the whole company.
2. Functional decisions in other parts of the organization that require a specified degree of accuracy.
3. Intracomponent performance improvement.

Recalling the systems approach, one division may require considerable detail from its departments to predict performance and costs for the next four quarters, while another may not.

Summarizing, detail in a plan usually grows from need arising from the three users: top management, other functional components of the organizations, and the component using the plan as an internal tool. If something is wrong, top management or executives from other parts of the company will complain sufficiently to generate revisions in approach to increase accuracy. Over a period of time plans evolve in more or less detail, and management must keep the planning process under control so that adequate but not excessive work is involved.

Objectives, Guidelines, and Forms

People must be given instructions for what is expected of them in planning. For example, in completing part of SROP the purchasing agent should know whether raw material costs should be estimated at $10.00±5\%$ or take the time to analyze sources and derive the more exact forecast of $9.86. The sales representative needs clarification on degrees of detail on size of customer, product and geographic breakdowns, intracompany competition for customers, other competitor developments, and net prices realized. Several examples could be cited to demonstrate that those participating in the planning process need guidance beyond the headings and instructions on forms.

Important steps in generating willingness to plan throughout an organization are:

1. Clearly stated support for SROP by middle and top management.
2. Communicating appreciation and results from applications involving extra work.
3. Explicit details about SROP in memos and meetings (which also give guidelines on individual assignments) so that employees will give greater effort to planning.

Forms evolve from revisions and the need for more or less detail. Improvements become apparent with usage. Figure 6—6 gives an example of the repetitive planning cycle and the modifications that result. In marketing, both cash inflows and outflows are involved

Figure 6-6. The Evolution of SROP

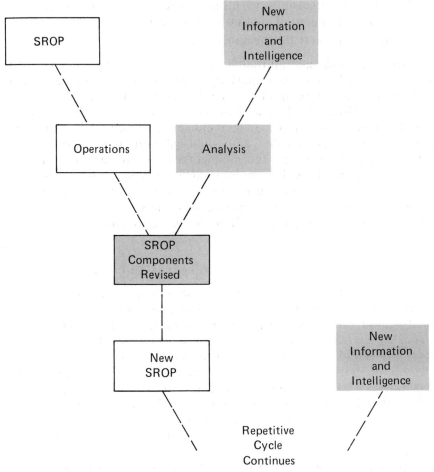

while a department in operations, for example, might have budgets and units of production. Consultants who have had the opportunity to compare SROP in several companies confirm significant differences in the mechanics of planning. The approach reflects the individuals in the firm, the type of business, and the intensity of competition within the industry.

Management Summaries

Each segment of the organization can use portions of SROP, but will be inundated in paper if it receives the whole plan. The purpose of planning is defeated if managers do not get the information they need to carry out their responsibilities successfully. Consequently, one of the most critical elements in designing a plan is the content of summaries that communicate what managers need—no more, no less. Providing the correct amount of information requires a formal system of communication between those responsible for SROP and management, which is similar to the "give and take" process for selecting flow from MIS.

Five levels of management are to be considered in designing summaries:

1. Top executives charged with responsibilities for overall performance.
2. General managers having been delegated the responsibility for a division or subsidiary.
3. Functional executives managing marketing, production, personnel, accounting, and so on.
4. Lower level managers handling departments such as advertising, inventory control, accounts payable, and so on.
5. Special situations such as the economist, manager of environmental relations, the Washington D.C. office representative, corporate counsel, and so on.

Note that some firms do not have all five levels, while others have an organizational structure that does not readily fit all the points discussed here.

Top executives should have enough planning forecasts and statements to compare with reports on actual performance. This means that the design of SROP and MIS on operations should be as similar as possible. When alerted to a problem, this system should have back-up information that enables them to: (1) identify the cause and to authorize corrective measures without having to use time searching for what is needed to make a decision, or (2) call up more details because the situation is complex, there is disagreement between a top executive and the general manager, new unexpected developments have occurred, or a combination of the three. In these latter situations, copies of planning summaries, which the general manager (or staff executive) receives, plus studies that have been compiled from raw data in the system will usually provide sufficient information for a decision—sometimes too much. Judgment is very important in expanding flow of SROP and MIS to avoid "overkill," that is, overspending on accumulation of too much information.

General managers are similar to entrepreneurs. They concentrate on operations and performance standards by which they are measured. Less time is spent on the long-range future as compared with top company executives. More emphasis is placed on earnings in SROP. General managers want to know about sales, cash inflows, budget position, inventories at key stages, workforce developments, and so on. Their tendency will be to concentrate on problem areas, and they will go through the process of getting sufficient decision-making information described in the previous paragraph. Through an appropriate incentive system, they may be able to offset the resistance to planning by rewarding those who are bettering predicted performance. While this tends to encourage conservative estimates that are relatively easy to exceed, the regular flow of comparisons between SROP and actual performance will sort out those who are overly conservative.

Functional managers get details on their responsibilities, and often they request information on another function. For example, the sales manager will have an individual plan but will request production output and finished goods inventory to be certain of being able to service customers. If invoicing and cash inflows are handled by the controller, the sales manager should know about the performance of customers in paying for products ordered. Having selected the necessary information from the administrator of the plan, the sales manager will coordinate with these other functional managers both in the formulation of the plan and in managing specific responsibilities as the SROP period involved yields actual results to compare with forecasts. When serious deviations occur, meetings are usually necessary to resolve the problem most efficiently. In the real world, personality clashes, rivalries, historical inability to reach a compromise, and similar human problems make an apparently simple planning process quite complex. However, the framework of SROP assists in achieving an acceptable solution.

Lower level managers have a narrower scope of interest. While often concerned with other departments, coordination is on a smaller scale. Generally they are concentrating on their own responsibilities, and summaries must support this work. The ultimate objective is for these departmental managers to meet standards in an approved plan so that the company will equal or better predicted performance. Realizing this objective occurs less often than one would expect because of some combinations of strategic variables, planning incompetence, management incompetence, human factors, and the structure of the plan. Therefore, before operations based on these summaries go into action, computerization and experimentation are important means of achieving effective planning and good management performance.

Special departments probably will plan with words more than with numbers. Environmental relations, the legal department, and technical research are examples of organizational components that will have budgets to prepare, but will measure short-range success in goals not easily quantified. An important exception is the economist who will be concerned with strategic variables and will prepare extensive forecasts on the economic framework. The administrator of the plan will normally work with management running these departments on the design of summaries and the flow of both information from other departments, which they need, and details needed by other departments.

Computerized Models

There are two primary reasons for utilizing the computer in SROP: (1) While possibly increasing accuracy and desirable detail, workloads and cost of planning can be reduced. The repetitive process of short range operational planning is programmed so that the computer does more in much less time and this relieves people who had been producing the plan manually. (2) The speed and simplified procedures enable managers to experiment with decisions to determine their impact on performance. It is thereby feasible to make mistakes in the experiments instead of actual operations.

Citing a 1970 article by K.W. Bennett in *Iron Age*,[1] the size of a company that can gain from a model is about $20 million in sales. However, the amount is getting smaller as commercial programs for SROP are refined. Several consulting firms are now offering tailored models on a one-time basis for $25,000± or on a continuing basis for $2,500± down and $1,000 per month for a minimum of two years. The important point is that models are not the exclusive advantage of big corporations. Both timeshare terminals and improved small computers permit firms with as little as $5 million in sales per year to have effective SROP models (computer manufacturers such as IBM have free programs that can be modified for use on their equipment.)

Sun Oil Corporation was an early leader in developing computerized planning. It took 13 man years to plan and 10 man years to train management in the 2000 equation model built by the company. George Gershefski, as a result of building the models at Sun Oil, has written an important reference in the field, "The Development and Application of a Corporate Financial Model."

THE CONTENT OF SROP

Differences between companies within industries and industries within an economy make it necessary to generalize the content of short-range operational plans. A table of contents will serve to summarize a typical situation, recalling that details are given for time periods discussed earlier in the chapter.

[1] Bennett, K. W., *Iron Age*, October 29, 1970. Information in this article has been updated to reflect circumstances in 1974.

Part	Section	Title	Content
I	a	Statement of General Company Objectives	This is "boiler plate" material, but it serves to remind users of overall direction and purpose.
	b	Statement of Specific Short-Range Objectives	Current factors affecting competitiveness and profitability are identified, and strategies to combat these situations are referenced by location in the plan and organizational responsibilities for execution.
	c	Measures and Standards	Measures such as earnings per share and standards such as unit cost per product before administrative overhead are identified so that operating managers are making the same comparisons.
II	a	Forecasts of Economic Indicators	This provides the economic framework, and clarifies whether the company is operating in a time period when the trend is up, down, or stable. Prosperity, recovery or recession is predicted.
	b	Industry Forecasts	Breakdowns by geography, product, price condition, and inroads of competitive materials are usually included.
	c	Assumption on the Business Climate	Government actions, community developments, international situations, etc., potentially affecting the business are identified.
III	a	Management Summary of Companywide Performance	This is often a financially oriented executive summary with restricted distribution. Confidential comments on segments of the firm may be included.
	b	Management Summaries by Specific Areas of Responsibility	Company organizations vary. The breakdown could be by divisions, subsidiaries, product managers, regions of operations, type of customer, manufacturing process,

			or combinations. Distribution is restricted to top management, the manager involved and organizational components affected directly.
IV	a	Cash Inflow from Sales	Totals in IVa are detailed by type of product, and breakdowns between dollars and units. Other appropriate sections would be geographic and physical distribution data on type of transportation, warehouse involved, etc.
	b	Cash Inflow from Other Sources	Interest income, sales of assets, rent, and miscellaneous sources such as return of purchases are identified.
V	a	Production	Output by products by plant corresponding to the sales breakdowns.
	b	Production Unit Costs and Gross Margins by Product	The unit comparisons usually clarify performance by product. Product interrelationships are included to eliminate impractical comparisons.
	c	Inventories	The breakdowns will give finished goods by location, raw materials and parts at plants, and related items such as orders placed with suppliers and expected arrival dates.
VI	a	Companywide Budget Summary	This summary reconciles cash out flow for the appropriate time periods by the major categories shown in VIb and the entities in VII.
	b	(Refer to the areas of responsibilities in IIIb for the number and type of organizational entities involved.)	These summaries by major organizational component give full cost details, including the smallest department, in most SROP's.

VII SROP for Special Organizational Components a. Legal Department b. Research & Development c. Engineering d. Corporate Planning e. Industrial Relations f. etc.	Not many companies force managers of staff components to plan, particularly short range. It is, however, an excellent means of gaining efficiency and establishing priorities.
VIII SROP for Projects and Programs a. Acquisition of XYZ b. Construction of Plant Z c. Diversification through Product R including Pilot Plant Operations and Market Testing	These projects and programs relate to long range plans being implemented outside the responsibility of managers for existing operations. Distribution of the information is usually very restricted.
IX Appendixes	Charts, graphs, tables, and supporting calculations are placed where only persons working with details can refer to the information.

Nearly all of the content in a plan is a forecast. SROP provides a starting point. Throughout the time period involved actual performance will be compared with expectations. This up-to-date information is quickly and accurately obtained if the plan is computerized. Daily and weekly reports on the period of SROP completed are analyzed for deviations. Personnel affected are alerted that adjustments are needed. Coordination between organizational components may be necessary because of disbalances between sales and shipments to warehouse by location, production at plants requiring raw materials from other plants, and so on.

Emphasis is placed on the computer because of speed of information flow, capability to make complicated comparisons of performance, reliability of data (mistakes occur especially in the early stages of use, but accuracy is far better than manually prepared plans over a period of years), and capability to experiment before finalizing the plan. In addition, alert systems can be programmed whereby key people are informed as soon as deviations beyond a certain minimum limit occur.

Looking back on the years in which calculators and weeks of 20-hour days were an integral part of both SROP and long-range planning, the advances are significant. Utilization of modern methods will increase the probability of making good decisions in a greater number of organizational components. This, in turn, should result in better company performance.

Contingency Planning and Executive Management in SROP

Executive management traditionally spends most of its time plotting the future course of the company and handling relationships with shareholders, board of director members, the financial community, community leaders, and others who affect the future. A smaller portion is given to supervising daily operations. As stated in Chapter One, key executives delegate operational authority to subordinates. However, dramatic changes took place in the structure of world business in the mid-1970s. The sharp rise in the cost of energy, shortages of key materials, and rampant inflation are at the core of the changes. These and other factors related to specific firms forced greater participation by top executives in SROP. One result was formal plans providing guidance on what to do when unusual events occur.

A method to cope with extraordinary change is called *contingency planning*. It calls for plans prepared for immediate substitution in SROP when a serious situation arises. Preparation of these plans involves:

1. Identifying the critical success factors in the company's business.
2. Completing an analysis which pinpoints major developments that could occur and would affect these success factors significantly, and estimating the varying degrees of magnitude of their actual occurrence (for example, 50%, 100%, or 200+% increase in the delivered price of iron ore).
3. Determining the impact of the major developments on the success factors and resulting profits in the existing SROP.
4. Conceiving alternatives for optimizing under the new conditions.
5. Executive judgments on the number of conditions to be covered in contingency plans to narrow the number of alternatives to be selected for optimization.
6. Completing the stand-by plans in a form which enables effective rapid insertion in SROP as necessary.

Most of the six steps require major input by top management. Otherwise, the end result could be inadequate or misleading. Motivation to allocate time to contingency planning instead of other high-priority jobs is best summarized by T. D. C. Anderson, Managing Director of Lawson and Co. (Merchants), Ltd. in London, England: "It is a matter of making certain that a company has a 'tomorrow.' If those responsible permit the foundations of a business to be undermined in the present, long-range planning is a worthless exercise."[2]

---

[2] Quote from a personal letter to the author.

The computer is an immense help in selecting the alternatives with the best probabilities for optimizing during steps three, four, and five. Through use of corporate models and quantitative techniques such as simulation and optimization, the thousands of variables can be handled efficiently and quite rapidly. In addition, when conditions actually change, the computer can be programmed to sort through components of contingency plans and to select the best of these components for the specific situation that occurred.

This refinement in approach requires the development of plan segments in step six, which give flexibility in coping with a change that could have widely ranging degrees of magnitude. Most contingency plans are monolithic, and while beneficial, they may not provide the optimum solution. Figure 6–7 illustrates the concept.

Normal Roles for Executive Management in SROP

The competence and experience of top management can play an important role in the planning of daily operations. These operations actually earn the profits, and contributions to contingency planning for SROP can keep the company growing and profitable.

In addition, executive management can directly contribute by having their staff analyze plans made by lower levels of the organization and by making contributions to plan content in discussions with both their staff and the managers responsible for executing the plans. This talent should be particularly applied to strategy formulation. Staff input will improve quality and coordinate these plans with long-range strategies. Executive management normally does not get involved in back-up detail and could be out of touch with existing conditions, but their involvement plays a critical role in subordinates: (1) knowing their plans will be reviewed; (2) preparing for meetings on content and revisions, and (3) feeling an obligation to check out suggestions by top executives. The resulting refinements lead to profits.

Regarding executive management's role in establishing a link between SROP and the long-range plan, Peter Drucker points out, "Decisions exist only in the present. The question that faces the long-range planner is not what his organization should do tomorrow. It is: What do we have to do today to be ready for an uncertain tomorrow? The question is not what will happen in the future. It is: What futurity do we have to factor into our present thinking and doing, what time spans do we have to consider, and how do we use this information to make good decisions now."[3] This places SROP in perspective with the long-range plan, and initiates programs and projects.

[3] Peter F. Drucker, *Management: Tasks, Responsibilities, Practices.* Harper & Row, 1973. Chapter 16.

Figure 6—7. Two Approaches to Contingency Planning

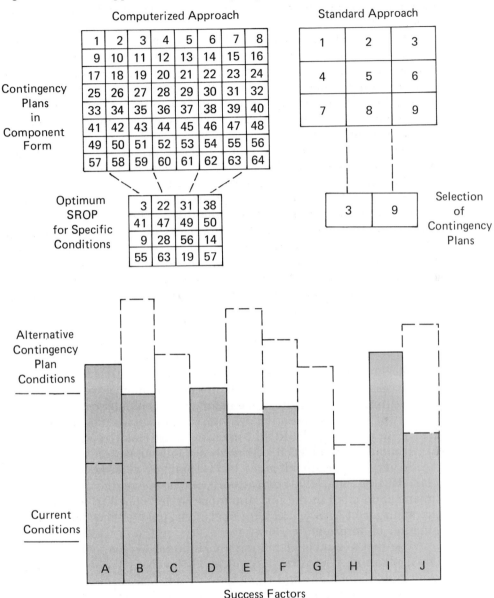

SUMMARY

There are two fundamental motivations for short-range operational planning (SROP): (1) superior operating performance, and (2) implementing long-range plans through programs and projects. The plan provides a framework for decision making at all levels of the organization.

A definition for SROP includes: (1) a time span of no more than one year; (2) variables for the business environment and for each major component of the organization based on assumptions and forecasts for strategic variables; (3) assignments to identify responsibility for both planning and carrying out the plan, and (4) policies on degree of detail required to communicate the information needed to improve performance.

Within the year's coverage for SROP there are breakdowns such as quarters or months. More detail is contained in the period closest to going into action than those at the end of the year. Objectives will be developed for each major entity in the organization, and critical factors and assumptions will be identified. The operating variables will include strategies as well as forecasts of sales, production, and other aspects of a going concern. Computerized planning models best handle the volume of data and permit experimentation before putting the plan into action. Contingency planning is essential and the approach can vary from (1) awareness about developments which could affect the business' success factors and informal plans to counter each situation, to (2) sophisticated, computerized plans that permit iterating through alternatives and selection of the optimum plan.

Three factors are critical in making assignments: (1) personnel should know what they are expected to do through clear instructions and access to guidance while planning; (2) managers should make every effort to match the assignment with competence, and (3) the degree of real cooperation within organizational components is critical to accuracy of SROP. Managers must make an effort to identify trouble spots in each of the three and take corrective action.

A very important element is the policies guiding design of the plan. Content must be compatible with needs of the five levels of organization cited in the text and must be developed in the same way the manager of MIS works with executives to give them the best combination of information flow.

The two extremes of planning techniques are bottom-up and top-down planning. The former requires all levels of the organization to contribute their ideas and capacities. In most cases, supervision sorts out unrealistic forecasts and suggestions and attempts to develop a workable SROP. Top-down planning is an approach where top management makes most of the decisions and the remainder of the firm is given assignments to carry out although they have had little voice in the content. Full-resource planning utilizes the talents, experience and current knowledge of all people in the company. However, proper administration of this approach is important if full benefits are to be gained.

An example of content in SROP is given in the form of a table of contents in the text along with explanatory comments.

The role of executive management involves a large proportion of time devoted to long-range planning and external relationships. However, the motivations of SROP deeply involve the top executives of a company. Profit performance improves from their inputs, particularly in contingency planning and the formulation of strategy. Equally important, programs and projects to achieve long-range objectives are implemented under their direction.

DISCUSSION QUESTIONS

1. Why should the structural design of SROP and MIS be compatible and identical if possible?
2. Explain the differences between *top-down*, *bottom-up*, and *full-resource* planning, and give the advantages and disadvantages for each, selecting different types of companies.
3. What is meant by "rolling SROP"?
4. What are the primary reasons for using a computer in SROP?
5. Defend or criticize this statement, "All levels of an organization should receive the whole SROP to gain maximum efficiency."
6. What are the five levels of management to be considered in designing management summaries?
7. What are the critical factors in assigning people to specific responsibilities in SROP? Relate these factors to setting up and maintaining support for SROP.

SUGGESTED READINGS AND BIBLIOGRAPHY

Ammer, D.C. "Side Effects of Planning," *Harvard Business Review*. May—June, 1971, pp. 32—34.

Bagley, Edward R. "How to Avoid Glitches in Planning," *Management Review*. March, 1972, pp. 4—9.

Bennett, K.W. "Company Plan Models—A Must," *Modern Age*. October 29, 1970, p. 35.

Bennett. "Who Will Do It Is Planning's Big Problem," *Iron Age*. June 17, 1971, p. 41.

Carson, I. "Computer Power for Planning," *International Management*. May, 1972, pp. 36—38.

Christopher, William F. "Marketing Planning that gets Things Done," *Harvard Business Review*. September—October, 1970, pp. 56—64.

Dible, Donald. *Up Your Own Organization.* Entrepreneur Press, Santa Clara, California, 1971.

Egerton, H.C. and Brown, J.K. "Some Perspectives and Business Planning," *Conference Board Record.* August, 1971, pp. 32–36.

Godfrey. "Short Run Planning in a Decentralized Firm," *Accounting Review.* April, 1971.

Hanan, M. "Manpower Management," *Sales Management.* January 24, 1972, pp. 36–37.

Irwin, Patrick H. "Why Aren't Companies Doing a Better Job of Planning?" *Management Review.* November, 1971, pp. 11–16.

Kastens, Merritt L. "Who Does the Planning?" *Management Review.* April, 1972, pp. 48–49.

McCartney, H.P. "Planning via the Top Down Method," *Public Relations Journal.* January, 1970, pp. 11–13.

Miller, Ernest C. Advanced Techniques for Strategic Planning. *American Management Association,* 1971.

Parker, George G.C. and Segura, Edilberto L. "How to Get a Better Forecast," reprint from *Harvard Business Review.* March–April, 1971, pp. 99–109.

Pogue, C.A. and Bussard, R.N. "Linear Programming Model for Short Term Finance Planning under Uncertainty," *Sloan Management Review.* Spring, 1972, pp. 69–88.

Salmon, Kurt. "How Short-range Planning Can Make Long-range Plans Work," *The Office.* January, 1970, pp. 64–66.

Steiner, George A. *Top Management Planning.* Macmillan, 1969.

Stokes, Paul M. "How to Make Plans that Work," *Supervisory Management.* January, 1970, pp. 2–5.

" 'Sword Thrust' Planning has just one Target: ROI," *Industry Week.* July 3, 1972, pp. 42–44.

Zager, Robert. "Getting into the Habit of Planning," *Director.* March, 1971.

Case: Trenton Industries, Inc.: Designing and Implementing SROP

Fundamentals of SROP are covered in this second case on Trenton. Subtleties arising from the characteristics of company personnel, and refinements required to apply the fundamentals to a specific company develop the student's understanding of SROP.

On February 1, 1976, Trenton distributed two policy manuals, one for executive management and the other for operating personnel reporting to directors. (See Figure 3C–1, p. 77 on company organization.) Hank Trenton, executive vice president, had devoted considerable time to the revisions developed from the trial in 1975. The final proposal to the board of directors was well received. He then turned his full energies toward designing and implementing a coordinated short-range operating plan (SROP).

Hank Trenton and his two vice presidents were encouraged by the informal planning that led to the Wichita plant exceeding expectations in 1974 and achieving the forecast for units produced and sales volume in 1975. However, several factors indicated the need for SROP.

First, the outlook for 1976 was excellent. Sales of $7.6 million and after-tax profits of $700,000 were possible. However, top management estimated a rate of 12% profit on sales was feasible with greater volume, more emphasis on efficiency, and controls on increases in overhead. The possibilities were encouraging because the learning curve for new personnel at both plants and the sales force had been slightly better than predicted.

Second, the first year of full-scale operations at both plants was to be in 1976, and this increased the need for coordination on shipment of orders. It was important to meet delivery promises, especially in the new territory (see Figure 3C—2), and this meant a tight rein on production schedules from week to week. In fact, some distributors had customers who would be wholly dependent on new equipment to harvest their crops because of food policy programs.

Third, some plant operations at Wichita were going to require the services of employees normally working in Omaha. Rather than employ people with skills that would not be fully utilized during large portions of the year, Trenton paid a premium to diesel engine mechanics and vacuum welders to spend three to four weeks per quarter in Wichita. This policy saved a significant amount of expense but required coordination between the plants.

Fourth, inflation had eaten into profit margins in the 1973-75 period. If price increases were justified, considering productivity improvement and greater proration of overhead, 1976 was the year to make such decisions because of strong demand. Also, Trenton did not have sufficient unit cost information to make selective increases instead of using the previous practice of raising the prices of all items by a single percentage.

Fifth, customer service and repairs could be a problem in a year when operations are expected to be at full capacity. It was essential to coordinate promises being authorized by the manager of customer service with plant managers at Wichita and Omaha. SROP would give a framework for making these decisions.

Executive management at Trenton was convinced that several efficiencies would result from a functional operating plan. Also, their cash position would be clear in the event of any expansion opportunity coming in 1976 although the company would concentrate its energies on a more efficient Trenton through short-range planning.

DESIGNING THE PLAN

Hank Trenton believed it would be best if SROP had major input from personnel in lower levels of the organization. However, the executive vice president was uncertain about the exact method of achieving this and began by proposing a detailed study of their newly designed Trenton combine. Pricing of this self-propelled vehicle in two sizes would justify the expense of learning:

1. Existing methods of determining unit costs at the Omaha plant.
2. Organization at the plant level to manufacture this important product.
3. Lead times on purchasing including the cost basis for make or buy decisions.
4. Shipping costs to various distribution points.
5. The best approach to proportioning selling, customer service, administrative, and other expenses such as interest and rent paid in order to have accurate unit costs.
6. Timing factors associated with each phase of making and selling the combine including receipt of cash from the distributor.

The information from this study would provide the basis for the executive vice president and the two vice presidents to draft an approach to SROP, which could be modified by other levels of management. Timing was important because the plan's value would be most critical in the current year. As a result, Hank authorized the combine study on February 9, 1976 and a draft was to be completed by March 31. The work would be conducted by John A. Hotchkiss, a bright management prospect who had left Trenton in 1973, but had returned to the company as Manager of Market Research February 1. It was feasible that Hank would place John Hotchkiss in charge of planning and development if the study and drafting of SROP went smoothly.

Results of the Combine Study

The costs and suggested price structure are given in Table 6C−1. The details were developed from original work by John Hotchkiss because he found thorough cost ac-

Table 6C−1. Self-Propelled Combines

	Medium* Capacity Combine	Full* Capacity Combine
Retail List Price	$23,250	$26,250
Standard Equipment per Vehicle	Diesel 130 hp, or Gasoline 145 hp	Diesel 150 hp, or Gasoline 165 hp
Full Range of Grain Platforms, Corn Heads, Feeding Equipment, Threshing Type Cylinders, Separating Straw Racks, Cleaning Systems, Conveying and Storage Tailings Elevator.	Width 114 inches	Width 126 inches
Trenton Industries, Inc. Price to Distributors	$15,500	$17,500
Profit Contribution before Taxes	4,500	5,500
Total Expenses	$11,000	$12,000
Depreciation (Prorated: 25 medium, 20 full; $112,500/$1,285,000 for medium=8.75% $110,000/$1,285,000 for full=8.5%		
Cash Expenses	9,235	9,855
Pre-tax Cash Contribution Per Unit, 1976	$ 6,265	$ 7,645
Total Cash Contribution, 1976	158,625	152,900

* The closest competition for these combines is the International Harvester Company Series, specifically the 815 and 915 respectively.

	Medium* Capacity Combine	Full* Capacity Combine
Cost Breakdown Per Unit (Cash Only):	$9,235	$9,855
Components Purchased (Diesel engine, frame, wheels, and miscellaneous items)	3,715	4,180
Subtotal	$5,520	$5,675
Production Direct Wages and Salaries $1,125		
Trenton Manufactured Parts 725		
Proration of Supervision 315		
Inventory and Quality Control 185		
Dispensable Materials 25		
Utilities Prorated at 8.625% 110		
(Note: Charges for space and equipment are included in depreciation; return on this investment is included in the profit contribution)	2,485	2,485
Subtotal	$3,035	$3,190
Marketing: Proration of Budget at 8.625%	775	775
Subtotal	$2,260	$2,415
Service and Repair Forecast	325	510
Subtotal	$1,935	$1,905
Administration, Cash Management and Financial Charges	$1,935	$1,905
	0	0

* The closest competition for these combines is the International Harvester Company Series, specifically the 815 and 915 respectively.

counting on totals such as electricity or wages and benefits for the overall plant but no attempt had ever been made to identify unit costs. One result was the suggestion that another study be conducted later in the year after obtaining SROP results to determine if distributors would object to Trenton dropping any unprofitable products identified in the plan.

One important point uncovered during the research was that the space allocated to the combine in

Omaha could be utilized for customer service projects during four months of the year and, when coupled with the seasonal downtime for the hand operated hilldrop planter, the entire service and repair program could be handled at one plant.

Another point was that nearly all Trenton distributors paid the company late. The average was 87 days, almost twice the regional average. This practice developed in the 1969-70 period when Trenton Industries carried the distributors for as long as six months as a gesture of goodwill during a recession. Hank was annoyed at the controller for not being on top of this situation.

Finally, research for the study determined that a shift in price position had occurred during 1974-75. Until that time Trenton products were 5 to 10% more expensive than competitors, but sold well on the basis of quality. Now the major companies in the industry had increased prices to a point where they averaged 3 to 5% more than Trenton products. This information indicated that marketing had no feedback system which would permit inputs by field salesmen who were probably aware of this fact. SROP, if properly designed, might correct this problem.

Structure of the Plan

Hank delegated responsibility for preliminary design of the plan to John Hotchkiss who was then on special assignment to the executive vice president. The timetable and steps to include the contributions of everyone in management are given in Table 6C-2.

The most significant step for the executive vice president was to obtain the cooperation of his father who had delayed implementing the policy framework for a year. In addition, members of middle management might resist the accountability resulting from SROP. Too much could be accomplished in 1976 to delay any aspect of the timing in Table 6C-2. He decided against using any of the points revealed in the study as a basis of gaining support. This could be interpreted as a criticism of management in the early 1970s. Instead he decided to express concern about adequate cash for both operations and also loan obligations since this

Table 6C-2. Timetable for SROP

February 9, 1976	Initiate Combine Study
March 31	Review of Conclusions on Combine Study
April 9	Design Concepts for SROP
23	Instructions for Management
30	Final Draft of Design and Instructions
May 3	Distribution to Management
21	Companywide Meeting on SROP
June 15	Preliminary Estimates from Management
30	SROP I
December 13-17	Review of Results

was the first year of capacity operations at both plants. At lunch on Monday, March 29, he asked, "Would there be adequate working capital?" Without additional prompting from Hank, short-range planning was authorized. Using the same tactic, but being certain that there could never be an accusation that he had misled his father on scope of the planning, the son asked to put together something that could be useful to operating personnel as well as top management. This suggestion was thought to be "constructive."

John Hotchkiss had the design concepts for SROP within a week.

His suggestions for instructions were ready two weeks later. These were amended by Hank and relayed to the vice presidents for comments. The final draft was ready by April 30. Table 6C−3 gives the contents and the introduction for each major section. Hank Trenton decided that, while the remainder of the instructions were prepared, SROP would get greater support if the directors and other managers made a major contribution to the content. As a result, the companywide meeting to discuss the concepts was moved to May 27−28 instead of the previous Friday.

Table 6C−3. Table of Contents and Introductions to SROP

Table of Contents

III Marketing Operations
3.1 and 2.4 Marketing and Customer Service Summary
3.2 and Other
     Within policy guidelines, develop optimum efficiency in: (1) selling and servicing Trenton products and (2) coordinating the payment of receivables with the Controller's office. It is the responsibility of marketing to maximize cash inflow, and through coordination with production, emphasize products yielding the greatest after-tax profits.

Regarding budgets, examine all expenditures including wages and salaries for their contribution to the primary objective — selling. No ceiling is placed on spending. Budgets can be increased if sales are increased. If, on the other hand, sales forecasts do not indicate substantial improvement in volume, every effort must be made to increase efficiency and reduce expenditures.

IV   Production
4.1 and 2.5 Production Control Summary
4.2 Omaha Plant Operations — Summary
4.2.1 Omaha Department Summaries (4.2.2, 4.2.3, etc.)
4.3 Wichita Plant Operations — Summary
4.3.1 Wichita Department Summaries (4.3.2, 4.3.3, etc.)

Within policy guidelines, develop optimum efficiency in the production of Trenton products, given existing facilities. No ceilings are placed on spending for equipment and structures which can be quickly added to the plants if such additions substantially reduce costs. All budgets should be examined for their contributions to the primary objective — making high quality farm implements at the lowest possible cost.

Recall that decades of tradition are behind many operating practices. It is time for Trenton to determine if production methods are modern and the most efficient ways to achieve unit volume. Coordination with marketing will be essential in this process in order to concentrate plans on the best product-mix.

V   Cash Management
5.1 and 2.3 Cash Management Summary
5.2 Cash Flow — Short Range
5.3.1 Cash Inflow Analysis (5.3.2, 5.3.3, etc.)
5.4.1 Cash Outflow Analysis (5.4.2, 5.4.3, etc.)
5.5 Money Management — Half Year
5.6 Capital Allocations — Half Year
5.6.1 Capital Allocations — Next Calendar Year
5.6.2 Capital Allocations — Five Year Forecast
5.7 Dividend Summary

Four purposes guide cash management: (1) Monitor payments to suppliers and creditors in order to retain the highest credit rating while avoiding early dispersements. (2) Develop the maximum amount of interest income from company cash. (3) Provide the cheapest possible capital for the company, and (4) Plan capital allocations for decisions for executive management. This places on management the necessity of being continually conscious about the receipt and disposition of the Trenton company money.

In carrying out its primary objective, those responsible for cash management must use prudence in preparing and adhering to departmental budgets. Directors reporting to the Vice President and Controller have the obligation to increase use of the computer in establishing programs in repetitive data processing and operating control. Summarizing, all changes in cash outflow must be justified on the basis of contribution to profits.

VI   Administration and Other Functions
    6.1 Summary of Other Company Functions
    6.2 Research & Development Programs and Projects
    6.3 Personnel Control and Programs (Includes Benefits)
    6.4 Miscellaneous Operations

      All functions involved in cash outflow must consider their responsibilities and possibilities for improving efficiency. Particularly, Research & Development is obligated to uncover new market opportunities to retain the competitive position of Trenton. This necessitates coordination with marketing and Production.

Management Support for Planning

Rumors about formal planning circulated the offices in Omaha and Wichita. The schedule for introduction of SROP was common knowledge. No one had a clear idea about what was involved. Nearly all the managers and supervisors were concerned about any overload that might interfere with their work.

In mid-April Trenton personnel were uncomfortable waiting for planning to begin. Few had anything to hide. However, many were uncertain that they had the training and experience to carry out their obligations satisfactorily. They recognized that specific policies had helped the company, but the general feeling was that SROP was an unnecessary exercise. The primary objections being raised were:

1. The time it would take to provide information, budgets, and forecasts during the busiest period for operations.
2. The implication that some people were not doing the best they could because, otherwise, changes were unnecessary.

3. The dislike for having to account for details and routines that had never been reviewed by top management.

No organized resistance had developed. An alliance of "old timers" had formed casually during recent weeks. They sympathized with the president having to cope with these programs and talked about the "good old days." Some speculated on a battle between Hank and his father on the planning issue.

The general attitude toward SROP was summarized by Mike Sloane, the general sales manager, who said he was measured by sales volume without discounts that cut into profit margins. Hank Trenton could expect him to spend his energies selling. Time spent on planning would have to receive second priority.

Executive Management's Perspective on Support for Planning

Hank Trenton realized that most of management would look on the analysis required to prepare an accurate, efficient SROP as an overload to their normal work. He was considering a two-pronged approach to generate enthusiasm for planning.

First, it was important to develop an open mind toward the added work versus benefits obtained in better performance in their normal jobs. This meant attention to written releases, orientation of key management, and presentations to the remainder of the company contributing to the plan.

Second, profits were expected to increase as a result of SROP, and participation of the entire organization in a portion of these profits would give incentive to work at realizing planning commitments. The idea of employees knowing about profit performance would be contrary to policy in this part of the country because ownership of most local companies was closely held. This meant that H. S. Trenton V, as a prominent industrial leader in the Midwest area, might resist such a proposal. Hank knew that modern management concepts were not readily accepted as logical in his father's circle of friends, and that if he pushed too hard his incentive plan would be jeopardized. Communications were entirely under his control, but he was worried about early disclosure of cash incentives.

The bonus system could only be justified if the gains in efficiency as expressed in after-tax earnings significantly exceeded the costs in wages and salaries paid as an incentive. Since 1976 was a transition year, gains in profits resulting from SROP could be attributed to economies of scale, normal improvement in managing the operation and favorable market reaction to the selfpropelling combine rather than SROP. As a result, Hank had to have a means of identifying planning benefits.

Base Point for SROP

In late April Hank Trenton held a "budgets meeting" to forecast performance during the last six months of 1976. His tactic in bringing together the two vice presidents and the five directors was to have budgets and sales forecasts that were acceptable to everyone including the CEO and the board of directors. Because there was a meeting of the board in early May, Hank could present the results and obtain a commitment that performance during the period was satisfactory. Later, the April forecast of operations prepared using the normal approach at Trenton Industries would be compared with a plan prepared in May and June which would examine all present practices and give revised sales forecasts, cost estimates, and statements of strategy in the July–December period.

The base point forecast made by the eight-man management team is summarized in Table 6C–4. This updated the projections made in late 1975 given on the third page of the case.

The base point forecast and the concept of an "Employee Participation Bonus" program based on improved performance were accepted by the board of directors on May 5. Hank Trenton was charged with the responsibility of developing SROP without disrupting the company in a way which would jeopardize the accepted forecast.

Table 6C-4

| | $ Millions $ | | | | | | | | |
| Sales | | Predepreciation Expenses | | Depreciation | | Taxes | | After-Tax Profits | |
12 Mos.	2nd Half	12 Mos.	2nd Half	12 Mos.	2nd Half	12 Mos.	2nd Half	12 Mos.	2nd Half
$7.715	$3.965	$5.925	$3.005	$ .505	$ .245	$ .595	$ .335	$ .690	$ .380

May and June

The contents and introductions for each of the sections in Table 6C-3 were distributed to the directors. They were asked to take complete leadership for their area of responsibility in order to develop the maximum amount of bottom up contributions to the plan. As previously mentioned, the meeting for reporting on proposals by these parts of the organization was set back to May 28.

It was never certain that, in the process of putting SROP together, personnel of Trenton were motivated by the rumors about bonuses. Many liked expressing their own ideas. Many more were thoroughly annoyed at the diversion from normal duties and the overtime. Morale dropped to an all time low by the end of May.

Regardless, the summary of Trenton performance under the first draft of SROP was overly optimistic, and there was an disbalance between what marketing wanted to sell and what the two plants wanted to make. Greater coordination was necessary between these key departments, and portions of the plan were returned to the directors by Hank with specific areas for revision and suggestions on better communication between departments.

The second draft was presented to the Executive Vice President and the two vice presidents by the key managers on June 18 after revisions which resulted from what was expected to be a "rubber stamp" coordination meeting with the directors on June 14. The results are shown below.

Improvement under SROP was not spectacular. Sales were slightly less because more money could be made by making four more self-propelled combines instead of 32 cultivators. The most encouraging aspect was the many ideas for

| | $ Million $ | | | | | | | | |
| Sales | | Predepreciation Expenses | | Depreciation | | Taxes | | After-Tax Profits | |
12 Mos.	2nd Half	12 Mos.	2nd Half	12 Mos.	2nd Half	12 Mos.	2nd Half	12 Mos.	2nd Half
SROP $7.710	$3.955	$5.785	$2.875	$ .505	$ 245	$ .650	$ .385	$ .770	$ .450
Normal 7.715	3.965	5.925	3.005	.505	.245	.595	.335	.690	.380

greater efficiency coming from the process of planning. Examples are:

1. Space for inventory of components limited capacity in Omaha. Double stacking would increase inventory space by 40% through simple racks and a retriever accessory on a tractor. The entire system was installed in December 1976 before Christmas.
2. Purchasing had not been coordinated between the two plants. Volume had now reached a point where discounts were significant. Savings of 4% would be achieved in 1977 although not much could be gained in 1976 with accumulated inventory. Also, examination of parts and materials uncovered sufficient duplication to save 3% in volume of purchases.
3. Salesmen's routes and number of calls per week had never been considered. No one would be fired, but sales for the capacity being added could be generated by fewer people with greater efficiency. Previously a sales representative was allowed to plan his own time with no coordination by Mike Sloane.
4. Running in diesel engines after mounting had occupied floor space and limited capacity on several production lines. Investigation with suppliers of the engines indicated that improved tolerances enable the time to be reduced 80%, or a 2% increase in capacity.

The actual proposal to the CEO and board in early July was to create an "Employee Participation Bonus." The calculations for the payout had been based on comparisons between the normal forecast and a thoroughly prepared SROP. If the new approach realized significant gains in July–December, 1976, SROP would be continued. Regardless, an incentive bonus of 25% of the gain in pre-tax profits between the second and first forecast would be paid in January. The on-going bonus would be 25% of the gain in pre-tax profits over the previous calendar year distributed through a procedure which could be developed in 1977. The CEO and the board approved the proposal. One board member summarized their position, "You can't go wrong giving away 25% of something you wouldn't have had anyway."

PERFORMANCE OF SROP

Trenton achieved a $68,000 increase in after-tax profits in the last six months of 1976 based on reliable but unaudited accounts, or $2,000 less than the SROP addition. Cash flow was slightly greater than the $695,000 in the forecast because of additional write-offs. This meant that pre-tax and depreciation earnings were actually higher than expected in SROP.

Hank Trenton was encouraged, and a bonus fund was created based on 25% of the gain in pre-tax earnings during the second half. This would be $133,000 times .25 or $33,000. Wages and salaries excluding the president and vice president in the same period were $685,000. As a result, everyone received a 4.85%

		$Million		
Sales	Predepreciation Expenses	Depreciation	Taxes	After-Tax Profits
$8.100	$5.665	$ .545	$ .870	$1.020

bonus on their gross income for six months.

The general attitude toward planning had improved. Potential gains from SROP in 1977, which were discovered in last year's planning process but not fully realized, will yield new and substantial gains in pre-tax profits. From the company's viewpoint, this meant a significant improvement in after-tax profits because the bonus fund is deductible, and taxes payable are reduced 50¢ for each $1.00 paid to employees. On January 9, 1977 the Board of Directors approved the possibility of $179,000 in bonuses based on the above forecast.

Administrative Controls

John Hotchkiss was appointed director of planning and development reporting to the executive vice president. Hank Trenton's concept was to have John administrate the plan and clear strategic and problem areas with the vice presidents. He would be involved in important meetings on revisions. In addition, John Hotchkiss could conduct venture analyses for expansion and acquisitions. This would give some momentum to growth.

To improve coordination between line and staff departments, a planning committee was formed by John Hotchkiss which included all the directors. In the first meeting of this group they decided on only two revisions per year. The director of research and development also wanted to know about long-range plans which would affect his work. Since this type of planning was compatible with growth programs Hank Trenton had "only in his mind," the planning committee was authorized to develop a format for a Trenton Long-Range Plan during 1977 which could direct growth programs.

STUDENT PROBLEMS

1. Place yourself in the position of Hank Trenton. Looking back, is it prudent to divert company personnel from operations into planning during 1976, a very pressure laden and busy year?
2. Identify points in the introduction of SROP undertaken by Trenton Industries which you would change. Clarify the part that self-propelled combines played, if any, in the steps you took to formalize planning.
3. Switch roles and place yourself in the position of John Hotchkiss. Recognizing conditions at Trenton, and the existence of a new planning committee, design a feedback system that assures better communications in the company. What

steps are needed to improve employee attitude toward planning in addition to "buying" their support?

4. Now play the role of a non-Trenton shareholder. You have objected to the design of the "Employee Participation Bonus." Defend its elimination and offer another incentive system to gain the support of managers and supervisors for SROP.

Long-Range Planning

The elements and objectives of long-range planning are identified. The part of strategic variables and allocation of resources in the planning process are explained. Personnel doing the planning and administration of the plan are discussed. Finally, intracompany steps required for successful long-range planning are outlined. This chapter develops another dimension of planning which is critical to continuous profit performance.

7

Long-range planning involves a different time period and less detail than SROP. Generally, a company's management analyzes a future period and develops plans with the objective of taking full advantage of the predicted strategic variables and company resources. The goal is to earn maximum profits within self-determined constraints such as geographic areas and other constraints such as laws on pollution control. These plans are implemented through programs and projects in SROP.

THE ELEMENTS OF LONG-RANGE PLANNING

This brief definition needs to be expanded to gain a better understanding of long range planning. Let us examine each portion of the definition separately.

Time Period

Forecasts normally become less accurate as they probe farther into the future. A guide to whether the plan should be immediately following SROP, three, five, or ten years in advance of present operations can be obtained by estimating the following:

1. *Vulnerability.* What is the possible impact of technological innovation, subsidized foreign competitors, and so on? Can significant portions of the existing business be quickly hurt by a new product or service offered by a competitor, shortages, or a sharp increase in the cost of an important item? Or, will it take years to make an inroad into a company's cost structure and markets. If management judges vulnerability to be great, long range planning focuses on a period immediately after SROP, through three years from the present. If the company is deemed to have adequate time to diversify, employ counterstrategies, and so on, the time period would be a typical four to six years in the future.

2. *Capital Intensive Facilities.* Contrast the planning needs of a firm or division typically constructing a $10 million plant that has an expected life span of 15 years with one leasing space and equipment and existing from contract to contract. If financial feasibility depends on an assumption that the minimum competitive life of facilities is more than five years, it is prudent to have a planning framework for an extended time period.

3. *Financial Structure.* If there are no long-term loans, a company has financial flexibility on its long-range planning. It loses some of this flexibility when borrowing money to be repaid in three or more years. Most institutions lending major amounts to companies will require cash flow estimates for the life of the loan substantiated by extensive research on probable operating results.

4. *Characteristics of the Industry.* Some industries have a short life cycle for their products like toys while others continue for decades such as steel products. It is normal to concentrate planning on SROP and the two to three years immediately following if products generating current cash inflow will not exist next season. Master strategies to extend the life of products a few more years sometimes force planning to include periods farther into the future than required by current operations.

Top management will use these or similar factors to assess its position and set the timing parameters for long-range planning. It is feasible that diversification (different products and/or industries — see Chapter Eleven for details), and the time period for existing operations will have to be modified to accommodate the programs and projects to enter new businesses. The average long-range plan will estimate company operations five years into the future, as shown in Figure 7—1.

Figure 7-1. A Projection of the Company's Future

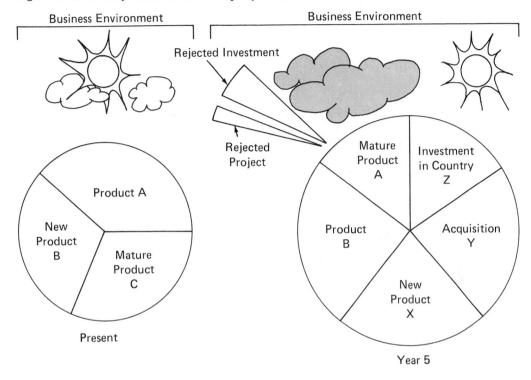

Updating Plans

Most firms update their long-range plan once each year, but there are numerous exceptions. For example, one major American company revises both SROP and its five-year plan twice a year at a week long meeting of the top executives in the company. A few review the long-range plan with each revision of SROP to coordinate programs and projects needed to realize forecasts in the years ahead.

Another consideration is the time required for preparation of objectives, forecasts, strategies, and assignments of responsibility. This varies with the method of planning and complexity of the plan. Weeks of information gathering, analysis, coordination meetings, and careful attention to details are usually necessary if long-range plans are to be of value. For most executives, the work is an extra responsibility in addition to running the business. To support these decision makers, staff personnel are continuously involved in analyzing components of the plan.

Complying with deadlines for completion of forms supplying raw information only takes a few days in most departments, but refinement of information, forecasts, and assumptions is a full-time job. This would involve considerable time in departments such as market research, production planning, and financial analysis.

Types of Objectives

Executive management usually develops long-range planning objectives from internal and external pressures rather than selecting from a list. However, some portion of the following list summarizes a firm's long-range planning goals:

1. Existing Business
   a. Maintain and strengthen product lines predicted to exceed minimum profit standards.
   b. Screen and phase out product lines with profit potential less than standards.
   c. Acquire going concerns, patents, licenses and other assets to expand operations.
   d. Support internal development of new concepts for the existing business.
   e. Allocate resources to programs and projects that expand, consolidate, and otherwise improve profits.
2. Diversification
   a. Identify new businesses and product lines growing at a high rate which are countercyclical and counterseasonal to present operations and acquire going concerns in these fields as a means of entry.
   b. Develop new product lines internally through research, or in combination with acquisitions, and allocate funds to realize the potential of those products exceeding minimum profit standards.
   c. Organize new operations to optimize use of company resources and facilitate control of new product lines.
   d. Act on acquisition opportunities which, after research and analysis, are judged to be attractively priced.
3. Support and Other Programs
   a. Employ and develop managers who are capable of carrying out assignments needed to expand the existing business and to manage new operations profitably.
   b. Develop systems and programs which minimize work stoppages, maximize esprit de corps, and profitably upgrade the workforce.
   c. Assume social responsibility in ways that do not conflict

with profit objectives but enhance the company's image with the public, employees, and institutions important to successful operations.

d. Anticipate contingencies and plan actions that optimize the company position.

Some companies will have special objectives that will control their long-range decision making. For example, the shareholders of a small or medium size firm may wish to be acquired so that they can realize a substantial capital gain when "cashing out." Therefore, resources will be allocated in a way that allows them to make the highest profits at the planned time of sale. Another situation might involve a coordinated five-year plan to establish operations in other countries with equipment being phased out in highly competitive countries.

It can be seen that objectives give direction to both planning and implementation. Managers should know the acceptable level of profitability for proposals, the types of investments needed to comply with corporate goals, budgetary constraints affecting decision latitude, and similar guidelines for successful businesses.

Identification of Strategic Variables Affecting the Company

Strategic variables are those variables outside of management control,[1] and in combination, make up the business environment in which a company will operate. They involve, as mentioned in Chapter Six, government actions, the economic, labor, and social framework for business, and the strategies of competitors. It is fundamental in long-range planning to forecast these variables first, and then make decisions on the operating variables the firm can control.

The forecasting capability for strategic variables has improved with the use of complex computer-based models that assist the decision maker in assessing: (1) interrelationships between variables, and (2) the degree of accuracy needed for individual variables to forecast the operating environment in the future period selected. After World War II, when formal long-range planning became more prevalent, it was common practice for operating divisions to take a number of forecasts prepared by staff experts on gross national product (GNP), income per capita, and so on as well as consuming industry forecasts such as construction, automobile sales, electrical sales, electrical equipment, and so on, and make estimates for future production and sales.

[1] Components of a strategy involving decisions within company control, such as selection of a geographic alternative or the combination of personnel to carry out aspects of the strategy, are sometimes referred to as strategic variables. This book uses the definitions given because they are the differentiations most common in business.

The situation in the 1970s is much more complex. Many economies around the world are more dynamic than the American economy. Government decisions can have lasting impact on volume and profit margins. Communication systems permit almost instant knowledge of business information by institutions, particularly the financial community. Complying with social responsibility has become a major factor in the allocation of resources. A web of inter-relationships between strategic variables has resulted from these and other developments that are the realities of the evolving business environment.

Forecasting under these conditions is difficult. However, it is particularly important to estimate the company's future business environment because of two related factors: (1) global competition in most products, and (2) a rapid rate of technological obsolescence. Decisions on operating variables have an increasingly higher probability of being correct as a company progresses from:

1. "Seat of the pants" judgment based on a few forecasts in trade publications to,
2. Estimates prepared by staff and/or top management with the defined goal of predicting the company's environment, to
3. Computerized models built from hundreds of interrelationships between strategic variables expressed quantitatively.

Contingency Plans for the Long Range

The structure of the long-range plan must have a mechanism to allow for unexpected events and changes in directions by outside influences. Therefore, the design and forecasting methods should result in management having knowledge of and means of coping with extraordinary developments through some form of contingency planning.

A different timeframe is involved than that discussed in Chapter Six on SROP, and the need for a detailed alternative ready for immediate implementation is not present. There is reason, however, for not only regularly revising forecasts of strategic variables, but also updating assessments of developments that could seriously affect profitability. Preparation of this type of contingency plan involves:

1. Reviewing success factors in SROP as a start to identifying the factors applicable in operations planned for the future.
2. Identifying developments which could seriously affect these factors, the manner in which the affect could occur, and alternative means of optimizing under the predicted conditions.

3. Executive judgments on the best alternatives by specific operation if the developments actually take place.

4. Completing this aspect of the formal plan that usually includes only summaries of the decisions in steps one, two and three.

Executive management must participate in the preparation of these special plans because of the impact on decisions involving the allocation of resources. If certain investments and programs are vulnerable to developments which could seriously affect profitability, and the probability of the development occurring is high, they could lose their priority. Top executives must also participate because of the quality of brainpower in steps one, two, and three is extremely important.

Formulating Strategy and Allocating Resources

Executive management, after concurring with forecasts for the company's business environment, makes two broad categories of decisions in long-range planning: (1) formulation of master strategies that provide direction for and influence the (2) allocation of tangible resources such as personnel, money, equipment, materials, and properties.

Master Strategies

Master strategies involve multi-pronged courses of action towards an objective (see Chapter Eight) and necessitate key decisions made by top executives on such items as expansion, diversification, approaches to complying with social responsibilities, concentration on automation, methods of financing new operations, and other fundamentals required for growth. These key items set the course for the company's future and guide many of the decisions on operating variables.

EXAMPLE OF A MASTER STRATEGY Preliminary forecasts indicate 35% of existing products will drop below the company profit standard in the next five years. Before returning the long-range plan submitted by the divisions involved, top management must devise a means of offsetting declining earnings. The strategy conceived involves five parts:

1. The 35% portion of the existing product line with unacceptable profits will be placed on a "maintain facilities/stabilize budgets/no expansion" basis.

2. The remaining 65% will be given "applied research/market development" resources to increase the profits from this source. An objective of 15% gain in profits from expenditures of $3 million in

the first year diminishing to $2 million in the third year, with cash inputs in years 4 and 5 dependent on progress in the first three years. All developments involving the 35%, particularly those elevating profits on these products to acceptable standards, are to be approved by top management before any amounts are allocated to projects that develop the ideas.

3. Forecasts submitted by the divisions indicate a 3% annual rate of growth. The company objective is 6% excluding major acquisitions. To achieve the 6%, research and development will be strengthened with a supplemental $750,000 budget to extend existing product lines through new discoveries in processes, materials, cost reducing equipment, customer oriented innovations, packaging, and transportation. Management has also allocated $15 million for special experiments, pilot plants, and other testing during the five years beginning with $3 million in year 2.

4. Executive management wishes to diversify through acquisitions. The first three substrategies concentrate 40% of forecasted capital resources on improving performance in familiar markets. An aggressive acquisitions program will be initiated in year 1 as the fourth substrategy with an expense budget of $100,000 excluding legal fees. Increases in budget will be justified by progress in earnings relative to capital expended.

5. Financial flexibility will be needed to take advantage of: (a) innovations in familiar markets, and (b) large-scale acquisitions. Research on methods and preliminary negotiations on sources of both equity and debt capital are to receive a special expense budget of $50,000 (One professional and staff). At the end of year 2, $75 million will be available in addition to forecasted resources.

This five-part strategy will give direction to a major portion of the company. There are, however, other strategies that are important to realizing this master strategy. Social responsibility is a basic issue for very practical reasons. Some decisions are still discretionary, but many are not, and the degree of decision-making latitude is narrowing. Consequently, companies are formulating strategies with multiple components to anticipate problem areas and not only comply with laws, community pressure, internal employee programs, and so on, but also to optimize operating requirements. The broad area of social responsibility is a critical factor in profit performance.

Master strategies normally cover a time period that spans both the formal short- and long-range plans and serves as inducement for executives to make decisions in the present needed to realize goals for the future. Therefore, a systematic review of the organization is needed periodically to be certain that each segment is planning and formulating strategies needed for expected performance.

Formulation of master strategies also results in allocation of resources. Decisions on distribution of money and the deployment of personnel and facilities are either part of formulating strategies or influence the characteristics of the strategies. When taking these steps, top management divides company resources and distributes them to the organizational components that will earn the greatest profits.

The first phase of allocating resources involves money. Revised forecasts are prepared which reflect the master strategies resulting from their original estimates. New projections must be made to obtain cash inflows and outflows for expenses. This will derive estimates for the after-tax cash generated from both the existing business and those to be added in the time period between SROP and the long-range plan. Allocations of this capital will be to: (1) shareholders in the form of dividends; (2) reserves for meeting company obligations to tax authorities, lenders, and other potential liabilities; (3) maintenance of assets owned currently and those to be acquired; (4) development and expansion of product lines in operation during SROP, and (5) acquisition and development of new assets.

The second phase is the numerous discretionary decisions on how to spend the money remaining in the business. For example, a manager could be concerned about allocations to expensive but talented personnel as compared to many more people with fewer proven talents, and/or contracted services from consultants. Another possibility is computer-based automation or more people and equipment with less sophisticated capabilities. The options include funds for insurance, supplies, leasing, and tens of other alternatives. Decisions on spending money force many other decisions on the best methods to manage the business.

The third phase involves nonmonetary decisions. Organization of the company to carry out the long-range plan is essential. In fact, it may precede or be an integral part of allocating money. Refer to Figure 7−2 for an illustration of this possibility. Other aspects of the third phase may be revisions to policies, updated information systems, office locations, compensation plans, and similar refinements to reflect the changes in operations that have been added. The use of facilities is a direct result of decisions on money and personnel.

One point to emphasize is the order in which phases of long-range planning take place. Common sense and experience with one or two annual revisions will establish the most efficient sequence of tasks. Even experts who have designed and implemented planning systems in other companies find the need for adjustments to the order in which phases are completed when taking on the assignment in a new firm.

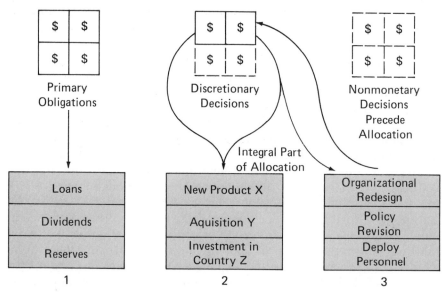

Figure 7−2. Stages of Resource Allocation

Primary Obligations	Discretionary Decisions	Nonmonetary Decisions Precede Allocation

Integral Part of Allocation

Loans	New Product X	Organizational Redesign
Dividends	Aquisition Y	Policy Revision
Reserves	Investment in Country Z	Deploy Personnel
1	2	3

Constraints Affecting the Company

There are two categories of constraints on long-range planning over which the company has little or no control. First, it must operate within the law. Second, competitors, labor unions, suppliers, and customers usually act independently. These constraints have been considered in forecasts and assumptions for strategic variables.

Other constraints within control of management are important to identify. A decision to comply fully with the spirit of social responsibility and initiate pollution control projects, training and development programs for women and minorities, community involvement, and so on could lead to a complete revision of the long-range plan because of the need to reallocate money, personnel, and other resources.

Shareholders and executive management may place limitations on geographic scope, risk exposure, degree of leverage in financing, latitude of diversification, and size of a single acquisition. These constraints reflect the judgment of people at the top, and support of these decisions is not always universal within the company.

Difficulties can arise from reluctance to communicate the reasoning behind self-imposed constraints. Confidential information with restricted access is often behind the decisions. Company personnel can be confused by seemingly arbitrary actions that do not make sense from their perspective. On the other hand, leakage of information on these decisions can give the competition an advantage.

Customers could become worried about supplies. Other adverse developments could occur if top-level judgments become public knowledge.

Executive management must carefully consider the full impact of self-imposed constraints. Assuming they are prudent and based on adequate information, it may also be necessary to conceive programs to communicate sufficient background to retain the support and loyalty of company personnel. A thorough long-range plan will consider sensitive areas such as these and other major impacts on employees such as implied transfer of offices and elimination of operations.

PERSONNEL PARTICIPATING IN LONG-RANGE PLANNING

It has been repeated in previous chapters that executive management spends a considerable portion of its time planning the future course of the company. In Chapter Six it was also mentioned that SROP is best accomplished with full-resource planning in which top management inputs are balanced by extensive contributions from the rest of the organization. In long-range planning, the importance of decisions on self-imposed constraints, master strategies, and key allocations of resources forces more involvement by top executives.

Figure 7–3 summarizes the change in executive management participation between SROP and the long-range plan. It can be seen that there is a shift toward top management as the time period changes from the present to "blue-sky" planning 7 to 10 years into the future. This latter type of planning attempts to foresee major developments affecting the business such as changes in types of energy or shifts in technology. The concept originated in the 1950s when company executives became concerned about being put out of business by the increasing rate of technological obsolescence. Blue-sky planning is almost exclusively undertaken by executive management and its staff.

Figure 7–3. Management Participation in Planning

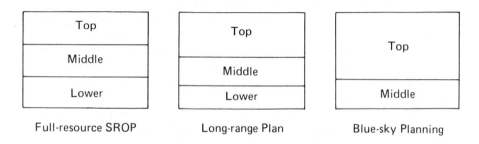

| Full-resource SROP | Long-range Plan | Blue-sky Planning |

Some long-range planning experts will prescribe a version of full-resource planning to include a broad portion of the organization in key decisions. This is evident in the five-step master strategy formulated earlier in this chapter as an example of strategic long-range planning. In that situation, various managers have submitted preliminary forecasts which indicated 35% of the company's products would fall below profit standards. This is a major input for executive management. It is feasible that a five-year plan prepared solely by executive management and their staff would have projected existing profit margins and much more cash than would have actually been generated, thus placing the company in jeopardy. However, as a result of full-resource planning after formulation of the strategy, a revised after-tax cash flow was developed by the divisions.

Attitudes Toward Planning

The normal manager in the organization is concerned with current performance as measured against historical periods or an established standard. SROP is logical and tangible to most management personnel in that it represents a current yardstick against which performance is measured.

As planning shifts into the future, beyond one year, fewer managers give complete support. One of the major causes for this reaction stems from regular revisions that substantially change the estimates before they become part of SROP. It is common to hear, "Top management is always playing games with us and the numbers. Last week they wanted to do it one way. Now they want it just the opposite way. A month from now it will change again." Another typical remark in middle or lower levels of the organization is, "If I owned this company, I would fire those guys who are always worrying about five years from now and get down to decisions about today and next week."

Most complaints are a normal reaction to a combination of extra work and lack of understanding about how these plans affect individual careers. More enthusiasm can be generated by communications from executive management on how effective long-range planning can help the company and the individual.

In smaller companies without the complex organizational breakdowns and multi-industry product lines, it is often practical for executive management to prepare the complete long-range plan. However, it is unusual to find a small business with a long-range plan. The attitudes of most entrepreneurs toward the future is a reflection of todays' receipts. A few of these companies have plans in the minds of key executives, but rarely in writing. Generally sophisticated long-range planning is undertaken only by large companies and appreciation of the benefits increases as one progresses up the organizational ladder.

Administration of the Plan

The long-range plan can be administered in several ways. A few of the possibilities are illustrated in Figure 7–4. The consistent part of the organizational relationships for long-range planning is placement of responsibility at the top of the chart.

Planning Department

A director or vice president is placed in charge of planning and often reports to the chief executive officer. The person could have responsibility for SROP as well as the long-range plan. If there is not full support for planning, the manager could report to the executive vice president or another officer such as a vice president in charge of staff activities.

The executive in charge of planning administers either (1) a new planning system, or (2) a tried and proven planning design. In both instances there is a framework that prescribes what managers are to do in the process of planning. The normal planning department makes few decisions on strategy or allocation of resources. It designs the planning method. It expedites so that timing objectives are achieved. It physically prepares the final plan resulting from revisions and controls distribution. Finally, it plays an important advisory role.

Personnel in planning gain perspective on current developments in the company, the viability of proposals, and the probability of forecasts being achieved. It can be a position with great power, regardless of place on the chart, because of the interpretations that can be given to plans passing through the office from either direction. Also, forecasts of strategic variables are either prepared by the planning department and/or gathered from components of the organizations contributing expertise.

Planning Committee

In some firms a committee replaces the department,[2] as in 2 of Figure 7–4. It is usually composed of top executives who are responsible for the organizational components that carry out the plans. The authority of their positions permits them to make decisions on strategies and allocation of resources. Differences in judgment are

[2] Note that many companies have both a planning department and committee. In these cases, the committee is not involved in administration of the plan.

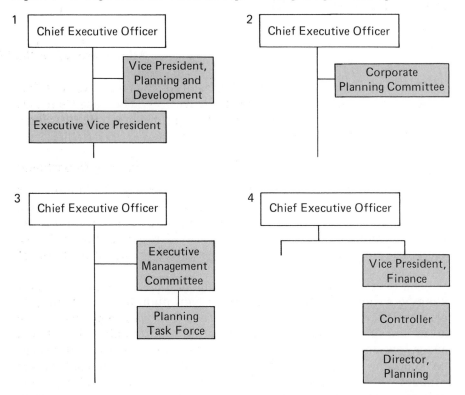

Figure 7-4. Organizational Relationships in Long-Range Planning

mediated by the members. Theoretically, this concept for developing a long-range plan is sound if supplemented by a committee secretary who assumes many of the assignments handled by the head of a planning department.

Many companies endorse this approach, particularly in establishing a new approach to long-range planning. For others it has resulted in lack of efficiency, friction between departments, and compromises detrimental to the firm. In choosing between a department and committee, top management must assess: (1) needs in leadership and motivation; (2) personalities involved, and (3) practical aspects such as difficulty in getting several people together sufficiently often. Executives committed to planning will tend to avoid major dependence on the committee approach.

The Task Force

Sometimes a group of managers is given the special assignment of designing and implementing a new long-range plan or revising the existing methods, as in 3 of Figure 7-4. It is a committee but importance is given to the objectives by calling it a *task force*. Also, the personnel are only temporarily working full-time at planning and will resume their regular jobs when the assignment is completed.

A member of executive management should head this type of task force, and other members should be representatives of the company functions plus specialists such as those formulating assumptions or an expert on strategic variables and forecasting techniques.

The relative success of this approach depends on clearly stated goals, a defined timetable with interim checkpoints on progress toward the goals, capability combined with compatibility among the members, and superior leadership. Selection of the members is important for another reason. Subsequent support of long-range planning within organizational components may reflect the status, respect, and character of the individuals picked for the task force. Omissions would diminish enthusiasm in divisions or departments which are bypassed.

The Role of Executive Management

The chief executive officer and those in the top levels of management have three primary responsibilities in long-range planning:

1. They must understand the concepts and methods, and fully support them in ways that communicate their support to the rest of the organization.
2. They must make the key decisions that give direction of profit objectives, product lines and service, financial means of achieving growth, organizational changes, and important policies.
3. They must assure success by having programs and projects implemented in SROP which will realize the long-range plan.

Judgment is paramount in the decisions that lead to fulfilling the three responsibilities. Given the same set of facts and similar levels of education and experience, different executives will plot different courses for their companies. The spectrum of results ranges from spectacular success to complete failure. Another factor is the way in which plans are carried out by lower levels of the organization. The company is composed of many degrees of *competency*, and executives are dependent on subordinates to do the necessary planning and implementing. Unless top management is closely monitoring critical components of the plan, reassignment or termination of an employee comes too late and execution is poor.

A third factor in success is the *ability to respond to change*. Forecasts and assumptions for strategic variables are totally accurate very rarely, and this affects forecasts for operating variables. Many executives feel the excitement of managing a business comes from problem solving and converting a problem resulting from changes in conditions to an advantage. They revise or fine tune their programs and projects in SROP and modify portions of the long-range plan to reflect new information in a dynamic environment.

Finally, executive management must *achieve balance* between being: (1) sensitive to developments around them but unemotional about decision making; (2) creative in generating alternatives but practical about selection, and (3) personable in developing relationships helpful to the company but detached in carrying out responsibilities. This balance is an intangible factor in planning day-to-day managing.

THE INTRACOMPANY PROCESS OF LONG-RANGE PLANNING

The steps discussed here are essential to successful long-range planning.

Corporate Self-Analysis

The point of departure in short- and long-range planning is the present position of the company. Corporate self-analysis is not a simple inventory of assets. A superficial approach can be misleading. For example, a company considers itself secure in a market to which it sells 35% of the total demand. The firm is the low cost producer and innovations emerging from R and D would increase participation to a probable 45%. However, competition surfaces from a totally different concept answering customer requirements. It sells for half the price of our company's product and is easier to handle.

Should market intelligence have given early indication of this possibility? Should management have assumed a limited life cycle for the established product? The formal corporate self-analysis in contingency planning tends to reduce the possibility of this kind of serious surprise.

In addition to market and technical developments, managerial competence may not be sufficient to carry out plans. Yet these managers may see themselves as being fully capable of achieving or exceeding company goals for profit growth, yet be unable to complete assignments satisfactorily. Moreover, the situation may be more complex. Let us assume top management is doing a creative, capable job of deciding on future courses of action. The personnel reporting directly to these executives are also top caliber managers. However, below these upper levels of the organization competence deteriorates sharply. There is a high probability that performance will not achieve goals in the plan.

Summarizing, corporate self-analysis means evaluation and conclusions about a company's present position. This includes vulnerability analysis and assessment of the marketplace, personnel, physical facilities, finances, technological status, and required resources. Problems arise from unfounded optimism, underrated opportunities, misplaced responsibilities, and inadequate flow of intelligence to make the proper decisions.

Comparisons of Performance with Previous Plans

Clues to the future can be gained from comparing past plans for operations and the actual performance. A surprising number of companies fail to use this information. Most of the large corporations monitor the progress of individual investments and require reports on deviations from predicted performance. However, with increasing computer capacity it is now practical to expand this practice to companywide plans.

One of the primary reasons for not thoroughly examining past plans and actual performance is the immense volume of data involved. The cost and time were prohibitive in larger companies. Now computer programs can scan data and alert management in time and provide input for qualitative evaluation.

Another reason executives do not probe past long-range plans is the exposure of serious errors by managers who have subsequently been promoted to important positions. Rather than unearth past embarrassments, the opportunity to improve the planning process is bypassed.

Variables in the Design of the Plan

The *first* group of variables to be considered by the designer involves who will participate in long-range planning and the organizational approach that defines who will administrate the plan. These people-oriented decisions include subtitles on degree of participation. The delicate question of power to be given the organizational entity administering the plan must be decided in a way which retains checks and balances in the system. The correct decisions vary by company. They are often made directly by the chief executive officer, but it is essential that the system has the CEO's complete approval.

The *second* group of variables involves the format of the plan. Experienced planners will usually separate strategic and operating variables into separate sections. Summary statements on the forecasts and assumptions for the business environment are needed to make operating decisions and formulate strategies. Cooperation in preparing the plan and usage on a regular basis will depend in part on ease of reference and layout of details. The format of summaries and the binder distributed to users has a bearing on attitude. However, the most important point is limiting the amount of details to the minimum that still meets the needs of decision makers.

The *third* group of variables involves timing. This includes: (1) the time period most appropriate for the long-range plan such as the five years mentioned previously in the chapter; (2) the frequency with which the plan is revised such as every 12 months in the Honeywell case following this chapter, and (3) the number of weeks in the network model controlling the revisions each year. Careful attention must be paid to all three aspects of timing.

The fourth group of variables involves developing the cooperation and support of top management and other executives participating in preparation and usage. It should not be assumed that the reasons for planning are apparent, or that the advantages of the concepts and format selected are evident to key personnel. If time and budgets permit, presentations and personal contact are superior means of communicating ideas as compared to memos and other non-personal approaches. Any change from tradition necessitates extra thought about gaining support for the new method.

Mechanisms for Transition between Short- and Long-Range Plans

Success in long-range planning as measured by profit performance depends on implementing programs and projects in SROP that will achieve the end result desired in future years. This means a translation of forecasts and strategies into specific goals, responsibilities, and assignments to accomplish in the present.

A mechanism is needed in the long-range plan that establishes the method for programs and projects to become reality. One approach involves placing each "thing to do" in a strategy, and control of the strategy means control of the programs and projects. This method is discussed in Chapter Eight.

It is possible, however, that overlapping purposes, no relationship to a strategy, and so on could require another control method.

The design of the plan should include a component that defines the programs and projects involved in the predicted growth. This assists in the process of allocating and controlling capital and other resources in SROP. This mechanism provides a second bridge between short- and long-range plans in addition to strategies. In fact, it could help top management monitor and refine the company's strategies. Figure 7–5 summarizes this concept.

Figure 7–5. Realizing Long-Range Planning

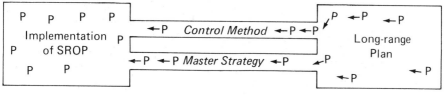

←P = *Direction of Programs and Projects*

Compromises in Design Based on Experience

The ideal plan for a company's products and facilities may not be ideal for personnel managing the firm. If experience with sophisticated planning systems is limited, it is advisable to begin with simple designs that will act as the foundation for steps toward more complex systems. The timing for introducing the preferred concepts can depend on performance in handling the simple design and support for long-range planning within the company.

Simplicity is generally preferred because of advantages shown in Figure 7–6. Sophistication and complexity can only be justified by needs for more information to make important decisions. Executive management must be cautious about expanding the plan because of the impact on cost, commitments in time, power given to planners, and overall attitude by line managers.

SUMMARY

The time period selected for the long-range plan will depend on vulnerability to competitor action, the scope and operating life of facilities, the financial structure, and special characteristics of the business. Usually five years in the future is used as the basis of the plan.

Figure 7-6. Compromises in the Design of the Company Plan

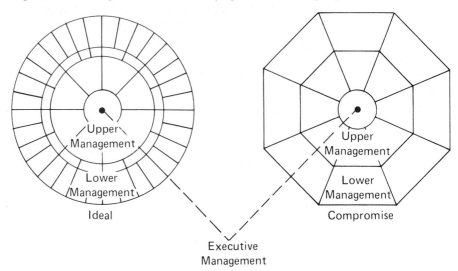

Definition of objectives is critically important. Top management must decide on the course the company will follow in future years including rate and method of growth, diversification, reorganization, and specific programs such as divestiture of existing assets.

Strategic variables, those factors that are beyond company control, make up the business environment for a firm. Forecasts and assumptions on what will occur in the future are the basis for predicting the outlook for existing operations. Some strategic variables are constantly changing such as labor union demands, and others are noncontinuous such as a sudden shift in government controls. Techniques to forecast the business environment in five years have improved with increasing use of the computer and the application of complex mathematical models.

Strategies formulated by a company's management and strategic variables are different terms. The former has been defined in Chapter Six and provide a bridge between short- and long-range plans. While the end result is given in the long-range plan, specific programs and projects to realize objectives in the strategy begin in SROP.

The plan normally contains a complete balance in cash flows, disposition of assets, borrowing, and capital spending. Reorganization to adjust for growth, changes in product lines, and so on is part of this balancing.

Most of the major decisions in long-range planning are made by top management. There is a distinct shift to the upper levels of an organization as compared with the full-resource planning recommended for SROP. However, there is a need for participation by the remainder of the company in order to have realistic plans.

Administration of the plan usually takes place in a planning department with a director or vice president reporting to the chief executive officer or someone reporting to the CEO. There are numerous variations such as the controller being responsible for planning. Companies sometimes use committees or a task force to carry out this work.

Top management has three responsibilities in long-range planning: (1) they must understand the concepts and methods and fully support them; (2) they must make the key decisions that give direction to others in the planning task, and (3) they must make certain programs and projects are formulated to take the steps needed in the present to achieve the future.

Some of the important elements to consider in designing a plan include: (1) corporate self-analysis as the point of departure for planning; (2) comparing actual performance with previous plans to uncover weaknesses in the current design and problem areas in the organization; (3) the four groups of variables; (4) mechanisms to bridge SROP and the long-range plan, and (5) compromises related to inexperienced personnel, attitudes toward planning, and support by executive management.

DISCUSSION QUESTIONS

1. Identify companies with products that justify different time periods for long-range plans. Explain your examples to make clear distinctions.
2. Executive management has major responsibilities in long-range planning. List and clarify the implications of these responsibilities.
3. Corporate self-analysis and performance evaluation are important steps in long-range planning. Do you see any difficulties in a company developing an accurate picture of itself? What steps would improve these analyses?
4. Businesses usually operate in an environment over which they have little control. Identify five strategic variables and constraints, and explain how they could seriously affect long-range plans.
5. Figure 7—4 shows four different organizational relationships in long-range planning. List the advantages and disadvantages of each. Identify a fifth approach. Which would you use?
6. What are the variables in the design of a plan?
7. Discuss the factors involved in the transition between the long-range plan and SROP.

SUGGESTED READINGS AND BIBLIOGRAPHY

Bennett, K.W. "Company Plan Models — A Must," *Iron Age.* October 29, 1970, p. 35.

Carson, I. "Big Leap in Corporate Planning," *International Management.* April, 1972, pp. 25—28.

Carson, I. "Computer Power for Planning," *International Management.* May, 1972, pp. 36—38.

Ehrhardt, S.P. "Five Year Plan, a Year at a Time," *Administration Management.* July, 1973, pp. 65—66.

Glaser. "Outline for Long Range Corporate Planning," *Advanced Management Journal.* January, 1971, pp. 51—56.

Hall. "Corporate Strategic Planning; Some Perspectives for the Future," *Michigan Business Review.* January, 1972, pp. 16—21.

Herold. "Long Range Planning and Organization Performance," *Academic Management Journal.* March, 1972, pp. 91—102.

Irwin, Patrick H. "Why Aren't Companies Doing a Better Job of Planning?" *Management Review.* November, 1971, pp. 11—16.

Kastens, Merritt L. "Who Does the Planning?" *Management Review.* April, 1972, pp. 48—49.

Litschert. "Structure of Long-Range Planning Groups," *Academic Management Journal.* March, 1971, pp. 33—43.

LoCascio. "Financial Planning Models," *Financial Executive.* March, 1972, pp. 30—34.

LoCascio. "Long Range Planning, Seance or Science," *Sales Management.* January 15, 1969, p. 31.

McGuire, Patrick E. and Earl L. Bailey, "Factors in Corporate Growth," *The Conference Board Record.* February, 1970, pp. 30—34.

North. "Simulation for Planning and Control," *Management Review.* February, 1972, pp. 18—27.

Pennington. "Planning Takes More than a Little Planning," *Industry Week.* December 20, 1971, p. 35.

"Planning Terms and Functions," *Management Systems.* January, 1971.

Renner. "Business Quality Triangle: A Guide to Planning," *Management Review.* April, 1972, pp. 26—32.

Rue, L.W. "How and Who of Long Range Planning," *Business Horizons.* December, 1973, pp. 23—30.

Schollhammer. "Long Range Planning in Multinational Firms," *Columbia Journal of World Business.* September, 1971, pp. 79—86.

Schoonmaker. "Why is Corporate Planning Resisted?" *International Management.* October, 1971, pp. 26—27.

Scott, Brian W. *Long-Range Planning in American Industry.* American Management Association, 1965.

Steiner, George A. Top Management Planning. The MacMillan Co., 1969.

Tebay, James E. "Planning that Begins and Ends with People," *Management Review.* January, 1973, pp. 47—51.

Vancil. "Accuracy of Long Range Planning," *Harvard Business Review.* September, 1970, pp. 98—101.

Waghorn. "Five Barriers to Company Planning," *Director.* March, 1972, pp. 330–333.

Warren, E. Kirby. *Long-Range Planning; The Executive Viewpoint.* Prentice-Hall, 1966.

Zager, Robert. "Getting into the Habit of Planning," *Director.* March, 1971.

Case: Long-Range Planning at Vintage Enterprises

Structure and type of planning at Vintage and recent performance of the company bring out principles regarding who should participate in long-range planning.

INDUSTRY

Production in the mobile home industry has increased rapidly in the last decade. Industry sales expanded from $1.071 billion in 1964 to over $4.515 billion in 1973 (see Figure 7C–1). A setback occurred in 1974–75 due to the recession.

A major factor in sales volume is a change in attitude among older people. Traditionally, they were reluctant to leave the homes where they raised their children. As indicated in Table 7C–1[1], people are now realizing that owning a mobile home has all the comforts and con-

veniences necessary, while being the best buy in housing on a monthly cost basis. Details are for the monthly cost for a $7000 mobile home, complete with appliances and furnishings, assuming a 15% down payment and a 7-year contract at 6% add-on interest. Average monthly cost/10 year use—$180. Apartments rent from $125—$200/month with no tax advantages or net equity. A $20,000 house averages $200—$250/month with more care involved.

The Federal Home Loan Bank has reacted to the recent mobile home boom by liberalizing its rules. In June, 1972, it allowed Savings and Loan Associations to invest up to 10%, instead of 5%, of their total assets in mobile home finance. Also, terms permitted 15 years instead of 12 years. Financially, the mobile home is the only outlet for certain

---

[1] Estimates reflect the situation in Georgia in 1974 (Standard & Poor's Industrial Survey B72 Copyright 1974. Used by permission of Standard and Poors Corporation, 345 Hudson St., New York, N.Y. 10014.)

Figure 7C-1. Mobile Home Industry Growth

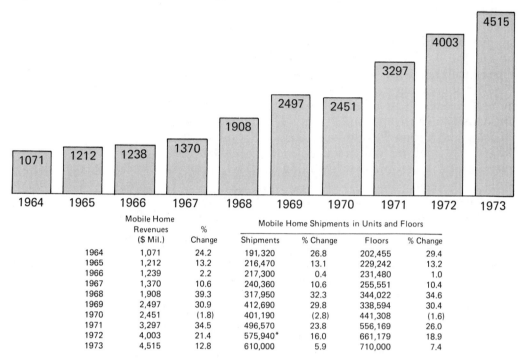

	Mobile Home Revenues ($ Mil.)	% Change	Mobile Home Shipments in Units and Floors			
			Shipments	% Change	Floors	% Change
1964	1,071	24.2	191,320	26.8	202,455	29.4
1965	1,212	13.2	216,470	13.1	229,242	13.2
1966	1,239	2.2	217,300	0.4	231,480	1.0
1967	1,370	10.6	240,360	10.6	255,551	10.4
1968	1,908	39.3	317,950	32.3	344,022	34.6
1969	2,497	30.9	412,690	29.8	338,594	30.4
1970	2,451	(1.8)	401,190	(2.8)	441,308	(1.6)
1971	3,297	34.5	496,570	23.8	556,169	26.0
1972	4,003	21.4	575,940*	16.0	661,179	18.9
1973	4,515	12.8	610,000	5.9	710,000	7.4

Note: A double-wide unit consists of two floors, and thus the increase in the number of floors more closely reflects the growth of the industry than does the increase in units. Double-wide units were first introduced in 1962.

*Excludes shipments of 16,725 to the federal government for disaster housing.

Source: Mobile Home Manufacturers Association: Oppenheimer and C. estimates.

Table 7C-1. Comparative Costs of Housing

Monthly Contract Payment	$107.00
Depreciation*	55.00
Maintenance	5.00
Park Rent and Taxes	50.00
Total	217.00

Monthly Cost After Year 7 — Paid For

Depreciation**	25.00
Park Rent and Taxes	50.00
Maintenance	5.00
Refurnishing	6.00
Insurance	10.00
Total	$96.00

* Depreciation is calculated on the basis of $1300 in the first year, $1000 in the second year, $700 in the third year and $400 per year in the fourth — seventh years.

** Depreciation is estimated at $300/year after the seventh year.

people due to low capital and monthly costs. Also, reluctant lenders have traditionally discriminated against women heads of households by making it very hard for them to secure mortgages for regular homes.

The increasing population naturally leads to an increased need for housing. The Department of Housing and Urban Development has determined that we will need an average of 2.6 million new dwelling units/year during the 1970s, and house ownership costs have continued to increase.

Since demand should be increasing while costs remain relatively stable, the future appears bright for the mobile home industry. Other reasons to expect a favorable future might be:

1. Recent moves to improve the condition of mobile home parks.
2. More young people being able to afford a second home.
3. The younger generation being less concerned with big homes.
4. Growth in the number of young marrieds and retirees who make up 75–80% of the market.
5. Introduction of FHA insured financing in 1970 on homes up to $10,000 for terms up to 12 years at rates between 8–10%.
6. Benefits in the Veterans Housing Act of 1970.
7. Increased willingness to change zoning laws.

VINTAGE ENTERPRISES

In the mobile home industry there are two basic areas of activity:

manufacturing and retailing. While the four top manufacturers account for almost 30% of the market, the two largest retailers sell less than 4% of the mobile homes.

Vintage Enterprises ranks second in the retailing of mobile homes in the nation. However, it is not one of the top manufacturers in the country, ranking twentieth in the United States.

History

In 1958 the company was founded by T. S. Cheek after leaving military service, by opening a retail outlet under the name of Colonial Mobile Homes in Atlanta, Georgia. One year later a second outlet was opened in Gainsville, Georgia. In 1964 Colonial Mobile Homes branched out with the establishment of retail outlets in Oxford, Alabama and Meridian, Mississippi. Two years later the company decided to enter into manufacturing operations and opened a plant in Georgia. By 1967, there were 25 retail outlets in operation throughout the states of Georgia, South Carolina, Alabama and Mississippi. The next year a second manufacturing plant was opened in Breckenridge, Texas.

In 1969 the name of the parent company was changed from Colonial Mobile Homes, Inc. to Vintage Enterprises, Inc. At approximately the same time the company became publicly held by the sale of 360,000 shares in a public offering. The company was subsequently listed on the American Stock Exchange.

In 1970 another manufacturing facility was completed and production started in Clarksdale, Mississippi. The year ending April 1, 1972 yielded record revenues and earnings in manufacturing and retailing. By the end of 1973 Vintage had added yet another manufacturing plant — this one in Montezuma, Georgia (now closed). Statistics in Table 7C–2 give an indication of performance through March 31, 1975 when the mid-1970s recession had had a major impact on operations.

center has a monthly and annual budget. There are monthly financial statements prepared showing comparisons of actual to budget performance. Managers are compared in reports and motivated by active competition at each level of management.

Manufacturing Division

The retail divisions management gives the manufacturing division a

Table 7C–2 Company Statistics

| | Millions | | | |
	Sales and Other Income	After-tax Profits	Earnings per Share	Shares Outstanding
1970	29.0	.95	.54	1,820,000
1971	34.3	.53	.29	1,833,000
1972	49.3	1.92	1.05	1,833,000
1973	61.3	2.97	1.56	1,904,000
1974	61.5	.18	.09	1,931,000
1975	39.7	−2.40	−1.25	1,940,510

Organization

Figure 7C–2 shows the basic organization at Vintage Enterprises. Additional details are given in the following sections.

Retail Division

There are three vice presidents in the field, each responsible for his geographic area. This is done through an organization of regional and district managers that supervise the retail outlets. At each level there is a profit center — retail lot, district, region, and division. In charge of each profit center there is a manager whose compensation is based on profit center performance. Each

direct line of communication with the ultimate customer. Manufacturing management meets regularly with the retail people to keep up with changing demands in style, design, price, and features.

Both divisions operate independently of each other. The manufacturing division contributes about 35% of volume and sells to independent dealers at the same price that it charges the retail division. The manufacturing plants try to keep their labor force relatively stable. They do this by selling a smaller percentage of production to the retail division in the summer months when independent demand is strong, and more in the winter months when demand drops. For ex-

Figure 7C−2. The Organization at Vintage Enterprises

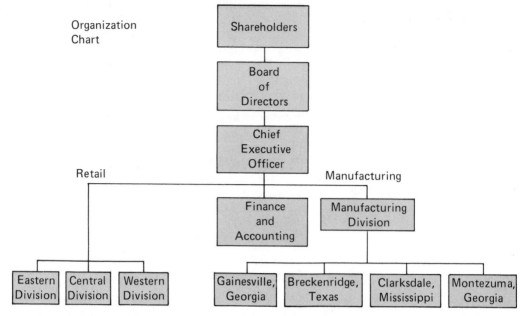

Organization
Chart

ample, in 1973 manufacturing sales to retailing were approximately one-third of its production.

Finance

Throughout 1973, as interest rates have continued to increase and money has become more scarce, the percentage increases in Vintage's three-month moving average of percentage changes in mobile home shipments have continued to decline.

The primary financial problem was not demand, which was relatively strong, but rapidly escalating raw material prices, such as wood products. Price controls prevented the rapid transfer of these costs to the consumer. Despite this problem (see the financial data in Table 7C−2 and Appendix A, p. 242), Vintage enjoyed strong profit growth in 1973. Only in the fiscal year ending March

31, 1974 does the real impact of the price/cost squeeze become evident. Results as of March 31, 1975 reflect both cost increases and a decline in demand.

Long-Range Planning at Vintage

Geographic Constraint

Vintage has confined itself to the Southeast and Southwest and has no plans of expanding beyond this region. The three people involved in long-range planning feel that the industrialization of many agricultural areas will continue to provide good business. There is a slightly lower per capita income here than in other areas of the United States as well as an abundance of mobile home sites due to less restrictive zoning codes.

Also, widespread interstate highways lead to low-cost rural living.

Although expansion, whether it be $100 million sales or $200 million, is always Vintage's objective; they feel it is to their best interest to remain within their existing geographic area.

Operating Constraints

In order to saturate the area and be profitable, they feel that good district managers are the key to future success. Very little advertising is done on a large scale, and the success of the company depends upon the motivation of its managers and the motivation they can generate in their lot managers. An extensive training program is being drawn up to achieve the full potential of new managers rapidly.

The Planning Committee

Vintage's long-range planning is basically the work of just three men: the president and founder of the company, Thomas S. Cheek; the vice president, secretary, treasurer, Dan Cashin; and the executive vice president, Gert Docterman. Mr. Cashin joined the company in 1969 after 12 years as a CPA in public accounting. He now heads all financial activities including the controller's office. Mr. Docterman, an accountant, took charge of manufacturing in 1968.

The forecasts are done for periods of three years. They feel that to push their long-range planning beyond three years would jeopardize the accuracy of their data. The long-range plan is then reviewed and updated every 12 to 18 months. The planning committee makes it a practice to compare their actual plans with past performance in order to seek out and correct problem areas.

The executive vice president initially does the long-range plans for the manufacturing division. The vice president, secretary, treasurer does the same for the retail division. Mr. Cashin then takes these two reports and molds them together into one plan to present to Mr. Cheek for his approval and suggestions. Mr. Cheek also does all corporate self-analysis and keeps constant track of the company's present position.

In 1973 the planning committee prepared a list of possible new ventures that Vintage may wish to undertake. Among them were:

1. The acquisition of land to build mobile home parks in order to promote sales.
2. The establishment of a life insurance company.
3. The establishment of a finance company to facilitate sales when there is a money crunch.
4. A land development project that would mean owning and developing lots for double-wides, which are readily accepted in real estate.
5. Improved flow of supplies to manufacturing, probably best established through acquisitions.
6. Acquire a supply house for parts.

Vintage has not incurred any long-term debts but, instead, has made a practice of getting short-term loans and paying them off with current cash flow. Since their labor force is nonunionized, there have been no labor management conflicts of any magnitude to upset long-range plans.

STUDENT PROBLEMS

1. Utilizing the information given in the chapter and this case, discuss the possibilities and necessities of revising the long-range planning process at Vintage.
2. Look up Vintage Enterprises' current financial position (1972–74 details are in Appendix A, below. Contrast the practical possibilities for the company to carry out the six ventures identified by the planning committee in 1973 considering its present condition. Establish priorities for undertaking these and other possible investments.
3. Based on your judgments in Problem 2 and research on the present conditions of the industry, assess the long-range possibilities for Vintage Enterprises.

Appendix A

FINANCIAL STATEMENTS OF VINTAGE ENTERPRISES, INC. AND SUBSIDIARIES

CURRENT ASSETS	1974[2]	1973[2]	1972[2]
Cash	$ 1,205,791	$ 738,270	$ 770,520
Accounts receivable			
Customers, net of allowance for doubtful accounts of $18,093 and $19,540	3,853,625	5,084,148	3,604,991
Financial institutions	539,863	487,971	307,308
Manufacturers	227,799	327,464	199,149
Other	57,050	79,930	97,714
		5,979,513	4,272,162
Inventories-partially pledged	11,433,066	13,731,361	7,893,761
Prepaid expenses	172,402	99,507	108,410
Total current assets	17,489,596	20,548,651	13,044,853
Refundable income taxes	1,549,429		
INVESTMENT IN UNCONSOLIDATED SUBSIDIARY	11,991	6,305	2,630

[2] Years ended March 30, 1974, March 31, 1973 and April 1, 1972.

PROPERTY AND EQUIPMENT — AT COST	1974	1973	1972
Transportation equipment	1,497,145	1,321,637	735,795
Office units and signs	742,774	632,074	431,119
Machinery and equipment	590,693	586,710	516,799
Furniture and fixtures	633,471	512,515	294,577
Buildings	1,595,720	1,584,934	1,465,560
	5,059,803	4,637,870	3,443,850
Less Accumulated depreciation and amortization	1,987,148	1,451,264	1,043,251
Leasehold improvements	612,362	526,138	318,064
Land	151,584	151,584	151,584
	3,836,601	3,864,328	2,870,247
OTHER			
Endorsement fees withheld	3,913,361	3,528,056	3,171,411
Goodwill	97,291	129,562	144,714
Other	60,473	42,001	54,365
	4,071,125	3,699,619	3,370,490
	$26,958,742	$28,118,903	$19,288,220

CURRENT LIABILITIES	1974[3]	1973[3]	1972[3]
Notes payable			
Floor plan	$ 6,567,408	$ 6,701,775	$ 5,557,604
Current maturities of lease contracts	37,301	28,554	27,389
Current maturities of long-term debt	215,599	214,635	219,843
	6,820,308	6,944,964	5,804,836
Accounts payable	2,079,655	3,677,475	1,884,430
Income taxes		425,255	1,027,411
Insurance premiums collected	252,018	446,790	339,018
Accrued liabilities			
Salaries and wages	268,051	462,906	264,605
Payroll and other taxes	117,201	166,001	98,946
Sundry	249,927	407,895	287,913
	635,179	1,036,802	651,464
Total Current Liabilities	9,787,160	12,531,286	9,707,159

[3] Years ended March 3, 1974, March 31, 1973, and April 1, 1972

LEASE CONTRACTS — net of current maturities	807,287	844,587	873,142
LONG-TERM DEBT — net of current maturities	427,787	643,387	869,956
RESERVE FOR GUARANTEED DEBT	1,422,349	871,387	667,778
DEFERRED INCOME TAXES	2,470,702	1,264,169	338,265

COMMITMENTS AND CONTINGENT LIABILITIES

STOCKHOLDERS' EQUITY

Common stock-authorized, 5,000,000 shares of $.20 par value	388,102	388,102	365,900
Additional contributed capital	3,616,785	3,616,785	1,481,348
Retained earnings	8,142,042	7,959,200	4,984,672
	12,146,929	11,964,087	6,831,920
Less 10,000 shares of common stock in treasury—at cost	103,472		
	12,043,457		
	$26,958,742	$28,118,903	$19,288,220

	1974[4]	1973[4]	1972[4]
REVENUE			
Sales	$61,516,415	$61,323,234	$45,270,609
Endorsement fees	4,052,399	5,474,793	2,676,307
Insurance commissions	1,528,799	1,932,875	1,223,931
Other	94,124	15,616	81,204
	67,191,737	68,746,518	49,252,051
COST OF SALES AND OTHER EXPENSES			
Cost of goods sold	55,581,736	53,408,911	39,284,129
Selling	5,722,177	5,241,095	3,366,866
Administrative	2,203,818	2,267,135	1,554,229
Provision for losses on guaranteed debt	2,485,805	1,226,999	603,154
Interest and floor plan	884,910	660,674	605,695
	66,878,446	62,804,814	45,414,073

[4] Years ended March 30, 1974, March 31, 1973, and April 1, 1972.

Earnings before income taxes and equity in net earnings of unconsolidated subsidiary	313,291	5,941,704	3,837,978

INCOME TAXES
Currently payable— principally federal	(1,070,398)	2,044,947	1,647,158
Deferred	1,206,533	925,904	271,831
	136,135	2,970,851	1,918,989

Earnings before equity in net earnings of unconsolidated subsidiary	177,156	2,970,853	1,918,989

EQUITY in net earnings of
unconsolidated subsidiary	5,686	3,675	1,130
NET EARNINGS	$ 182,842	$ 2,974,528	$ 1,920,119
Net earnings per share	$ .09	$ 1.56	$ 1.05

	1974[4]	1973[4]	1972[4]
COMMON STOCK			
Balance at beginning of year	$ 388,102	$ 365,900	$ 364,000
Sale of 11,010 shares		22,202	
Sale of 9,500 shares			
Balance at end of year	$ 388,102	$ 388,102	$ 365,900
ADDITIONAL CONTRIBUTED CAPITAL			
Balance at beginning of year	$ 3,616,785	$1,481,348	$ 360,998
Excess of proceeds over par value of shares sold		2,135,437	120,350
Balance at end of year	$ 3,616,785	$3,616,785	$1,481,348
RETAINED EARNINGS			
Balance at beginning of year	$ 7,959,200	$4,984,672	$3,064,553
Net earnings	182,842	2,974,528	1,920,119
Balance at end of year	$ 8,142,042	$7,959,200	$4,984,672

[4] Years ended March 30, 1974, March 31, 1973, and April 1, 1972

Case: Honeywell Information Systems, Inc.

The evolution of HIS, Inc. gives an opportunity to contrast the long-range planning and programming system that HIS has developed since the merger with General Electric's computer division in 1970 with planning at Honeywell before that time. Differing levels of sophistication are used at different times within the same company.

COMPANY BACKGROUND

The Minneapolis Heat Regulator Company, formed in 1885 to produce a new type of thermostat, joined with Honeywell Heating Specialities Company and incorporated under the name of Minneapolis-Honeywell, Inc. The present name of Honeywell Inc. was acquired in 1964.

From a small, one building company located in Minneapolis, Honeywell now has subsidiaries, affiliates, and distributors in 58 countries. Sales for 1973 totalled $2.41 billion with an after-tax income of $104 million (see Appendix B, p. 255).

Prior to 1955, Honeywell manufactured industrial, high-temperature, measuring and control instruments, pneumatic control systems, switches, and thermostats. Honeywell entered the promising new field of electronic data processing (EDP) when it formed Datamatic Corp. in 1955 as a joint venture with Raytheon. The Datamatic Division was created when Raytheon sold its 40% interest to Honeywell in 1957.

Background on Division Growth

In order to gain an insight into Honeywell and HIS planning techniques, it is necessary to describe the development of the computer business.

Before 1953, electronic data processing (EDP) was used only for government priorities. Industry estimates in 1953 indicated that perhaps 50 companies could use computers. Honeywell had not entered the field, but elaborate studies showed a $10 million investment would return profits by 1957. A survey in 1958 showed 1,700 computers already in use across the country.

By 1962, industry sales totalled $1 billion annually with predictions of $4 billion in four to seven years. Every company but IBM was losing money in computers, but most of them felt they were in too deep to get out. Honeywell had already invested $95 million. Sales had grown to $47 million, but there were no profits. In 1965, the industry estimated sales of $5 billion in Europe alone and rentals of $1.4 billion.

Honeywell determined that it wanted to be No. 2. IBM already had claimed first place with approximately 70% of the market, and there was little chance of catching them. Competition had become fierce and several companies already had dropped out of the race, leaving only about 15 companies sticking it out. Few of those 15 could afford to take on IBM in all markets, so many tried to pick an area where their own experience could gain a segment of the market. Honeywell, going the other way, decided to round out its lines and compete directly with IBM. In 1966, 11 years and $300 million after Honeywell's initial step into computers, the EDP division turned the profit corner (before interest and other corporate allocations).

President Keating announced 1967 revenues from computers to be $207 million, and for the first time,

all computer operations, foreign and domestic, earned a profit. In 1968 the EDP division had sales of almost $300 million. However, the market share dropped from 7.4 to 5.4%. Honeywell fell from second to third place in value of equipment shipped.

In 1969 industry estimates for software and timesharing were $2.7 billion annually and growing by 25% per year. Honeywell started the Information Service Division and added product lines to become a full supplier of hardware, software, and timesharing but still lacked capacity in the larger systems.

Except for IBM, Honeywell had the broadest market line and largest marketing organization in the industry. Most of the other companies tended to specialize. Honeywell, although not aggressively acquisition-minded and preferring growth from within, began looking at many companies to increase its scope of operations in the industry.

President Keating said that the computer industry had grown almost independently of the forces of the economy and expected the growth to continue. Honeywell spent 25% of their $139 million R and D budget in 1969 on computers. Revenues for computer sales and services totalled $351 million.

Computer Developments Leading to the General Electric Merger

Honeywell profits in computers came far later than expected. The reasons for this were: (1) time to achieve technological competitiveness; (2) costs higher than had been estimated, and (3) market penetration that fell short of expectations. However, Honeywell was beginning to learn more and more about computers and their users.

In the early 1960s many companies, seeing the promising market for EDP, saw computers as a good possibility for diversification and growth. At that stage the business was young and IBM was the only veteran. Considering the industry's optimistic forecasts, all it would take to get into the business was a group of talented scientists, some good electronic and mechanical engineers, a staff of bright sales representatives, electronic manufacturing facilities, and enough cash to survive until sales or rental fees began to offset costs.

These criteria were accurate except that only the largest corporations in the world could have afforded to pay out the amount of money required.

Only a fraction of the costs of getting into the computer business are in engineering and producing the computer hardware. Also, the equipment must be programmed for every job, and customers expect and get a great deal of help from the manufacturers. This assistance involves programming personnel and programs taking thousands of hours to prepare and prove. This software service is actually just as important in selling systems as the hardware and a major reason why many companies, including Honeywell, experienced a long road to profits rather than the expected quick path.

Repeatedly as IBM raised the stakes in the computer game by introducing new machines, Honeywell would follow, unveiling their own family of computers. Honeywell also began developing software to allow customers to translate or shift programs written for IBM machines to Honeywell's line.

In the mid 1960s Honeywell aimed for number two in Europe through its own local R and D efforts, and by forging its European operations into a self-sustaining overall unit. The company even upset the usual pattern by exporting products developed in Europe to the United States. Vice president John McCardle said, "Through functional autonomy, Honeywell encourages management to participate in setting objectives for the continent. Then, we leave it pretty much up to them as to how they intend to achieve these goals."

In 1968, Honeywell began upgrading the systems of its customers. As the needs of customers grew from punched card equipment, to small computers, to large computers, Honeywell hoped to gain more business. In terms of growth Honeywell wanted to get in at the lowest level and let their customers grow and continue to be loyal. In this way the company would continually expand its base.

With the introduction of Keytape in 1968, Honeywell sought to bypass punched card equipment with which the vast majority of computer buyers start. IBM had a virtual monopoly on punched card equipment and most customers continued with IBM when they moved into computers. Also, in 1968 Honeywell began branching out more into peripheral equipment. It brought out three new products weekly±, like the new disc pack storage system and solid-state computer keyboards.

In order to gain a larger share of the market Honeywell added timesharing and software services in early 1969. Ten data service centers across the country offered processing, service for computer owners, and timesharing services through these centers. Honeywell also began studying possible acquisition of software companies, but also realized its lack of depth in the larger machines.

Formation of HIS

On October 1, 1970, Honeywell Information Systems (HIS) was created in a historic merger that joined Honeywell's computer operations with the business computer equipment operations of General Electric.[5] The latter company acquired $1.10 million in Honeywell notes, and 1.5 million± shares of Honeywell in the transaction which it must sell by 1980. GE also acquired the 18.5% ownership in HIS, and these shares must be sold to Honeywell by that year. Either party can initiate steps to sell or buy with proper notice.

Some Details on the Merger

GE wanted out of a business in which they had lost over $200 million. At almost the same time but completely independent, studies at

Honeywell concluded that a larger customer base of at least 8 to 10% of the market was needed to stay competitive with the huge IBM.

Honeywell successfully achieved their critical mass with GE's $412 million in revenue and $351 million[6] of their own, and the product combination was almost a perfect fit. This size and type of customer base was critical because Honeywell had previously estimated 80% of future computer revenues would come from trade ups.

GE was a natural for Honeywell because of strength in the large-scale machines where Honeywell was weak. In medium and small machines Honeywell was strong and GE was weak. GE was quite strong overseas and weak in the United States with Honeywell just the opposite. Manufacturing plants in the United States and abroad were neatly distributed. In addition, the combination would achieve Honeywell's goal of having over 10% of the market. Elimination of costly duplication in R and D and corporate staff, plus savings from sheer size also favored the merger. In October, 1971, one year after the merger Honeywell had proved their planning and strategy worked. There were no mass layoffs of GE personnel and no complaints from GE customers.

The new company employed 48,000 people in 50 countries and had a total of 10,000 installations original-

[5] See Chapter Five, p. 148 for information on GE.

[6] Profits were estimated by Fortune Magazine to be $3 million at the start of merged operations. Rentals were about $400 million, or 52% of total revenue of $763 million. In 1973 rentals were $681 million, or 58% of HIS revenue.

ly worth $3.5 billion. Table 7C–3 gives a brief financial performance through 1973.

In April 1974 HIS introduced System 60, which it expects to have the answer for anything IBM can offer. While not a major technical innovation, a comprehensive programming system provides a common thread from the largest to the smallest machines. This step greatly reduces the postmerger problem of consolidating 10 product lines with 20 central processing units, 12 programming systems, 33 design families, and 157 peripheral equipment products.

Products, Services, and Organization

HIS products include six series of general purpose computer systems, as well as time sharing and minicomputer systems. The company also markets frontend network processors and communication equipment, data preparation equipment, application products, computer services, educational programs, products for original equipment manufacturers, and general supplies.

Honeywell Information Systems has the same corporate officers and top executives as Honeywell Inc., and an executive vice president of Honeywell Inc. has operating responsibility. HIS is organized into five operating groups responsible for marketing, manufacturing, design and development, and financial control within their respective territories:

1. North American Operations, Waltham, Massachusetts — United States and Canada.
2. Compagnie Honeywell Bull, Paris, France — Continental Europe, (except Italy) Scandinavia, French-speaking Africa, Mexico, and South America.
3. Honeywell Information Systems Italia, Milan, Italy — Italy, Yugoslavia, Turkey, Libya, and Iran.
4. Honeywell Information Systems LTD., Brentford, England — the United Kingdom, and Ireland.
5. HIS Pacific, Tokyo, Japan — Japan, Australia, New Zealand, and South Africa.

PLANNING TECHNIQUES

Honeywell Information Systems is decentralized, and the heart of Honeywell's management approach

Table 7C–3. HIS Financial Performance

	$ Millions $		
	1973	1972	1971
Revenues	1,177	1,061	950
Pre-tax Earnings	93	73	33
Computer Rental and Service Revenue (Included above)	681	601	570

to coordination is painstaking planning.

Pre-HIS Planning at Honeywell

Prior to the GE merger and creation of HIS, Honeywell had five major operating groups with several divisions in each group. Twice a year the group vice presidents met with the corporate chairman, president, controller, and the heads of marketing, research and new business development department. In December, the group vice presidents presented their tactical one-year plans and budget requests. In July they returned for review of their long-range strategic plans.

Most groups planned three years ahead but Mr. Davis, then head of the computer division, planned five years into the future. To do that, Davis explained "you make a seven year forecast of trends, map your strategy for five and lay down an operations plan for one."

The July review sessions took two to four days per group because carefully detailed plans were presented to corporate executives for questions and comments. After all five presentations the corporate executives retired to weigh the proposals and then returned for a summary session.

Each group vice president then learned, in writing, to what extent top management had bought his plans. He may have been asked to change his plans but by the end of the July sessions top management knew the precise goals of each division and group.

Planning Technical Research

Each division and group went about their planning process in the way that best suited their needs. The problem of directing research in a technology-oriented company as Honeywell under these conditions was also complicated by the wide variety of products and the geographical distance between divisions. Keeping in mind that many of Honeywell's 18 divisions (1967) were quite autonomous, it was decided that the company's growth could be improved by better coordination of research at corporate headquarters between the applied research and design programs and the marketing and engineering needs of the many divisions.

In 1968 a plan was implemented to coordinate the fundamental research of this large multidivisional company. Top management correctly contended that, if corporate research scientists worked with little attention to overall needs and goals while research in the divisions concentrated on already developed products, this failure to tie together these parallel research programs could easily stunt Honeywell's growth.

Previous long-range planning for technical research had been ineffective mainly because of failure to obtain broad participation in choosing alternative directions. To alleviate this, sources of inputs in the new procedure included:

1. The divisional engineering and marketing groups that make use of the actual results.
2. The research scientists who are in

closest contact with new scientific ideas and trends.

3. The top financial, legal, and other corporate staffs.

The divisions had previously been accustomed to sending random research requests. Different departments from the same division could submit projects that were conflicting in direction and this led to a less than optimal allocation of R and D funds.

The new plan in 1968 was to dispatch memos to each group, including top officers requesting their recommendations for research. Each was asked to:

1. List two or three areas of research and technical problems of greatest importance to his division.
2. Briefly state how research done in these areas could improve profits.
3. List possible alternative solutions.
4. Obtain requests that would represent a joint effort on the parts of marketing and engineering.
5. Select only persistent problems that are likely to continue if not attended to.
6. And finally, pick topics suited for research and not for engineering and design.

The scientists enlisted to predict scientific and technological trends were asked to tell how their recommendations would be related to Honeywell's present and future business objectives. They also were to estimate the manpower needs, achievement schedules and probabilities for achieving goals.

Management provided their five year trend and budget along with their recommendations. Efforts were divided into: (1) exploratory research; (2) research coordinated with specific developments of divisions, and (3) research on specific technical areas that previous research indicated was attractive.

Again many requests overlapped so the total number could be reduced. A Research Planning Team ranked proposals by two factors: Honeywell's present and future market penetration, and whether the area in question would be dominated by (1) price competition or (2) performance.

If Honeywell already commanded a large portion of the market, the possible gain in market share would be small so research would tend to be wasted unless technological obsolescence would jeopardize the company's future position. The second ranking factor led to the conclusion that research payoffs will be greatest if results lead to radical improvements or provision of a previously unavailable service. Price competition and price reduction would be a third consideration which might result in smaller contributions to profit. And finally, the proposals were evaluated in terms of their suitability for research work.

Technical success was not enough. If success only generates the need for more research then profits would continue to lag. The interaction of manager, engineer, marketing expert, and scientist leads to projects that will not be only scientific successes but will also strive to achieve goals for sales and profits. It stimulates innovation and makes obsolescence less likely.

Innovation and technical achievements translated into new products and services are the basis of growth for a company like Honeywell.

HIS Planning Methods

Honeywell Information Systems' new long-range planning system integrates each new product into the company's long-range plans and strategy. Strategy and planning changed after the merger with GE because of multinational operations. HIS had to consider a "pipeline" of products going both ways rather than the old system of shipping from the United States to markets in other countries. HIS has established a companywide strategic guide that lists objectives by profit, market share, volume, return on investment, and so on.

Details on the Methods

This planning approach is backed by a series of strategies for each product line, and each of the product line strategies varies according to the particular part of the world where it will be marketed. A product calendar is constructed to guide funding, production, and availability dates. This calendar coordinates product availability at certain times with specified price position and assumed market participation.

Each of HIS's organizational components are given subsets to identify their expected profit contribution. They then proceed to put together their long-range plan using selected measures of performance such as sales, leases, installations and other forms of cash inflow as compared to cash and operating budgets.

The organizational component's five-year plan may or may not agree with corporate HIS long-range objectives. If not, the plans are worked and reworked until a compromise is found.

Honeywell calls this their closed-loop planning process. They tie each individual product plan with long-range plans for the entire company. It is a continuous process, adjusting to changes in each individual product plan using impact analysis versus anticipated results. It is a full-facility method (top-down/bottom-up) that is continually updated and revised.

In the computer industry it is important to know exactly how you stand at the beginning of each year. Consequently, forecasters, using historical data based on each market situation, determine customer potential, key customers, and new accounts. A mutation table gives estimates on changes in hardware configuration as each customer's needs change. In the computer industry, because of the high number of rentals to sales, it is basic that more capital must be invested as operations expand.

Rental sales cause unique cash flow problems. Small changes in forecasts and plans can abruptly change HIS's financial picture. Therefore, this planning factor model has been programmed into a computerized model with cash generation as a key input. Since the plan is a continuous concept, managers are always somewhere between review and revision. The data are then fed into a financial model and the computer simulates future operations in the form of expenses, budgets, cash flows, and so on. Within a matter of seven minutes, (the time needed to change inputs), details of possible events can be placed in the model and adjusted to allow for possible changes.

Once assumptions for strategic variables are fixed as a result of experimentation with the model, the same computer program also prints the long-range plan for HIS. These occupy three, two-inch-thick volumes.

STUDENT PROBLEMS

1. Contrast the pre-HIS planning approach with that used after the merger. What are the primary reasons for differences?
2. Review the company background of Honeywell. Actual performance in computers was not consistent with forecasts in long-range plans for sales and profits in the 1950s. If you were the CEO at that time, would you have stayed in computers or sold the operation? Defend your decision. (The Olivetti decision on its computer division could provide insight for the analysis).
3. Give your opinion on the differences and similarities between HIS and CDC. Which appears to have the strongest long-range planning program?

Appendix B

Summary of Income for Honeywell Inc.
(81.5% owner of HIS)

For Year Ended December 31, 1973

Revenue:	
Sales	$1,727,259
Computer Rental and Service Revenue	663,333
Other Income	17,844
Total	2,408,436
Costs and Expenses (Including Depr., 1973; $270,289)	
Cost of Sales, Rentals, and Services	1,506,918
Selling, General and Administrative	671,204
Interest — Net	31,891
Total	2,218,013
Income Before Income Taxes	190,423
Taxes on Income (Including Deferred Income Taxes, 1973, $35,734; 1972, $38,646)	78,454
Minority Interests	14,634
Income Before Extraordinary Item	97,335
Extraordinary Item (Tax Benefits of Operating Loss Carry Forwards, Net of Minority Interests)	6,550
Net Income	103,885
Earnings Per Common Share	
(Based on Average Number of Shares Outstanding)	
Income Before Extraordinary Item	5.12
Extraordinary Item	.34
Net Income	5.46

Appendix C

Some Characteristics about the Merging Companies

Computing Equipment Installed	General Electric	Honeywell	Total
Large computers (more than $30,000 average monthly rental)	101	30	131
Medium computers ($5,000-$30,000 average monthly rental)	988	1,840	2,828
Small computers (less than $5,000 average monthly rental)	2,700	1,446	4,146
Manufacturing Plants			
U.S.:	Phoenix, Arizona Oklahoma City, Okl.	Wellesley Hills, Mass. Framingham, Mass. Marlboro, Mass. Tampa, Fla. Minneapolis, Minn. San Diego, Cal.	
Foreign:	France (2) Italy Netherlands	Canada Germany Scotland England Japan	

Data: International Data Corp. estimates

Bylinsky, Gene. "Happily Married in Computers," reprint, *Fortune*. 1973.

"Challenging the Jolly Gray Giant," *Time*, January 3, 1972.

"Computer Sales Soar in Europe," *Business Week*. April 28, 1965, pp. 63–66.

"Computers Go Commercial — by Degrees," *Business Week*. November 21, 1953, pp. 68–70.

"Europe's No. 2," *The Economist*. April 27, 1974.

Gardner, D.W. "Anatomy of a Merger," *Datamation*. November 15, 1970, pp. 22–31.

"G.E. and Honeywell Test their Match," *Business Week*. May 30, 1970, pp. 30–31.

"G.E. Goes Out," *Newsweek*. June 1, 1970.

Honeywell Annual Report, 1970.

"Honeywell Builds on the G.E. Line," *Business Week*. February 20, 1971.

"Honeywell Calls a Computer Bet," *Business Week*. February 13, 1965, pp. 102–104.

"Honeywell Closes the Gap," *Duns Review*. February, 1968, pp. 67–68.

"Honeywell Inc.," *Moody's Industrial Manual*. 1972, pp. 2078–2079.

"Honeywell in Control," *Time*. October 18, 1968, pp. 99–100.

Honeywell Information Systems, 1973, fact book, June, 1973.

"Honeywell Rounds Out Its Line," *Business Week*. February 1, 1968, p. 18.

"Honeywell Tries to 'Get Them Young'," *Business Week*. February 3, 1968, pp. 88–92.

"Honeywell Tries to Makes Its Merger Work," *Business Week*. September 26, 1970, pp. 92–97.

"Honeywell Unscrambles Its Computer Mix," *Business Week*. April 27, 1974.

"Hot Race for Far-Off Profits," *Business Week*. March 31, 1962, pp. 62–72.

Levy, Robert. "The Heat's on at Honeywell," *Duns Review*. June, 1969, pp. 44.

McGlauchlin, L.S. "Long-Range Technical Planning," *Harvard Business Review*. July–August, 1968, pp. 54–64.

"Still a Dark Horse," *Forbes*. October, 1968, p. 64.

Strategy: Formulation and Execution

Strategy is defined, and the approach to formulating strategy is outlined. The character of a strategy and the role played by executive management in the process of strategy formulation are explained. This chapter interrelates formal plans such as SROP and strategies that are more flexible and are not limited in time span. A careful understanding of what an executive means by strategy is needed because the business application is defined differently by different managers.

DEFINITION OF STRATEGY

8

The word *strategy* stems from the Greek word *strategos* and has its origin on the battlefield. Military strategists differentiate between tactics to win a specific battle and strategies to win a war. In business, tactics usually entail actions to cope with and/or capitalize on immediate situations. A strategy is:

A multiple-step approach to achieve a specific objective. It is controlled by a plan, involves coordinated use of selected components and resources of the company, and covers the time frame necessary to accomplish the objective.

This business definition of strategy has four elements. They are explained in greater detail here.

1. *Definition of an Objective.* The objective can range from a broad goal such as diversifying the company's operations to a narrowly defined objective such as optimizing company performance in a specific situation. The important point is that the objective is stated in a way so that success or failure can eventually be measured.

2. *Multiple Components.* A strategy consists of deploying person-

nel, capital, and other resources in ways to accomplish the objective. More than one function is usually involved. Even in strategies that might be wholly confined to a specific function such as marketing or finance, more than one person or department is participating.

3. *The Time Framework and Strategic Plan.* Timing in a strategy is usually a critical element. Weeks, months, or years could be involved in achieving the objective, and the length of time is not constrained by periods in formal company plans such as SROP. Interrelationships of components usually necessitate completion of components on schedule and a strategic plan controls progress as time elapses. For example, problems could result from one or more of the multiple components going smoothly while others encounter unexpected problems.

4. *Coordination of Changes between Actual Conditions and Forecasts.* The dynamic character of the business environment makes it mandatory to monitor each component and identify differences between: (a) assumptions and forecasts in the original strategy, and (b) actual conditions and performance. Changes will always take place, and modifications in the strategic plan are essential for success.

It is important to emphasize the contribution of training, experience, and judgment in formulating a strategy. Each of the four elements required in a strategy increases the possibility of an executive making a wrong decision. In some cases, everything could be correct but the timing. In other situations, executive management might formulate an intricate means of combatting a symptom instead of the basic cause of the problem. The purpose of pointing out these potential difficulties is to clarify that a strategy is not an automatic solution. However, adjustments resulting from monitoring and coordinating components can convert a bad strategy into a solution.

Example of a Strategy

Let us consider the following case to see how a complicated strategy fits together. Company ABC has just discovered that competitor XYZ has introduced an outstanding new product that will have a serious impact on sales of an ABC product line. Testing of the competitor's product indicates that modifications and accessories will revolutionize the industry. The product will do a better job of meeting the customer's needs and cost less while offering XYZ an improved profit margin. There is high probability that XYZ is aware of the potential for these additional improvements and is holding them in reserve for future marketing programs. The situation could not be worse for ABC.

The president of ABC calls for the formulation of a master strategy that will minimize the short-term impact of XYZ's new product and assure ABC long-range leadership in this particular market. The following are substrategies within the master strategy.

Defensive Substrategies

1. *Short-Range*. Improvements developed for future models of ABC's product are to be adopted immediately. Concepts proven in prototypes will make ABC's product appear competitive with XYZ for approximately one year. Part of this counterstrategy includes modifications in the appearance of ABC's product components to modernize them rather than using the present, practical design. Subsequently, it is expected that XYZ will introduce modifications that will confirm superiority over ABC's product.

2. *Short-Range*. A stand-by plan must be developed to soften the impact of XYZ's next moves. A product promotion and advertising campaign is designed to emphasize ABC's reputation for quality and technical service. One tactic would be to time the greatest campaign intensity to coincide with XYZ's introduction of the improved product to offset initial sales impact.

Both 1 and 2 are defensive substrategies which make up a counterstrategy to retain ABC's share of the market during a one- to two-year period. XYZ acts and ABC reacts. Despite competitor superiority, ABC's objectives are to minimize loss of sales and to gain time for offensive steps to be developed and implemented.

Offensive Substrategies

3. *Short-Range*. A completely new concept for answering the customer's needs was uncovered by the basic research group. No funding was authorized for development because it would have rendered obsolete several millions of dollars of capital invested in the present products concept. However, a detailed network model now indicates a crash program including construction of a plant that could produce the product resulting from the new concept in 30 months. The program is authorized.

4. *Long-Range*. The XYZ development has influenced top management of ABC to shorten product life cycles and to be aware of the need to develop new ideas to supplement the new product being introduced in 30 months. Therefore, a greatly increased budget for Research and Development is authorized to explore alternative means of servicing not only the direct customer but also the retail customer, thereby broadening the scope of possibilities that could arise from this investment in research.

Both substrategies seek to regain leadership in the market place for ABC's product. The firm recognizes that while a defensive counterstrategy is required to counter the XYZ innovation, the authorization of research funds is the beginning of future technological strength within the product line. Hopefully this will force XYZ into the position that ABC currently finds itself.

5. *Long-Range.* The threat of a sharp loss in sales and profits within a specific market has motivated ABC's executive management to assign the director of acquisitions to propose a plan within 90 days for strengthening the company's position in the market. Upon approval of this plan designating specific directions for acquisition moves, the director will proceed with implementation.

Figure 8–1 summarizes the five substrategies of ABC's master strategy. There is a clear distinction between: (1) the counterstrategy, which concentrates on the product in jeopardy and seeks to hold participation in the market and gain time, and (2) the three-pronged development strategy, which will strengthen the overall company in future years through research projects that could render existing product lines obsolete, and by acquiring going concerns that make ABC less dependent on its present industry.

Note that both the counterstrategy and the development strategy have components that extend well beyond the time limit of SROP.

Figure 8–1. Strategic Objectives

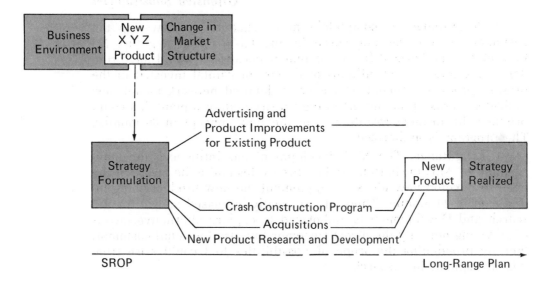

Fundamental Techniques in Planning and Strategy Formulation

These components become a bridge between the short-range plan in which they are implemented decision by decision and the long-range plan in which the results of realizing goals are portrayed in operations expected at that future time. Figure 8–2 illustrates this important point about the nature of strategies.

Substrategies are part of the master strategy to maximize the potential of existing product lines and to strengthen the long-range future of the company. This demonstrates another characteristic of strategies. You will recall that systems analysis stresses interdependence of components in a system and that each component is a system with its own subsystems, and so on. Strategies are similar. Once

Figure 8–2. Integration of the Master Strategy with Plans

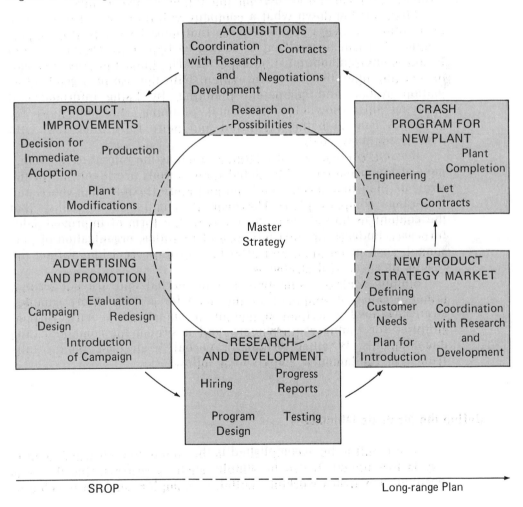

there is agreement on the definition of the objective for the master strategy and the major components are identified, such as in substrategies 1, 2, and 3 of our example, each substrategy becomes a strategy within several substrategies as the process of delegating responsibilities is carried out in appropriate parts of the organization.

FORMULATING STRATEGY

Short- and long-range plans are integrally involved with company strategy. This can be seen from the following two points.

First, writing down what a company will do now and in years to come often uncovers problem areas that must be resolved or opportunities that can be realized by taking certain steps. Changes in the business environment must be expected. The impact of these changes on existing operations is more evident with the use of a good information system and competent planning. By being informed and applying this knowledge to formal planning, the objectives for strategies can be better identified and more fully integrated with overall company goals.

Second, components of a strategy such as the role of each component of management within stated time periods are identified in the strategic plan that is separate from and more flexible than short- and long-range company plans. However, it is important to realize that the content in formal company plans in the form of improved sales forecasts, budgets, product mix, use of facilities, organization of personnel, cash generation, and after-tax earnings, revisions reflect the results of successful strategies.

Simple strategies sometime remain verbal and are not written either because of simplicity or the need for secrecy. More complex strategies need a written statement of objectives, specific responsibilities for timing requirements, and a system for communicating developments. Whether written or verbal, a strategic plan results from five fundamental steps which follow.

Define the Strategic Objectives

The result to be accomplished is the foundation on which a strategy is formulated. It can be simple, such as restructuring the composition of a firm's working capital, or complex, such as developing product lines that counterbalance a strongly seasonal cash flow. In many business situations the definition of a strategic objective initiates the process of identifying the means of achieving the objective. For example, the seasonal cash flow problem could be solved through varying combinations of acquisitions in new fields, development of new markets, and diversification through internal research.

As just discussed, the process of planning, which provides information and perspective, when combined with executive management experience and training, adds to the probability of making a good choice. The purpose in stressing use of information systems and modern planning techniques is the critical need to identify all the strategic objectives open to the company for a given problem or opportunity.

For example, a firm wants to market an electric car that is competitive with the performance of combustion engine compact cars and that generates cash out of season with the remainder of the business. This objective can be refined to include decisions on the venture being: (1) a joint venture or sole ownership; (2) international, nationwide, or regional, and/or (3) compatible with a segment of existing operations.

Identify and Analyze the Strategic Variables

The problem or opportunity has been isolated and the objective has been defined. It is now necessary to forecast the environment in which our strategy will operate. This must precede any consideration of deploying company resources.

Strategic variables are of two types: (1) extracompany and (2) intracompany. Extracompany variables are those involving decisions by government, financial institutions, competitors, communities, foreign parties, and similar influences that are clearly beyond company control.

Intracompany variables involve a distinction that is necessary in modern business. For example, a firm has theoretical control over wages and salaries it pays. Yet, in reality, union contracts, competition for skills, regional cost of living developments, and governmental "freezes" eliminate some of discretionary decision making by management. The right to hire and fire has been greatly affected by pressure groups seeking progress for minorities and women, labor union resistance to automation, government restrictions, and community outcries against major layoffs.

The forecasts of strategic variables in SROP and the long-range plan are basic resources that provide a starting point. Additional analysis, and special forecasting techniques may be justified, however, because of a different time framework.

Figure 8–3 shows the importance of estimating what will occur in each strategic variable that could affect the objective of the strategy. Management has the responsibility of choosing which ones they are, forecasting what will happen, and accurately assessing what impact the prediction for the variable will have on the strategy. For example, within the objective of marketing an electric car, the following strategic variables could affect success and must be considered in formulating the master strategy.

OUTLOOK FOR ENERGY Petroleum availability, refining capacity, and price of gasoline per gallon. Electrical power availability for charging and impact of predicted "brown-outs."

GOVERNMENT REGULATIONS Pollution restrictions on combustion engines and potential for innovations on exhaust control. Highway restrictions on speed, vehicle design, and safety regulations. Price, wage, interest rate, dividend, and other possible controls.

COMPETITOR REACTION The existence of a competitive electric car by major auto makers or electrical equipment producers. Dealer organizations and parts distributors aligned to combustion engine car producers that could affect market penetration. Supplier alignments. Use of labor union support for counterstrategies by competitors.

FINANCIAL INSTITUTIONS Bank alignments with competition. Company financial relationships and their dependability. Geographic situation on distribution financing.

COMMUNITY RELATIONSHIPS Assessment of true public support for an electric car distinct from market estimates. Specific response by localities in providing electrical charging facilities. Social responsibility aspects involving minorities, women, and other pressure groups.

Figure 8–3. Strategic Variables in the Electric Car Strategy

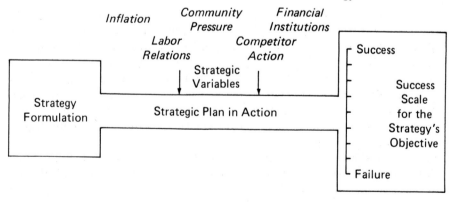

CONSUMER REACTION   Assessment of true consumer support for pollution control considering necessity to recharge nightly. Sales forecast in units by geographic area, by time period, by model for market penetration estimates. Essential features for buyer acceptance.

In addition to these extracompany strategic variables, the electric car manufacturer must realistically evaluate the following intracompany variables. In the past, some of these variables were under greater control of the company and could be considered operating variables. However, this is not true in today's business environment.

DEALER DISTRIBUTION NETWORK   Suitable dealers by geographic areas the same as the sales forecast. Potential of establishing wholly new dealerships with no combustion engine car affiliation. Resistance from established dealers other than normal competitive tactics.

LABOR UNION SUPPORT   Flexibility in work assignments for selected personnel from the workforce in building prototypes. Potential support if pressured by affiliated organizations to resist commercial output of the electric car. Work contract features that assist or complicate production, particularly the impact on costs.

SOCIAL RESPONSIBILITY   Community pressures affecting the strategy and necessitating capital allocations that divert needed funds. Possible company decisions conflicting with social responsibility. Advantages in introducing the electric car.

SUPPLIERS   Potential problems because of supplier/customer relationships with combustion engine car producers, the petroleum industry, and others. Interrelationships that could be advantageous.

The result of this process is the identification of all factors out of company control that could affect the strategy, development of available information on each factor, analysis of this material, and forecasts of probable impact on components of the strategy. Interrelationships, existing and potential, will be clarified. This step provides the framework for examining operating variables.

Identify and Analyze Operating Variables

Operating variables include those a company can control to a significant degree within the limits of contracts and the law. Examples are sources of financing, appointment of management personnel, and allocation of after-tax cash flow. Some operating variables strongly influenced by strategic variables are: (1) pricing of products, affected by government regulations, competitor decisions and consumer acceptance of the value offered; (2) deployment of the workforce, limited by flexibility in the union contract and competition for availability of skills; (3) purchasing of materials, restricted by relationships of preferred suppliers with competition.

Many company strategies involve revisions of plans for existing operations. A primary step in this situation is to identify the main components in the present strategy, the variables involved, and specific responsibilities delegated to portions of the organizations. Analysis of what has occurred will clarify problem areas and eliminate the possibility of attempting a new strategy similar to one that has not achieved the desired objective. Sometimes sensitive organizational relationships are involved in the revisions, and executives formulating new strategies try to avoid personal fault finding whenever possible.

In the case of the electric car, which is wholly a new venture, a vast number of operating variables must be analyzed. In addition, facilities for production, warehousing and transportation, working capital, personnel, organizational relationships, and so on must be balanced to achieve both short- and long-range plans for existing operations and the strategic plan for the electric car. Pages 254 and 255 of *Top Management Planning*[1] give an excellent checklist of operating variables. These are repeated in Appendix A of this book (p. 00).

An important part of this analysis is the identification of competitive advantages and disadvantages. In the case of strategic variables, the company can only make forecasts and assumptions and hope they are correct. Operating variables can be modified by management to optimize advantages and minimize disadvantages in marketing the electric car. Success may depend on finding a niche, and intuition can play a role. Figure 8–4 completes the diagram begun with Figure 8–3, and illustrates the full range of variables that could effect our strategy.

At this stage in strategy formulation the company has identified the resources required to undertake the venture and the potential problem areas from definition of both strategic and operating variables.

Competitive advantages have been evaluated for their contribution to potential profits.

Formulate a Strategic Plan from the Variables and Alternatives

Timing is critically important in decisions required to construct a strategic plan. Being correct about an event occurring but being wrong about the time is usually disastrous. Consequently, the fourth

[1] Steiner, George A. *Top Management Planning*. The Macmillan Co., 1969.

Figure 8–4. Variables in the Electric Car Strategy

step requires final judgments on the composition of the master strategy will take place.

Testing the impact of different decisions is feasible through simulation. Experimenting with the forecasts for individual strategic variables can clarify whether more studies are required. If timing will not permit more deliberation, simulations will alert management to the importance of monitoring those which are critical. In some cases, executive management has been misled by simulation because the model did not adequately reflect the environment being studied. These tragedies emphasize the need for thoroughness in building models so that the composition truly simulates existing conditions.

Let us assume that the judgments have been made which predict the environment for the master strategy on the electric car. This environment spans a 48-month period of time, and the influence of each strategic variable has been evaluated over this time period to give the company an assessment of the effects of outside influences.

Decisions about operating variables can now be made. As each component is placed within the timetable, an interrelationship is established. For example, advertising is aimed for the weeks just before introduction and during the initial sales period. However, preparation of the campaign and selection of media will take place well in advance. Coordination with dealers, production, budget control, and so on is essential. Figure 8–5 is a summary schematic that portrays the master strategy and some of the substrategies. It is important to realize that there may be substrategies and tactics within the substrategies to market the electric car successfully. The reason for the complicated structure of this strategy is the simple fact that many people are involved. As assignments are made at progressively

Figure 8–5. Modifications to Reflect Influences of Strategic Variables

Influences of Strategic Variables

Master Strategy Initiated

Campaign Design	Customer Research	Product Improvements	Budget Planning	Engineering	Sourcing of Finance	Equipment Selection	Research Goals	Executive Search
Initiation	Coordination with Research and Development	Hiring for New Plant	Monitoring Cash	Let Contracts and Begin Construction	Loan Negotiations	Installation	Expertise Added	Screening
Evaluation		Production Planning	Progress Payments	Plant Completion		Running in	Testing	Selection
Redesign	Distributors Selected	Purchasing	New Product Budgets	Plant Start up	Takedown	Full Scale	Refinements	Staff Added
				Production Begins				

Master Strategy Completed Successfully

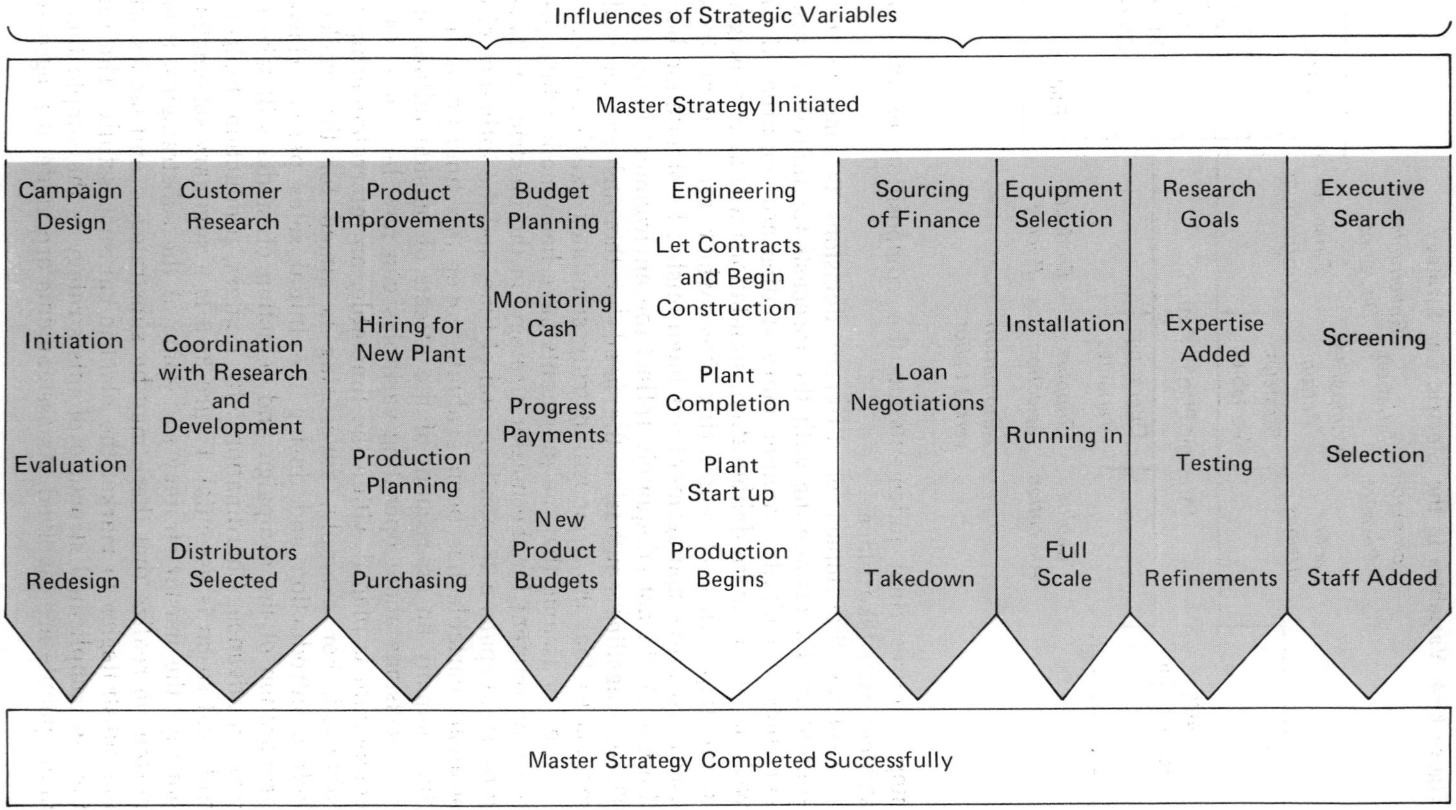

lower levels of the organization, substrategies will be designed to complete the individual assignments.

The element missing from the strategy up to this point is organizational responsibilities for the master strategy and each component. A manning table is needed. The scope involved in marketing an electric car will probably necessitate recruitment of special talents in the automotive industry. Other voids in the table will be identified in completing the process of selecting people for important roles in the strategy.

Timing can be a critical factor in developing a manning table. New assignments made too early could hurt the company's other operations. The financial burden of hiring new employees before the car is generating cash could be a serious cost problem. On the other hand, the "right" person is difficult to find, and it is sometimes prudent to accept the expense of an early appointment in the expectation that performance will justify the decision. A time allowance for screening candidates, interviewing, transfers, and orientation to the objectives and interrelationships is needed for major undertakings such as an electric car. It may be less important for simple strategies involving a few people and a short time period.

The budget is a fundamental part of the strategy. Problems can arise from: (1) being inadequate to achieve the objective, or (2) allocation to the various components, that is, "starving" one portion while "overfeeding" another. In addition, procedural aspects should be identified including cross-charges for personnel on loan, account numbers, timing of cash availability, and similar factors. It is important that appropriate budget details be fully communicated to personnel in charge of each component in the strategy.

At this stage, the master strategy has been completed, and substrategies for specific functions and responsibilities have been included in the time framework. The assessment of overall risk for marketing an electric car can now be estimated because forecasts of after-tax profits can be compared with risk to judge whether the return to the company is adequate. Figure 8–6 illustrates the concept. The diagonal line is the norm. Operations above this line exceed expectations. While it is difficult to quantify risk, some companies have developed systems to provide measurable assessments to weigh with return.

Summarizing, the fourth step integrates the work accomplished in identifying and analyzing strategic and operating variables. Specifically, (1) a timetable is established in which the objective of the strategy is to be accomplished. (2) Decisions are made on the most probably occurrences for the strategic variables to provide an environmental framework. (3) The operating variables are then given times for start-up and completion, amounts in dollars and units,

Figure 8-6. Risk Assessment

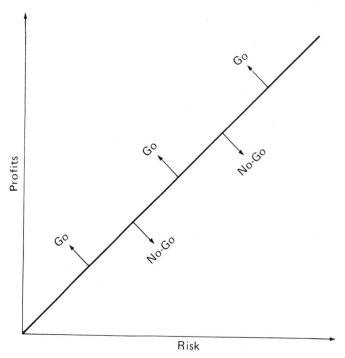

geographic locations, divisional and departmental assignments, and clarification of policies, principles, philosophies, and so on. (4) The financial support for the strategy is resolved from the point of source, timing, budgetary control, and procedures to deviate from budgets. (5) The manning table is developed outside of existing organizational relationships to assure getting the best man for the assignment considering plans for other operations, the need to transfer employees, and recruitment of new management personnel. Finally, (6) a clearly defined system for feedback is established to communicate important information, including market analysis.

Monitor and Modify Strategy Based on Observations and Feedback

Actual conditions rarely coincide exactly with the assumptions and forecasts in the strategy. The fifth step modifications needed optimize as the timetable unfolds. There are four elements involved in realizing the strategic objective while reacting to the dynamic business environment affecting the master strategy:

BASIS FOR MEASUREMENT   The first four steps of formulating the strategy give a frame of reference for evaluating expected performance as compared to actual progress of the strategy.

Fundamental Techniques in Planning and Strategy Formulation

FEEDBACK AND ANALYSIS   The electrical car strategy is an integral part of the company's plan for future growth. Key executives have spent considerable time on the project. However, initial formulation is only the beginning. Once the strategy is in action, information must flow on what is actually happening as compared to forecasts.

AUTHORITY FOR, AND RESPONSIVENESS TO CHANGE   When management has feedback indicating change, it is critical that it occur promptly. The personnel responsible for the strategy must have the authority, competence, and willingness to implement the prudent modifications.

IMPLEMENTATION OF CHANGE   Coordination in making changes is essential to avoid the possibility of conflicts in priorities, timing, organization, budget allocations, and similar elements. These changes must fully consider the feedback system designed into the strategy originally because future adjustments are very probable.

Because deviations between plans and reality happen regularly throughout the life of a strategy, original formulation must be followed by competent management demonstrating judgment in initiating appropriate changes. The first four steps provide the framework for success, but the fifth step is primarily responsible for ultimate success.

THE CHARACTER OF A STRATEGY

Strategies can be categorized by their aggressiveness, level of ethics, degree of complexity, time span, and financial commitment. After completion, it is also possible to characterize the creativity of the concept. As can be seen in Figure 8–7, the total character of a strategy is a combination of the five categories and this character can affect success.

The character of a firm strongly influences strategies formulated either at the top of an organization or in one of the divisions. Established traditions and conservative management practices tend to discourage very aggressive strategies. In contrast, young management with ambitions for above average growth in earnings might be quite daring in their strategies. Analysis of situations where leaders formulate strategies with questionable ethics, justifying the approach by the results, usually uncovers a history of executive management that tolerated such thinking.

It is difficult to change the character of a company. The process takes years, and the end result is not always the one desired. For example, executive management of companies with agressive expansion programs have attempted to integrate an acquisition into the more dynamic parent organization to realize their full potential. Even

Figure 8-7. Seeking the Correct Combination of Characteristics

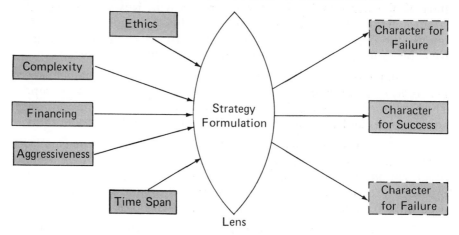

Lens

replacement of key personnel and creative redesign of the organization has failed to change the character from overly conservative, or highly political, or slow moving, or the many other words used to describe an unwanted situation in a company.

Managers must make a conscious effort to assess the character of the firm in which they work. Their thought processes and actions should be in concert with this character. If they are not, their strategy formulation will involve ideas that have a lower probability of success because others in the firm may regard them as risky, unethical, or other interpretations influenced by adhering to what has been acceptable and unacceptable approaches within the company over extended periods of time.

EVALUATION OF STRATEGIES BY EXECUTIVE MANAGEMENT

Within the range between those having short duration with a narrowly defined objective and those with a long time span and broad objectives, strategies move the company towards its primary goal of adequate return on invested capital. If the strategies being formulated are not achieving this goal and others specified by the company, a thorough reexamination must take place.

The evaluation being discussed pertains to the net effectiveness of company strategies. There is a preimplementation phase that permits initial input by top management and a postimplementation phase that allows them to refine suggested modifications.

It is possible that judgments by lower level management on the basic assumptions and forecasts for strategic variables have been consistently wrong in either timing or actual occurrence. This pin-points a portion of the organization that may need additional talent. A problem can also result from the selection of objectives for the strategies by company personnel. Regardless of specific reasons, top management must be certain subordinates are plotting the correct course for the company. Serious problems result from the following.

Incompetence. Executive management has the obligation to replace executives whose performance on strategy formulation and implementation is poor. Whether by termination or transfer, a company has to have its best team making important decisions. An almost insurmountable problem arises when the incompetence is at the highest levels of management. They can be forced from their positions only through actions by the chief executive officer and/or the board of directors. This step usually occurs only after gross mis-management.

Poor Deployment. Complex strategies sometimes involve com-promises on use of personnel and other resources. For example, com-petent executives in their own areas of expertise can fail in special assignments. Inadequate budgets for important components could be a factor. Access to company facilities needed for success could be restricted due to priorities given to other operations. Poor deploy-ment of personnel, money, and/or facilities can defeat a strategy even when every other component is correct.

Lack of Control. Initial timing for each component rarely holds throughout the life of a strategy. As timing for one component changes, adjustments must be made in all the others. Without some formal method of control such as a network model, management can lose perspective and not realize the strategy is in trouble.

In extreme cases, companies fail due to consistently poor strategies or a low level of effectiveness resulting from poor deploy-ment and/or lack of control. Usually, it is a matter of not achieving full potential. Disasters are avoided, but the company misses op-timum performance. Top management often deals in centimeters rather than meters in seeking improvements that will yield profits equal to or better than expectations. This places importance on per-formance in formulating and implementing strategies at all levels of the organization.

SUMMARY

A business strategy is the deployment of multiple resources of a com-pany towards accomplishing a defined objective within a specific time framework. The objective can range in time and complexity from a single product development in an existing division to be achieved in a few months, to a companywide change in product balance with diversification to be achieved in several years.

Formal company planning can assist strategy formulation in two ways:

1. Changes in the business environment must be expected, and the impact of these changes on existing operations become easier to see with the use of a good information system and competent planning. This process clarifies objectives for strategies.

2. The results expected from strategies, which are separate from and more flexible than short- and long-range plans, are portrayed in these latter plans through improved sales forecasts, budgets, product-mix, use of facilities, organization of personnel, cash generation, and after-tax earnings.

The first four steps in strategy formulation involve: (1) defining the strategic objective; (2) identifying and analyzing applicable strategic variables; (3) identifying and analyzing operating variables, and (4) deploying operating variables having made judgments on the risks and returns to the company. Specifically, a timetable is established. Priorities, amounts in dollars and units, geographic locations, and divisional and departmental assignments are placed within the time framework. Details for financial support of the strategy are completed. The manning table is developed.

The fifth step is dependent on feedback. Deviations between plans and reality happen regularly throughout the life of a strategy. Monitoring progress and initiating appropriate changes is essential to achieve the objective of the master strategy.

Strategies may be categorized by their aggressiveness, level of ethics, degree of complexity, time span, and financial commitment. Creativity can only be judged in retrospect after success or failure. The character of the firm strongly influences strategy formulation. For example, young management with ambitions for above average growth in earnings might be quite daring in their strategies while a conservative firm with entrenched traditions might be more conventional.

Top management has the responsibility to plot the correct course for a company, and selection of appropriate strategies is critical to achieving company goals. When performance on strategies is consistently poor, three reasons are involved: (1) incompetence; (2) poor deployment, and (3) lack of control. The difference between success and failure can be decisions by individuals and executive management must continually probe for facts on what has occurred.

DISCUSSION QUESTIONS

1. Relate substrategies to master strategies. Develop an example that includes offensive and defensive components.
2. How are strategies related to short- and long-range plans? Explain specifically how you implement a strategy through the planning framework.
3. Simulation offers a manager the opportunity to experiment with a strategy prior to it being implemented. What problems do you foresee in this approach to refining strategies before implementation?
4. Identify the people who formulate and who approve strategies. How are your ideas related to the portions of Chapters Seven and Eight, which discuss who participates in planning? Could a young aggressive manager, for example, have problems in a conservative company?
5. What role could social pressures play in strategy formulation? Give two examples of major impact on a strategy.
6. How many of the categories describing the character of a strategy can apply to a single strategy?
7. Is it possible for a fundamentally good strategy to fail? Why?

SUGGESTED READINGS AND BIBLIOGRAPHY

"Dunlop-Pirelli: A Troubled Marriage," *The Economist.* February 3, 1973, pp. 54—55.

"Forecasting the Decline of the Corporation," *Business Week.* June 23, 1973, pp. 12—13.

Gilmore, Frank F. "Formulating Strategy in Smaller Companies," *Harvard Business Review.* May—June, 1971, pp. 71-81.

Hall. "Corporate Strategic Planning; Some Perspectives for the Future," *Michigan Business Review.* January, 1972, pp. 16—21.

Hutchinson, John G. *Management Strategy and Tactics.* Holt, Rinehart, and Winston, 1971.

Katz, Robert L. *Management of the Total Enterprise.* Prentice-Hall, 1970.

Miller, Ernest C. *Advanced Techniques for Strategic Planning.* American Management Association, 1971.

Nierenberg, Gerard I. *The Art of Negotiating.* Hawthorn Books, 1968.

Steiner, George A. *Top Management Planning.* The Macmillan Co., 1969.

"Talcott Winds up in Sindona's Stable," *Business Week.* April 7, 1973, p. 27.

Wheelwright. "Strategic Planning in the Small Business," *Business Horizons.* August, 1971, pp. 51—58.

Case: A Steel Industry Strategy in the 1970s

Historical development of the steel industry permits the student to formulate an industrywide strategy for obtaining a sufficient flow of raw materials in the years to come.

AMERICAN STEEL INDUSTRY THROUGH 1972

Historical Overview

The American steel industry has changed radically in the 25-year period after World War II. Before the war it was considered indefinitely self-sufficient in its supply of iron ore and coal. Annual ore consumption in the 1930s averaged approximately 40 million tons, but this figure rose to 100 million tons in the 1940s. As a result of this sharp increase in use of iron ore, estimates prepared in 1947 revealed a 25-year supply[1] of high-grade ore and the need to search for additional resources.

The situation was compounded by a post war surge in steel production sparked by pent up demand for consumer durables. Departments of the government under the Truman administration contended that the steel industry should expand and modernize in order to meet estimated demand. The steel industry, on the other hand, had doubts about committing $2.5 to 3 billion for 10 million[2] tons of new capacity for what they believed to be a temporary "post war boom." To justify the investment, a high operating rate would have to be sustained for 10 to 15 years, and the steel industry was not willing to invest in plants that

[1] William T. Hogan, S.J., *Economic History of the Iron and Steel Industry in the United States*, vol. 4, p. 2089.

[2] Ibid., p. 1447.

might be idle in a few years.[3]

During a 1949 recession operating rates declined, and steel companies were hit by a six-week strike. After this strike consumers began to stock pile to avoid being caught by another crippling strike. Then in June 1950 the Korean War broke out. People, remembering the shortages of World War II, feared a cut in civilian production and accelerated purchases of consumer durables. With the end of the Korean War in 1953, controversy over steel capacity came to an end, and the industry began to expand ingot capacity.

Periods of steel shortages in the 1950s originating with strikes and boom years created discontent among steel industry customers. Several turned to imports, particularly on the West Coast. Steel also began losing ground to substitutes such as reinforced concrete in the construct/on industry, aluminum in the container field and plastics in a number of uses.

The 1960s witnessed a sharp increase in the population of the seven western states and demand for many types of steel products. Although the industry tried to capture the market there, import tonnage increased from 196,000 net tons in 1957 to 2,582,000 net tons in 1969. Much of the steel imported on the West Coast comes from Japan, and in 1969 imports constituted 13% of the national market and 28% of the West Coast market.[4]

Shipments of steel in the United States have increased from 49 million net tons in 1946 to 99 million net tons in 1975. Table 8C–1 gives details on product shipments, imports, and raw steel output.

Industry Structure and Technology

The steel industry includes over 200 companies. Less than half turn out steel ingots. Others operate rolling, wire drawing and other finishing mills. The industry is dominated by the giants identified in Table 8C–2. These companies have integrated back through the blast durnace and coke oven stages, and account for over three-fourths of domestic shipments. Modern steel mills require immense sums of capital. Table 8C–2 gives an idea of the scope.

The newest rolling mills are wider, faster, more powerful, computer controlled, and yield a greater volume of a higher quality product. (See Figure 8C–1 for a "Flowline on Steelmaking"). Blast furnaces are larger, hotter, charged with high-iron content pellets and helped out by fuel and oxygen injection. As a result, they turn out more iron per day, with a much smaller consumption of coke and fluxes.

Computer Developments

"Virtual" storage, a recent development of IBM, vastly increases the size of the memory available. The practical result is that more sophisticated—and often very lengthy—computer programs can fit into the main memory. Large batch processing jobs and on-line, remote inquiry systems can be processed by the system at the same time. More systems simulation is possible. Not only can detail orders be processed

[3] Ibid., p. 1448.
[4] Ibid., p. 1471.

faster and more accurately, the on-line system also allows immediate quoting of stock availabilities, delivery schedules, and in-process order status.

Advanced computer systems of this type can explode individual order requirements to metallurgical, size and surface finish specifications, set up the routings, and schedule production. Then it will track each mill order from release to completion. Production planners can call out a terminal display on a cathode ray tube or a printout showing the status of any order at any time. Computer-based communications brings the steel company's remote mills, fabri-

Table 8C–1. Steel Industry Statistics

Year	Total Net Shipments	Imports (000 tons)	Raw Steel Production
1975*	95,000	15,000	137,500
1974	109,472	15,970	145,525
1973	111,430	15,150	150,799
1972	91,805	17,681	133,241
1971	87,038	18,304	120,443
1970	90,798	13,364	131,514
1969	93,877	14,034	141,262
1968	91,856	17,960	131,462
1967	83,897	11,455	127,213
1966	89,995	10,753	134,101
1965	92,666	10,383	131,462
1964	84,945	6,440	127,076
1963	75,555	5,446	109,261
1962	70,552	4,100	98,328
1961	66,126	3,163	98,014
1960	71,149	3,359	99,282
1959	69,377	4,396	93,446
1958	59,914	1,707	85,255
1957	79,895	1,155	112,715
1956	83,251	1,341	115,216
1955	84,717	973	117,036
1954	63,153	771	88,312
1953	80,152	1,703	111,610
1952	68,004	1,201	93,168
1951	78,929	2,177	105,200
1950	72,232	1,014	96,836
1949	58,010	291	77,978
1948	65,973	148	88,640
1947	63,570	32	84,894
1946	48,775	23	66,603

* The figure for 1946 is from the American Iron and Steel Institute, *Annual Statistical Report*, 1963. The figure for 1975 is the author's estimate, based on industry estimates.

cating plants, warehouse, and sales offices together into a centralized order entry system. This can help optimize utilization of a company's total resources.

Finance

The industry has had very little investor appeal and articles in financial magazines favorable to steel do not fully reflect the problems stated in this case. Its peak profits before the 1973–74 surge came back in 1957 at $1,132 million. Thereafter, the companies have complained about high wages, material costs, and interest charges, not offset by productivity nor price boosts.

Starting with the 1959 strike, domestic mills had to contend with an increasing volume of imports. More recently, they have been forced to pay for expensive pollution controls. Consequently, for several years steel has ranked near the bottom of a list of 41 manufacturing industries in return on net worth, and was at the bottom in the 1970–72 period.

Diversification into Other Industries

Most companies have diversified into other fields. Ten, in fact, have dropped the word "steel" from their corporate titles. Probably half of these corporations wanted to improve their image with investors more than reflect the addition of other activities.

Not all nonsteel activities have been profitable. Bethlehem, for example, suffered a decline in earnings in 1972 solely because of losses by its shipbuilding division. Allegheny, Armco, and U. S. Steel have part ownership in leading producers of titanium, but none have yet been consistent earners. National Steel's venture into the magnesium business has yet to turn a profit. On the other hand, its aluminum interests have consistently been in the black. On the balance, diversification has been a very small plus for the profits of steel makers.

Table 8C–2. Company Information

	1972 Shipments (000 tons)	Sales 1972 (millions)	Sales 1971 (millions)	Net Profit 1972 (Per Share)	Net Profit 1971 (Per Share)
Allegheny Ludlum	680	$ 571.7	$ 484.0	$2.45	D$1.06
Armco Steel	5,722	1,910.8	1,696.2	2.28	1.44
Bethlehem Steel	12,494	3,113.6	2,969.1	3.02	3.14
Inland Steel	5,186	1,469.8	1,253.6	3.43	2.44
Jones and Laughlin	5,070	1,189.4	1,074.0	2.43	0.93
National Steel	7,496	1,660.2	1,522.1	3.81	2.46
Republic Steel	7,096	1,595.7	1,384.8	2.66	0.01
U.S. Steel	20,800	5,401.7	4,928.3	2.90	2.85
Wheeling-Pittsburgh	2,874	607.8	528.0	2.78	0.44
Youngstown	3,780	999.5	901.7	0.43	D0.27

D–Deficit.

282

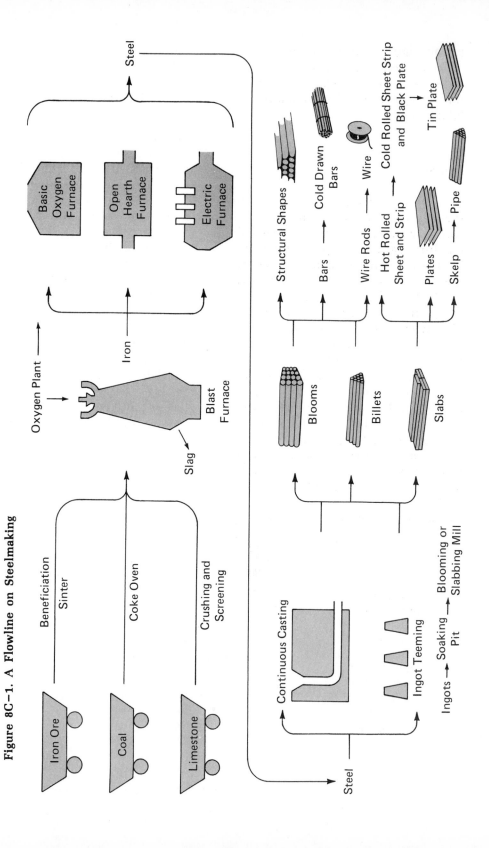

Figure 8C–1. A Flowline on Steelmaking

Labor

Management–labor relations have been, on the whole, quite satisfactory except for major strikes in 1949, 1952, and 1959. Management and the United Steel Workers of America (U.S.W.) have joined to come up with new and better ways to handle problems.

During 1971–72, the handling of local complaints was causing a great deal of dissatisfaction within the U.S.W. Arbitration systems were overburdened and cases were lingering on, often for months at a time. Consequently, local union officials insisted that arbitration be eliminated and that workers have the right to strike over a grievance. To avoid this threat to the industry, senior U.S.W. leaders took steps to cooperate with management in a program to: (1) boost productivity in the plant; and (2) use outside umpires to resolve basic contract questions.

The improved spirit is attributed to a new method of handling grievances. Called *instant arbitration* or *expedited arbitration*, this features a simplified procedure for minor cases.

Under this system, there are no written briefs. Hearings are very informal—in motels or plant conference rooms—and no formal record is kept. Local company and union people present the cases. Since they cannot turn the problem over to headquarters specialists, the local officials have an incentive to find a solution with arbitration. More cases are getting settled without going on to second and third steps.

To assure prompt hearings, the steel companies have recruited 200 arbitrators. These are mostly young law school graduates. A special effort was made to get fresh talent rather than people whose thinking has been shaped by years of conventional arbitration. By pooling the problems of 10 major mills, the steel companies are able to afford maintaining a 200-man panel. This large force is considered necessary in the interest of speed.

Neither party has the right to choose the arbitrator. This is of some importance, for apparently the selection process has been lengthy in the past, sometimes as long as a year.

Imports

The National Commission on Materials Policy says in its final report, "the administration of the United States antitrust laws should be altered to permit mergers of firms encountering serious difficulties arising from import competition in order to sustain domestic production."[5] The steel industry is asking whether it qualifies as one encountering serious difficulties arising from import competition.

Steel imports rose from about one million tons (1.5% of domestic consumption) in 1957 to a record breaking 18.3 million tons of steel (18% of domestic consumption) in 1971.

Significantly, the imports had a

[5] Final Report, The National Commission on Materials Policy. Public Volume 91–512, Title 2, Section 201. June, 1973. Available through the Superintendent of Documents, U. S. Government Printing Office.

tremendous impact in certain vulnerable areas such as the West and Southwest, where they took over 25% of the total market and as much as 90% of the market for some steel products.

The U.S. government is pursuing a free trade policy. However, in 1971–72 the steel industry was asking questions like, "What would happen to steel prices once foreign suppliers control led the market? Would they exercise restraint? What assurances would American steel users have of a continuing source of supply in the event of an international crisis? What about national defense?"

Another fundamental question was "How have imports reached such levels?" A partial explanation was given by *Nations Business*.[6] The biggest threat of steel imports is from Japan. Japan's steel strategy could best be characterized as aggressive and global in scope. Private industries and government are working together.

"In Japan virtually unlimited capital is made available (however indirectly) by the government, and the installed cost of integrated steel plants is about one third that in the United States. This great advantage in capital costs results from low financing and hourly employment costs in construction.

Labor is a major factor in the cost of steel plant operations. In other words, the much lower hourly employment costs of foreign producers give them a double advantage—both in capital costs and in operating costs.

It would be well to take a look at Japan's

6 *Nations Business*, July 1971, p. 54–57.

national goals in steel. Japan wants an output matching that of the United States (and doubling our per capita production) by 1975! Further, this expansion contemplates doubling steel mill exports every four years. Clearly, the Japanese nation recognizes the desirability of a strong and growing steel industry.

Most of the remainder of steel making capacity in other countries is government supported and nourished to a degree unheard of in the United States. Mergers and cartels are condoned if not actually encouraged. Steelmakers are insulated from some or all of the rigors of domestic free capital markets. Tax policies are designed to assist growth and to enhance export of steel.

And virtually all of these countries have erected nearly unsuperable barriers to unwanted steel imports. To cite a typical example, the "cost of entry"—total of duties, taxes, etc.,—to get $100 worth of U.S. made carbon steel bars into France is over $33; but it takes only $7 to bring $100 worth of French-made bars into the United States."

Because of their inability to fend off imports, domestic mills did not have a good market between 1965 and 1972. This static situation caused steel profits and productivity to lag. Consequently, big pay hikes have meant big price hikes. These price increases further hindered the ability of steel companies to expand their markets through 1972.

Counter Action by U.S. Steel Companies and the U.S.W.

The president of the U.S.W., I.W. Abel, felt that this situation meant one thing for certain, job losses in the industry. As a remedy he advocated the push for productivity and labor peace described earlier. In addition, the union joined management in an effort to restrict imports. The incentive was thousands of man-hours of potential employment. For the year 1971, imports represented the loss of roughly 100,000 job opportunities, according to Mr. Abel.[7] "At the local level, he notes, the steelworkers have made progress in awakening the public. At the federal level, the union is simultaneously pushing for trade legislation and voluntary steel import quotas."[8]

Testifying before the House Ways and Means Committee in April, 1973, the chairman of the American Iron and Steel Institute endorsed the concept of expanding commerce through international negotiations.[9] Also, while he supported the idea of giving the President the power to raise and lower tariffs, he also felt special attention should be given those sectors contributing heavily to the U.S. balance of payments deficit. In talking about the Trade Reform Act the chairman said "Incorporation in the Act of clearly defined conditions under which import limits are to be imposed would create the degree of reasonable certainty that is an essential condition for American industry to commit capital for improvement and expansion."[10]

Table 8C−1 shows that imports declined in 1969, 1970, 1972 and 1973, partly reflecting two devaluations of

[7] *Iron Age*, February 3, 1972, p. 47.
[8] Ibid.
[9] The information contained in this paragraph is paraphrased, and in cases, directly quoted from *Iron Age*, June 14, 1973, p. 17.
[10] Ibid.

the dollar but more because of a sharp surge in demand for steel abroad. This reduced the tonnage available for shipment to the United States and raised the price of foreign steel.

Environment

One serious question facing steel mills is the potential loss of future earnings from substantial additional efforts which must be made to control pollution of air, land, noise, and water. Since 1966, operators have laid out or committed nearly $1.3 billion for this purpose, including $200 million spent in 1972 and $336 million in 1973. Operating pollution control facilities costs another $150± million a year.

The Council on Economic Priorities, which calls itself an "organization dedicated to analyzing the performance of U.S. corporations," released a 500-page report on the environmental performances of the nation's seven largest steel companies in 1972. The C.E.P. says the steel industry doesn't measure up to standards.

The C.E.P. says it found vast differences in the degree of pollution controls at the 47 mills examined. Their impact on the environment ranged from "negligible to devastating." It estimates that the seven major steel producers could bring their mills into compliance with environmental protection agency standards over a five-year period with an average increase in the price of a ton of steel of approximately 1.1% a year or reduction in dividends of approximately 40 to 90 cents per share during the program period.

In Ohio, things began warming up when in 1972 the state EPA gave companies 30 days to submit plans for coke oven cleanup. The directive called for all ovens to be in compliance by July 1, 1975. The EPA closed the door on technical arguments by saying there was plenty of technology for controlling emissions.

Some plants are making great strides in an effort to comply. Jones and Laughlin will spend about $14 million in putting in an expanded water treatment and recirculation system for the blast furnace and sinter plant area and expanding the clarification facility and recirculation system in the steelmaking and rolling mills area.

Another plant, Inland Steel, has a similar three-year program. It is installing oil skimming and settling basins, a coke battery ammonia recovery still and additional clarifier and chemical treatment units. Also included are recycling systems for blast furnace gas scrubbing and cooling water, cascade rinsing systems and deep well disposal of pickling line rinse water, and a recycling system for a 56-inch tandem cold mill.

One executive said privately that due to the profit squeeze in past years, firms will wait until it is more economically feasible to install the necessary pollution control equipment. Another executive comments, "If you can show the inspector you're on top of it by having a list of what you're actually doing to comply, he won't be looking as hard because he'll know you're in command of the situation."

DEVELOPMENTS IN 1973–74

Steel industry profits set a record high in 1973 with $1.255 billion. Table 8C–3 shows the performance of selected companies and the overall industry. In 1974, profits were $2.437 billion despite the fourth quarter which included cutbacks in production due to the coal strike, the sharp decline in demand for automobiles, and the slowing of the overall economy.

Reasons for Improved Performance

The primary reason for record profits was price increases of approximately 44% during 1973–74 after the lifting of price controls by the federal government. This greatly improved margins. Also, sustained volume played a major role. As a result, the steel industry moved out of last place in return on net investment reaching 6.5% as compared to 3.9% in 1972. In 1974, steel achieved a ranking in the middle third of all 41 American industries with its $2+ billion year. It is interesting to note, however, that although the record was achieved, performance on earnings after taxes was less than the previous record of $1.132 billion in 1957 in deflated dollars.

Demand for steel during 1973–74 exceeded supply. Customers were on allocation. Softness in one industry and a decrease in buying was offset by another needing more steel. For example, when demand for consumer goods fell in 1974, the steel industry was relieved because more raw steel could be diverted to mills

Table 8C-3. 1973 and 1974 Company and Steel Industry Information

	1974 Shipment (000 tons)	1974 Sales (000)	1974 Net Income (000)	1974 Earnings per Share
U.S. Steel Corp.	25,518	$ 9,337,573	$ 634,858	$11.72
Bethlehem Steel Corp.	16,256	5,448,709	342,034	7.85
National Steel Corp.	8,790	2,727,774	175,764	9.44
Republic Steel Corp.	8,156	2,741,370	170,706	10.55
Armco Steel Corp.	6,561	3,219,508	204,260	6.31
Jones and Laughlin Steel	6,087	2,216,646	141,529	NA
Inland Steel Co.	6,121	2,450,289	148,009	7.96
Youngstown Sheet & Tube	4,362	1,556,052	96,366	NA
Wheeling-Pittsburgh Steel	3,297	1,043,715	73,418	19.23
Kaiser Steel Corp.	2,008	812,050	66,491	9.45
	*	*	*	*
Industry Totals	109,472	37,808,660	2,437,486	9.29

	1973 Shipments (000 tons)	1973 Sales (000)	1973 Net Income (000)	1973 Earnings per Share
U.S. Steel Corp.	26,066	$ 7,044,683	$ 325,758	$ 6.01
Bethlehem Steel Corp.	16,627	4,174,833	206,609	4.72
National Steel Corp.	9,142	2,103,279	98,072	5.27
Republic Steel Corp.	8,501	2,068,605	86,744	5.36
Armco Steel Corp.	6,872	2,416,125	107,454	3.38
Jones and Laughlin Steel	6,013	1,534,354	50,220	3.12
Inland Steel Co.	5,891	1,828,951	83,129	4.39
Youngstown Sheet & Tube	4,479	1,088,760	43,283	—
Wheeling-Pittsburgh Steel	3,476	763,815	19,324	4.45
Kaiser Steel Corp.	2,381	614,507	52,694	7.53
	*	*	*	*
Industry Totals	111,430	$28,328,797	$1,242,229	4.86

turning out products for machinery, oil and gas drilling and transmission, and so on.

The supply situation was aggravated by a drop in imports accompanied by sharply increased prices. Japanese and European demand was also near steel industry capacity. In addition, the American dollar's devaluation in 1971 and 1973 meant that domestic producers were much more competitive across the board.

Finally, inflation greatly increased costs abroad. In Japan, for example, wage concessions were 25% ± in both 1973 and 1974. Although an extreme case, developments in baling wire tell the story of supply/demand and prices. In 1972 a spool of 100 lbs. cost $13.00. At the end of 1974 the domestic price was $21.00 and foreign suppliers wanted $54.00 per spool. Regardless of price, bailing wire was in short supply.

The boom was over in 1975. Steel production was off nearly 30%, and earnings fell below $1 billion. Sluggishness in the domestic auto industry caused reserve concerning the outlook for 1976 despite increased steel consumption in the search, production, and transmission of oil, gas, and coal.

Other Developments During the Period

The steel companies have announced various plans for expansion as a result of their improved cash position. These plans, if they proceed considering the decline in 1975, total 18 million tons of added raw steel capacity for a net total of 170 million tons (according to the AISI). The cost will be about $7 billion because most of the projects are extensions of existing facilities. A "green field" expansion (starting a wholly new facility) of 1 million tons capacity would cost $800 million in 1974 dollars. Allowing for 10% imports, the industry will be able to supply approximately 125 million tons of finished product in 1980 as compared to 110 million in 1973 (actual shipments were more in that year due to depletion of inventories).

Binding Arbitration on Contract Negotiations

A major development occurred in labor relations during 1973 which will yield several significant benefits. Up to then, the steel industry's contract with the U.S.W. led to "crisis bargaining" every three years, and this encouraged strike-hedge inventory buying by steel users. The period of negotiations involved a boom that stimulated imports, followed by a lengthy slump while stocks were worked down to normal levels.

The industry says this pattern should be broken by an experimental agreement to submit unresolved contract issues to binding arbitration. Hopefully, the pact will guarantee labor peace at least through the contracts of 1974 and 1977.

Some observers question whether labor peace is desirable if it leads to major wage concessions. In 1971 for example, a contract was signed forcing labor costs up by nearly a $1.00 an hour increase in the first year with additional automatic raises in 1972 and 1973. The agreement was immediately followed by one of the biggest steel price increases in recent times, a full 15%.

Thanks to huge capital expenditures ($17.25 billion between 1962−1973), it has been possible to shave steel employment from a high of 650,000 in 1953 to 478,000 in 1973 and still boost production. The effect has been a slowing of the rise in labor costs. Total payments per hour (wages and fringes) have nearly tripled during the same years from an estimated $2.90 in 1953 to an estimated $7.60 in 1973.

Global Developments

Supply will be augmented by 35 to 40 million tons of raw steel capacity being added outside the U.S., Europe and Japan. Brazil has announced 12 million tons of expansion and "petro-dollars" will be invested in about 15 million tons of new capacity in Arab countries in North Africa and the Middle East. Egypt and Australia are each planning 3.6 million ton expansions.

Various combinations of ownership are involved. Large multinational firms are normally involved because of need for technology. Very often they have joined in partnership with the host country. In many cases the primary market is local, but exports will be important for at least 40% of the new capacity. This means 10+ million tons of finished product will be looking for buyers in addition to output from the United States, Europe and Japan.

Political Environment

At the close of the third quarter, 1974, earnings of the steel industry were averaging more than double the same three quarters in 1973, which had been a record year (nondeflated). Sales had increased about 50%. This motivated Senator William Proxmire of Wisconsin, as vice chairman of the Joint Economic Committee, to ask the companies to provide data on capacity and capacity utilization.

The capacity issue was raised because of steel industry claims that improved earnings are needed to support expansion needed in future years. A staff member of the Joint Economic Committee, viewing the serious downturn in steel demand begun in late 1974, claims that promises to add capacity could evaporate with problems in key consuming industries.

Senator Proxmire's surveillance means steel companies could have difficulty sustaining improved profit margins and return on net investment. The difficulty encountered by U.S. Steel in holding a price increase in December, 1974 and a Federal Trade Commission investigation in 1975 are examples of the problems the steel industry is experiencing.

A STRATEGY FOR SURVIVAL[11]

The steel industry realized in the 1970s that it was facing serious problems in maintaining sufficient flow of raw materials at a reasonable price during the foreseeable future without decisive action. However, individual companies had been reluctant to join together in taking the necessary measures due to retaining competitive advantages and fear about government accusations of collusion. After years of leadership and hard work by Yankee Steel, the first step toward united action was an industrywide meeting of the leaders of the U.S.W. and ten of the large steel firms in the United States on January 3, 1975. Also present were representatives of the Justice Department and Federal Trade Commission.

The purpose of the meeting was to form an industrywide strategy for raw materials while staying within antitrust guidelines and the competitive spirit of the American economy. Following the initial introductions and the preliminary necessities, the meeting began with a presentation

[11] *Third National Seminar Steel Industry Economics*, AISI, p. 42.

by H.J. Reifschneider, President of Yankee Steel, Inc., describing what he considered to be the necessary industrywide strategy.

Gentlemen, while I don't pretend to have all the answers, I think I have some of them. I would like to start out by saying that regardless of the strategy that we in the steel industry adopt, it must be one in which the union, management, and federal government work together. We are familiar with the crucial role that each of the three plays in maintaining the competitiveness of the industry.

Maintaining the survival and competitiveness of the industry is critical to the U.S. economy. According to the International Iron and Steel Institute, world steel consumption will grow to over a billion net tons by 1980, and by 1985 it will double the record set in 1970. However, steel consumption in the United States is projected to increase by only 50% between 1970 and 1985. Consequently, if the U.S. Steel industry is to remain profitable and to improve world market share, the objective of our strategy must be to make available to American companies adequate volumes of raw materials at reasonable prices.

In 1973 Bethlehem and U.S. Steel were forced out of their Venezuelan iron ore operations. Legislation was introduced in the U.S. Congress to place an embargo on Rhodesian chromium ore. Litagation was initiated against Armco and Republic's iron ore benefication plant[12] to prevent dumping in Lake Superior. Tens of other examples could be cited as you know.

Furthermore, since OPEC[13] successfully tripled the price of crude oil, countries are considering joining together in similar organizations for iron ore, manganese, nickel, tin, and others. We could be dealing with cartels on most of

[12] Ibid., p. 50.
[13] Ibid., p. 51.

the imported materials. It would be disastrous if we negotiated individually.

In the interest of time, I would like to briefly outline my proposed strategy through some slides and subsequently open the floor for discussion.

The following appeared on the screen during a 40-minute period. Mr. Reifschneider narrated the presentation.

Status on Raw Materials

My staff has put together some numbers which will give us some insight on our dependence on foreign raw materials. Table 1, based on U.S. Government statistics, shows the situation in 1973.

Table 2 statistics also come from the U.S. government and they show which countries have important raw material reserves. This table indicates, in my opinion, that the steel industry must move to establish secure sources of key items such as nickel and chromium. Otherwise we will not be able to make alloys and stainless steel. Yet it will take federal government influence and support to make arrangements with both an unpopular country such as South Africa and one with opposing racial policies such as Gabon.

The supply situation is critical in my judgment. It is essential that we unite to secure sources good for at least 50 years.

Domestic Sourcing

The steel industry must acquire funds to modernize and expand domestic facilities for every raw

Table 1. U.S. Dependence in 1973 on Imported Raw Materials

	Imports as a % of Consumption		Imports as a % of Consumption
Chromium	100	Manganese	100
Cobalt	100	Nickel	92
Copper	8	Tin	100
Iron Ore	29	Tungsten	56
Lead	19	Zinc	50

Table 2. Countries with Major Reserves of Raw Materials

	Percentage of world reserves		Percentage of world reserves
Chromium		**Manganese**	
Republic of South Africa	62.9	Gabon	15.0
Southern Rhodesia	32.9	Republic of South Africa	8.5
United States	—	United States	—
Other Free World	2.8	Other Free World	35.0
Communist Countries	1.3	Communist Countries	41.5
Cobalt		**Nickel**	
Zaire	27.5	New Caledonia	33.3
New Caledonia & Australia	27.1	Canada	13.6
Zambia	14.0	Cuba	9.1
United States	1.0	United States	0.4
Other Free World	8.5	Other Free World	21.9
Communist Countries	21.9	Communist Countries	21.6
Copper		**Tin**	
United States	22.4	Thailand	33.5
Chile	15.7	Malaysia	14.4
Canada	8.9	Indonesia	13.2
Other Free World	41.6	United States	0.1
Communist Countries	11.4	Other Free World	21.8
Iron Ore		Communist Countries	17.1
Canada	14.5		
Brazil	10.8	**Tungsten**	
United States	3.6	United States	6.4
Other Free World	24.5	Other Free World	16.1
Communist Countries	46.6	Communist Countries	77.5
Lead		**Zinc**	
United States	38.9	Canada	26.0
Canada	13.2	United States	22.9
Australia	8.3	Other Free World	35.9
Other Free World	22.2	Communist Countries	15.3
Communist Countries	17.4		

material we can produce here in this country.

Sources of Funds

1. *Internally generated funds* for raw material capacity expansion and gains in productivity can result from steel price increase commitments and support from the federal government.
2. *Decrease use of equity financing*, and in cases of unusually low stock prices, reacquire the stock to avoid acquisitions by foreign based investors.
3. *Debt financing* is to be the principal source of funds. Seek and obtain government guaranteed financing to reduce the cost of money. Seek Congressional legislation for favorable tax policies to assist in servicing debt.

Costs

1. *Employment Costs.* Decrease through investment in automation that increases required skills but decreases employment. Limit wage increases to productivity and cost of living changes. Improve relations between the workforce and management resulting from these decisions through a joint educational program with the U.S.W. on the present position of the industry on raw materials. Increased use of fringe benefits in place of salary and wage increases; maximize economies from industrywide programs in insurance and other related group benefits including tax savings for employees.
2. *Technology.* Collaborate on joint

research programs focused on reduction of both capital costs per ton of raw material capacity and operating costs per ton. Also seek material benefication processes that will make it economical to produce from a broader range of American deposits, such as the recent process introduced in the Mesabi Range.

Foreign Sourcing

The industry must embark on a concentrated effort to seek government aid in negotiating imports of raw materials produced from non-American owned deposits. Use of political influence is also needed to establish new American operations owned jointly by several cooperating firms, and to protect existing facilities from nationalization and other forms of expropriation. This is to be accomplished through:

Lobbying

Obtain the support of Congress and other forms of government through intensive use of contacts and power available to the industry.

Industry Public Relations

Influence public opinion and the government by showing the need for, and the negative consequences of not getting, coordinated federal government intervention in transactions involving foreign governments.

1. Explain how foreign nations have stolen American investments, agitated inflation, and jeopardized

national security by forcing depletion of domestic supplies.

2. Communicate the need for government cooperation in the formation of consortiums and joint ventures in new facilities at home and abroad. The negative consequences of laissez faire policies by the federal government would be shortages, higher prices, and aggravation of the balance of payments. This concept is especially explosive when you consider that the suppliers of materials, especially the less developed countries, may insist on more processing of those materials before they are exported. This could mean the conversion of iron ore to semi-finished steel in countries like Australia and Brazil, potentially adding further to the price of steel and the already aggravated balance of payments.

Environment

Relax pollution-control enforcement and reduce the economic impact on American raw material operations.

Influence Public Opinion by:

1. Publicizing that in 1971 the President's Committee on Environmental Quality pointed out that the steel industry has spent twice the average percentage of capital spending as manufacturing and three times the average of business and industry combined.
2. Publicizing that steel plants are 90% effective in pollution control now, and that the remaining 10%

is prohibitively expensive. Creating awareness about the financial impact of government objectives and regulations. See Exhibit A (p. 294).

3. Publicize other impacts on society. Choose popular examples such as government limits on sulfur content of fuel which causes a drastic reduction in the use of coal and an increase in gas and oil consumption, complicating the already critical energy crisis. See Exhibit B (p. 295).

Influence Congress and EPA by:

1. Bring more E.P.A. and other officials to selected raw material facilities for pollution control tours.
2. Push for unusually favorable tax treatment on investment in pollution control devices. For example, Japan is granting liberal tax and other concessions for pollution control investments, with a special depreciation schedule that permits the write-off of one-half the purchase price of the equipment the first year.

Administration

Establish a special Raw Material Coordinating Office in Washington, D.C. Each component of the "Strategy for Survival" would have a top manager directing activities toward specific goals according to specified timing. Financial cost of the office would be prorated on the basis of company capacity.

Upon conclusion of the presentation, the chairman of the meeting called a 15-minute recess, after which members of the meeting were to return for discussion and evaluation of the "Strategy for Survival."

STUDENT PROBLEMS

1. Analyze the strategy considering current conditions, and formulate

changes which reflect your position on the situation.
2. Take one of the companies in Table 8C—2 and do sufficient research to interpret the impact of the industrywide strategy on your company.

Exhibit A

How Pollution Abatement Creates Pollution

The following, a study submitted to EPA by AISI, shows how much added power is needed for complete removal of electric furnace emissions.

It also shows how much pollution is generated by this power as compared to pollutants removed at the steel plant.

	Direct Furnace Evacuation System	Canopy Hood System	Closed Shop With Total Building Evacuation
Gas cleaning system	Baghouse	Baghouse	Baghouse
Fan volume, ACFM	155,000	600,000	515,000
System pressure drop, in H2O	14.5	14.5	14.5
Fan horsepower	274	1956	1682
Dust collected, lbs./ton steel	22	2.4	0.023
Electricity required			
KW hrs./ton steel	2.55	18.2	15.7
Kw hrs./lb. dust collected	0.12	7.7	680
Generation of electricity			
BTU required/ton steel	29,000	207,000	178,000
BTU required/lb. dust collected	1320	87,000	7,750,000
Emission of new pollutants at power plant			
Lbs. per lb. of electric furnace dust collected	0.003	0.17	15

In terms of the dust collected, it takes nearly 6000 times the energy per pound of dust to remove the last trace as it does to remove the first major portion of the pollutant.

It's also noteworthy that collection of the last trace of visible emission for the case illustrated results in a negative environmental impact in that 15 pounds of new pollutants (SO2, nox and particulates) are legally emitted at the power generating station for every pound of electric furnace dust controlled in the final increment.

Source: *Iron Age*, November 22, 1973

We have only one proven source of energy for now...and the next 400 years

OIL

Known U.S. oil reserves are being depleted. The search is on for new discoveries. Meanwhile, we grow more dependent on imports.

GAS

Our known gas reserves are dwindling fast. Unless new sources are found, demand may soon exceed existing domestic supply.

SOLAR

We would need perpetual sunlight. As yet, there's no full-scale, practical way to store energy from the sun.

COAL

There's enough U.S. coal to last an estimated 400 years. Based on BTU values, coal makes up 88 per cent of the nation's energy reserves. Greater utilization of coal can keep our lights burning and our industry humming both now and for centuries ahead.

WIND

Too primitive. Windmills still work in some areas, but they're unreliable and inefficient.

Coal is vital to steel

Coal is needed in vast quantities to make steel. And the steel industry is a large consumer of electric power, of which coal is by far the largest source. Bethlehem mined more than 14 million tons of coal last year, and most of this was used in our own blast furnaces.

What about surface mining?

Surface-mined land can be reclaimed responsibly under present state reclamation laws. About 20 per cent of Bethlehem's coal is surface-mined while more than 50 per cent of the nation's coal is surface-mined. If unreasonable restrictions on surface mining are enacted, the nation may be in trouble. That includes all coal users. And steel users. And all who use electric lights and appliances would feel the pinch.

WATER

Only about 4 per cent of the nation's energy comes from water power. And we've already harnessed our best sources.

Why restrict our most abundant fuel?

We favor legislation that will make it possible to meet the nation's energy needs and reasonable environmental goals at the same time. More coal is needed now to avert steel shortages. Why cut coal production by unreasonable restrictions on surface mining at a time when all other energy sources—except coal—are in critical supply?

NUCLEAR

Promising but slow in developing Atomic power *may be* our best bet in years to come. Nuclear power today contributes about one per cent of U.S. energy.

Bethlehem

BIBLIOGRAPHY

American Iron and Steel Institute. "Annual Statistical Report," 1952, 1963, 1972.

American Iron and Steel Institute. "A Selected List of Articles-Speeches-Studies on the Steel Industry," Education Department, AISI, April, 1973.

American Iron and Steel Institute. "Steelmaking Flow Charts," Public Relations Department AISI, 1972.

American Iron and Steel Institute. "Third National Seminar Steel Industry Economics," 1972.

Black, Ira G. "EPA-Industry Palaver Dissolves into Open-end Mumbo Jumbo," *Iron Age.* June 28, 1973, p. 19.

Broude, Henry W. *Steel Decision and the National Economy.* New Haven, Connecticut: Yale University Press, 1963.

Burn, Duncan. *The Steel Industry 1939-1959.* London: Cambridge University Press, 1961.

Cathey, Paul J. "Labor Goes Right for the Jugular in Drive on Multinationals," *Iron Age.* May 24, 1973, p. 49.

Cort, Stewart S. "Free Trade? Yes—But." *Nations Business.* July, 1971, pp. 54—57.

Cort, Stewart S. "The Steel Industry Today and Tomorrow," American Iron and Steel Institute.

Drapkin, Michael K. "Japan, Long an Exporter of Steel to U.S., Now is Building a Mill in New York State," *The Wall Street Journal.* June 20, 1973, p. 38.

Fenninger, Laurence, Jr. "World Trade In Steel . . . Past, Present and Future," Committee on International Trade American Iron and Steel Institute.

Hogan, William T. *Economic History of the Iron and Steel Industry in the United States.* Lexington, Massachusetts: Lexington Books, 1971.

Hussey, Allan F. "Steel's Mettle," *Barrons.* July 2, 1973.

Kaufman, Kenneth A. "Steel to Congress: Save Us from Imports-Again," *Iron Age.* June 14, 1973, p. 17.

Manners, Gerald. *The Changing World Market for Iron Ore 1950—1980.* Baltimore, Maryland: Johns Hopkins Press, 1971.

McManus, George J. "Don't Sell Phase II Short, Asks USWA's Abel," *Iron Age.* February 3, 1972, pp. 45—48.

McManus, George J. "Steel's Utopia: New and Better Problems," *Iron Age.* May 31, 1973, pp. 28—29.

Pounds, Norman J. G. *The Geography of Iron and Steel.* Tiptree, Essex: Anchor Press, 1966.

Tracy, Eleanor Johnson and others. "Facing the Future in a Troubled Industry," *Fortune.* July, 1971, p. 13.

Case: Powerite Tools, Inc.: A Strategy for Market Retention

With the accumulated background on Powerite, a student can evaluate a strategy preferred by executive management of the company.

In the Chapter Two case, a serious problem of foreign competition developed for Powerite Tools. On page 000 decisions were made which were not unanimous among executive management, nor were they full supported by the outside shareholders. The two chief executive officers disagreed with a proposal to compromise on quality to reduce costs while implying to customers that the product continued to have the same utility and reliability.

Many shareholders supported the quality cutting proposal and considered the executive decision to be idealistic and indicative of management not giving sufficient priority to profits and an adequate return on investment. The alternative introduced by Charley Bobzin would have resulted in a very low-cost base and minimal losses to foreign competition in 1975 and future years.

The purpose of this case is to formulate a strategy for the company utilizing the background information in Chapter Two and the added details given here. Foster and Huggins are motivated to succeed in proving the wisdom of their decision.

STRATEGY COMPONENTS

Components of a master strategy are identified in the following paragraphs.

Marketing

POWERITE LINE   The marketing position for the firm in 1975 is as follows:

1. Quality for the average unit retail price of $49.95 (see Figure 2C−1, p. 46) is the best in this range of the market, particularly after correction of minor defects publicized by Yamasuki.
2. As incentive to retain and promote the Powerlite line, the profit margin for distributors is increased to $11.00 from $9.00 per unit assuming retailers will buy for $35.00. This would give a margin of 46% to distributors, whereas retailers would retain a 43% margin.
3. Powerite has a proven record for service and honoring guarantees promptly. Proximity of manufacturing and warehousing operations to distributors and retailers is a marketing asset, and the "Buy America" concept will support this advantage in campaigns.

To realize the full potential of this market position, vice president R. A. Bobzin was allocated $.40/unit of predicted total increase in cost of $1.25/unit. According to forecasts in late December, 1974, this would mean a budget addition of about $280,000 for sales respresentative incentives, advertising, promotion, and other ideas needed to attain better sales objectives for the Powerite line of hand tools.

QUALITITE LINE   The contract with Mooney Mart calls for 150,000 units in 1975, and general sales manager Ken Resnick is confident of not losing this customer despite the Minoni-Ware offer. A concession in price to $17.00 from the $20.00 in the agreement is given in his sales forecast, but he has confided to Charley Bobzin that he expects to get at least $18.00 in the negotiations.

To expand the volume of this line and reduce unit costs, Mr. Resnick has opened discussions with AMSELL and ELCHEAPO. The year-end forecast for 1975 included 31,000 units to these potential buyers, but this is also less than the probable volume. Ken Resnick is expecting to achieve at least 100,000 units in sales to the two companies.

The primary reason for keeping estimates low is that Marketing looked bad when Powerite Tools found out about the attempted penetration by Minoni-Ware, Yamasuki and other less important companies weeks after discussions had started. Also, no attempt had been made in previous years to develop new customers for the Qualitite line. If sales can exceed both volume and unit price estimates in 1975, the confidence of top executives in marketing management will be improved. This "harmless" deception was regarded as a department secret to be given to Charley Bobzin as a surprise present next year.

Operations

Four main goals concern manufacturing in late 1974:

1. Squeeze every cent out of costs

for both product lines to a maximum of $21.25 for Powerite (based on 700,000 units) and $13.00 for Qualitite (based on 180,000) units.

2. Achieve quality represented in the advertising. This involves: (a) procedures for quality control and (b) modifications in assembly and parts specifications to counter Yamasuki criticisms.

3. Rectify industrial designs to permit use of contoured grips, modern looking housings, and thicker colored cords. Regarding housings, top management does not want "cheap plastic solutions".

2. Schedule changes and report on purchasing requirements after receiving final sales forecasts.

Bob Allan does not feel that increased inspection and testing is practical nor justified based on historical performance. His management team is putting together a workable proposal to eliminate these capital expenditures and the estimates which added $1.25 to the $20.00 in costs experienced in 1974.

Finance and Administration

Central purchasing is trying to negotiate discounts on purchase orders flowing from manufacturing. As soon as the list for materials and purchased components of both lines is complete, the manager will conclude contracts. He has had to develop at least two alternative sources for each item on the preliminary lists in order to retain negotiating position in the event there are delays in final decisions on designs yet initial orders must be placed.

A crash study is underway to determine which is lowest in cost:

1. Two suppliers; lower volume per supplier; opportunity to double order quantity with both suppliers in the event of emergency; 50% reduction in safety stocks of components.

2. One supplier; greater volume and unit discounts; 60-day notice on inability to supply and damages on contract performance failures; 25% increase in safety stocks.

Accounting is collecting the data from all of the departments. The December 31, 1974 estimates are:

	1975 Sales & Profit Objectives	
	Powerite	Qualitite
Average Price/Unit	$ 24.00	$ 17.00
Units Sold	701,000	181,000
Net Sales	$16.82 million	$3.08 million
Pre-tax Margin/Unit	$ 2.75	$ 4.00
Pre-tax Profits	1.93 million	724,000
Companywide Performance:		
Net Sales	$19.90 million	
After-tax Profits	1.35 million	
% of Sales	7%	

STUDENT PROBLEMS

1. Place yourself in the position of Dick Foster and Joe Huggins. Pull together a strategy with the following:
   a. January 1975 components.
   b. 1975 components (remainder of the year after a.).
   c. Long range components to protect the growth potential of the business.
2. Lay out a network model with a time line (target dates within the periods involved) for a, b, and c in Problem 1.
3. Compare the content of your strategy with possible counter-strategies by Minoni-Ware and Yamasuki, and devise contingency components in your strategy.

Computerized Techniques for Strategic Decision Making

Complexities in business forcing greater use of the computer in top level decision making are discussed. Fundamentals needed by the executive are identified. Potential applications of the computer are explored, and the strategic decision center is described.

The primary objective of strategic decision making is to achieve company goals, and this usually means maximizing profits. The complexity of major decisions has increased sharply during the past decade, and this has motivated use of the computer to identify decision alternatives and experiment with the alternatives before commitment to a course of action. The following factors have contributed to complexity:

1. *Social Constraints.* Companies have options which include: (a) voluntarily complying with the needs of the community whenever possible; (b) complying because of government regulations that are costly to ignore, or (c) implementing a policy of avoiding and delaying while publicizing gestures of social responsibility. In large corporations a variation of all three could be in action at the same time due to the individual perogatives of top executives and the absence of a company-wide policy for social responsibility.

2. *Multinational Operations.* Most American companies have some involvement in international business. Market opportunities, sources of raw materials and energy, and financial transactions are among the motivations for operations outside the United States. The complexity of controlling international business involves: (a) strategic variables that are less predictable than in the United States; (b) the

9

intensity of global competition in all markets, even the United States; (c) multiple currencies, most having floating values or restrictions on flow across borders; (d) employees who think differently than the American executives and direct their activities; (3) long distances and the need to control logistics such as inventories, lead times, damage in transit, etc., and (f) communications dependent on verbal and tele-exchanges and extensive executive travel.

3. *Government Regulations and Influence.* The free society protected by natural systems of control and a laissez faire government policy described by Adam Smith in his *Wealth of Nations* has disappeared. The government taxes, regulates, protects, buys, influences, and provides services. Its politicians play the game of power and trade for support in elections and struggles for survival. Lobbyists maneuver to get bills passed which could seriously hurt some businesses and result in a windfall for others. In this atmosphere, companies and industries implement strategies based on selection from complex sets of assumptions and alternatives.

It is feasible to cite other strategic and operating variables that have significant impact on the profits of a specific company, particularly with an accelerating rate of technological change and the existence of double digit inflation. All of these factors have caused many firms to redesign information systems, forecasting methods, planning techniques, and organizational relationships, and to introduce the computer for top-level decision making.

This discussion on computer uses by executive management *excludes* common applications in: (1) payrolls, invoicing, and other repetitive functions required in running a business; (2) control systems for cash, inventories, quality, scheduling, personnel deployment, and transportation, and (3) aids to managerial decision making below the level of executive management such as linear programming for raw material usage and network models for research projects.

COMPUTER KNOWLEDGE REQUIRED BY EXECUTIVE MANAGEMENT

There are three important elements involved in using the computer for decisions by executives at the top of the organization:

1. Technical knowledge of statistical and quantitative techniques.
2. Business knowledge accumulated by top management.
3. Creative programming knowledge that optimizes 1 and 2.

Very few people have adequate knowledge in all three elements. Even with the best training in college, modern information systems, training to update techniques and applications, and business experience in applying quantitative methods, it is doubtful that a top executive can keep sufficiently current to design computer programs that optimize in problem solving. Usually it would take someone who regards the computer as a fascinating avocation. On the other hand, the computer analyst who has the technical knowledge usually does not have the business acumen of a top executive.

To achieve the objective of having computer programs that increase the probability of correct decisions, a communications link must be established between executive management and computer analysts. This can best be accomplished by creating a position(s) that makes a computer expert part of the support staff for executive management. This individual refines knowledge of business problems through day-to-day contact, and begins to see the array of techniques and computer capabilities in terms of top management.

Figure 9—1 shows that some of the burden still remains with the executive. Efforts to design computer programs cannot be a one-way conversation. Each has to overlap the other's field of expertise. As in other professions with important responsibilities such as medicine, it is an obligation for top management to be informed about modern methods and use these developments where applicable.

One complication for executive management in the late 1970s and early 1980s is that computer analysts with a good overlap in Figure 9—1 will be scarce. Executives who depend heavily on the computer expert to tell him how to improve the accuracy of decisions will be hurt because this specialist is difficult to find and retain. For periods of time an executive may be left to personal resources. As a result, business executives with ambitions to gain executive management positions will improve their probability of success if they strengthen their capability in quantitative problem solving and computer know-how.

The Role of Information in Model Building

Model design and computer program construction is dependent on reliable information. The task of collecting, sorting and selecting this information is awesome when you consider:

1. *Interrelationships.* Developments in social constraints, multinational operations, global operations, global competition, government regulations and influence, inflation, technological advances, and specific company situations affecting one another.

Figure 9–1. Overlap of Understanding

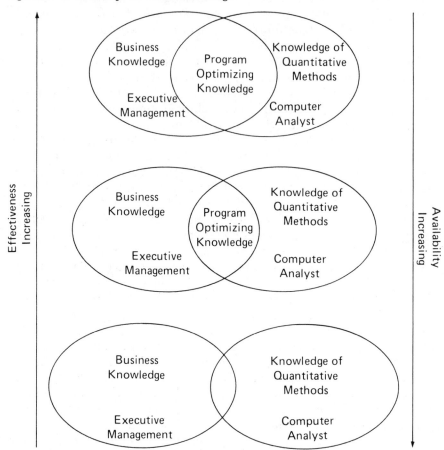

2. *Volume of Information.* Data, judgments, opinions, forecasts, confidential releases, reports, news in periodicals, memos, letters, summaries, and so on can bury an executive in paper.

3. *Full Development of Alternatives.* Identification and definition of all decision alternatives including content, tangible and intangible costs and benefits, and probability of outcome within the range from complete success to total failure improves the possibility of making good decisions.

A modern executive must strive for the knowledge of all the alternatives available while guarding against being inundated by information flow. Major corporations are making progress toward this goal by having the facilities and support personnel to computerize greater portions of the decision-making process. The small business owner usually does not have the resources to respond with computerized techniques.

During the next decade, it is likely that people in executive management will not know technical details about the way in which a computer system works and the nature of the software and hardware involved. The executive might regard the details as interesting, and they could provide "gamesmanship material." However, with the presence of computer analysts, absence of this technical knowledge will have little impact on the executive's performance.

Expectations about the Computer by Executive Management

Let us list what the computer is expected to do for a person in executive management:

1. Through advanced information storage methods and refinements in information selection processes, a computerized MIS will give an executive the information needed. This may be too much or too little based on individual judgment, but the system is available and can be adjusted.

2. Interrelationships can be identified through cross-referencing. The computer does not forget, and it can be programmed to relate previously stored information with new developments to clarify the impact on selected strategic and operating variables. This significantly improves perspective in the decision-making process.

3. Alert systems are important. Some developments have zero or only minor implications for a company's plans and strategies. However, tactics by competitors, government rulings, technological advances, and so on can require immediate revisions. The speed of the computer and the systems involved in the Strategic Decision Center concept discussed later in this chapter, can earn millions of dollars from prompt action by management.

4. Simulation and optimization models provide the opportunity to experiment with a decision and make mistakes on the computer rather than in actual operations. The simulation models in common use today are deterministic, and will dutifully report back what happens, given what data has been put in the program. Less frequent use is made of Monte Carlo simulation which takes into account the probability of strategic variables occurring and optimization models that search for the best plans by automatically adjusting operating variables.

5. An executive desires, in addition to good decisions: (a) specific numerical values to justify the decision he is making, and (b) an image as a competent member of executive management. Realiz-

ing these desires can be aided by programs tailored to the problems of an executive which reoccur frequently, application of standard programs available on the system such as regression analysis for forecasting, and accessing portions of master models such as simulations.

6. Many qualitative components of business problems cannot be transformed to a language the computer can understand. However, this excuse is overused in companies to disguise inadequate knowledge of what can be done. While each situation is different, many seemingly complex situations composed of qualitative information can be simplified through numerical weighting systems.

Figure 9—2 summarizes what executive management should expect to get from computer systems. This diagram is a reference for present and future executives to determine their company's current position.

Figure 9—2. Expectations for Computer Assisted Decision Making

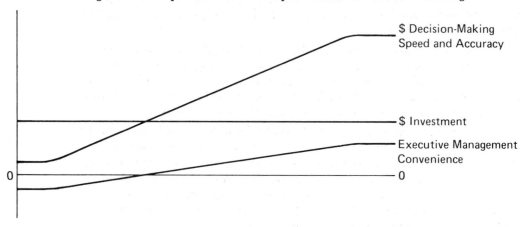

POTENTIAL APPLICATIONS

Table 9—1 is an example of a deterministic simulation of operations for Division Z of a company during the next 12 months. It can be seen that there are millions of calculations involved in building this model.

The experimentation that preceded agreement on the structure and variables probably required billions of calculations. In the 1950s the task would have been uneconomic and consumed months of work by an immense staff. Today, much more time is spent on experimenting and deciding which relationships and methods will provide the most reliable model. The actual calculations will take only a few

Table 9-1. Example of a Simulation Model for the Long-Range Plan of Division Z

Tier	Content	Qualitative Methods and Comments
1. U.S. Economy	Nationwide forecast of economic activity by an independent source, XYZ Economic Analyses, Inc.	Nationwide growth rate is weighted by independent variables used below to obtain a "relevant" forecast for the company.
	Alert System:	MIS monitors current news to find any important forecast which deviates from those of XYZ.
2. Industry	Market forecast of each product or product grouping to make up the industry in which Divison Z competes.	Approach for each product or product grouping: Multiple correlation, every other year sampling for the past 10 years: exponential smoothing forecast of correlations to Year Six of long-range plan; most suitable forecasting method for each independent variable including input-output analysis (data permitting). Independent variables fixed from previous experiments; different forecasts of independent variables can be substituted for adjustments.
	Alert System:	MIS monitors assumptions for forecasts; an example of a deviation would be: A revision of the economic forecast by XYZ is higher (or lower) than previous estimates.
3. Company: A. Operations	Sales Forecast in Units and Dollars; Derivation of Gross Revenue.	Approach for each product or product grouping; Exponential smoothing forecast of historical participation in the market weighted by

Table 9–1. continued

Tier	Content	Qualitative Methods and Comments
		sensitivity analysis to design revisions (quantified), price/cost/quantity fixed relationships, and brand loyalty assumptions. Program iterates to identify ideal participation between the constraints of minimum production required to service the market and practical capacity.
	Alert System:	MIS monitors for: Competitor developments coded for degree of impact on the forecasts; new transportation possibilities also coded, and so on.
	Forecast of Division Z Costs.	Budgets are developed by departments and fed into the computer after revisions and approvals. Variable cost differentials are calculated on a fixed formula basis.
	Consolidation	Individual forecasts are integrated into a Division Z position for each of Years Four, Five, Six, and an average for the three years.
B. Resource Allocation	Executive Decisions on Level of Plowback: a. Zero-Closing down b. Maintenance-Phasing out of business c. Historical expansion—Keeping pace with competitors. d. Aggressive expansion—Increase market participation.	Opportunity loss analysis is integral in the iteration to identify gain in pre-tax profits if capacity constraint is removed.

minutes on the computer. Keep in mind, however, that the specific software (computer programs) may require weeks of effort and thousands of dollars to prepare.

Most of the model can be used by functional managers below the level of executive management, and these managers can access segments of the model for their purposes. This improves the pay-out on the investment in building and updating the model. The total expense of the Division Z simulation could be $100,000±. While a cost/benefit analysis usually substantiates the expenses involved, most of pay-out is intangible as compared to other company investments.

Refer to Part 3B of Table 9—1. The modern executive will have a computer terminal with a cathode ray tube display screen in the office. The individual can then call up portions of the model, particularly Part 3B, for review and to jot down key numbers on expansion opportunities, growth rates, geographic coverage and so on. This enables the executive to:

1. Compare the performance of Division Z with its industry to identify discrepancies, and be informed in discussions with top management on the current as well as future profit situation.

2. Experiment with plowback of available capital to divisions, subsidiaries, and acquisitions. These experiments refine the investment priority system because major company strategies emerge from the grouping of investments by product and geographic area. By trying various combinations of capital allocations and determining the different growth rates resulting from the simulations, strategies can be formulated with a higher probability of success.

3. Explore ideas for outside sources of capital to realize more of the investments exceeding the company's minimum profit standard or an essential part of a company strategy. Terms and costs of the required capital vary, and a system of priorities is established through further use of simulation or optimization models.

4. Compare optimum alternatives derived from quantitative techniques with intuitive judgments by the executive. These might include assessments of managerial ability, hunches about competitors, and similar qualitative inputs reflecting his accumulated experience.

The ease with which an executive can gather concrete data for evaluating alternatives is an important advantage. The accuracy of estimates and the probability of good decisions is significantly improved by spending some time at a terminal and using the various programs provided by the computer. The advantages of this approach are illustrated in the following examples.

A Specific Example[1]

In Spring, 1973 Telex Corporation testified in a suit against IBM in Tulsa, Oklahoma that many of its problems were related to the pricing practices of that company. IBM countered by accusing Telex of pirating its employees and paying sizeable cash bonuses for trade secrets. The suit by Telex against IBM was the culmination of a market battle that began in the late 1960s.

Telex was one of several independent producers of tape and disc drives, printers, and other peripheral equipment that could be used on IBM computers. In 1970 an IBM study showed that 13% of its computers were "contaminated" by such equipment and that inroads into its traditional markets would get worse in the 1970s without corrective action.

By the end of that year IBM's counterstrategies were hurting Telex. First, a disc drive was introduced which performed essentially the same functions as an older model but at a substantially reduced price. Second, it offered two new long-term lease plans at substantial discounts. This reversed the trend. In fact, the 47 year old president of Telex testified that, "Before these moves we had the image of a growth company that was going to go to the moon. As the pressure (from IBM) built up, financing became expensive. It was hard to recruit new employees, and almost a feeling of hopelessness pervaded the company."

The basis of the IBM strategy was revealed by additional testimony. A financial analyst (playing the role of the computer analyst described earlier in the chapter) used computer modeling to determine the effects of potential IBM actions on the ability of the smaller company to get financing. The model indicated that the tactics involving the disc drive and long term leasing plans would reduce Telex volume. This would inhibit Telex from raising funds because it would "be seen by the financial community as a company with marginal viability." Details of other tactics in the counterstrategy evolved from experiments with the models.

Another Application

Methods for quantifying elements in projects fulfilling a company's social responsibilities can be the basis for a weighting system to adjust the minimal rates of return on these projects.

A logical approach to deciding on a course of action would be to

---

[1] *IBM Loses Antitrust Action for First Time As Telex Corp. Is Awarded $352.5 Million.* The Wall Street Journal, Tuesday, September 18, 1973.

have an executive concerned with social investments present the possibilities for the weighting system to a computer analyst. Two objectives are involved: (1) develop concepts that can be consistently applied to future as well as current investments, and (2) design a program sufficiently simple to enable executives with a broad range of backgrounds to use it regularly.

The computer analyst would, as a first step, work with the executive to identify the qualitative factors that would place an IMSR (investments to meet social responsibilities) properly on the priority list. After exhausting the possibilities for qualitative variables, the second step would be to assign weightings to signify importance. For example, one extreme would be compliance with a state pollution regulation with heavy fines for infraction. Less priority might result from a regulation that has no teeth in it. Voluntary investments with high visibility might have a heavier weighting than those with no public relations value. One heavy weighting might be reserved for projects that are the proper, honorable thing to do and which the executive judges to be a defensible decision.

The third step is experimentation with the computer program design. A link with existing plans is necessary to identify the impact of IMSR's on rate of return. The task of designing a program is likely to be difficult when both simplicity is required as well as an impartial, accurate system. Extra time to finalize computer programs to run flawlessly is essential to sidestep unnecessary objections to the underlying concepts. Communications between the computer analyst and the executive should be as frequent as practical to avoid the latter getting out of touch with the refinements.

When the concept for rating an IMSR is ready, the sponsors must take the fourth step, obtaining approval from the other members of executive management plus the board of directors. Figure 9–3 illustrates the steps and possible content of this use of the computer.

Still Another Application

Some executives use systems that establish a potential rating for subordinate managers on a zero to five scale for several performance evaluation criteria. These include college training, business experience, verbal communications, written reports, performance ratings on assignments, personality, physical appearance, and other appropriate measurements for the next level at the top of the organization. The method is comprehensive and probably is practical for executives with several subordinates only if information is computerized.

Goals	Factors to Gain Priority	Weightings Given To Factors Increasing Cost and Visability				Approval of the System
Generally Applicable Concepts	1. Legal Requirement	10	8	6	Experimentation	
	2. Probable Law in the Future	8	6	4	Executive Management Input	
Simple Implementation	3. Strong Community Pressure	8	5	2		
	4. Desirable for the Community	7	4	1	Experimentation	
Steps	1	2			3	4

The concept compares current actual ratings and total score against potential. Computer analysts have designed programs for timeshare terminals in executive offices to handle the system and receive data to keep it current. The confidential nature of the ratings are protected by passwords, call numbers, and various types of individual identifications such as voice, palm prints, and so on.

Executives above a certain level in the organization can use the program and establish both potential and current actual scores for each of the people reporting to them whom they judge to be promotable. A cathode ray tube display screen can give executives: (1) an individual's position; (2) overall comparisons with others, and (3) comparisons by criteria. Within a few seconds, and without requiring several personal files or exposure of the fact that the executive is interested in a person, the individual can pinpoint problem areas, identify development needs, and decide on candidates for new openings.

Concluding Comments on Applications

In the instances cited, the computer system becomes a tool to improve decision making. It makes no decisions. It only takes volumes of facts and opinions and, if the model is constructed properly, it sorts, calculates, and displays relevant alternatives in sufficient detail. Often a better decision results than if the decision were based on less information and more intuition. In addition to improving the quality of decision making, the use of computerized techniques can sharply decrease the time needed to reach a conclusion. This relieves pressure on executive management.

What *can* be accomplished and what actually occurs in most companies is often disappointing. John Hammond of Harvard University cites overcomplex models as a source of difficulty and stresses the use of models tailored to individual needs rather than attempting division- or companywide models. It is his contention that corporations will evolve toward successful use of more complex decision-making and problem-solving systems when a high percentage of executives in a company apply their own computerized techniques on a daily basis.

Another point of view is held by many managers involved in corporate planning. They contend that, while the evolutionary approach is logical, it could take too long to begin utilizing techniques that are needed and feasible now. Mistakes, often very serious ones, are expected from accelerated use, but the result will be realization of the computer's potential and a net gain in profit performance.

THE STRATEGIC DECISION CENTER

A wide and expanding range of computer equipment is available to members of executive management. However, this hardware is costly both in terms of an investment and operating expense. In order to utilize computer equipment most effectively, it should operate as a system rather than as individual pieces of equipment. In some companies this has led to centralizing equipment in a room called the *Strategic Decision Center* (SDC) and creating the optimum in a decision-making environment. In addition to remote terminals with cathode ray display screens, the following equipment can be included in the SDC.

1. *Computerized Display Screens.* Operating data from current cash position to workers in the company's Belgium plant can be shown in seconds by using a terminal in the room and calling up the data from the computer. The information can be displayed in tabular form on a screen that is usually 3 x 5 feet in size.

A pioneer in developing SDC's and refining equipment use, particularly in obtaining large clear graphics from computers, is Information Management International Corporation, New York. A diagram of their "CompuChrome" system is shown in Figure 9–4.

2. *Noncomputerized Boards or Screens.* These devices are also less complex and much less costly than an IMI system. For example,

Figure 9–4. IMI's CompuChrome

Computer-Controlled Large-Image Color Graphic Display

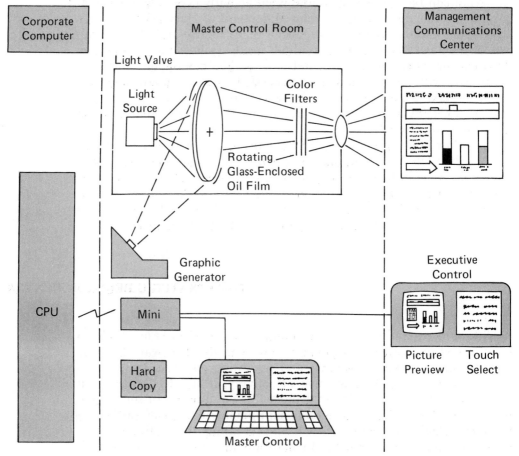

an English trucking company's board displays the location of every refrigerated unit at all times any place in Europe through radio signals. The system pays for itself in added business because clients in the Common Market countries try the firm for a low backhaul rate before contacting other carriers who have less control of their vehicles. This has led to a sharp increase in overall business and improved profits during a two-year period.

Dual display screens can be used permitting use of slides to compare new proposals with previous estimates, actual performance against forecasts, one investment's impact on profits versus another competing for available funds, and other strategic information. Rear screen projection from a control room retains the decision-making environment. Figure 9–5 illustrates the possibilities. It is feasible to ob-

Figure 9–5. One Approach to Strategic Decision Centers

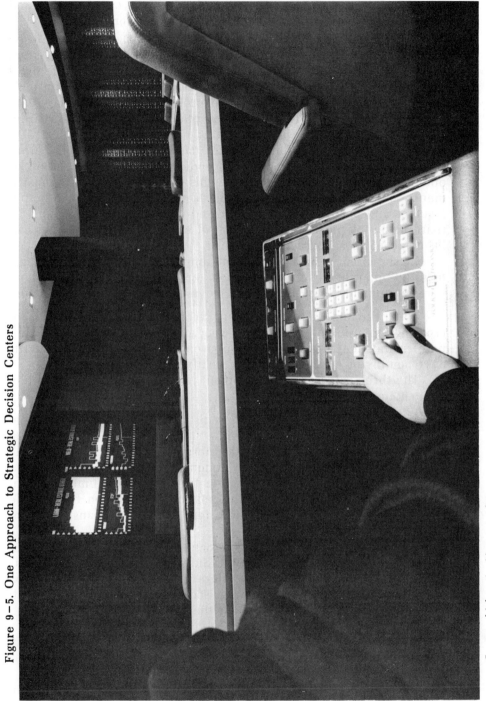

Courtesy of Information Management International Corporation. 425 Park Avenue. New York. N.Y. 10022

315

tain any slide at any time rather than depend on a certain order, and overlays can be programmed for emphasis and comparisons.

3. *Video Cassette Players, Organizational Design Boards, Closed Circuit Television, and so on.* Some visual display equipment is not expensive compared to electronic display screens but is an integral part of the SDC system. For example, a video-cassette of a division's previous presentation on a proposed project might reveal important facts on changes made to improve acceptability, or clarify the reasoning behind approval or disapproval.

A version of an opaque projector has been developed to permit key executives to experiment with redesigning the organization or other operating variables. Components such as divisions, departments, and key positions are like pieces of a puzzle. They can be put together and portrayed on a screen. Individuals make suggestions by rearranging the pieces. To avoid loss of a good idea, photocopies can be made of those designs with merit.

Closed-circuit television is sometimes included to give management an opportunity to see operations without having to visit a plant, view equipment ideas, pilot plants, advertising campaigns, and so on.

The principle and justification for investment in a SDC is increasing the probability of making good decisions. The value in profit performance may not always be apparent, but even tangible benefits over months of operation usually justify the money spent.

The three categories of equipment just described will be supplemented in the future by:

4. *Picture Telephones.* ATT has installed and tested phones that show the speaker on a screen while talking. By 1980, 27 American cities will likely have service with intercity conference calls feasible between most of them. The extra dimension is most important to executive management. Some executive travel will be eliminated, but the primary advantages are in the possible substitution for cathode ray tubes, the quality of communications, and direct transmission of data.

Service to Europe and Japan can be expected in the 1980s, depending on success in the United States. At present, the screen is about five inches square and registers in black and white. ATT experts do not foresee color, but larger screens with sharp pictures will be part of the expanded system in the future.

The Pioneer in the SDC Concept

Information Management International Corp. (IMI), based in New York City, specializes in designing systems to provide speed and quality in the flow of information to top levels of management. This company is originating new concepts that avoid mountainous piles of paper in the process of providing adequate facts and estimates.

"Today, information is primarily a management concern, for information technology is beginning to provide management with its most important set of tools. Those who know how to use information tools will take the lead; those who misuse, underuse or do not use information technology as a management tool will fall behind. If one can argue that this has always been true, then it can be argued that its importance may be second to none for management during the 70s, 80s and beyond."[2]

The IMI Concept

Traditionally, managers have relied on paper reports in making decisions. Increased use of computers for data gathering has led to immense volumes of paper printout for the executive to evaluate and interpret. Data in this raw form has caused frustration and has been a major obstacle in the transition to efficient, computer assisted managerial decision making.

There is a need, therefore, for presenting the data in a more streamlined form to allow management quick access, improved comprehension, and full development of alternatives in order to select a course of action. Two of the major means of exhibiting data are tabular and graphic form, the latter permitting improved identification of trends and better portrayal of the dynamic nature of business.

IMI's aim is not only to design the strategic decision centers, but to also conceive and manufacture the tools necessary for such rooms. IMI contends the traditional boardroom or conference room has many shortcomings and eliminates this type of room at client companies in favor of a "controlled environment." Incorporated in their center are paperless reports on slides and a relaxed atmosphere.

More specifically, IMI believes that a conference room with the traditional table is a hindrance rather than a help in decision making. The table does not encourage interpersonal communication and could encourage a "we versus them" attitude. To eliminate this structured atmosphere, IMI uses swivel chairs with the central focus of attention being a display screen. To complete the idea of a controlled environment, thement quick access, improved comprehension, and full development of alternatives in order to select a course of action. Two of the major means of exhibiting data are tabular and graphic form, the latter permitting improved identification of trends and better portrayal of the dynamic nature of business.

[2] Executive Summary, Information Management International, Inc. This is an excerpt from a company release.

IMI's aim is not only to design the strategic decision centers, but to also conceive and manufacture the tools necessary for such rooms. IMI contends the traditional boardroom or conference room has many shortcomings and eliminates this type of room at client companies in favor of a "controlled environment." Incorporated in their center are paperless reports on slides and a relaxed atmosphere.

More specifically, IMI believes that a conference room with the traditional table is a hindrance rather than a help in decision making. The table does not encourage interpersonal communication and could encourage a "we versus them" attitude. To eliminate this structured atmosphere, IMI uses swivel chairs with the central focus of attention being a display screen. To complete the idea of a controlled environment, the presenter has fingertip ability to control lighting and audio level, as well as the content, speed, and order of the presentation as shown in Figure 9—5. Since the presenter is in full control of the situation and there are no paper reports, the individual can proceed one step at a time without having the flow of ideas interrupted by someone leafing through a report.

Tools for the SDC Concept

Slides designed by IMI occupy the full 3 x 5 foot screen (single or double), are presented in graphic form, and are consistently color coded to increase perception by the viewer. They feel that this method aids recognition since management becomes used to always seeing revenues in red, expenses in green, projections in white, and actuals in yellow.

See Table 9—2 for a summary of the IMI systems and the capability of the console controlling the graphics. The latest and most advanced system developed to date is called "CompuChrome" (see Figure 9—4), and it is the first to be tied into not only a minicomputer, but also the corporate CPU.

The Decision-Making Process

IMI believes that group management is the way of the future and that effective group management is a direct result of a proper atmosphere. Therefore, the design of the strategic decision center (SDC) is a vital element to the success of this new management concept. Contrary to the traditional boardroom concept, spacious seating arrangement with comfortable swivel chairs will allow any person to become the focal point of attention. The company believes that many architects have yet to catch up with the new business environment and are still designing old concepts into modern buildings.

Before any firm can effectively employ a management information system similar to IMI's, they must first create a data base. This

Table 9−2. Chronological Development of IMI Systems

PHASE 1 :   THE TOUCHMATIC SYSTEM
1. Utilizes rear screen projections. Allows for presentations to be given in a lighted room.
2. Two or more synchronized slide projectors, as well as other items such as 16 millimeter film projectors.
3. Full audio control.
4. Control panels located at either lecturn, or at a console near the presenter.

PHASE 2 :   THE TOUCHTRONIC SYSTEM
1. Has all of the components as the TouchMatic system.
2. Random Accessibility — Allows for easy retrieval of information previously stored in the system. Makes this system more dynamic by allowing certain segments of the presentation to be skipped and recalled at a later time. Permits past programs to be used in aiding executive comprehension.

PHASE 3 :   THE COMPUCHROME SYSTEM
1. All the basics listed in the above two systems.
2. Does not rely upon a film base, as do the other two systems, but instead utilizes computer generated graphics.
3. Utilizes a mini-computer to aid in the random access feature. Once a graphic model has been introduced into the system, any time span for that model can be accessed almost instantaneously.
4. Hard-Copy printouts of computer generated displays are available. Permits review of the graph at a later time, and eliminates the necessity for the executive to rely upon his memory.
5. Picture preview, from the executive control panel, allows for the presenter to insure upcoming data to be that which was intended.

---

data base must reflect the actual elements needed for decision making by the firm's management. It is a synthesis of all internal operations data, plus the relevant factors of their business environment. A process of condensation, filtration, and summarization eliminates extraneous information. This data base is intended to be tailored to the level of management viewing it. Lower and middle management may require different components in their data base than would upper management.

Reactions of Selected Users

First National Bank of Maryland employs one of the basic systems produced by IMI, the TouchMatic System. The system is used for reporting purposes by top management and by the marketing department. The control room is centered between the firm's conference room and the executive dining room to allow presentations to be given in either room. First National prefers to discuss each slide fully before proceeding to the next slide and, therefore, their type of reporting does not need random access capability.

Bristol Meyers in New York has been using their TouchTronic system for three years. The vice president of planning was initially skeptical due to the costs involved, but the system has proved itself in his opinion. The company feels the most desirable characteristic is random access capability. At meetings where many division presidents are giving reports, if one person is late, the individual's presentation can be postponed. They are also pleased with the paperless reports, because the focus of attention is exclusively on the slide being shown.

IMPLICATIONS FOR THE ORGANIZATION

Key executives will be able to plan, organize, implement, and control through use of computerized aids for decision making. This could lead to centralization of power in the firm if computer capabilities are focused on a headquarters SDC. However, decentralizing computer facilities to permit decentralization of the organization and decision making utilizing the methods discussed in this book is economically feasible. Figure 9–6 gives a point of view in Robert L. Hicks' "Developing the Top Management Group in a Total Systems Organization."

To take full advantage of modern management systems some

Figure 9–6. Potential Shift in the Organizational Structure

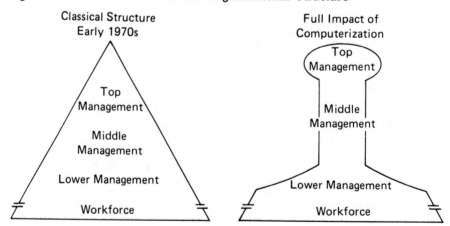

Fundamental Techniques in Planning and Strategy Formulation

changes are certainly going to occur. The disappearance of many staff jobs is likely to result as computers are put to full capability. Some positions will be downgraded to superclerical jobs, and technicians to keep equipment operating could become critically important for the company. Computer analysts may be centralized in a department headed by a corporate vice president, or integrated into the organization by being assigned to executives in top management. Titles, salaries, and places in the organization will reflect these changing roles in the decision-making process.

In addition to a new configuration in the organization, fewer personnel will be required for a given scope of operations. As systems are "debugged" and become reliable, certain jobs will be handled safely by computer controlled equipment.

CONTROL AND EVALUATION

Technological advances in the office of an executive and the strategic decision center are aimed at improving profit performance by the company while complying with both laws and social responsibilities. If this is not the result of these expenditures, then it is essential to carefully analyze the system and determine what is wrong. Figure 9–7 shows four diagrams illustrating the theoretical probabilities of advanced equipment.

The potential problem areas are:

1. The basic information is not adequate, relevant, and/or screened sufficiently. The executive and computer analyst are not getting what is needed to either define all of the alternatives open to them or know enough about the alternatives to make the best decisions on approach.

2. Computer programs utilizing statistical and quantitative methods, coding and weighting systems, and various kinds of hard- and software may not be designed to provide the executive with the input needed for good decisions. For example, the simulation may not accurately simulate a division's operations and could actually mislead management.

3. The executive is not communicating the business aspects of the problem to the computer analyst. The gap between each other's capabilities is so great that investment in computerized problem-solving is wasted.

Executive management should always beware of overly complex systems. Fewer tiers to a model and fewer quantitative relationships in a tier may often produce the accuracy needed, and minimize cost

Figure 9-7. Schematic Possibilities with Advanced Equipment

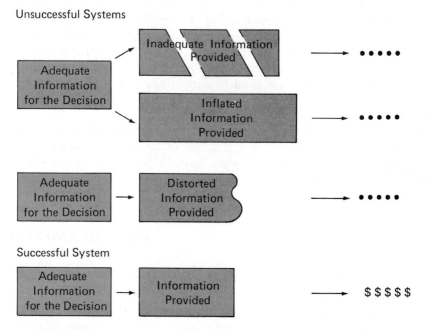

and frustration in usage. It is essential to avoid the temptation for unnecessary gadgetry and excessive refinements in software.

When problems surface, corrections are required. Research is necessary to assure that the proper steps are being taken. Each possibility must be explored through isolating and testing while other variables are controlled. Unfortunately, tensions build in an organization under problem conditions. There is a tendency for company politics and emotions to enter the process of rectifying the situation.

It is feasible that the executive is using poor judgment and that the hard- and software are not the source of the difficulties. Computer equipment will help an executive, but terminals and display screens in the office, the strategic decision center, and so on cannot convert an inferior manager into one of executive management caliber. Given the proper information and full development of alternatives, the optimum plan or strategy should be identifiable. However, some executives are not capable of making consistently good decisions.

Computerized Control Systems

Managers sometimes make forecasts and recommendations or take other actions for personal, rather than company, objectives. As a result, companies require executives to report on the accuracy of previously made: (1) forecasts; (2) investment evaluations; (3) personnel recommendations; (4) organizational changes, and (5) plans and strategies.

Considerable caution should be exercised by management during the design phase of a computerized control system of the five categories of actions, and later during input of data, to insure that information is not improperly altered before or after being inserted into the system. Reports have traditionally originated from the individual in the organizational entity that made the proposal. It follows that interpretation and assessment of problem situations are often biased justifications with questionable conclusions from the viewpoint of executive management.

Now, with the aid of good control programs, it is feasible to test actual developments against forecasts and assumptions through use of the computer. A program is designed for a major decision and the MIS automatically feeds the program appropriate data on a regular basis (for example, quarterly). Deviations from expected performance are identified to accomplish the following:

1. Analysis can assist members of executive management to correct their own errors, constructively develop subordinates, and minimize the possibility of the same mistake being made twice.

2. Early knowledge of a problem often permits counterstrategies, adjustments, and similar actions to optimize profit possibilities under current conditions. Without an evaluation system regularly monitoring performance, realization that a problem exists may come too late.

3. Sources of decisions that are consistently right or wrong are isolated by the system. Individuals who are over their head and frequently make the wrong decision or calculatingly distort facts and forecasts, will have trouble getting approval for future projects as a result of the system.

The advantage of an automated system for decision control and evaluation is that quantifiable elements in the decision are relayed to executive management without reliance on lower levels of the organization to supply the data. This free flow of information usually influences divisions and/or individuals to be as accurate as possible in preparing estimates and forecasts.

Qualitative elements in the five categories of actions also play a role. An automatic system will serve to alert top management about profit performance, sales, costs, and so on. However, there may be other factors involved such as an unexpected innovation by a competitor not expected at the time of approval. Executive management will logically have a reporting system that permits input of both quantitative and qualitative factors.

Refinement of Computer Programs

The executive and the computer analyst can potentially improve their performance by learning from each business situation. These situations normally fall into two categories: (1) the exchanges occurring in model building, testing, and early usage stage, and (2) the analysis resulting from the control and evaluation stage. A conscious effort is needed to gain experience from making mistakes and finding that your judgment was partially or wholly wrong. With experience over a period of time, the mistakes are fewer and judgment is better. Computerized control systems facilitate this process.

SUMMARY

The complexity of decisions is increasing because of: (1) social constraints; (2) multinational operations; (3) government regulations and influence, and (4) several other strategic and operating variables having an impact on specific companies such as technological innovations. This has caused increased dependency on the computer in redesigning information systems, forecasting methods, planning techniques, and organizational relationships.

In addition to the complexity, interrelationships and volume of information can overwhelm an executive. Executive management needs computerized techniques to develop the full range of possible alternatives in making decisions. Speed and accuracy are important, and companies not making full use of the computer are jeopardizing the shareholder's investment.

To become a member of executive management in the future, an executive must have knowledge of statistical and quantitative methods, and must remain current on developments that will improve the probability of making good decisions. It is not, however, critically important that the executive have programming knowledge. The most important point is the ability to communicate business situations to a computer analyst in a way that results in programs improving overall decision making.

The computer should assist in: (1) selecting, storing, and relaying information; (2) interrelating information to apply to specific problems; (3) alerting executive management to developments with implications for plans and strategies; (4) simulating decision alternatives; (5) solving repetitive problems, and (6) sorting qualitative information through numerical weighting and coding.

Review Figure 9–3 and the simulation example in the chapter.

The strategic decision center is an economic means of concentrating the aids to decision making. While key executives will have important equipment in their offices such as terminals with cathode ray tube screens and electronic display boards, the SDC gives all of executive management access to concise information pertaining to their responsibilities. Efficiency increases with this approach to formulating decision alternatives, and with the opportunity to hold conference calls on a picture phone, know the exact position of a division, possibilities for reorganization, and so on. IMI is a pioneer in SDC design.

One result of computerized techniques being used by top management is the increasing importance of the computer analysts. Titles, salaries, and rank in the organization will reflect their vital role in profit performance in future years. Many lower and middle management staff jobs will disappear.

Control and evaluation of techniques and resulting decisions are necessary to be certain that expenditures for equipment and expertise are producing the expected performance. Automatic systems permit: (1) correction of errors, development of subordinates, and minimizing of possibilities that the same mistakes will be made twice; (2) early knowledge of problems and opportunities arising from plans and strategies in action, and (3) identifying sources of decisions which are consistently right or wrong. The process of control and evaluation should lead to better combined performance of the executive and his computer analyst.

DISCUSSION QUESTIONS

1. Do all the factors that have contributed to the complexity of major corporate decisions in the mid-1970s have the probability of continuing in the future?
2. A communications link is needed between executive management and computer analysts. Do you fully agree?
3. The strategic decision center is an economic means of developing decision alternatives and selecting the best of the possibilities. Discuss.
4. How do you envision the following using the SDC?
   a. Board of Directors
   b. Executive Management
   c. Middle Management

5. Is the traditional board room obsolete?
6. Discuss the problems an organization can encounter using advanced concepts for decision making. Is there another source of difficulties?
7. Considering the material in Chapter Five, how do you see the developments in computerized strategic decision making affecting middle management?

SUGGESTED READINGS AND BIBLIOGRAPHY

Bierman, Harold. *Quantitative Analysis for Business Decisions*. Richard D. Irwin, Inc., 1965.

Brand, David. "I am a Computer," *The Wall Street Journal*. June 28, 1973, p. 1.

Chambers, John C., Mullick, and Smith. "How to Choose the Right Forecasting Technique," *Harvard Business Review*. July-August, 1971, p. 45–74.

Davis, Gordon B. *Computer Data Processing*. McGraw-Hill Book Co., 1969.

Emshwiller, John. "Eleven Named in Trade Secret Thefts at IBM," *The Wall Street Journal*. July 2, 1973, p. 4.

"Every Manager's Dream: His own Computer," *Iron Age*. January 8, 1970, p. 25.

Feltz. "Corporate Management's Tool of Control," *Personnel Journal*. June, 1969, pp. 459–462.

Ferguson and Jones. "Computer Aided Decision System," *Management Science*. June, 1969, pp. 550–561.

Gershefski, George W. *The Development and Application of a Corporate Financial Model*, The Planning Executives Institute, 1968.

Hammond, J.S. III. "Do's & Don'ts of Computer Models for Planning," *Harvard Business Review*. March–April, 1974, pp. 110–120.

Harvey. "Are Total Systems Practical?" *Business Automation*. June, 1969, pp. 72–76.

"IBM Loses Antitrust Action for First Time as Telex Corporation is Awarded $352.5 Million," *The Wall Street Journal*. September 18, 1973, p. 3.

"Japan: Computer Users Buy Time in the U.S.," *Business Week*. September 15, 1973, p. 76.

Lindsay, Franklin A. *New Techniques for Management Decision Making*. McGraw-Hill Book Company, Inc., 1963.

Lipperman, Lawrence L. *Advanced Business Systems*. American Management Association, 1967, Research Study #86.

"Management Communications Centers," *Information Management International Corporation*, New York.

"Management Decision Center," *Banker's Monthly*. July, 1969, pp. 34–35.

Miller, David W., and Martin K. Starr. *Executive Decisions and Operations Research*. Prentice-Hall, 1960.

"Perils of the Data Systems," *Business Week*. June 5, 1971, pp. 62–63.

"Predicting Earnings with More Precision," *Business Week.* June 30, 1973, p. 52.

Sanders, Donald H. *Computers and Management.* McGraw-Hill Book Co., 1970.

Westin, Alan F., and Michael A. Baker. *Databanks in a Free Society.* Quadrangle, 1973.

"Where Minicomputers Do All of the Job," *Business Week.* July 14, 1973, p. 38.

Plans, Strategies, and Reality

This is the last of five chapters on planning and strategy by top executives. Causes of problems are identified, particularly management competence. Changes and refinements in operating variables to improve performance, and the impact of personnel on the interpretation of strategic variables are summarized. The transformance of losers into winners is also discussed.

Plans and strategies never go exactly as conceived. Sometimes the variance is minor and no major problems arise which keep a company from achieving its goals. More often than necessary, however, planned growth is threatened. Figure 10–1 illustrates the range in actual performance as compared to plans, and uses an overlap to clarify that what is satisfactory for one company could be unsatisfactory for another more aggressive firm.

10

Figure 10–1. Individual Companies' Measures of Performance

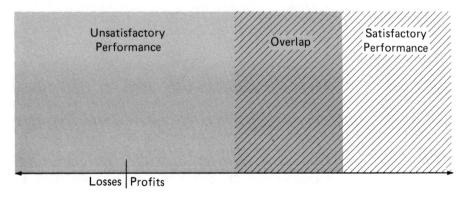

Reality can be defined as including two basic categories of results:

1. Plans and strategies on target or exceeding expectations.
2. Plans and strategies off target, or with predicted performance unsatisfactory to management.

Let us examine some of the reasons for the second category. The discussion may also give us some indications why many companies can consistently perform in the first category.

MANAGEMENT COMPETENCE

According to the Peter Principle,[1] people rise to the level of their incompetency. In corporations only a few executives have the overall competence to reach top management and have a good probability of doing a satisfactory job. However, more than the few are allowed to hold positions well above their capabilities. When this happens, creative problem solving and general effectiveness is at a minimal level, and the performance of the firm is below average.

Poor judgment can seriously damage a company. It can happen dramatically in a short period of time such as in the LTV case in Chapter Eleven or slowly such as in the Curtis Publishing case in this chapter. It is often difficult to pinpoint exactly when a manager consistently misses the optimum alternative. Inferior, but not obviously bad decision making, continues indefinitely in many cases. It follows that, as the number of people performing poorly increases, the slide toward breakeven operations or worse quickens.

In addition, when career paths are being blocked by people who are not respected, many good executives will leave a company. As a result, if this type of managerial problem is not corrected, the remaining managers are not adequate for an extended period of time.

Monitoring Performance

The possibility of having managers incapable of carrying out plans and strategies is always present. Therefore, it becomes important to know why, where, and how to make changes. Table 10—1 gives a framework for starting the process of change.

Some managers never seem to be aware of what is actually

[1] Peter, Laurence J. and Raymond Hull. *The Peter Principle: Why Things Always Go Wrong.* Morrow, 1969.

Table 10-1. The Stratigraphy of Monitoring Performance

Organizational Level Monitoring Performance	Organizational Level Whose Performance Is Being Monitored	Measures of Performance
1. Board of Directors (Shareholders sometimes place pressure on the Board for action.)	Executive Management	Earnings per share. Rate of growth of earnings, net worth, sales or others. Consumer and social goals. Other specific goals. Profit centers for divisions, departments, regions and subsidiaries.
2. Executive Management	Middle Management	Profit centers for regions and departments. Cost Centers. Specific assignments by job.
3. Middle Management	Lower Management	Cost Centers. Specific assignments by job.

happening. Feedback is not understood, encouraged, nor fully utilized. Predictable disappointments become surprises, and crises involving major decisions must be resolved in a desperation atmosphere. These are signs of incompetence and indicate an important fundamental of managment should have been applied and was not.

The monitoring level of the organization given in Table 10-1 must have tangible evidence before taking action to terminate managers for incompetence. Firing someone in an important position is a serious step for the company. It involves several kinds of risk, the most significant of which is causing insecurity among the competent managers whom the company wishes to retain. If an executive is fired without demonstrable proof of omissions or wrong doing, others can identify with the individual and protect themselves by starting the process of finding another job. Poor performance that can be measured and is easy for others to see, eliminates doubts. Figure 10-2 summarizes the concept of managing by defined objectives such as suggested in the chapters on strategy and planning.

With adequate measures at all levels in the organization and systems for monitoring performance against the measures, it is not necessary for executive management to find suddenly that the company is in serious trouble. Through timely corrections, adjustments, and replacements top management can keep their company on target.

332

Figure 10-2. Managing by Objectives

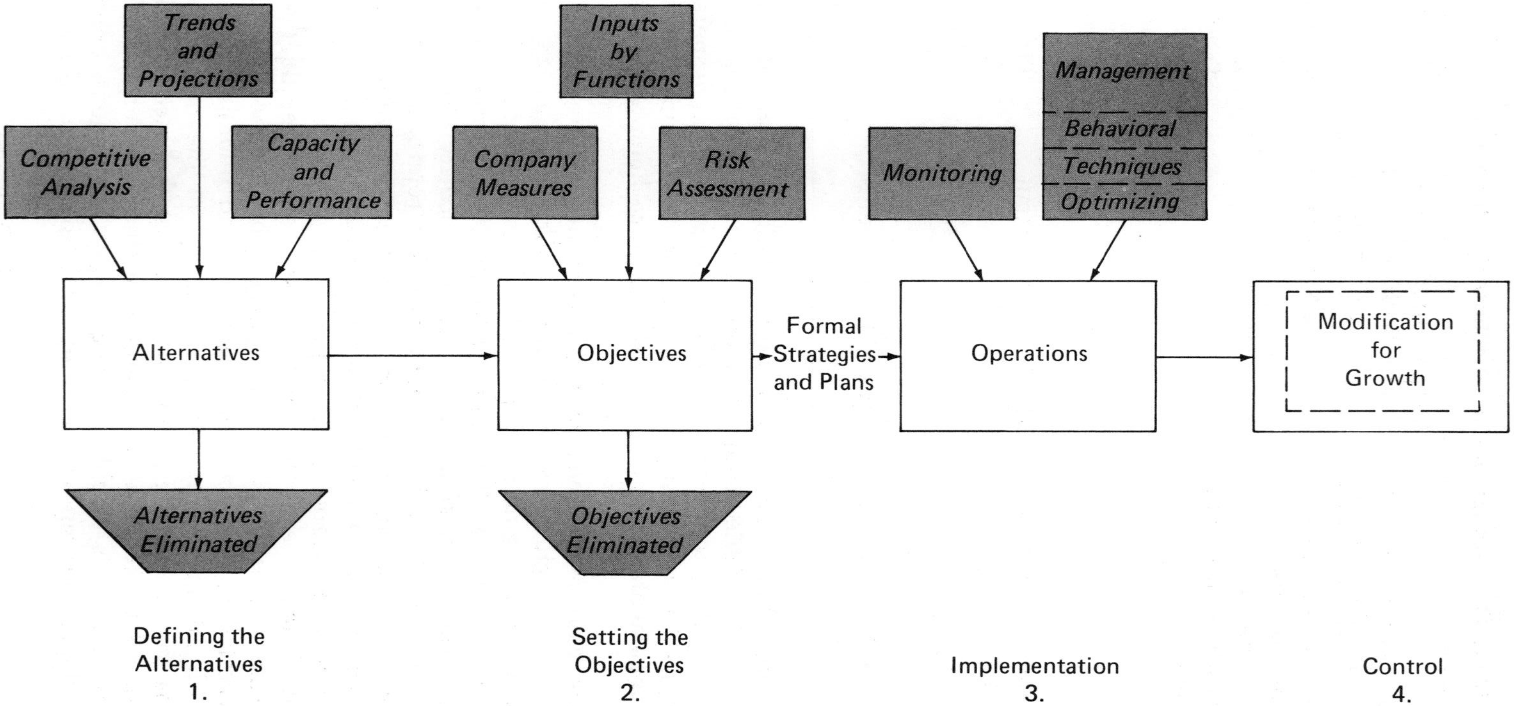

Competitive Analysis

Trends and Projections

Capacity and Performance

Alternatives

Alternatives Eliminated

Inputs by Functions

Company Measures

Risk Assessment

Objectives

Objectives Eliminated

Formal Strategies and Plans

Monitoring

Management
Behavioral
Techniques
Optimizing

Operations

Modification for Growth

1. Defining the Alternatives

2. Setting the Objectives

3. Implementation

4. Control

However, some executives do not like to be measured. Psychological and political reasons have led companies to the point where they do not regularly compare plans and strategies. This situation usually leads to substandard performance by managers and the possibility of dismissal.

Some executives agonize over the decision to fire a subordinate. It is an unpleasant experience, and they recognize it is a crushing blow to the individual regardless of cause. Personal discipline to take action is needed to avoid costly delays, and the rationale used most frequently in these instances is, "sacrifice one for the good of many."[2]

Organizational Structure

Not all problems traceable to poor management are related wholly to incompetent individuals. People must work together effectively, and it is possible that the existing company organization will not enable this to occur. Examples include marketing management needing prompt deliveries to retain customers, but not having authority over finished goods inventory. Or, the head of the management information system might have the responsibility for installing a total company system but have inadequate computer capacity and be unable to obtain funds for changes and expansion.

Complications can arise in correcting organizational design problems. New top management could recognize the situation but two factors might prevent them from making adjustments: (1) higher order of priority changes in operations, and (2) the judgment that the operating changes will be implemented most effectively without the disruption of changes in the organization. A conscious decision is made to accept the potential effects of organizational problems in order to have a higher probability of improving performance in the short-range.

It is important to remember that managers can be very effective in their normal responsibilities, and not be experts in the design of organizations. In other words, they are competent in their jobs, but may not recognize the need for a change in reporting relationships or application of new concepts in the organizational structure which could solve some of their "people" problems. *As one progresses up the organization, specific functional capabilities become less important and skills in planning, formulating strategy, and organizational design become more critical to success.* For this reason, the Peter Principle (rising to the level of one's incompetence) is a real possibility for top executives if they do not make a serious effort to develop top management skills to supplement functional competence.

[2] There are multiple sources. This phrase is used often in business.

Hiring and Development Practices

In Chapter Two we discussed the responsibility of executive management for developing competent personnel for important positions in the company. Figure 10–3 illustrates the general points of entry by managers into the firm, and the possibilities for development while with the firm.

Once policies for hiring and developing management are set and programs conforming to these policies are functioning, some qualitative points become important.

Figure 10–3. Manager's Entry and Development in the Firm

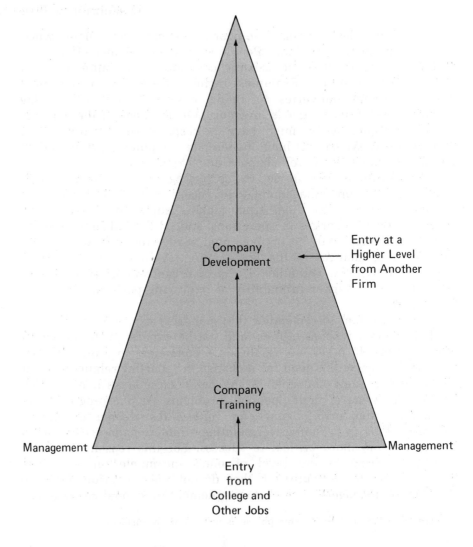

Fundamental Techniques in Planning and Strategy Formulation

1. At the point of entry, standards and procedures must be established and practices followed to permit the company to be competitive with other firms in employing the best people. This means compensation, benefits, assignment locations, and so on, but also includes systems to reach candidates that might not contact the company through normal channels. Whether college recruiting at the lowest level of entry or skilled executive recruiters at the top levels, a conscious effort is required to find people of top caliber for all positions if the company is to realize its growth potential.

2. Executive management should monitor resignations, terminations, and replacements to attain a goal of upgrading the quality of managers with each turnover. If a company does not do this it is possible to drift toward incompetence and mediocrity of performance. Most executives do not use the technique of having a system that matches an individual's potential against actual performance. As a result, a company could develop problems with quality of management slowly over a period of years and be incapable of responding to business opportunities.

3. Promotions of managers who appear to be very talented are often accelerated. In some cases they are pushed ahead too quickly and are not permitted to gain the experience needed at upper levels of the organization. After initial accomplishments, they leave serious problems for their successors to resolve. In this case the company induces the Peter Principle.

4. Managers with potential for top-level jobs may not be coming through the system. If a policy of the firm is to promote exclusively from within, unsatisfactory performance may be traceable to hiring and development practices. Most companies must look outside for special expertise, and it may be just as necessary to seek managers from other firms to retain the quality needed for growth. Some ideas for development of managers were mentioned in Chapter Two. It is advisable to establish these programs with the understanding that benefits are difficult to recognize except consistently good profit performance and even then, other reasons will likely be cited for progress.

PROBLEMS FROM OTHER OPERATING VARIABLES

Variables other than personnel have a major impact on performance. It can readily be seen that excellent labor relations can have a positive effect on profits or, on the other hand, the consistent failure of suppliers to provide necessary materials will have a negative affect on profits. Discussed in the following sections are less obvious variables that can be equally important and can strongly influence the quality of management.

Information and Communication

Management has a high probability of making good decisions if it is adequately informed. Chapters Five and Nine dealt with systems and techniques for the flow of information which are becoming increasingly important because of global competition, government encroachment on free enterprise, responsibilities to the community and the consumer, and the dynamic nature of other strategic variables. A change in business environment can mean that the decision that was proper yesterday is the wrong course of action today.

Executive management must be certain that the company has an adequate information system to support all levels of the organization. In addition, individual managers also have the responsibility to create sufficient flows of information to enable them to perform satisfactorily. This involves some fundamentals that need to be identified.

Attitude Toward Communications and Feedback

Employees will communicate opinions, rumors, and suggestions as well as facts if he knows management wants to know what is happening in other departments and divisions, in the market, with suppliers and the other people and organizations with which they come in contact. In some situations managers can be overwhelmed with communications that are no more than gossip, and, as a result, they tend to overreact and discourage feedback on anything which is not substantiated. Experience indicates that this may place too fine a mesh on the filter, and important intelligence on new developments, etc. may be cut off from people who need to know.

Common sense at all levels of the firm will usually lead to the proper balance between trivia and important information. However, it is often prudent to set standards for desirable feedback and that which should be discarded. The individual passing on the information could be cautioned to accumulate details and related rumors until there is sufficient substance to notify management. Another approach is to create a focal point for feedback and allow this individual to make judgments on validity and importance.

At the executive management level staff assistants can condense, filter, and summarize feedback if given the responsibility and emphasis is placed on the work. This personalized system supplements the MIS and establishes an attitude at the top which is critical to informed decision making.

The management technique of making major decisions by the consensus of key executives, such as in Japan, is having an impact on how information systems are designed. One school of thought revolves around the SDC (strategic decision center) and collective decision making by the board of directors and groups of executives in rooms such as those described in the previous chapter. The other approach focuses on the individual, and display equipment for personal access in the office to computer stored data and "canned" programs that assist in planning, forecasting, and allocation of resources. Table 10–2 compares the advantages and disadvantages of the two systems.

It is probable that combinations of the two will exist in most companies. Certainly MIS for highly centralized organizations will support key executives with personalized display equipment to avoid: (1) excessive "button pushing" and (2) the necessity of having sophisticated computer knowledge. The economics of a major investment in the system can be seen more easily when it is for the important decisions being made by top management.

Table 10–2. Advantages and Disadvantages of Collective and Individual Systems

Systems for Collective Decision Making	Systems for Individual Decision Making
ADVANTAGES	
1. Concentration of talent for a decision.	1. Executive gets a system tailored to personal needs.
2. Informal environment for relaxed communications.	2. Better control of individuals asked to participate in the decision-making process.
3. Full system available to a member of top management for a key decision.	3. Proximity to personal files, surroundings, and staff.
DISADVANTAGES	
1. Potential disclosure of confidential information to company personnel participating in a decision.	1. Less perspective on the alternatives when only an individual and personal staff are involved.
2. Collective systems sometimes do not provide the individual executive with what is needed for various responsibilities.	2. Several individual systems are often more costly than a single system.
3. Group most capable of making best decision may be difficult to assemble.	3. Individual may be blocked from needed information due to steps to provide security to the system.
4. Inability of some groups to make a fast decision.	4. Formal "across the desk" environment.

Justification for an expensive MIS, for example, $2 million for the entire organization, is often more difficult if the shareholders and top decision makers want evidence of tangible cash return. Also, debugging the pioneer information systems for companywide operations has taken time, and this has provided skeptics with reasons for delaying approval. Decentralized organizations have information needs as great, or greater than those with concentrated decision making. Many more people are involved and, as previously mentioned, the quality of these executives is not always certain. MIS is critically important to upgrading the performance of executives whom otherwise would be mediocre.

A system working as it was designed can make up for many deficiencies. However, it will not overcome individuals who refuse to break entrenched routines and fail to adopt the new improvements.

Coordination

Visualize an executive at a specific place and time in the organization. The individual would have to coordinate with the following categories of people:

1. Intradepartment personnel including the boss.
2. Intrafunction, region or similar organizational component within a larger component.
3. Interdivision communication volunteered through conventional channels or outside these.
4. Top management contacts with themselves and other personnel in the company channels.

Mandates from higher management to coordinate will not guarantee effectiveness. It takes loyal, motivated employees working for competent managers in a well-designed organization to achieve the desired results.

Something happens when people work well together. It is a combination of leadership, communication, good morale, proper use of the information system, and factors such as interesting products, customers, suppliers, and so on. People enjoy working long hours and performance of the entire group improves because several of the success factors are in action at the same time.

Plans and Strategies

Unsatisfactory performance can result from formulating poor plans and strategies. If this stems from incompetence, personnel assignments must be changed and/or personnel terminated. If techniques are the cause, modifications can be made according to concepts mentioned in previous chapters. However, it is possible that these two potential sources of problems need not be changed and other factors could be involved.

Planning Techniques and the Background of Executives

Executives in key positions in the mid-1970s probably graduated from a university years before techniques currently being used in SROP and the long-range plan were in common practice. It is, therefore, necessary for top management to devise methods of narrowing the gap portrayed in Figure 10–4.

Figure 10–4. Narrowing the Gap

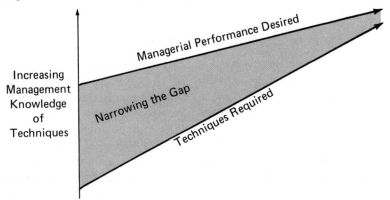

The most common approach to improving planning skills in business is learning by doing. No seminars or orientation meetings are held for the purpose of explaining methods expected to be used, specific goals, and other extra responsibility factors affecting reliability of the plan. A manager completes forms and meets deadlines set forth in instructions but without suggestions on forecasting and data gathering techniques or other refinements.

If the company, through some portion of the organization, takes steps to improve skills, the content of the plan is likely to be more reliable. This instruction takes time and money, however, and occasionally a dynamic business environment does not permit investment of either resource. Most often it is essential to provide management an opportunity to keep current techniques and develop potential capabilities. The alternatives to provide instruction include:

1. Meetings and orientation seminars at company facitities conducted by experts who are employees or consultants. The topics could range from a specific purpose to update a skill to continuous training.

2. Courses on topics related to company planning and strategy conducted at other locations such as universities and institutes that are either exclusively for company personnel or open to other applicants.

3. Programs designed for key executives involving cessation of company responsibilities for a sabbatical leave, concentrated courses, or similar tailored training.

The modern methods discussed in previous chapters need managers familiar with how to use them. A competent individual will strive for self-improvement, but executive management cannot depend on this occurring. Nor can it assume that self-training will focus on the correct topics. Some experts claim that the rate of obsolescence of management techniques is nearly as rapid as product obsolescence in the 1970s.

Refinements in Planning Structure and Techniques

Fine tuning the planning process is a continuing obligation of top management. This need is recognized in the Powerite Tools comprehensive case at the close of Part 2. It must be accomplished without participating personnel getting the impression that "the brass is always changing things." Minor adjustments can be introduced with each revision, and this will minimize the psychological impact.

It is better if top management assigns a staff assistant to analyze defects in the present methods and recommend the changes essential to retain SROP and the long-range plan as useful management tools. Accordingly, executives could determine that, for example, several adjustments might be desirable but, in their judgment, the complete revision might undermine support for planning within the company if implemented at one time. Often it is prudent to introduce major changes slowly over an extended period of time such as three years.

Techniques could require computers, other equipment, and/or data not available without excessive expenditures of time and money. Practical assessments must be made on the trade-off between information value and cost to avoid requests which require more detail than can be realistically used in management decision making. This is a serious diversion of company resources which places too much emphasis on the future and results in less accountability in day-to-day operations.

Sophistication of Personnel

Executive management should judge the degree of planning and strategy complexity company personnel can handle. This decision is a combination of capability and other developments happening at the same time such as organizational changes, government price controls, energy shortages, and similar stresses.

A progression of stages commonly found in companies in transition is:

1. *SROP only.* Getting operations under control and achieving the maximum efficiency possible.
2. *Extended SROP.* Encouraging participative planning by requesting an estimate for the year beyond the short-range plan. Parallel to this, executive management prepares similar estimates for comparison and a longer-range plan to guide capital allocations and other major decisions.
3. *Long-Range Planning.* SROP plus estimating the five-year outlook without details nor using sophisticated techniques. The information supports executive management resource allocation.
4. *Full-Resource Planning.* Covering all appropriate time spans, management at various levels prepares forecasts using MIS, computerized techniques, and thorough coordination.

Having adequate expertise in a company can be accelerated by: (1) training, and (2) employment of personnel from consultants, competitors, and so on. These people can act as a catalyst to improve understanding toward others in the company, and reliability can be greatly improved. If planning experts have a minimum of "people skills," it is still feasible to use the expertise for quality control, but support for planning by company personnel could receive a setback with excessive criticisms.

Timing in the shift from one of the four stages to another could be very important in achieving satisfactory profit performance. Business could grow in size, technology, geographic scope, and other dimensions, and require more details and preparation for the future. This judgment will depend on the competence of executive management.

Computers

The cause of many problems that executive management has with the use of the computer is GIGO, "Garbage in, garbage out." Simulations do not simulate and are misleading. Data is inadequate for the technique selected. The programmer/analyst designing the program fails to interpret the needs described by the manager.

Summarizing, this elaborate combination of equipment for storing, processing and reporting data does what it is told, and if the program or data input is bad, the output will sharply lower the probability of good decisions.

Part of the GIGO problem starts with upper management. They often have either a "black box complex", which takes various forms of resistance to computer use, or inability to communicate concepts directly or via the computer analyst to the computer. Executives may have the competence and the ideas, and they may even have some knowledge of quantitative methods. However, something does not happen and garbage goes in. Usually the computer analyst can keep extremes of poor communication from causing serious problems. However, when it occurs, executive management should not give up on the executive, the analyst or the computer. Some hard work will normally solve the problem.

Superior profit performance in the 1970s necessitates adoption of computerized methods. However, adjusting and fine tuning new programs to company needs requires management commitment and patience. In the end, the painful early stages are justified by the payout in tangible and intangible benefits in most cases.

STRATEGIC VARIABLES

Force Majeur is a clause that permits a party to an agreement to break the contract for reasons caused by events beyond his control. For example, the large oil companies refining crude oil used this clause to terminate all obligations to supply independent propane gas distributors in the 1973–74 heating season because of the Arab oil embargo. While most of these companies received nearly as much propane gas as before, the oil companies disclaimed any contractual obligation to amounts or timing specified in the original contracts.

This type of development covered in force majeur is out of the control of management. Whether it is a decision by the American or a foreign government, or a labor dispute at the plant of a supplier, the company is seriously crippled. Unpredictable events occur, and these are valid excuses for executives in reporting on their company's performance. The following points pertain to anticipating some of the strategic variables and both avoiding negative impact and taking advantage of opportunities.

Long-Range Plans

If long-range plans are based only on extensions of the existing business and a restricted examination of strategic variables, the process of making the forecasts will assist top management to a limited degree such as in the Vintage Enterprises case. However, a thorough analysis of success factors and outside influences that could affect each product line or service is fundamental in today's changing power structure in politics, energy, and materials. Also, while America has a definite lead in technology, competitors with viable new concepts are surfacing from all parts of the world. Consequently, executive management must attempt to estimate the business environment in which the company will operate in the 1970s in much greater depth than was required in the 1960s.

The techniques for planning several years ahead have been discussed in Part II, particularly the addition of formal contingency planning. The primary point in this discussion is recognition that not all setbacks need come as a surprise to the company. Perhaps the impact of some events cannot be avoided, but a stronger financial position through reduction of debt is only one example of several steps that can be taken to prepare for a problem. Simulation is very helpful in searching for the optimum alternative when management anticipates serious difficulties.

Pessimists, Optimists, and "Nothing-ists"

Personalities can have a major bearing on decision making within a company. Executive management must overcome confusion and conflicts created by differences between individuals and political intrigues. Also, interpreting forecasts of strategic variables when advised both by people who are regularly optimistic and by others who consistently see the worst is frequently a challenging problem. Both are accurate some of the time, and each set of conclusions could be based on identical facts and opinion. Management must seek a balance of input between pessimists and optimists.

Another factor is executives who are tempted to surround themselves with people who always agree with their bosses. This means these executives hear an echo, and the company is paying for paper pushing rather than bonafide counsel. Managers must make a conscious effort to keep the yes man out of important decisions.

WINNERS AND LOSERS

Companies that have had serious problems in the past often retain the "scars" of failure and do not respond to profit opportunities as rapidly or effectively as their competition. Executive management employed to "turn the situation around" encounter politics, lack of confidence and initiative, poor communications and, most serious, the attitude of a loser.

The words that describe a business loser are cautious, uncertain, wary, hesitant, supersensitive, highly critical, and defensive. Collectively, it means that a significant portion of the organization is not willing to take decisive actions to correct variances in SROP, formulate creative strategies, take risks in seizing opportunities, realign the organization, and so on.

Transforming a loser into a winner is not accomplished through a general formula applicable to every situation. Sometimes the transformation is never accomplished. Often years pass before there is significant improvement. Alternative approaches to accelerate progress toward optimum performance include:

1. *Clean House.* This approach assumes that a major portion of existing management must be fired to make room for executives who were not associated with past failures and will take the actions needed to convert the company into a winner. (NEM, Inc. in Chapter Four.)

2. *New Top Management.* This approach assumes that the majority of management can be motivated by a change in leadership at the top. Usually the new chief executive officer brings in a team of people compatible with his style of managing, and these company officers attempt to develop the support of those remaining in executive management and lower levels of the organization. (LTV in Chapter Eleven.)

3. *Reorganization.* It is assumed that the causes for previous problems are partly members of management and partly previous reporting relationships. A different organizational structure is created which eliminates those held responsible for past problems and creates new relationships for most employees of the company, thus eliminating reminders of past failures. (CDC at the close of Part I.)

Portions of these approaches have been applied to divisions and departments in order to improve performance.

Game Theory for Winners

The *zero sum game* assumes that an amount won is achieved by having an equal amount lost. When applied to management, it means that successes of individuals or groups must have a corresponding loss for some other component of the organization. In competing for the small number of jobs at the top and limited amounts of resources being allocated, managers under zero sum game conditions become political and self-centered rather than considering the overall performance of the company.

A more constructive attitude results from a *win/win* game. This concept is based on a dynamic growth environment in which an executive accepts the premise that successes of other individuals or groups will assist the individual's success. Growth creates the opportunity for rewards throughout the company, and it is essential to assist others rather than solely compete for promotions and presently available resources. The implications for improved communication and operating efficiencies are obvious.

The win/win game has improved performance in divisions of large companies and has not discouraged initiative. Its purpose is to create an attitude which acknowledges that one person can succeed without slowing the progress of others, and that more resources may be created from successes which increase the chances of others making it.

SUMMARY

Up to this point, chapters have dealt with those elements necessary for organizing and running a successful business. The company, however, operates in a dynamic environment and, no matter how good the organization and plans appear on paper, changes will occur which have an impact on the business.

Reality is defined as including two basic categories of results:

1. Plans and strategies on target or exceeding expectations.
2. Plans and strategies off target or with predicted performance unsatisfactory to management.

Some of the reasons that can cause a company to find itself in the second category are:

1. Lack of management competence to analyze data and make quick, accurate decisions.
2. Poor organizational structures that create inefficiencies.
3. Hiring and development practices that may not be adequate to assure that new managers are being brought into the system and provided with adequate training.
4. Other variables that can have impact on company performance including:
   (a) Poor utilization of information systems.
   (b) Management's attitude toward communication and feedback.
   (c) Coordination and handling of information.

In many cases unsatisfactory business performance can be traced to the development of poor plans and strategies. Provided plans and strategies are not caused by incompetent management or the use of poor planning techniques, other factors should be considered for action:

1. Upgrading management skills by bridging the gap in planning techniques through seminars, courses, and special programs.
2. Refining planning structures and techniques through fine tuning of existing plans.
3. Adjusting the complexity of the planning system to enable current personnel to handle the system. For example, if computers are being used, the input is critical to receiving meaningful output.

Management should continually examine the strategic variables on which the business plans are based and test the assumption being used to assure that the dynamics of situations have not undermined the long-range business plans.

A company continuing to suffer psychologically from previous failures sometimes requires drastic approaches to transform management attitude into that of a winner. Success in this objective is achieved when executives consider themselves in a win/win game instead of a zero sum game.

DISCUSSION QUESTIONS

1. Do you feel that in most cases managerial incompetence can be traced directly to the Peter Principle?
2. Assume you are an executive. What criteria would you use in terminating a manager reporting to you, and what help would you provide in relocating the individual?
3. Under what circumstances will management be reluctant to encourage constructive feedback?
4. Do you agree with the premise that collective decision making leads to better decisions in the business world?
5. What approaches would you use to increase management's knowledge of new business techniques?
6. How would you eliminate the GIGO (garbage in, garbage out) problem at the executive level?
7. Why is it more important to forecast strategic variables in the 1970s than in the 1960s?
8. What methods would you use in changing a company scarred with failures to one with high profits?

"Why Phillip Morris Thrives," *Business Week*, January 27, 1973, pp. 48–49.

"How Nestle Revives its Money-Losers," *Business Week*, January 27, 1973, pp. 44–46.

Haner, F. T. and Ford, James C., *Contemporary Management*, Charles E. Merrill Publishing Company, 1973. Chapter 12.

Humble, J. W. *Management by Objectives in Action*. 1970.

Kaufwan, H. *The Limits of Organizational Change*. 1971.

"Try Strategic Planning for Measurable Results," *Industry Week*, August 21, 1972.

Case: Problems at Curtis Publishing Company

A publishing empire established by the founder is destroyed by the managerial incompetence of his successors. The student is challenged to identify causes and to offer solutions that would have helped.

BUILDING AN EMPIRE

Curtis Publishing Company began in 1883, with the publication of a magazine entitled *The Tribune and the Farmer.* In the same year, a supplement to the *Tribune,* entitled the *Woman and Home,* was formed, and would later become the *Ladies Home Journal,* a completely separate publication. Cyrus Curtis, the founder of these magazines, based his success primarily on his ability to sell the product to advertisers, a knack which depended on strong circulation to the public. Curtis' wife was the editor of the *Journal* through 1889, when she relinquished the position to Edward Bok.

Expansion of the firm (it was in-corporated in 1892) occurred rapidly as Curtis was quick to purchase a magazine from another publisher entitled *The Saturday Evening Post* (1897). The purchase price was $1000, the low cost resulting from a lack of funds to continue operations by the previous owner. Again, Curtis concentrated on sales and the administrative end of the magazine, leaving the editorial job to George Horace Lorimer.

Because of a lack of competition from the start, these two magazines were especially sought after by advertisers. The content of the *Post* was primarily concerned with business and industry, and so, attracted the advertisers of manufactured goods. The *Ladies Home Journal,* of course, concentrated on the market attracting housewives, so competition between the magazines for advertisers was kept at a minimum.

Expansion in the different markets was one of Cyrus Curtis's basic objectives, and he continued this process as he purchased the *Country Gentleman* in 1911 for a price of $2 million, including both acquisition and reorganization costs. This was the advent of another new market for his company, because it attracted a completely new group of advertisers. The *Tribune and the Farmer* had been dropped after the success of the *Ladies Home Journal* had been assured.

These three magazines provided the basis for the Curtis Empire, which is claimed to have received 48% of the advertising dollars in the years through 1932. Shortly before his death in 1932, Cyrus Curtis relinquished the presidency to the *Post* editor, George Lorimer.

Basic Curtis Objectives

There were several basic stipulations that Cyrus Curtis left with his company. *First,* he stated that his company should not be sold except under extraordinary circumstances. *Secondly,* he left a group of owners, to be known as the Curtis Trust, which was comprised basically of Curtis' heirs and relations of Edward Bok, to control his objectives. (Edward Bok had married Curtis' daughter near the time of his joining the company). This group held effective controlling interest (30%), and would be responsible for keeping the operations of the company rather staid and conservative.

The Curtis program of expansion through reinvestment of company funds into the business was continued with each step policed by the Curtis Trust.

Another Curtis objective that had been with the company since its inception was to delegate full responsibility of the magazine's text material to each editor. This, of course, is a fundamental prerequisite for a successful magazine. Problems arise though when the audience, developing from text selection, and the market derived by advertisers do not match. Monitoring this activity is a function of top management, a fact that was later ignored.

Transition to Lorimer

George Lorimer's presidency (1932–1934) was an uneventful one. Profits and revenues continued their strong pace, as did the circulation of the Curtis magazines. Lorimer had been the editor responsible for the *Post*'s early success, and he continued to guide this publication as well as the company, during his three years as chairman of Curtis Publishing Company (1934–1937). He remained with the company until his death in 1937.

His major contribution to the firm was the establishment of the Curtis Circulation Company in 1932 as a wholly owned subsidiary. The basic task of the circulation company was the distribution of the Curtis magazines as well as magazines of other publishers. The circulation company was profitable from its inception through the 1960s.

Hidden Failures of Curtis Publishing Company

Walter Fuller, a Curtis Vice President, moved into the presidency upon Lorimer's promotion to chairman in 1934, and remained in the position until 1950. His inherited editor of the *Post* was to remain only until 1942 when he was fired for a controversial article entitled "The Case Against the Jew." This was a case of bad timing for such an article, but it proved fortunate for the *Post* as they promoted Ben Hibbs, the editor of the *Country Gentleman*, to the editorial position of the *Post*. He was very successful with the magazine and selected material which reflected the conservative American feeling prevailing after World War II.

Walter Fuller's decisions during his 16-year term (1934–1950) as head of Curtis Publishing played an important role in the company's downfall. At the beginning of his presidency, Curtis Publishing had three profitable magazines, *Post*, *Ladies Home Journal*, and *Country Gentleman*, as well as the Curtis Circulation Company.

New Competition

In 1936, increased competition for Curtis Publishing came in the form of two new publications introduced by other publishers. These magazines, named *Life* and *Look*, were directed at the advertising markets held by the *Post*. The strong position that the *Post* had held in the past was responsible for management's careless disregard of these magazines as a damaging force to their circulation and revenues. Only minimal attention was directed toward these magazines after their first issue had appeared and had been analyzed as being competitively weak. By 1942 though, the figures demonstrate the force with which these magazines entered the market. The advertising revenues of Time-Life company in 1936 were $9 million dollars, and in 1942 the revenues were $39 million. This compares to Curtis Publishing figures of $36 and $35 million for the same years respectively.[1] While Curtis revenues were floundering at their 1936 level, Time-Life took an aggressive stance and was able to surpass Curtis in advertising revenues within 6 years. Although *Look*'s performance was not as brilliant, it provided substantial competition through the 1950s and topped Curtis' ad revenues in the early 1960s.

Cyrus Curtis encountered similar problems upon entering the newspaper field early in his career (he quickly dropped this business), but he adapted much more readily to the situation. In order to defeat the competition, he bought out his competitors and kept the circulation for his own paper. His attention to competition was evident in all aspects of his business behavior, as this example demonstrates.

Still another form of competition was present throughout Fuller's presidency. This was the advent of television as an advertising medium. Once again, because of his belief

[1] Reprinted by permission of G. P. Putnam's Sons from *The Curtis Caper* by Joseph C. Goulden. Copyright 1965 by Joseph C. Goulden.

that television was a passing fad, he underestimated the potential of this new media and its input on Curtis. He believed that advertisers would soon be returning their dollars to magazines, especially as television rates began to rise. His analysis was proven faulty, as television, in the 1950s, became the most popular advertising medium. Competition from television became an industrywide problem, but many publishers fared much better than did Curtis Publishing Company.

Company Standing—1946

World War II was financially detrimental to the publishing industry, as advertisers directed their funds toward wartime production. The need for advertising during the period was small, as many resources were devoted to wartime products rather than consumer goods. Although Curtis Publishing Company had excellent profits during this period, as shown in Appendix B, the revenues of $39 million dollars in 1942 were small, especially in comparison to the $53 million in revenues taken in just by the *Post* in 1927.[2]

On the editorial side, World War II was beneficial in establishing the reputation and the image of the *Post*. Under Ben Hibbs, the *Post* earned recognition as the magazine which best professed the American spirit after the war, an asset promoting their circulation and leading to higher ad revenues for the magazine.

The economic expansion after the war greatly aided the revenues

[2] Ibid., p. 31.

of Curtis Publishing Company as well as the rest of the media. Companies that had devoted resources to the war effort were now concentrating on consumer products and were plowing money into magazines and television advertising very rapidly. A comparison of 1942 and 1946 (Appendix B) demonstrates the postwar changes. The Curtis revenues of $100 million in 1946 were two and one-half times the amount received 4 years earlier. Their decrease in net income though, from $4.3 to $4.03 million was a result of the costs of increased competition for the advertising dollar between the several types of media.

Both of the Curtis leading magazines were now showing great strength, as they were leaders in their respective categories, the *Post* through the number of ad pages per year, and the *Ladies Home Journal* in terms of its circulation.

Important Decisions

During the second half of Fuller's presidency, Curtis Publishing was capital rich and had the opportunity for several major investments. Four of their basic capital decisions are given below, and their other opportunities are described in Appendix A.

1. In 1941, because of a court ruling, the National Broadcasting Network was forced to divest itself of one of its two broadcasting networks. Curtis Publishing was offered the deal (1941), but they declined to invest the $3 million that was asked by NBC. Two years later, the network was sold for $8

million and became the American Broadcasting Company.

2. Three years afterwards, Curtis Publishing was offered the Columbia Broadcasting Network for a price of $10 million. Fuller and the Curtis Trust refused once again.

3. In 1944, Curtis Publishing was faced with the decision of either spreading its printing facilities geographically across the nation, or continuing their centralized operations, which were headquartered in central Philadelphia. The reasons for such a move would be a saving in transportation costs (not including mail costs) and also the plan would provide the opportunity for regional printing jobs that needed particular knowledge of the area. (Note the following story of TV Time.)

4. A decision that Curtis management accepted, and that was related to the three opportunities just cited, was the $40 million cash investment in their Sharon Hill Printing Plant located outside of Philadelphia. The plant could handle all of Curtis Publishing needs and still had excess capacity for handling other publishers' printing needs.

These four basic decisions represented the basic expansion choices available to Curtis Publishing Company between 1941 and 1947. The Curtis Trust and Fuller both held to the old strategic objective that profits should be reinvested in publishing. Therefore, they chose to build the Sharon Hill plant. Fuller's long-range plan for Curtis was to direct the company to the position of a vertically integrated firm, a completely self-sufficient unit that would not have a need to rely on outside suppliers. This plan rested on the assumption that if all operations were Curtis controlled, they could achieve better quality and cost control over their magazines and their company.

A major factor that did not seem to enter the decision process was the basically unstable environment of the publishing industry. Economic factors play a dynamic part in advertising dollars spent by companies, as witnessed during the war years (1942—Appendix B). Therefore, if economic recession occurs, dollars directed toward the publishing sector are reduced, accentuating the revenue decline, as all areas of the company are directed towards the single goal of publishing magazines. Since the recession affects all companies in the industry, opportunities for supplying outside firms with the excess capacity at hand are not available.

Such heavy concentration in publishing rested upon the assumption that television would not provide strong competition. Based upon this theory, Curtis management could expect to expand circulation and to begin new magazines as soon as the television fad had passed. The plan also presupposed the continued success of their current magazines both in circulation and profits. If these were to fall, Curtis would feel the effects throughout the company.

Secondly, the Curtis strategy took a unique path with its vertical integration pattern. In 1944, when

Curtis Publishing rejected the plan for geographic expansion, three of their competitors elected to expand their operations geographically as transport charges rose dramatically after World War II. Also, these competitors, particularly Downe and Cowles Communications, began to diversify horizontally, which lowered their operational and financial risk. Their diversification consisted basically of television networks, and communications opportunities other than magazines. This strategy also benefited their cash flow and supplied these companies with greatly needed funds in the early 1960s. Curtis Publishing therefore adopted a specialized pattern, whereas its competitors had chosen a more diversified route. Competition between these companies in the 1960s demonstrated that the most profitable strategy was the one accepted by the competition.

THE WHIPPING BOY

Robert MacNeal was the next person to be elected to the presidency (1950) as Walter Fuller was promoted to chairman. MacNeal had been with the company since the age of 20, and throughout his career, he had been responsible for several cost-cutting plans. MacNeal held many of the same management ideas that Fuller had held. For example, he, like Fuller, strongly held the belief that television was not a major competitor of the publishing business. His actions demonstrated that he also believed in vertical integration and that new magazines should be the source of added revenues. This same type of theory held by Fuller was the basic reasoning behind the Sharon Hill Plant construction.

The Status of Curtis Publishing Company at Takeover

Curtis Publishing was in excellent financial status in 1950, the year MacNeal took the presidency. Appendix B demonstrates that both revenues and profits had increased by 50% from 1946. Revenues jumped from $100 million to $149.5 million as net income rose from a $4 million level to $6.2 million. Magazine circulation was strong, but had not increased greatly between 1945 and 1950. Both the *Post* and the *Ladies Home Journal* had circulations of 4+ millions in both years. The *Post* continued to receive greater revenues than the *Journal* though, because of its greater prestige, as more advertisers desired space in it rather than in the *Ladies Home Journal*. Corporate expansion had occurred during the period as Curtis Publishing had bought several subsidiary companies which were also magazine publishing outfits (see Appendix C).

Expansion Attempts

MacNeal attempted to publish two new magazines, but both quickly failed. The first was called *TV Time* (1954), a publication intended to provide competition for the new *TV Guide*. Because of the heterogeneous material required for national circulation, the organization of the magazine text became too costly to handle from a centralized printing operation, and *TV Time* folded after 8 weeks.

The second attempt was the magazine entitled *Bride to Be*. This failed in 1956, a year after its inception. Again, the failure was due to excessive costs. The advertising revenues per page were small because of its limited circulation, and the cost of soliciting the large number of ads needed, made the attempt not feasible. Its circulation was sold to the publisher of *Modern Bride*.

Other Company Problems

Another of MacNeal's problems within the company was excessive manpower, yet he failed to rectify the situation during his term. MacNeal knew of the inefficiencies, as he had made several statements to the effect that only a small percentage of the personnel were productive. The excess did not prevent Curtis from producing a profit during the 1950s, but it laid the foundation for poor financial health as it eliminated funds that had investment and working capital potential, and both were sorely needed during the next decade.

TELLTALE SIGNS

As of 1958, the company was fully integrated, performing all of the functions of magazine publication. It consisted of the parent company and 13 subsidiaries, either totally or partially owned. Each one was related to magazine publication and production or the related aspect of advertisers aids, such as marketing research firms and their Premium Service Company.

The 1958 outlook was strong for Curtis Publishing but it was no longer enjoying a monopoly market. Competition from other magazines, especially *Life* and *Look*, forced Curtis into circulation wars involving cut rate subscription and newsstand prices. The wars accomplished their primary objective of increasing circulation. (Note Appendix C—compare 1955 and 1960.) Advertising revenues also jumped dramatically, as per page prices were increased because of the higher circulation. However, the lower price per copy received from each magazine no longer covered production expenses, and the slack had to be taken up by advertising revenues. Advertising revenues were increasing continuously in this period (1952 through 1960), but profit margins were falling, as well as actual profits earned. In 1961, Curtis Publishing Company posted its first loss. (Appendix B)

Many advertisers were forced out of this market because of the higher prices, so the actual number of advertising pages per magazine were reduced (primarily in the *Post*). This heavy concentration of the larger accounts hurt the *Post* in 1961 and 1962 when the advertisers began to lose confidence in the publication. Competitive advertisers tend to follow each other in and out of magazines and other media at the direction of their advertising agency.

NEW DIRECTIONS

The turning point of revenues and profits occurred in 1961, as Curtis Publishing Company posted a loss of $4.2 million. Management decided to change the *Post* format, hopefully to recall the advertising accounts that had disappeared. Concurrently, they changed the conservative viewpoints for which the *Post* was known, by replacing the editor. Advertisers proclaimed support of the new *Post*, but ad pages still dwindled. Between 1954 and 1960, the number of *Post* ad pages had shrunk by 900 per year, to a level of 2,788 in 1960.[3]

As a cost-cutting technique, MacNeal ordered that year end issues be combined, and that summer issues should be biweekly, rather than weekly. This plan backfired as it demonstrated to Madison Avenue that even Curtis Publishing Company did not have confidence in its own publication. By reducing the number of issues per year, it also reduced the business devoted to the Sharon Hill Plant by its own publications. This action went against their estimates of increased production business as the basis for building Sharon Hill.

MacNeal capped off these decisions, by removing the *Post* from the circulation race. The reason for the withdrawal was that Curtis was out of money and had gone heavily into debt for the first time since its inception. MacNeal had acquired $22 million worth of short-term debt by continuing the war. Revenues were not great enough to produce a profit, let alone pay off this debt.

[3] Ibid., p. 93.

A New Man

MacNeal was blamed for the recent problems causing the losses, even though he had inherited an operationally weak company. The board looked to Matthew Joe Culligan, a Madison Avenue executive, for help. Culligan took the presidency in 1962 and Robert MacNeal was fired. Culligan's most valuable asset for Curtis Publishing Company was his sales ability. He traveled to the major advertisers, soliciting business, and induced his editors to follow the pattern. The plan succeeded in the short run, as three of their four magazines increased or maintained their ad revenues as well as the number of ad pages from 1962 to 1963. The *Ladies Home Journal* increased its revenues from $23 million to $27 million. The newest of their magazines, *American Home* received a $2 million boost.[4] The *Post* was the only magazine that had decreases in each of these columns.

Culligan also introduced cost cutting techniques to the firm. Through his new financial vice president, J.M. Clifford, the staff was cut by approximately 2,000 from a previous total of 9,000. Departmental cuts of 20% were also ordered throughout the company.

Culligan convinced financier Sarge Samenenko to take a chance on Curtis, and they combined to rearrange the financial debt structure by raising $35 million from a syndicate of 5 banks, in order to pay the short-term debt accumulated under MacNeal. This plan also provided working capital to help

[4] Ibid., p. 143.

ease the money squeeze. The new cash was used to reenter the circulation race, again attempting to regain the position of each of its magazines. Comparing the 1960 and 1965 figures, the increases in circulation between these years were not comparable to the large increases seen in the previous 5 year period.

The vertical integration program now became a liability for Curtis Publishing as their major magazines were failing. Because about 90% of the Curtis payroll was devoted to the production side of the operation, the failures reduced the staff needed but left more and more unused assets.

Curtis Publishing was now faced with increasing costs and decreasing revenues as well as being in debt. The pattern of earnings shown in Appendix B, from 1962 through 1967, was clearly falling rapidly, as were the assets of the corporation. During this five-year period, several of their holdings were sold, primarily the partially owned and smaller subsidiaries, as a means of acquiring working capital to finance their declining publishing business. (Appendix A shows the large number of divestments occurring in the 1960s.)

In 1965, internal problems between the management and editor positions flared, resulting in the expulsion of both Joe Culligan and Clay Blair, editor of the *Post*. Blair, who had previously vied for the presidency, accused Culligan of mismanagement and giving inequitable discounts to certain advertisers. Board meetings were called to settle the matter, resulting in the dismissal of both Culligan and Blair.

Those who have analyzed this period feel that Culligan came very close to pulling Curtis out of its problems despite the damaging financial statements in the mid-1960s.

President Needed

The presidency was handed to J. M. Clifford, the financial manager Culligan had brought to the company. Clifford applied his technique again by cutting the budget. He successfully utilized the plan as Curtis had a profit of $347,000 at the end of 1966. The plan lasted only for that year as Curtis posted losses through 1970, while assets continued their decline.

A mineral discovery on the Curtis Canadian timberlands provided some financial relief as they sold the land to Texas Gulf Sulfur Company in 1965 for $24 million. They also sold two Pennsylvania papermill operations in the same year for an additional $11 million. This provided money to keep the operations going, as well as to pay off some of the outstanding debts.

RESTORING CURTIS PUBLISHING

Short-term salvation of the company came in the form of a man named Martin Ackerman, the new president, as Clifford took a very short term as chairman of Curtis. Ackerman, who was president of a firm named Perfect Film and Chemical Company, kept both positions upon entering Curtis Publishing. Ackerman came to Curtis in mid year of 1968 with possible merger plans between Curtis and Perfect Film, and soon afterwards arranged a deal with Time-Life publications that was intended to be beneficial to both participating companies.

The Plan

Time-Life would lend $5 million to Curtis in return for the *Post* subscriptions that Ackerman planned to eliminate with the new deal. In other words, as Ackerman was halving the circulation of the *Post* (concentrating the audience in the higher income area countries as an attraction for advertisers), *Life* would distribute its magazine in place of the *Post* and thereby increase their circulation. The new subscriptions taken by *Life* would boost its circulation above that of *Look*'s, its major magazine competition. The plan stated that *Time* would give their printing and circulation business to Curtis, thereby enabling the Sharon Hill plant to cover some of its overhead expenses, since the *Post* printing needs would be substantially reduced. The new lower costs of advertising in the *Post* would also be a change back to its previous stance, where the smaller companies would be able to advertise there.

Ackerman's Other Changes

Ackerman next divided Curtis Publishing and sold some of the parts. Some of the incentive for the scheme was to raise capital to pay back the outstanding loans that were still with the company. Ackerman

first took away the circulation company, the one unit that had always been a profitable operation and the one that had just benefited from the Time-Life arrangement. This unit was sold to Perfect Film Company for $12.5 million.

Ackerman then raised cash from a bank through Perfect Film Company to repay the remaining outstanding debt to the banking syndicate. This put Curtis in debt to Perfect Film Company in the amount of $13.2 million. Two months later, when Curtis could not pay, Ackerman sold both the *Ladies Home Journal*, (still a successful magazine today with Downe Communications) and *American Home* at the price of $4 million.

After the debt reduction, Curtis Publishing still owed Perfect Film more than $10 million. Ackerman then took over the *Post* and three other magazines (*Holiday, Jack and Jill,* and *Status*) and put them in the form of a new company, named the Saturday Evening Post Company. This unit belonging to Perfect Film, because of the unpaid debt, was put back under Curtis operations in return for $5 million taken from the Curtis Pension Fund.

Results

Ackerman's plan of reduced circulation of the *Post* was a disaster for the magazine and for Curtis operations, as the last issue appeared on February 8, 1969, a year after Ackerman's takeover. This was the symbolic end of the Curtis dynasty, although its obvious end had been seen several years earlier. Both Time-Life and old Curtis magazines, now owned by Perfect Film, took away their printing contracts, leaving Sharon Hill almost useless. It was later forced to close.

Ackerman's Resignation

Ackerman's presidential actions were regarded as illegal or at least unethical, (as all of Curtis' profitable operations were sold to Perfect Film), and there were several law suits that followed. He was charged with selling the Curtis assets below their real value, which was responsible for Curtis falling into as much trouble as it did. The battles resulted in Ackerman's resignation from Curtis (1969), and soon afterwards from Perfect Film.

The legal battles were aimed at the recapture of the assets taken from Curtis Publishing Company, and also the three existing magazines owned by Perfect Film. Curtis won the battle and was given back the magazines and some of its properties, but the Curtis empire was finished, as they had lost all of their profitable large scale operations. Both the Curtis headquarter's building ($8 million) and the Sharon Hill plant ($9.3 million) were sold between 1968 and 1970 because of their reduced current needs.

SKELETAL REMAINS

The presidency was taken over by default in the legal battles until Beurt SerVaas was elected president. SerVaas then bought controlling interest from the Curtis Trust a few

months later that year. He published three issues of a quarterly *Post* in 1971 as he had planned to do upon coming into the company. Subscription to the newest of the *Post* magazines was totalling 70,000 in that year.

Under the new president, Curtis Publishing Company has had the following profit performance:

	$Millions		
Year	Receipts	Net Income	Total Assets
1971	5.894	2.244	2.798
1972	6.134	0.041	2.639
1973	9.052	0.111	3.555

Three principle officers in the present day Curtis are:

Beurt SerVaas, Editor and Publisher
(His wife) Cory SerVaas, Executive Editor and Publisher
Julie Nixon Eisenhower, Associate Editor

They now have eight advertising offices:

6 in the United States,
1 Toronto, and another in the Netherlands

The basic format of the *Saturday Evening Post* magazine has not changed, and it still attracts many famous writers such as Ray Bradbury, Isaac Asimov, and Kurt Vonnegut, Jr. In 1974, it began being published monthly, in March to May and October to December, and bi-monthly in Jan./Feb., June/July, and Aug./Sept.

Holiday and *Jack and Jill* are also being published by the SerVaas organization, the latter being a consistently profitable magazine.

STUDENT PROBLEMS

1. Devise the steps you would have taken over the years to prevent the actual end result. Do some research and give details on what you would have done and why. (The answer depends on identifying turning points in the history of Curtis.)
2. Assume you replaced Fuller as President in 1941, and three years later Curtis is offered ABC and CBS. What criteria would you use in making a decision? Can you defend the decision not to purchase? (Research on the status of the companies and the progress of radio and television in the early 1940s is essential to answer this question.)
3. If Curtis had been interested in mergers and acquisitions, what other industries might be prospects in the 1950s? Relate your suggestions to seasonal cash flows, industry trends, and the company's financial capacity.
4. During the reign of Robert MacNeal, what strategies could have been formulated to reverse apparent trends? Were these fundamental problems related to the Curtis Trust, which prevented him from succeeding?
5. Do you believe Martin Ackerman was dishonest? What exactly were his motives in your opinion?

Appendix A. Chronological Log of Events

Major Capital and Operating Decisions		Disposition and Results	
CYRUS CURTIS (1883–1932):			
1883	Tribune and Farmer — a four-page weekly	1884	Given to old editor of magazine
1883	Woman and Home — Began as supplement to above but soon separated to become independent magazine named the *Ladies Home Journal*	1969	Sold to Downe Communications
1892	Incorporation of the Curtis Publishing Company	1973	Has changed hands (controlling interest) but name remains the same
1897	*Saturday Evening Post* — was purchased from another publisher for $1000 because of funds problems	1969	Last issue until reorganization

Major Capital and Operating Decisions		Disposition and Results	
1911	Erection of Curtis building on Independence Square	1968	Sale of building for price of $7,300,000
1911	*The Country Gentleman* — Purchased by Curtis for $2,000,000	1955	Sold because it was unprofitable

GEORGE LORIMER (1932–1934)

1932	Curtis Circulation Department became a subsidiary corporation	1968	Curtis Circulation Company sold to Perfect Film and Chemical Company

WALTER FULLER (1934–1950)

1936	*Life* and *Look* magazines are introduced as competition for Curtis	1936	Curtis management takes no action after first appraisal of new magazines
1938	*Jack and Jill* magazine started by the Circulation Company	1969	*Jack and Jill* went with the *Saturday Evening Post* to Perfect Film Company
1938	Began the Premium Service Company as a subsidiary company — aid to advertisers.	1964	Sold the Premium Service Company
1941	Opportunity to purchase operation which later became ABC — Purchase price would have been $3,000,000	1943	Decide against purchase — Later sold for $8,000,000
1944	Opportunity to diversify printing operations geographically — competition followed this route	1944	Decision not to expand printing in this direction — were centrally located at this time
1944 1945	Opportunity to purchase CBS for $10,000,000	1945	Declined this opportunity
1943	Started National Analysts — a research firm for Curtis and outside	1966	Sold National Analysts

Appendix A. continued

Major Capital and Operating Decisions		Disposition and Results	
1946	*Holiday* magazine was started — aimed at leisure market	1969	Followed group of magazines to Perfect Film Company
1945 1952	Purchase of 5 subsidiaries to be partly owned by Curtis	1954 1966	Sold whole or partial interest in each of these subsidiaries
1947	Build Sharon Hill Printing Plant — 108 acre site — most modern in world	1970	Sold to General Electric for $9.3 million

ROBERT MACNEAL (1950–1962)

1950	Invested $20 million in paper mills of which they held controlling interest — 1956 they held complete ownership	1965	Sold the paper mills and Canadian land for $35 million
1954	Introduced new publication called *TV Time*	1954	Lasted only eight weeks until found not feasible
1955	Introduced *Bride to Be* magazine	1956	Lasted only a year before sold to *Modern Bride*
1958	*American Home* was purchased	1968	Sold with *Ladies Home Journal* to Downe Communications

MATTHEW CULLIGAN (1962–1965)

1958 1968	Sale of several partially owned subsidiaries	1968	Attempts to raise working capital, cut costs and pay off debt

J.M. CLIFFORD (1965–1968)

MARTIN ACKERMAN (1968–1970)

1968	Ackerman comes in and sells off most of existing pieces of company	1968	Many of profitable part going to Perfect Film because of debt foreclosure by Perfect
1968	Stock delisted from New York Stock Exchange	1968	Listed on PBW Stock Exchange
1970	Controlling interest of Curtis goes to Beurt SerVaas	1970	Plans for continuation of *Post* and carries out plans

Appendix B. Financial Data on Curtis Publishing

$ Millions Year	Receipts	Net Income	Total Assets	$ Millions
1942	$ 39.475	$ 4.361	$ 52.704	
1946	100.001	4.034	72.578	
1950	149.553	6.212	88.267	
1954	174.366	4.516	90.743	
1958	217.070	2.512	121.487	
1959	243.043	3.960	124.204	
1960	248.607	1.079	133.481	
1961	243.164	−4.193	135.535	
1962	149.284	−18.917	127.810	
1963	152.030	−3.393	122.966	
1964	139.401	−13.947	112.675	
1965	122.738	+10.954	88.921	
		(14.306 − special credit)		
1966	128.897	+.347	94.555	
1967		−4.839		
1968	98.685	−20.886	43.622	
1969	32.031	−19.433	20.255	
1970	6.915	−.010	10.293	

(See the text of the case for details on Curtis after it was sold to Beurt SerVaas.)

Appendix C. Circulation and Advertising Revenue Data

	Millions			
	1950	1955	1960	1965
Saturday Evening Post				
Circulation	4.220	4.702	6.301	6.661
Advertising Revenues	$75.372	83.449	103.930	36.867
Ladies Home Journal				
Circulation	4.722	4.893	6.414	6.661
Advertising Revenue	19.517	23.642	28.366	29.479
Country Gentleman				
Circulation	2.376	Sold	None	None
Advertising Revenue	8.572	Sold	None	None
Holiday				
Circulation	.861	.849	.936	1.029
Advertising Revenue	4.895	5.890	11.126	10.299
Jack and Jill				
Circulation	.741	.715	.834	.833
Advertising Revenue	None	None	None	.865
American Home				
Circulation			3.689	3.390
Advertising Revenue			8.341	12.795

Books

Culligan, Matthew J., *The Curtis Culligan Story*, New York; Crown Publishers, Inc., 1970.

Friedrick, Otto, *Decline and Fall*, New York; Harper and Row, 1970.

Goulden, Joseph C., *The Curtis Caper*, New York; G. P. Putnam's Sons, 1965.

Wood, James P., *The Curtis Magazine*, New York; The Ronald Press Company, 1971.

Periodicals

"Curtis Starts to Change," *Business Week*, March 31, 1962.

"New Bundle of Hope for Ailing Post," *Business Week*, May 25, 1968.

"Perfect Wants a Better Image," *Business Week*, June 28, 1969.

"Return of Curtis Publishing," *Fortune*, July 15, 1966.

"Robert MacNeal of Curtis Publishing: Rousing the Giant of Philadelphia," Part I: *Printers Ink*, October 31, 1958.

"Robert MacNeal of Curtis Publishing," Part II; *Printers Ink*, November 7, 1958.

"Robert MacNeal of Curtis Publishing," Part III; *Printers Ink*, November 14, 1958.

"Still Fighting over Curtis," *Business Week*, May 17, 1970.

"The Resurrection of the Saturday Evening Post," *Business Week*, November 14, 1970.

Advertising Age Articles

February 10, 1969, p. 4.

February 10, 1969, p. 8.

September 8, 1969, p. 64.

June 1, 1970, p. 6.

Reference

Moody's Industrial Manual, Curtis Publishing Co., 1953, 1956, 1960, 1961, 1966, 1970, 1971, 1972.

Wall Street Journal

1958:
April 22, p. 12.
August 28, p. 2.

1959:
February 26, p. 1.
March 20, p. 6.
November 4, p. 19.

1960:
March 1, p. 1.
October 6, p. 25.

1961:
April 14, p. 21.
May 10, p. 15.
May 11, p. 11.

June 21, p. 4.
July 19, p. 5.
August 14, p. 5.
August 15, p. 5.
October 3, p. 17.
October 23, p. 5.

1962:
March 26, p. 12.
June 4, p. 26.
June 22, p. 3.
June 26, p. 28.
June 27, p. 19.
June 29, p. 28.
July 3, p. 4.
July 10, p. 12.
October 11, p. 15.

1963:
February 13, p. 16.
May 7, p. 12.
June 11, p. 30.
July 19, p. 13.
August 9, p. 9.
August 13, p. 9.
September 9, p. 8.
November 1, p. 6.
November 6, p. 14.
November 7, p. 7.
November 19, p. 17.
December 11, p. 6.

1964:
January 9, p. 14.
February 13, p. 3.
March 16, p. 14.
April 21, p. 6.
May 27, p. 2.
July 22, p. 5.
October 12, p. 2.
October 14, p. 19.
October 20, p. 2.
October 21, p. 2.
October 26, p. 8.
November 2, p. 5.
November 6, p. 3.
November 11, p. 3.
November 13, p. 28.
November 16, p. 4.
December 24, p. 5.

1965:
March 18, p. 8.
May 7, p. 8.
May 25, p. 10.
June 10, p. 5.
October 27, p. 4.
December 13, p. 30.

1966:
April 11, p. 6.
April 15, p. 11.
May 2, p. 5.
May 20, p. 4.

1968:
April 17, p. 33.
April 22, p. 8.

April 23, p. 24.
April 25, p. 4.
April 6, p. 9.
May 9, p. 11.
May 10, p. 34.
May 20, p. 4.
June 26, p. 10.
July 18, p. 2.
August 14, p. 5.
August 15, p. 3.
August 23, p. 1.
October 16, p. 36.

1969:
January 8, p. 2.
January 13, p. 10.
January 17, p. 24.
January 21, p. 36
February 12, p. 7.
March 3, p. 6.
March 4, p. 27.
March 28, p. 4.
April 4, p. 29.
April 14, p. 10.
May 1, p. 36.
May 20, p. 15.
June 4, p. 3.
June 5, p. 4.
July 3, p. 21.
September 25, p. 24.
December 3, p. 16.

1970:
January 14, p. 2.
February 5, p. 16.
March 18, p. 5.
March 25, p. 20.
May 6, p. 31.
May 19, p. 31.
June 30, p. 10.
November 6, p. 9.

1971:
June 3, p. 31.
June 23, p. 5.

1972:
January 31, p. 7.
June 13, p. 9.
September 15, p. 5.

Comprehensive Case: Powerite Tools and the Constructo Line

This case is intended to review techniques in the five chapters of Part 2. It will be essential to study information and conclusions on Powerite covered in Chapters Two and Eight.

Profits from operations during the first five months of 1975 were somewhat less than those predicted in SROP. The entrance of Yamasuki into the quality electric hand tool market had had greater impact on the Powerite line than expected. Volume through May held to the targets for each product. However, retailers had to discount the line and offer special promotions to keep from building inventories. This led to cooperative advertising and special displays adding $87,500 to Charley Bobzin's marketing budget.

Qualitite sales to Mooney Mart stores were slightly less than planned, but Ken Resnick had completed negotiations with a $0.15 per unit increase in the price used to develop SROP for 1975. This had

eliminated Minoni-Ware from this outlet, but the Italian firm intensified efforts to obtain a contract with AMSELL and EL CHEAPO. The marketing department was still reporting progress in discussions about three-year supply contracts. However, the probable volume was going to be 60,000 units per year each instead of something similar to the 180,000 sold to Mooney Mart. Both AMSELL and EL CHEAPO had taken 5,000-unit trial shipments and customer reaction had been better than expected.

Dick Foster and Joe Huggins were, however, deeply concerned about the long-range outlook for Powerite Tools. The company was struggling instead of expanding. Confrontations with shareholders earlier in the year had resulted in the two executives making statements which, when summarized, said the decisions on Powerite and Qualitite were the best for long-range growth in profits. In June, 1975 they were uncertain about this position. The markets for the company's two lines had changed fundamentally, and it would be difficult to achieve any improvement in profits during the foreseeable future.

PLANNING AND ORGANIZING PROJECT CONSTRUCTO

In reviewing notes on the December meetings which formulated Powerite Tool's present strategy, Dick Foster became interested in the suggestion that had been made to upgrade the Powerite line to service a segment of the market that wanted multiple-speed drills, more precise cutting alignments, and so on. Reference had been made to contractors who were incurring serious losses of equipment from job sites as a result of stealing. Calls to three friends in the construction business confirmed that it was a major problem. Two of the three felt that cost was less of a factor than the daily frustration of not completing scheduled work. Dick Foster proposed having less expensive but a larger inventory of tools at the site. All three agreed to the concept's merit.

"Project Constructo" developed quickly after the discussions with the contractors. The true potential of a new line of hand tools and, perhaps, other equipment for work stations at a construction site, had to be determined more accurately. Long hours and two weekends resulted in a series of interrelated network models to coordinate the activities of several parts of the organization. Morale improved throughout the entire organization because at a time when Dick Foster and Joe Huggins could have turned cautious and indecisive, they were demonstrating the capabilities that led Powerite Tools to a $20 million business.

The strategy for a go/no-go decision on a Constructo line involved use of both internal and external resources. The role for each resource is described in the following paragraphs.

Internal—Market Research

A comprehensive study had to be completed by mid-August, and the responsibility was given to Steve Keiser, director of marketing services. However, feedback to other components in the strategy during July was necessary in order to have specifications on the products for costing. Also, some information could substantially change assessment of the potential and/or necessitate redeployment of external resources. Specific objectives of market research were:

1. *Definition of the Product Line.* What constituted a line of products for this market? Is it only more powerful units of the existing line with a greater range of capability or will stationary drill presses, saws and sanders be re-

quired? Identify specifications in the first stage of the study. What are expansion possibilities? Guidelines for a product plan should result from research which gives the line at time of entry, additions feasible in each of the subsequent three years, and longer range possibilities to identify a dynamic "path of growth."

2. *Pricing.* What do buyers expect to pay for the proposed Constructo Line in order to solve their problems? Using $100 as the initial dividing point, determine whether products less than $100 have images of fraility, inadequate capacity or any other damaging characteristic in the buyer's mind.

3. *Geography.* What areas offer the greatest potential? Are there limitations for the company to service specific areas such as established local producers, distributors with exclusive contracts, unusual transportation costs, contractor attitude or other factors? Make recommendations on the geographic areas to be serviced initially and those to be included in future expansions.

4. *Distribution Channels.* Are special outlets required at each stage of distribution? Can Powerite Tools sell directly to large volume businesses servicing contractors, or is it necessary to establish exclusive regional territories for wholesalers? Will regional centers be needed to repair equipment and honor guarantees? What is the nature of selling to the selected distribution channels?

5. *Sales Methods, Advertising, and Promotion.* Who would sales representatives call on and what would be the objective of each call? What media is most effective with contractors and those selling to contractors? What copy will catch favorable attention? Will salesmen act as field troubleshooters? What budgets are needed to penetrate the market and what are the on-going costs?

The result of this research will lead to a complete marketing plan, including a forecast of sales in units by month for the first six months, by quarter for the remainder of the year, by half years for the second year, and annual estimates for three years allowing for product additions. The timing assumes full-scale operations beginning on January 1, 1976. The forecast would also have price per unit in each period, and the net effect of discounts, special promotions, returns based on necessary guarantees, and similar allowances required for accurate cash flow totals.

Internal—Operations

The market research study would give Bob Allan and his staff in operations information by mid-July on the product specifications required by contractors. Make or buy decisions would be completed by the end of the month, and central purchasing would have preliminary prices on purchased items by mid-August for information to be relayed to the controller.

In addition, operations had to review facilities to determine space availability. Capital requirements for alterations, extensions, foundations, special equipment moving, and so on were to be identified. Alternative courses of action such as leasing or buying a nearby plant for the Constructo line would be reviewed. Recommendations should be finalized by September 1st.

A critical element in the final decision will be cost of each unit. All wages, salaries, utilities, materials, supplies, insurance, other services and items needed by the Constructo line must be estimated. Forecasts received from marketing services in mid-August would be the basis of a report to be ready by September 1st. If Jim Ford, director of administration, coordinates with Steve Keiser, the flow of information between these components in the strategy should improve the accuracy of forecasts.

Internal—Controller's Office

Les Chadwick was placed in charge of pulling together estimated sales and costs to prepare reports on cash flows and capital estimates. He will assist coordination by meeting with Steve Keiser and Jim Ford periodically in July and August. This would also improve his interpretation of the forecasts and assure that the separate teams of people were acting on the same assumptions.

During August Les Chadwick will also inform Austin Hartfield, his boss and vice president of finance, about the capital estimates so that alternative plans for having the necessary money would also be ready on September 1st.

Finally, Les Chadwick will evaluate the proposal received from Information Management International, Inc. (IMI) to install a computerized strategic decision center during fall, 1975. The idea was finely tuned to the needs of Powerite Tools, especially when there was concern about the Powerite and Qualitite lines of the company. In addition, they were very likely expanding into another related business. Foster and Huggins thought the SDC might be a means of tightly controlling the business under these conditions.

External—Executive Recruitment

The two top executives did not want to disrupt the existing assignments at Powerite Tools to establish a new line. It would be better if they could employ someone with experience in the field who would be compatible with management. As indicated in Table CC−1, the new person would have a profit center and enter at the vice president level. He would be hired effective October 1, 1975, and would build his own organization during the remainder of the year.

The interviewing process, which included the three vice presidents, could also improve everyone's knowledge about the business in which the Constructo line would be operating. Allan, Bobzin, and Hartfield were fully informed of developments in this important step, and all agreed to note any comments or intelligence that would assist Steve Keiser's study.

Powerite Tools retained Nowlin and Nowlin on July 1st after review-

Table CC-1. Details on the Constructo Position

Position Description
for
GENERAL MANAGER, CONSTRUCTO PRODUCTS DIVISION

Title:	Vice President and General Manager, Constructo Products Division
Reports to:	Office of the President
Responsibilities:	*Primary* — Profit performance equaling or exceeding that which is expected for the Constructo line of products.
	Facilitating — Employ competent personnel to carry out the work of the division. Optimize use of funds, equipment, and other assets. Plan for operations in the approaching twelve months and an average year three to five years in the future. Conceive investments, programs and projects which achieve profit growth and selects the best alternatives for inclusion in plans. Assure continuous operations through adequate supplies of materials and components, good labor relations, a working environment leading to the attraction of needed talent, and conformance with laws and regulations.
Duties:	Communicate progress toward objectives to the Office of the President regularly both through routine formal reports and informal verbal and written contacts. Establish policies and procedures for the orderly management of the Division. Develop personnel to carry out their regular assignments more effectively and to replace those who are promoted or who leave. Institute an information system that assists management to make good decisions. Design an organizational structure, and update this structure, in order to allow personnel to carry out their assignments in the most efficient manner. Attend the monthly executive management committee to communicate the divisions current position, coordinate business activities with other committee members, and receive information on the company.
Location:	Open — Either at Chicago headquarters, or at a separate division office, the choice depending on the most effective means of managing the division.
Compensation:	Salary — Range of $36,000 to $54,000 per year. Company car of any make up to $8,000 in cost to replaced every other year. Full company paid maintenance and insurance. Incentive of 0.5% on pre-tax division earnings.

ing possibilities with four executive recruiting firms. Joe Nowlin seemed to understand the situation at Powerite Tools very well, and his organization had had assignments in related fields as well as having a computerized candidate file for immediate screening. The first interview was scheduled for the third week in July and the final decision would be in September after two reinterviews at Chicago headquarters and the go/no–go decision on Constructo.

External—Market Research

A sensitive decision was made in June by the top executives. They wanted an outside estimate on the market potential for a Constructo line. In addition, they wanted to know whether it was feasible for Powerite Tools to introduce a line that would have acceptance among contractors as compared to market entrance through an acquisition which would be offering a lower grade of products than the level which had established the firm.

Marketing could interpret the decision as lack of confidence in them after problems with sales, market intelligence and forecasts in 1974–1975. Foster and Huggins had not lost faith in Bobzin, Keiser, and Resnick, but they knew shareholders could be less critical if an outside firm assisted them in developing their opinion.

Rather than the top executives retaining a market research firm, they explained their position to Charley Bobzin. Did he agree? Would he select the firm? Could he handle it without involving Steve Keiser until early August? The tactic of delegating the study to marketing paid off in that Bobzin agreed with the idea and seemed to feel complimented that he had been included in Foster and Huggin's confidence.

It was agreed that the outside firm and Steve Keiser would exchange information and forecasts before the final estimates were prepared by Les Chadwick. The three also wondered if the company's research would uncover the fact that another firm was investigating the market.

Summary of Project Constructo

Figure CC–1 gives the timing of the principle components of the strategic plan to enter the market for tools and equipment required by contractors.

THE IMI PROPOSAL TO POWERITE TOOLS

Powerite Tools was small compared to users of the IMI systems. However, the company particularly needed daily current information on the Powerite line. In addition, it seemed prudent that steps be taken in the 1970s to improve profit performance. If the Constructo line was not the answer, other avenues would have to be selected from various alternatives. Even if the company entered the market for contractor tools, some diversification in related fields appeared appropriate in June, 1975.

It was a coincidence that Bill Haesche, vice president of marketing for IMI, was in the offices of First National of Chicago. Joe Huggins had been discussing Project Constructo

Figure CC–1. Summary Model for Project Constructo

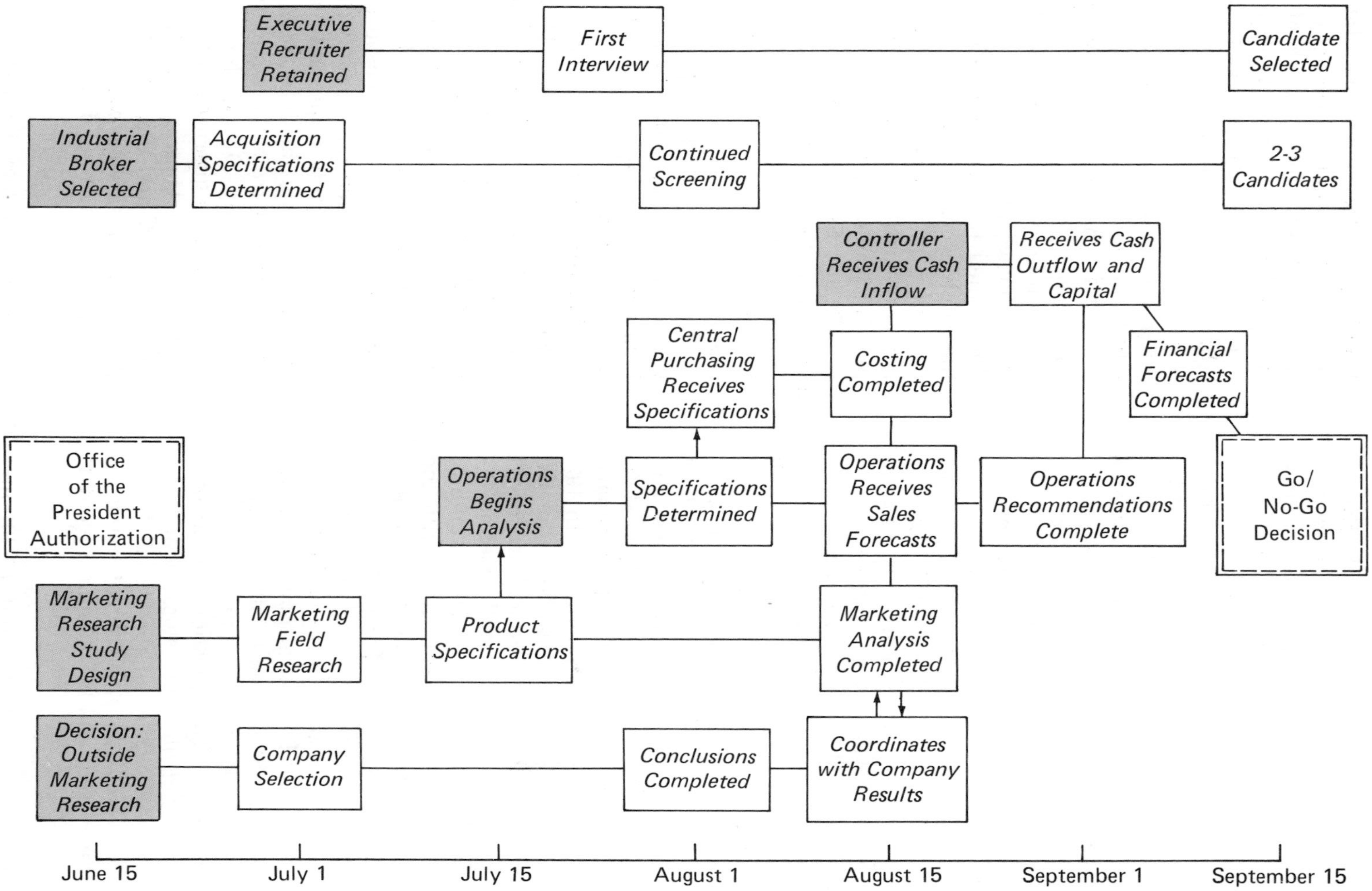

Candidate Selected

2-3 Candidates

Go/ No-Go Decision

Financial Forecasts Completed

Receives Cash Outflow and Capital

Operations Recommendations Complete

First Interview

Continued Screening

Controller Receives Cash Inflow

Costing Completed

Operations Receives Sales Forecasts

Marketing Analysis Completed

Coordinates with Company Results

Central Purchasing Receives Specifications

Specifications Determined

Conclusions Completed

Executive Recruiter Retained

Acquisition Specifications Determined

Operations Begins Analysis

Product Specifications

Industrial Broker Selected

Marketing Field Research

Company Selection

Office of the President Authorization

Marketing Research Study Design

Decision: Outside Marketing Research

June 15   July 1   July 15   August 1   August 15   September 1   September 15 with an officer of the bank. Even then, it was shareholder pressure aimed at lack of aggressiveness about profit growth that led to Huggins suggesting lunch with Bill Haesche that week. This led to additional discussions at Powerite's offices with the top five executives and a demonstration of the concept in New York.

Present Status of the Computer at Powerite Tools

In 1969, when Powerite Tools installed a new assembly line to supply Mooney Mart, sales volume and number of employees reached the point where it was essential to use a computer service company to invoice customers, control orders, and pay employees. The service was expanded in 1970 to relate receivables, receipts, disbursement salaries, and wages into a pre-tax cash flow statement available to executive management each Monday morning. In 1972 this reporting system added details on the geographic breakdown of orders, receivables and receipts to assist the controller and marketing.

An IBM System Three with the PICS program package (Production Inventory Control System) was installed at the plant in late 1972. The motivation was problems being encountered by central purchasing due to shortages of materials affecting the consistency of shipments by suppliers. The questions posed on the level of safety stocks which would be prudent for "EIs" (endangered items) were not being answered, and the manual inventory

keeping was too slow. Also, determination of optimum product cycles for the various tools in each of the two product lines was a problem; and the combination induced Bob Allan, vice president of operations, to ask for assistance from the computer service company. Instead of attempting to resolve the matter with their staff, the firm recommended IBM.

With consulting assistance from IBM Chicago office, Powerite Tools determined the basic numbers for the safety stock and reorder point of each item purchased from vendors. After an audit to establish the company's inventory position on January 1, 1973, the System Three program began monitoring usage and signaling a need for an order at three levels of inventory: (1) safety stock + 10%; (2) first use of safety stock, and (3) safety stock less 50%. Central purchasing can judge the supply situation for the item and decide to order or wait for a later warning.

Bob Allan contracted for the System Three when he saw that it was a "stretch system", and that Powerite Tools could obtain the BICARSA program package (Basic Invoice Control Accounts Receivable Sales Analysis) which would improve utilization of the leased system. After a successful year with PICS, the company requested assistance to duplicate the information being received from the computer service company. During the January–March quarter in 1974, Dick Foster and Joe Huggins decided to run BICARSA and the output from the computer service company in parallel. This was an incentive to

IBM to remove the "bugs" from their package, and it served ample notice for termination of the contract for data supplied by the computer service company.

In mid-1975 both PICS and the modified BICARSA were running well. The information proved to be the basis of coordination between operations and marketing which reduced the inventory level of finished tools without disrupting flow to customers. It also identified distribution channels being most severely affected by the Yamasuki line. Duncan Colgate, planning director, made a cost/benefit analysis of the System Three at the time when Powerite Tools received the proposal from IMI, and the net results were that quantifiable benefits exceeded total costs by approximately 3.5 times after the first year. The situation was breakeven in 1974.

Summary of the IMI Proposal

The concept involved conversion of executive management's conference room to a seven chair strategic decision center. The screen would be 3½ x 6 feet. On the same wall would be a map of the area within a 600-mile radius of Chicago; this map would be linked to a minicomputer which, in turn, would be connected to the System Three. Six colors for lights designating distributors for the Powerite line (and Constructo if approved) would show those with sales on target, above or below target, and the same three categories with deeper shades designating special promotions needed to

achieve the sales volume. The modified BICARSA program would feed the necessary data with no changes, and the minicomputer would simply activate the appropriate colored lights. This device would give Foster and Huggins, the four vice presidents, the planning director, and others authorized to use the room a visual indication of the condition of the business.

The screen would also be connected to the Systems Three, but programs in a second minicomputer orienting data will display graphics of operating performance by selected segments, comparisons with SROP, and long-range plans on file in the computer. Colors in the graphics would be coordinated with those on the map. There would also be a small control room that would permit slide presentations through rear screen projection. This feature would assist board of director meetings and marketing in their attempts to develop new contracts for Qualitite and distributors for other lines.

A picture phone link with plant operations, especially if the Constructo line would be managed and produced at another location, would round out the aids to decision making. Figure CC–2 shows the floor plan and the proximity to the other offices.

The turnkey cost of the SDC would be $315,000 including supplementary hardware (mini-computers, light values, and so on), peripheral equipment, and furnishings and services (design, supervision of installation, programming and testing). Guarantees on actual performance according to specifications were

Figure CC-2. Executive Floor Plan at Powerite Tools

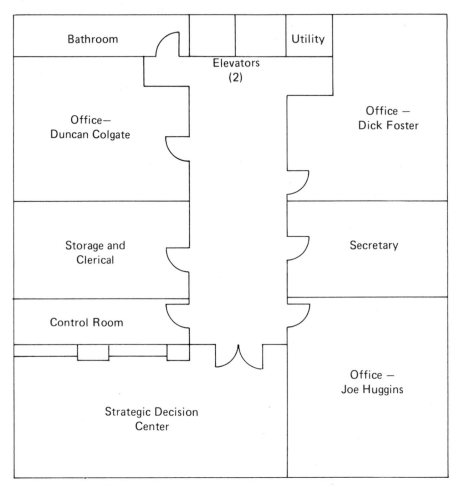

reassuring, and checks with companies and banks with more complex systems confirmed IMI's reliability.

Status of the Decision on the IMI Proposal

Dick Foster and Joe Huggins met with their three vice presidents and planning director in mid-July, 1975. The result was approval of the installation contingent on board of director agreement with the concept. The outlook was hopeful because one of three outside board members had a similar IMI system.

At a luncheon meeting on July 22 with this member it was determined that he would consider joining with Foster and Huggins in voting for approval. He also commended the two on their decision to investigate the Constructo possibility and the strategy implemented to reach a go/no-go decision. The atmosphere at the luncheon was friendly, and the concern about support in future confrontations with shareholders, if they occur, was lessened by the compliments on the steps being taken.

A second meeting of the six executives led to agreement that the SDC decision would be made in September at which time full specifications would be known. The addition of the Constructo line would add $22,500 to the cost of the strategic decision center.

RESULTS OF PROJECT CONSTRUCTO

On Monday, September 15, 1975 Messrs. Foster and Huggins had detailed reports on the Constructo line. Table CC−2 summarizes the sales forecast and the outlook for pre-tax cash flow from the business. In general, the outlook for the Constructo line was encouraging; top management could focus on the optimum approach to entry. Summary sections of the lengthy feasibility study are given below.

Marketing

Timing is critically important. Powerite Tools must be in the market by March, 1976 or risk loss of a major opportunity. While sales can be made during the prime construction season, overall volume will suffer in the first year by being late. In addition, tool companies are observing the actions of Powerite Tools to learn from their response to the entrance by Yamasuki and the threat posed by Minoni-Ware. A poorly timed move by the company at this stage will accelerate entrance into this new market by their present competitors, foreign firms, and manufacturers at the top end of tool quality and precision who, as yet, are not reacting to this opportunity.

Heavy advertising and promotion will be needed at the beginning of 1976, and prototypes must be ready in the stores of sales outlets in February. This campaign must be timed with actual availability; consequently, if any difficulties arise in production which slows or stops the flow of the Constructo line to retail outlets, it will be necessary to modify the intensity of advertising quickly to avoid the loss of sales and damage to company image from stock-outs.

Pricing of the two categories of products determined as required and viable, hand and stationary tools, are given here:

	Hand Tools	Stationary Tools
Price Paid by the Customer	$99.00	$140.00
Price Paid to Powerite Tools	63.50	99.00

A contractor or other buyers of quality hand tools identifies $100 as the breaking point for general purpose equipment as compared to either special purpose tools or the extra quality that is being stolen from tool sheds. It is likely that, with inflation increasing the costs of existing producers, Powerite Tools

Table CC-2. Estimated Cash Flow for the Constructo Line

	1st Half, 1976						2nd Half,
	Jan.	Feb.	March	April	May	June	3rd Qtr.
CASH INFLOW							
Hand Tools:							
Units Sold	—	—	3000	7500	1000	12500	29000
Price/Unit[1]			$63.50	$63.50	$63.50	$63.50	$63.50
Sales	—	—	190500	476250	635000	793750	1841500
Stationary Tools:							
Units Sold	—	—	—	—	—	—	—
Price/Unit	—	—	—	—	—	—	—
Sales	—	—	—	—	—	—	—
% of Market	—	—	1%	2%	3%	3%	4%
Cash Inflow	—	—	—	95000	333625	555625	1931500
CASH OUTFLOW							
Purchased Components	50100[2]	105250	147000	188750	180400	147000	260600
Adv. & Promo.	125000	175000	175000	125000	100000	60000	100000
Admn. & Ovrhd.	35000	35000	35000	35000	35000	35000	120000
Selling, Srvs, Guarantees & Repairs	29575	29575	29575	34575	39575	44575	148725
Operations:							
Wages/Salaries	21150	52875	70500	88125	84600	81000	204450
Mat'ls, Suppls	7800	19500	26000	32500	31200	26000	52000
Utilities	3900	9750	13000	16250	15600	13000	26000
Depreciations	45000	45000	45000	45000	45000	45000	135000
Learning Curve & Contingencies	22500	20000	17500	15000	12500	10000	15000
Expenses	340025	491950	558575	580200	543875	461575	1061775
Pre-Tax Profit	(340025)	(491950)	(558575)	(475200)	(210250)	94050	869725
CASH FLOW	(295025)	(446950)	(513575)	(430200)	(165250)	139050	1004725

Prices and costs are in 1976 dollars. Forecasts assume that increases in costs can be offset by increases in prices to maintain profit margins.

[2] Some totals for January 1976 include expenses incurred in late 1975.

1976		1977					
4th Qtr.	1976 Totals	1st Half	2nd Half	1977 Totals	1978	1979	1980
16000	78000	55000	50000	105000	125000	140000	150000
$63.50	$63.50	$63.50	$63.50	$63.50	$63.50	$63.50	$63.50
1016000	4953000	3492500	3175000	6667500	7937500	8890000	9525000
—	—	17000	20000	37000	45000	50000	55000
—	—	$99	$99	$99	$99	$99	$99
—	—	1683000	1980000	3663000	4455000	4950000	5445000
4%	3%	4%	4%	4%	5%	5%	5%
1428950	4344700	4490000	5160000	9650000	11707000	1314500	14285000
424100	1503200	1318750	1420000	2738750	3257500	3638000	3935000
75000	935000	450000	475000	925000	950000	950000	950000
150000	480000	300000	325000	625000	650000	675000	700000
158725	514900	337500	354500	692000	700000	710000	720000
194500	797200	451375	520375	971750	1376250	1537000	1662500
59800	254800	196500	212600	409100	505000	564000	610000
29900	127400	98250	106300	204550	252500	282000	305000
135000	540000	270000	270000	540000	540000	540000	540000
30000	142500	60000	48000	108000	60000	50000	36000
1257025	5295000	3482375	3731775	7214150	8291250	89460000	9458500
171925	(950300)	1007625	1428225	2435850	3415750	4208500	4826500
306925	(410300)	1277625	1698225	2975850	3955750	4748500	5366500

might be one of the few suppliers offering products at $99.00 or less.

The breaking point for stationary tools is $150, according to surveys. Most contractors felt that between $135 to $150 you could buy sufficient reliability, power, and so on to do most jobs at the site. More expensive equipment would be used in factories where work required higher speeds, greater preciseness, and intricate angles.

Distribution channels by existing producers vary from direct outlets owned by the manufacturer to wholesaler/retailer avenues of sale. It was encouraging that both company personnel and the consulting firm decided that Powerite Tools could reach the stores supplying contractors in an area through direct sales. The sales force would call on 15 to 18 outlets per week beginning in January, and repeating the cycle in the 4th, 7th, etc. week. Consequently, each sales representative would have 50± stores in each territory. By the end of the second year, 1977, there would be 14 territories with an average sale of 180± units per store per year.

A strong distributor/Powerite Tools relationship would also slow the inevitable entry into the market by some form of direct competition. By reducing the options for "late comers", the Constructo Division will have a strong position as contractors shift to the new line and turn to distributors who are tied to Powerite Tools.

The same territories would be used for stationary tools, but the outlets would vary. A few stores would carry the full line. Others would specialize in either stationary or hand tools. Some sales would be made directly to large corporations. It was the magnitude of the task of setting up a distribution channel for the stationary tools, as well as the time to get production into gear, that influenced management to recommend waiting until 1977 for start up of this operation.

The distribution concept depended on the contractors in each area habitually using a major supplier for many of their needs. Research confirmed that there were four to six stores of this type within one day's driving. After initially securing agreement to sell the Constructo line, the salesman would develop a good relationship with the buyer through repeat calls, and work with the outlets on advertising and promotion.

Image of Powerite Tools was a major point of disagreement between company personnel conducting market research and the consulting firm. Steve Keiser, manager of market research, encountered people who had doubts about the company's ability to sell in a higher quality market. Some outlets stated that contractors might consider the Constructo line as "beefed up" versions of the Powerite line, and these were "toys" in the opinion of those interviewed.

The consulting firm surveyed contractors directly. Many had the Powerite line in their homes. Nearly all had a favorable impression of the equipment for that use. Regarding a "jump" to the Constructo line, 77%

of the replies thought it would be easier to upgrade to meet their needs satisfactorily than to downgrade from a very high quality line. In response to the question. "Would you buy a Constructo line made by Powerite," 81% answered "yes." 11% would want to see the specifications. Only 8% said "no," or had serious doubts.

Interpreting this divergence of opinion would be difficult. Company personnel had concentrated on the buyers of Powerite Tools while the consulting firm went directly to the ultimate customer. It was possible that the people selling to contractors knew their preferences better than the user. On the other hand, it was a comparatively new market with little historical data, and the firms incurring the losses from pilfering at job sites might be the best source of information.

Geographic distribution of the regional headquarters for sales territories would be:

Chicago (incl.
   Milwaukee)   6 territories
Detroit   3   "
Indianapolis   2   "
St. Louis   3   "

After these regions were functioning according to plan, it would be feasible to consider other areas where the Powerite line had distributors such as Ohio, Kansas, and Minnesota.

Each of the four cities would have a warehouse office to serve and supply outlets. Marketing decided to have a senior sales representative who would have a territory within each of the four regions, and he would receive extra compensation for supervising the performance of the other sales representatives and monitoring supply and service. By paying well and offering an incentive compensation plan, Charley Bobzin felt little supervision would be needed and secretarial office support would be adequate. This decision could be modified by the new general manager.

Advertising should be concentrated in trade magazines. The approach recommended would go directly to the papers, magazines and journals which the contractor and sales outlet reads for business reasons rather than broad coverage in popular publications. The concept was to build a highly professional image, and distinguish the line from campaigns that might be undertaken by the Powerite line.

Promotions at each outlet would establish a "Constructo Corner" from the beginning of the relationship. The sales representative would work with the store to obtain maximum benefits from cooperative local advertising paid fully by Powerite Tools during the February—March, 1976 "kick-off" campaign. In future months the company would share on an equal basis the cost of ads in which the store would have latitude to promote other non-competing products.

Budgets shown in Table CC—1 involve very intensive coverage in the territories during early 1976. For seasonal reasons, as well as the avoidance of oversaturation, the campaign eases throughout the year. A similar campaign is then begun again in 1977 for stationary tools.

Operations

Coordination with marketing during summer, 1975 was quite good. Product specifications were received on schedule July 14 and preliminary designs were completed by August 1st in order for purchasing to identify the cost of components. Operations was then able to forward its portion of costs to the controller, Les Chadwick.

Capital Expenditures were estimated by a different team under the direction of vice president Bob Allan. The total excluding any spending on buildings would be $5.4 million excluding working capital. An allowance for price escalation and contingencies of 15% was included in the numbers.

The assembly line could be set up in a straight line, a "C", or serpentine configuration. Flow required no construction of overhead material handling equipment. Inquiries with suppliers of the required machinery, bins, tables, and so on which could not be made in the Powerite Tool shops indicated the line could be functioning in January, assuming an approval of the project before October 1st.

Recent experiences in refining the costs of production for the Powerite and Qualitite lines led to a highly efficient product design. Some components would be universal to all three lines and still have no effect on quality or performance specifications. Consequently, these items would be received from company inventories. Other purchased components would be wholly different and require about 40,000 sq. feet of floor space for inventories. Expansion of the Constructo line could be accomplished later by taking half of the inventory area and using more expensive stacking systems which could triple component storage in half the space.

The location of the line was a major question. The present plant could house the Constructo line for hand tools plus required inventories with some realignment. Economies would be possible by having the operation under the same roof as the other two lines. In addition, when the company begins making stationary units, another building would need to be constructed. This would exhaust the land available at the Chicago plant.

An alternative would be leased property two blocks away in an industrial park. A plant very similar to that which would have been designed by the Operations staff was available on a 40-year lease. Rent would be $6,500 per month for 85,000 sq. feet plus office space that would have headquartered a small manufacturing company. It was more office space than what was needed to run the plant, but, if the General Manager of the Constructo line elected to locate outside the downtown offices, it could house his personnel. Access by truck was good, but there was no possibility for a rail siding. This did not disturb Operations because the siding at Powerite's plant was rarely used.

Another alternative was four miles away. It had 100,000 square feet, minimal office space, a rail siding, and good access for truck flow in and out. Rent would be $5,750 per month. It was ideal for basic assembly and manufacturing with no frills or unnecessary facilities. The lease would be for 25 years.

The Controller's Estimates

The unit costs derived from Table CC–1 are given here along with profit margins. Volumes and expenses for the first three years of business are prorated as the basis of the data.

Because the proration of overall expenses is based on sales volume of the two product categories, marketing management might consider lowering the $99 price of stationary tools to $95± if a volume increase would result. The pre-tax profit margin on sales also indicates a possible adjustment.

Controller Les Chadwick also pointed out that a lag of 45 days is included in the cash flow estimates, and that large amounts of working capital, approximately $1.9 million,

will be needed before operations begin to contribute cash to the Constructo line division. Normal working capital would be about $1.2 million after the start up year of 1976–77.

The discounted cash flow rate of return on the $5.4 million in new assets and $1.2 million in working capital would be 14¼% after subtracting: (a) 10% of Constructo pre-tax profit for contribution to the overhead of Powerite Tools, and (b) 50% of the remainder for taxes payable to state and federal authorities.

The DCF was based on 100% equity, and interest expense on loans would reduce the percentage ROI by the amount borrowed and the interest rate. Regardless, if the sales forecasts were accurate, the proposed venture was attractive.

Finance

Austin Hartfield, vice president of finance, had been discussing ap-

	1976	1977	1978	Weighted Average
Hand Tools	$64.81	$43.14	$41.63	$48.01
Stationary Tools	–	66.06	63.28	64.53
Pre-tax Profit Margin @$63.50	−2%	+47%	52½%	+32%
" " " @$99.00	–	+33%	36%	+35%

	1976–78 Avg. Pre-tax Profits	Avg. 1976–78 Sales Volume	Pre-Tax Profit on Sales
Hand Tools	$1,590,000	$4,929,000	32%
Stationary Tools	$1,413,000	$4,059,000	35%
Total	$3,003,000	$8,988,000	33%

proaches to raising the money needed for the expansion. He had been informed about the $6.6 million needed for the Constructo line. The plan that evolved was designed mostly by a vice president of First National Bank of Chicago.

First, Powerite Tools could safely invest $2 million in cash in autumn, 1975. By carefully allocating cash in early 1976, the company could add another $1 million during the deficit months of the Constructo line. This meant a 1:1.2 equity/debt ratio for this expansion.

Second, the cash flow estimates in Table CC–1 justified bank loans to the Constructo venture. The First Chicago officer recommended establishing the loan for "takedown" on December 1st. Although potentially early considering company cash going into the expansion, the money would be ready for contingencies such as accelerating completion of the assembly line.

First Chicago knew Powerite Tools from the beginning but the bank had gained confidence in Foster and Huggins in 1975 because of the dynamic way in which they reacted to pressures in the market and from shareholders.

Executive Recruiting

Nowlin and Nowlin had exposed Powerite Tools to eight realistic candidates to head the Constructo profit center. One person stood out, not because of previous experience or college training, but because he had interpreted the situation at the company correctly and gained the con-

fidence of the three vice presidents with whom he would have to work. All agreed George Middleton was first choice.

George Middleton had been Regional Sales Manager for Dark and Necker Tools, a West Coast firm comparable to Powerite. He was then given an opportunity to develop a product line sold to contractors which secured structural and other materials to concrete by firing a fastener into the concrete through force created by a .22 shell. Middleton had been successful in planning and organizing the expansion, and had begun making a profit when Dark and Necker spun off the operation to a competitor. Investigation confirmed that the company ran into cash problems in winter, 1974–75 and was forced to sell to retain the core of their business. The company did not wish to lose George Middleton, but it had no openings at the vice presidential level which he deserved.

Discussions with the candidate had been candid, and he knew that the go/no–go decision was September 15. While he had another offer, he assured Joe Nowlin that he would wait until Foster and Huggins decided on Powerite Tools' course of action.

STUDENT PROBLEMS

1. You are either Dick Foster or Joe Huggins. Evaluate the feasibility study reports, and decide whether to go ahead with the Constructo

line and accompanying investments, stating your degree of confidence in the cash flow estimates
in Table CC–1.

2. Select the components of the
strategy you will use to enter the
market with the Constructo line.
Assume a "go" decision for this
question, and also assume that it
is September 15, 1975. Outline

each major detail. Then, relate
each component in your entry
strategy to SROP and the long
range plan.

3. As a member of the board of
directors, would you approve the
IMI proposal to install a strategic
decision center? Defend your position.

Realizing Plans and Strategies

The next four chapters involve methods employed and situations encountered by executive management in realizing plans and strategies. Cases illustrate the impact of management competence on company performance and develop understanding of control methods that prevent or minimize potentially serious problems.

PART THREE

Acquisitions, Mergers, and Divestitures

Terms are defined, and attention is given to product and industry life cycles. Techniques for identifying, pricing, and negotiating acquisitions and mergers are discussed. The difference between acqusitions and mergers is clarified, and methods of handling the transition phase in both situations are covered. Aspects of divestitures, spin-offs, and going "private" are outlined. This chapter brings out the fundamentals involved in generating growth from sources outside the company.

To gain needed technologies, penetrate new markets, broaden or narrow product lines, and generally improve profitability, executive management will sometimes buy and sell company assets. The principle terms used for these activities are *acquisition*, *diversification*, *merger*, *spin-off*, and *divestiture*. Concepts and techniques involved with these terms are critically important for achieving profit goals.

Before discussing the concepts and techniques, let us clarify the five terms in order to be precise in their usage.

1. *Acquisition.* Purchase of all or a portion of ownership of an asset. The business connotation is the purchase of a controlling interest in a company so that it becomes part of the acquiror's operations in the role of a division or subsidiary. Eighty percent ownership or more permits financial consolidation for tax purposes. Sometimes identity is completely lost while occasionally a trade name, company image, managerial factors, and so on, influence retention of identity.

2. *Diversification.* Expansion through the additions of new product lines and services which are countercyclical, counterseasonal and/or offering opportunities to offset the impact of technological change or global competition. Internal development, acquisitions, and mergers are approaches to diversification.

11

3. *Merger.* Joining of two or more separate entities into one company to achieve one or more of the following: (a) minimizing administrative expense; (b) linking product lines that are potentially complementary to growth; (c) accomplishing diversification; (d) taking advantage of financial/tax advantages such as abundance of cash, tax-loss carry forward, and attractive cash flow; and (e) realizing gains from other situations such as managerial talent, access to raw materials, site location, and similar business factors. A synergetic effect $(1 + 1 = 2\frac{1}{2})$ is expected from the merger.

4. *Spin-off.* Sale of assets that are segments of the business but can function as a separate operation. This means sale of a going concern and not, for example, only land or plant and equipment. After an acquisition or merger, some components are commonly spun off to recover capital and unload operations not part of future plans.

5. *Divestiture.* Sale of a whole division or subsidiary that has not been significantly divided or reorganized after an acquisition or merger. The integrity of the original operation basically has been preserved and not recently combined with another asset to make up a more salable package. Justice department rulings frequently motivate a divestiture.

The decision to grow and diversify through acquisitions, mergers, spin-offs, and divestitures should be part of both strategies and formal plans. Specific criteria compatible with these plans should be developed for each move. Strategies should be formulated to accomplish each of the five points just given and bridge the time span between SROP and the long-range plan. Alternatives not meeting the criteria should be disregarded.

Simulation models can test acquisition possibilities in combination with forecasts on what the existing company is expected to be in the years after acquisition. Modern management techniques such as those discussed in Chapter Nine permit analysis that portrays the impact of undesirable possibilities such as sharp increases in interest rates, a recession, or technological advances.

ACQUISITIONS FOR GROWTH

The business environment is dynamic with almost unlimited opportunities. In order to attract and hold investors, a company must continually grow and increase its earnings. Broadly, there are two primary sources of this growth: (1) internal—improvement of existing products, geographic expansion, and new products flowing from company research, or (2) external—allocation of resources to acquire rights and assets capable of making a product new to the firm, the rights to market a new product or service, and going concerns currently earning profits.

Most companies use a combination of both internal and external sources to achieve profit goals. The aspect of internal development that disturbs executive management is the large sums of capital applied to research which have not resulted in significant new products and services. While these investments are the basic source of new technology and many firms depend on growth from this source, executives often opt for the acquisition of a going concern because they are buying a proven product or service and immediate profits.

Figure 11–1 illustrates a typical result of combining internal and external sources of growth.

Figure 11–1. Plan for Growth

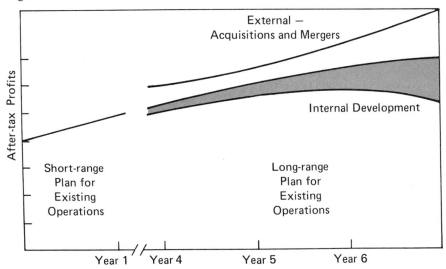

Influences on Acquisitions Programs

Product Life Cycles

During the past 20 years global competition has increased sharply. Strong, innovative companies have emerged in other countries. An American product or service that fulfilled a purpose in the 1960s may still satisfy the buyer's need but not as cheaply or with comparatively less quality, or at the expense of higher transportation cost, and so on. Figure 11–2 shows schematically the shrinking life cycle for American products. As this development became apparent, management in many companies felt that they could not develop new products fast enough internally to remain competitive.

Acquisitions, Mergers, and Divestitures   389

Figure 11-2. Shrinking Product Life Cycles

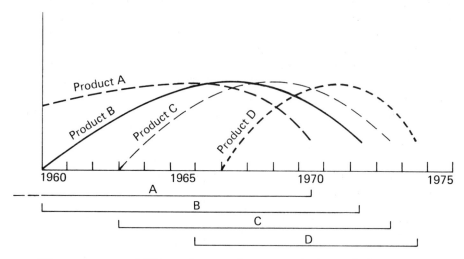

The concepts of life cycles can be expanded to whole industries. The time span from infancy to maturity is becoming shorter because of the technological changes and global developments such as changes in control over key raw materials. Ease of entry and intensified competition accelerate the pace toward maturity. In the end profits are eliminated and/or customers can satisfy their requirements by buying from wholly new industries. Perceptive management will recognize maturity and take steps to direct the company toward industries in an earlier stage of development.

Distribution of Earnings

A company can achieve growth most readily through a cash plowback program which:

1. Uses current cash flow to build the future and minimizes distribution of earnings.
2. Blends the proper combination of growth from internal sources and acquisition of existing operations.
3. Picks a significant majority of winners instead of losers in the allocation of capital.

Management has the responsibility to provide investors with an adequate return on their capital. In the simplest terms, this return can be in the form of cash through dividends, appreciation of the investor's capital, or a combination of the two. The company's policy is established by tradition, the board of directors, or management, and places a constraint on the amount of cash that can be reinvested in growth programs. For example, deciding to pay out 40% of the earnings in dividends means less cash for plowback than a 10% policy. Under a 40% policy the firm eventually has less equity and a smaller base on which to borrow for funding future growth programs.

Decisions on Internal Development Programs

Figure 11—1 simplifies the options open to executive management. Without the direction of proven ideas or existing operations, some businesses will not attain growth objectives. However, most companies allocate a substantial portion of their resources to internal development through:

1. Improvements in their existing products.
2. Improvements in processes, packaging, handling, and transportation of their existing products.
3. Research on new related product lines.
4. Development of wholly new concepts for growth.

Applied research in (1) and (2) lengthens the product life cycle and is basically a good use of funds. In some cases, however, new projects conceived within a company such as in (3) and (4) do not meet expectations. Normally there will be little or no historical data available to support estimates of the market, product acceptance, and costs. In these situations millions of dollars are spent on projects that are logical and well researched, but the forecasts are wrong and the money is lost. These experiences contrast with many success stories that justify $32 billion in expenditures on research and development in 1974.

Resources Gained and Given in Acquisitions

Resources Gained

The benefits of an acquisition can be broader in scope than the direct after-tax profits of the seller. Figure 11—3 serves to illustrate these possibilities.

Resources gained in blocks 1 and 2 are straightforward. However, those gained in block 3 can include: (1) patents, nonpatentable products and services, trademarks, copyrights, good will, and systems; (2) territorial rights to or market penetration for potentially profitable products and services; (3) competitors with innovations which would endanger growth; (4) plant locations in modern condition, and (5) special situations such as sources of raw materials, water, energy, and need for expansion.

Usually it is not possible to acquire a firm that has both a high rate of current earnings and a tax loss benefit. Occasionally it is

Figure 11–3. Building Blocks for Company Growth

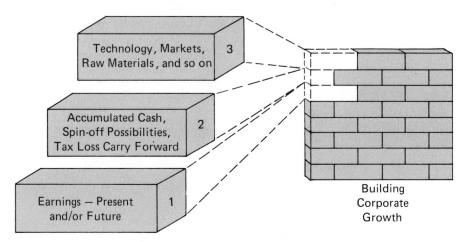

feasible to buy a firm emerging from a loss period but is realizing its earnings potential.

Is it realistic to expect all three building blocks to exist in one acquisition? Rarely, but it is feasible. For example, imagine a firm that is currently profitable and gaining momentum, but in the recent past it has piled up significant losses that now provide a write-off against current earnings. The firm also controls important raw materials and property locations.

Resources Given

To gain the benefits of an acquisition, a company must give up resources. Each asset acquired is made on the assumption that the trade-off is beneficial to the buyer. Figure 11–4 summarizes resources used.

The student will recall from courses in finance that the buyer can obtain all the assets of a firm without buying the shares to avoid hidden or unknown liabilities of the corporate entity. Mention should also be made of the need for advice on the tax implications of each approach, especially multinational transactions. Creative design of the acquisition framework can result in significant tax savings for both buyer and seller.

The Price Paid for an Acquisition

In judging losers and winners, profit performance is compared with the price paid. Shareholders are generally impatient with intangible benefits. The capital used must yield a return in dividends and/or share appreciation.

Figure 11-4. Resources Given

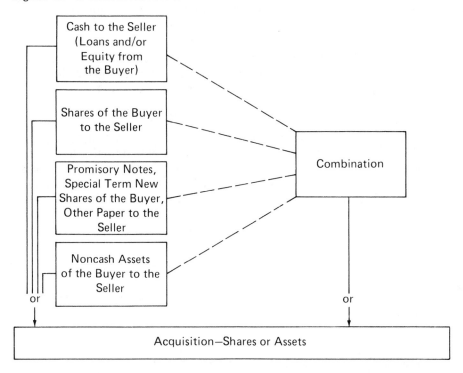

The basic point of emphasis is that companies buy present and future earnings, not assets. For example, a firm has invested $1,000 and is earning $10 per year after taxes. This is a return of only 1%. A potential buyer investigates whether there is overinvestment or underperformance. Suppose that studies conclude that earnings after taxes should be $150 per year and specific steps can be taken to achieve this potential. What should the buyer pay? Let us consider the negotiating results that could occur.

RESULT 1 The seller is unaware of the true potential but is motivated to bargain intensively because of (1) the magnitude of the original investment and (2) some knowledge that earnings are below full possibilities. The buyer uses the seller's ego to claim it could not be much greater than present performance. Negotiations about price concentrate on the return a buyer will receive. If the buyer's objective is 10% per year after taxes, he can pay only $100 on the basis of published earnings. A 10% objective means 10 times earnings. A 12½% objective means 8 times earnings and so on.

The buyer can concede the possibility of $50 per year in after-tax earnings and also concede to permit the "times earnings" standard to slip to 12. This results in an acquisition price of $600. The seller may be upset about the loss of $400 of capital on one hand, but relieved to obtain a price as high as $600 on the other.

The buyer pays 60 times present earnings. Concessions are based on the assumption that $150 per year can be earned. If the studies are accurate, the buyer has paid four times the after-tax profits and will earn a 25% simple rate of return on capital invested (23% discounted rate of return based on present values).

An important point to keep in mind is the time needed to achieve the $150 potential. If, for example, 5 years are required to improve from $10 to the optimum instead of a few weeks, and the life of the investment is 12 years, the discounted rate of return based on present values is only $9\frac{1}{2}\pm\%$, a considerable difference and much less of a bargain. The following table illustrates the results.

	Year 1	2	3	4	5	6	7	
Earnings per year	$10	20	40	80	150	150	150	
	8	9	10	11	12	Average Earnings—12 Years		
Earnings per year	150	150	150	150	150	$112.50		

RESULT 2 The seller is fully aware of the potential and, in fact, foresees $400 per year in earnings in 5 years. The seller insists the business is in the embryonic stage of the life cycle for its products, and views a $150 estimate as extremely conservative, perhaps even contrived to obtain a lower price. To allow for contingencies and the present value of money, the seller is magnanimous and is willing to discuss earnings of $200 per year despite current performance of $10. The buyer started with a standard of 10 times earnings, but this would result in a $2,000 price—over twice the maximum. Instead, the buyer counters with 5 times the estimate of $150 in profits or a $750 price.

The seller by a negotiating approach has maneuvered the buyer into an initial offer 25% greater than the price concluded in Result 1. The facts have not changed, only speculation about what might occur. If the buyer can walk away from the bargaining table and does not need this particular acquisition, the final price could range between $750 and $1,000. If not, the buyer will probably pay between $1,500 and $2,000 because the company is eager to obtain the seller's company.

Between the two extremes of Results 1 and 2 are a spectrum of possibilities. It is necessary for the buyer to maintain perspective on what should be paid for an acquisition. With no risk, a firm can earn

5% after taxes by drawing interest on its capital at the bank. If it elects a balanced portfolio of stocks, dividends and share appreciation might yield an average of 8% after taxes. Why incur the risk of conducting business for less than 10% or 10 times earnings?

During the height of the conglomerate acquisitions boom the price earnings ratios for companies acquired averaged: 1966—16.5; 1967—17.6; and 1968—20.6 respectively.[1] The objective of most buyers is a net price of 6 to 7 times earnings or 14 to 17% rate of return, and this was the price earnings ratio of many firms in the mid-1970s. How then can companies justify 20 or 40 times earnings? These buyers visualize the following:

1. The seller's firm fills out a strategic plan and enables other operations to earn greater profits as well as improving the acquisition's performance.
2. Management has been inadequate. The present potential is appraised as in Result 1. Specific changes will yield the improvement that justifies the apparently high price.
3. Profit potential is in the future because products are in the early stage of their life cycle as per the contention in Result 2. Estimates for growth in earnings provide the incentive to buy without major changes in management or additional investment.
4. Lack of captial has restricted scope of operations. Investment in addition to the purchase price will yield an overall return justifying both phases of capital allocation.

These reasons enable a company to pay an apparently high price and still remain within its standard for return on investment.

Buyer Research

The more a buyer knows about a firm being considered for acquisition, the better position he is in to make a decision. Also, the study is the foundation for negotiating strategy. Summarizing, the purpose of buyer research is to identify:

1. Facts about the business such as present market position, financial details, and technological condition.
2. Managerial competence and attitudes toward the possibility of a new owner.
3. Forecasts of what will occur in future years to estimate after-tax earnings per year.

[1] W. T. Grimm and Co., Chicago, Illinois.

4. Probability of government intervention and the impact on both the acquisition and the overall company.

5. Components of the acquisition not part of the strategic plan which can be spun off to lessen the net price.

6. The "downside out" position or the situation if the worst conditions forecast occurred and the company had to: (a) sell under these distressed circumstances or (b) operate the assets.

This information gives executive management what it requires to decide if the company should buy. If the buy decision is made, a negotiating strategy can begin to be designed. Important points necessary in the agreement other than price are identified and a minimum position is decided for each item.

Intelligence

Methodical buyers attempt to uncover more information about the seller than audits, technical appraisals, and so on, normally reveal. They wish to be certain nothing is overlooked or being withheld. The seller has made statements on why he wants to sell, and the buyer should be confident the reasons are valid. Selected sources of information are queried in a way that develops intelligence without a tactical indiscretion. However, some risk of disclosure is always involved in contacting people outside the company even through third parties.

Going farther than these inquiries involves practices that are questionable to most business executives. However, occasionally investigative services are authorized to unearth information on personal habits and background details of the seller and the negotiator that can later be used during negotiations. These investigations sometimes lead to damaging disclosures, and this tactic is viewed as highly unethical.

Comments on the Acquisition Approach to Growth

Most of the foregoing discussion assumes that executive management will competently analyze the specifics of an acquisition within the guidelines of their plans and enter into agreements that achieve written goals. However, several factors can cause problems: (1) being misled by the seller; (2) overestimating the upward thrust of the operation particularly when diversifying, and (3) changes in company plans that altered the "fit."

One common problem area concerns firms that have an aggressive acquisitions campaign. Occasionally they find themselves without a company to acquire which meets specifications. To keep up earning momentum, management changes its requirements rather than pass over a possibility with an acceptable return on investment. This leads to a poor "fit" and complications that should not have occurred.

The most frequent loss of earnings potential occurs during the transition stage when the acquired company is being absorbed into the buyer. Insensitive decisions made by the acquiring firm often damage intangible assets of a going concern such as management talent, customer goodwill, historically good labor relations, and similar intangibles. Less often the buyer will reorganize in a way that tangible assets are rendered useless.

MERGERS

The difference between an acquisition and a merger is explained on pps. 387—88. Students will sometimes hear the two terms used as if they are interchangeable when, in fact, they are not. This confusion arises many times as a result of the psychological tactic of a buyer or seller to label an acquisition a merger. In these cases it is decided that a better attitude toward the new owners and executives can be generated by portraying a pooling of talent and resources rather than a takeover by powerful outside sources.

Technically, a merger is a joining of companies resulting in revised goals, plans, and policies. New organizational relationships are created; assignments are given to the most qualified personnel but with attention to balancing selections between the merger participants. Improved financial capacity is normal. A new company name may be selected to avoid the appearance that one company has taken over the other. The combination eliminates some old problems and gains some new ones. However, the purpose of a merger is to improve the probability of a higher rate of earnings by proceeding together rather than separately.

When a question arises about which of the merging companies gained the dominant power, the answer may be found in one of the following:

1. Did either firm surrender identity? Does a new name, company identification symbol, and/or trademark favor one company? Where is headquarters? Who is moving where? What reasons are given for changes, if any?

2. What percentage of the power structure does each management team have in the new organization? Are those appointed to important jobs similar in background, methods, outside interests, and

other indicators that could denote compatibility with new executives in key positions rather than a balancing of assignments between the merging entities?

3. What percentage do former shareholders have in the surviving entity as compared to their previous position? Which faired best? If one portion is less than 40 per cent, did that firm have large blocks of shares which can effectively unite to have an impact on decision making, or is ownership dispersed among small investors?

4. Do disclosures on plans for expansion, use or disposition of physical facilities, consolidation of product lines and brand names, geographic emphasis, and selection of approximately equal assets for development indicate a significant bias toward one of the previous companies?

A picture emerges from answers to these questions. It could mean an opportunity for the careers of astute employees who read the signs and make the appropriate move. The recommended assessment will also give an indication of possible shifts in power that usually occur as the merger matures and factions develop.

Motivations for Merging

The general incentive to merge is an improved outlook for after-tax earnings. This improvement originates with both offensive and defensive motivations. Figure 11−5 shows the basic concepts.

A motivation for one party is usually not a motivation for the other party in a merger. It is feasible, however, that two strong aggressive firms will join to dominate a market or two weak companies join as a means of becoming competitive. Most often it is a mixture of defensive and offensive reasons which leads to a merger.

Some examples will clarify the points. Imagine an oil company with good distribution in the eastern United States, adequate modern refineries to service this market, and the prime source of its crude oil has just been nationalized. At the same time, picture a company with distribution the western states, surplus crude oil sources, and a desire to expand nationwide. The match is obvious, and some of the facts (not all) fit the Atlantic Refining/Richfield Oil merger completed in January, 1966.

Another merger situation arises when a successful product spurts in demand, and the company uses its capital to add new capacity. However, it does not adequately plan for working capital to cover the increased cash outflow from the expanded volume. The company borrows money to pay its bills and then borrows some more. Management begins to realize that profits are seriously diminished by in-

Figure 11-5. Motivations to Merge

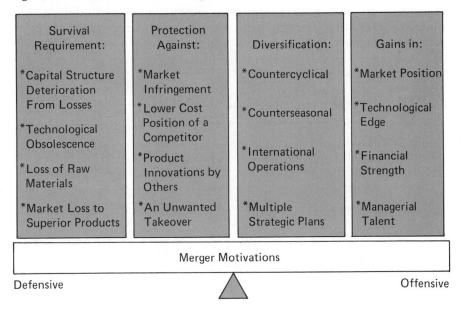

Survival Requirement:	Protection Against:	Diversification:	Gains in:
*Capital Structure Deterioration From Losses	*Market Infringement	*Countercyclical	*Market Position
*Technological Obsolescence	*Lower Cost Position of a Competitor	*Counterseasonal	*Technological Edge
*Loss of Raw Materials	*Product Innovations by Others	*International Operations	*Financial Strength
*Market Loss to Superior Products	*An Unwanted Takeover	*Multiple Strategic Plans	*Managerial Talent

Merger Motivations

Defensive   Offensive

terest payments and that the bank from whom they borrowed working capital might own the business if the situation is allowed to continue. The high growth rate makes the firm an excellent merger candidate, and an established competitor with surplus cash opens negotiations. These conditions would have resulted in an acquisition but the growth company developed a refinancing plan with its bank to strengthen its negotiating position.

Price of Shares in a Merger

Each of the two merger candidates appraises the value of the other through studies. When the shares are traded on a stock exchange, a day-to-day value is established. However, the market value may not accurately portray the true value of one or both parties. Yet, the price on the stock exchange will strongly influence negotiations and has often been the reason for terminating discussions between companies that would have benefited from the proposed merger.

Sellers and buyers in the stock market drive share prices up or down through speculation and/or emotional reactions in addition to capital investment. The price of one merger candidate changes disproportionately to the other, and the idea is sometimes dropped. Another potential partner is identified or negotiations are tabled until stock prices permit a reasonable agreement. However, merging parties are not always limited to the stock market price nor are they restricted to exchanges of shares. The price is a guideline, and shareholders have the right to decide if management proposes different arrangements to conclude a merger. Figure 11–6 illustrates alternatives involving an exchange of shares and problems with current prices of shares.

Figure 11–6. Mergers Involving Exchange of Shares

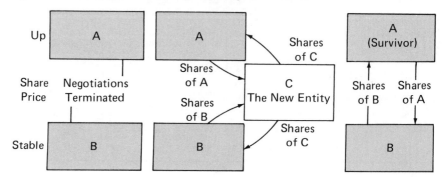

Variations in the Mechanics of a Merger

Recall that the companies in a merger are joining to achieve a synergetic effect on earnings performance (1 + 1 = over 2). Normally, all the resources of both companies are needed to attain this objective. Consequently, cash to shareholders of one of the participants is a rare occurrence; so is giving other assets of a participant to satisfy the shareholders of the other party. Both of these approaches have a second disadvantage in that the recipient must pay taxes on the cash. This is the primary motivation to exchange some type of shares.

Instead of dealing only with common stock, variations have been devised to convince reluctant merger participants. These include the following:

1. Convertible, Cumulative Preferred. The fixed dividend rate gives some control in fluctuations of share price. Less amplitude in the fluctuations means protection on the downside while the convertible feature places no limits on the upside. The stockholder temporarily trades voting rights for a measure of protection in an uncertain situation. The concept can be applied to both a new survivor corporation and when the entity of one of the participants is the survivor.

2. Participating, Voting Preferred. One or both of the participants

in the merger trades common shares for an issue that provides voting rights. The fixed dividend is usually set at a lower than normal rate for preferred shares. However, the holder of the new issue participates in other distributions of earnings according to the merger agreement. In this approach some share price control and dividend protection benefits are gained, while little or nothing is lost.

3. Subordinated, Convertible Debentures. This concept involves a trade of voting rights for excellent downside protection. The fixed interest rate guarantees an income to debenture holders because these are debt instruments and default is a public indication of serious troubles. In the event of failure, the subordination places them last in the line of creditors but ahead of all equity issues. With success the convertible feature allows the debenture holder to convert to common shares and voting rights.

There are other combinations that have been discussed in your finance courses. These approaches are used when problems arise in the process of merging companies. Rather than a comparatively simple exchange of shares, a portion of the owners are uncertain about the net gain and need inducement in the form of one of the three examples.

Disclosure of Merger Discussions

It is a fact that 13 officers, directors, and employees of Texas Gulf Sulphur were prosecuted by the Securities Exchange Commission in 1965 for failing to disclose publicly a 1963 copper ore find in Timmons, Ontario until they had purchased several thousand shares of the company's stock. In August, 1966, a judge upheld the SEC accusation but released 11 of the 13.

The history of subsequent court actions and counteractions in this case is not pertinent to mergers, but the reactions of corporation officers and directors in the United States to this SEC prosecution are important: (1) management tends to disclose serious merger possibilities much earlier than in the past. This means that public speculation on share prices can change the basis on which the negotiations were initiated; (2) rival candidates for a merger can move into the picture and make offers that might be more attractive to one of the original discussants, and (3) personal speculation by executives of prospective merger participants has almost completely stopped and conflict of interest in negotiations is minimized.

If the stock market operated wholly on a rational basis, the results would be completely positive. However, emotion and the accelerated rise and fall in the price of shares because of speculation means that early disclosure can destroy a potential merger which should rationally take place.

Merger Factors Other Than Price

Philosophies and methods of management and interpretation of responsibilities to shareholders can be so different between two firms well suited on paper that the results are far below expectations. Questions of integrity and ethical behavior need not be involved. It could simply be approaches to making operating decisions and formulating future plans.

Examples of Contrasting Management Methods

Management of what was formerly Longview Industries has been integrated into key positions of the new entity resulting from a merger with Highroller Corporation. Longview was owned by the Long family and they are 43% owners of Longview Highroller. The management of Highroller implemented their stock options, but the total shares owned by executives is less than 3%. Picture the first joint meeting of management on reorganization. Each group has submitted a plan to realize economies from the merger. There is basic agreement on what has to be done. However, Longview wishes to give termination notices with a settlement based on length of service and rank. Highroller proposes to give each management employee 30 days and other personnel 2 weeks. They contend that the economics of the merger are set back months by the generosity proposed by Longview. This difference of approach may be symptomatic of other serious clashes that could occur between two groups of executives in the future.

In another situation, it is discovered that several members of Highroller's management are the owners of a company offering to buy property from the new entity. Investigation reveals that a report confirming valuable mineral deposits on the land has been "misplaced." It is obvious that there has been an attempt at fraud, but the worst fact is that those dismissed were part of the assets in Longview's assessment of the merger. Also, "likes" attract "likes" and reorganization may create a serious conflict between management teams.

In a third situation, Longview has always maintained a high level of cash balances with its bank. While the interest rate received is lower than other alternatives, the bank has been extremely cooperative in syndicating long-term loans for expansion programs. Highroller, however, believes shopping will result in the same terms or better for long-term money and that it is prudent to invest cash in commercial paper and other relatively liquid alternatives to earn the maximum rate of interest. Both approaches are defensible but represent significantly different philosophies.

In addition to management methods and philosophy, several factors should be studied before a contract to assure shareholders, directors, and key executives that they will get from the merger what they hope to get. These factors include:

1. *Audit of Accounts.* Degree of detail will depend on the negotiating position, timing planned for closing on the contract, and human factors such an an intuitive feeling points are being exaggerated in the discussions. Validation of earnings is fundamental. Also, unearthing significant liabilities could change the structure of the merger.

2. *Survey of Personnel.* Depth of the survey will depend on the importance of management and special skills in the merger. The training and experience of key personnel should be identified: (a) for initial discussions on organization; (b) to be confident about achieving forecasts for earnings, and (c) to gain insight on the attitude of employees toward the company. Also, the firm's agreement with unions could be a problem area.

3. *Market Position.* Research should include trends in customer attitude, estimates on product life cycles, infringement by competitive materials and products, geographic scope at present and in the future, and forecasts of cash inflow by region and product category. Optimism about the outlook for the merger candidate must be investigated by qualified personnel who are not emotionally involved.

4. *Inventory of Facilities and Properties.* Assessment of the company's equipment and its position on an appropriate range of production costs per product category. This determines whether facilities are going to be competitive. In addition, are the major expenditures required to be competitive or remain in operation? A thorough analysis of tangible assets is basic.

5. *Financial Appraisal.* A *before* and *after* analysis of the earnings outlook is essential. Also, an appraisal of financial structure is needed for working capital requirements, degree of leverage, and possible new issues to persuade reluctant shareholders or strengthen the equity position. Accuracy of the analysis will, in part, depend on the conclusions of 1 through 4.

6. *Compatibility Test.* Upon completion of these analyses, a reassessment of the reasons for mergers should be made. After a "hard" look, is what you get what you need? In most cases it is much less expensive to terminate discussions than attempt to recast the merger to meet expectations.

Within each of the six points on the checklist there is another checklist that is long and detailed. It identifies specific steps to take if you are on the auditing team, the marketing team, and so on. Summarizing, these analysis are similar to a feasibility study for a new investment or buyer research for an acquisition. It is essential for all parties involved, particularly shareholders and management, to have these appraisals conducted by competent personnel. If the other participant does not agree to in-depth studies and appears to be hurrying negotiations, it is often as sign that there is something hidden.

DIVESTITURES AND SPIN-OFFS

As defined in the first section, a divestiture is the sale of operations that were originally independent of the selling company. While some modifications are usually made during the period of ownership, the operation being divested is similar to what it was before being acquired by or mergered with the seller.

A spin-off is the selling of a segment of an acquisition or possibly a group of segments from numerous acquisitions to unload operations not compatible with company plans and to regain some of the capital used to acquire the overall company. To be a spin-off instead of a sale of selected assets, the component being sold must be able to operate as an independent division.

There are situations when it is difficult to decide whether a sale is a divestiture or spin-off. Modifications have been made but trademarks and other components of the original entity have been retained. The primary point to consider is that both are variations of sales which can operate independently.

Motivations for Selling

Listed here are typical reasons for companies to sell off part of their business.

Divestitures

1. Government Action. Antimonopoly decrees or irregularities in the transaction result in a company having no other choice. (See the case in this chapter.)
2. Financial Reorganization. Defensively, the firm may have overcommitted to make this or another acquisition (or merger) and needs to sell to lessen debt and strengthen its financial

structure. Offensively, the operation being sold may not be as good a fit with future plans as other acquisitions, and management cannot financially do both.

3. Shift in Company Direction. The purpose for which the acquisition or merger was made is no longer a major factor in future plans. Cash and borrowing power are required for other investments. Also, dilution of managment time is often a factor.

4. Special Situations. Trades with other companies to obtain important links to future plans for growth, geographic withdrawals, conflicts in policies and methods, and similar developments motivate a sale.

Spin-offs

1. Recovery of Capital. Streamlining components of an acquisition not part of your plans to make them salable is usually a first step toward a successful spin-off. Some of these sales have gained more than the cost of the original acquisition.

2. Earnings Improvement. Unloading a loser to a careless buyer is a common occurence. This is the fundamental reason for the emphasis on thorough analysis of an operation being considered for purchase.

3. Government Action. It is feasible that a compromise solution with authorities will result in a spin-off instead of a divestiture. This solution may leave the buyer with the primary elements he originally wanted, or it might lead to additional acquisitions and spin-offs to get the government out of the picture and achieve balance in operations.

4. Special Situations. Problems with labor unions, management hardened against change, destruction of a portion of the facilities, and community problems are typical of developments leading to a spin-off.

The Deconglomerates

In the late 1960s a number of firms were famous for aggressive acquisition programs. Table 11–1 shows a partial list of firms forced through the full cycle of acquisition and divestiture. Some conglomerates were successful despite having to divest a few companies. Others, such as L-T-V, nearly went bankrupt. Investors lost millions of dollars as the stock market became disenchanted with these high rolling firms.

Table 11-1. Reversing the Acquisition Course

Conglomerate	Divestment (Completed or pending)
Avco Corp.	Moffats, Ltd. (appliances)
Bangor Punta	Metcalf & Eddy (water treatment)
	Connell Associates (water treatment)
	Sunn, Low, Tom & Hara (water treatment)
	Bangor & Aroostock (railroad)
Brunswick Corp.	Concorde Yacht Division (boats)
	School Equipment Division
Commonwealth United	Real Estate Division (realty)
(under Chapter X,	Wenner & Kane (insurance)
Bankruptcy Act)	Commonwealth United Music (music)
	Betty Petroleum (oil and gas)
	Seeburg (vending machines)
Aqua Industries	Ward Mfg. (camper trailers & coaches)
	Vattco Panden (metal buildings)
	Natco Division (ceramic tile, brick)
	Producers, Inc. (warehousing)
Glen Alden	RKO Stanley Warner Theatres (theaters)
Gulf & Western	Transnation (sports complex)
	Norma Hoffman Bearings
	Famous Players (entertainment)
Kidde (Walter)	U.S. Lines (shipping)
	Globe Securities
	Siltron (lighting equipment)
Kinney National Service	Kinear Corp. (auto rental)
	Ashley Famous Agency (talent agency)
Ling-Temco-Vought	Wilson Pharmaceutical (drug products)
	Wilson Sporting Goods (sports equipment)
	Braniff International (airline)
	Okonite (copper & wire products)
Litton Industries	Clifton Division (metal products)
	Koehler & Dayton (fuel valves)
National General	CAIV Systems (television operations)
	Columbia S & L (S & L association)
National Industries	Southern Tank Lines (trucking)
	Retail Centers of America (discount operators)
	GIS Gouco Stores (discount operations)
	Merry Mfg. (impulse toys)
Northwest Industries	Chicago & North Western (railroad)
Republic Corp.	CC Plastics (display equipment)
	Gale & Thompson (display equipment)
	Shelmac (telephone equipment)
	Duco (engineering)

Table 11–1. Reversing the Acquisition Course cont'd.

Conglomerate	Divestment (Completed or pending)
Signal Companies	Signal Equities (realty)
	American Independent Oil (oil)
	Houston Refinery & various oil properties
Textron	Amster Morton (steel products)
	Caroline Tools Division
	Peat Mfg. Co.
	Randall Division's housewear unit
Whittaker Corp.	Metal Resources (metal products)
	Hol Gal (power equipment)
	Universal Battery (power equipment)

Used by permission of *Financial World*, Macro Publishing Corporation, New York.

Some special reasons for the problems developed in addition to government interference and overleveraging. They underline some of the principles in this chapter.

First, takeovers were often ruthless and people's careers were destroyed. The acquiring company drove out badly needed management. The blood baths were frequently accompanied by an arrogance that greatly magnified the resentment of remaining management. While streamlining was usually required, the approach used frequently diminished the value of the asset acquired.

Second, research into the potential and characteristics of an acquisition candidate became superficial as pressure increased to buy more and more companies. People qualified to conduct thorough venture analyses had too much to do. Most importantly, there was a feeling that if time was taken to undertake a thorough analysis, the seller might conclude an agreement with someone else. A frantic atmosphere developed that resulted in many of the fundamental research steps being bypassed.

Third, tender offers[2] were made to shareholders of firms whose management did not cooperate in supplying data before the offer. As a result, acquisitions were made with little more information than an individual investor buying a few shares. Once enough stock had been purchased, the conglomerates got a look at the business. Several were shocked at what they had bought.

Fourth, executive management of conglomerates often took the position that good managers can manage anything, and that

[2] Tender offers are public offers to buy shares of a company at a price which is usually above the stock market price. This is a means of obtaining ownership when voting stock is owned by many dispersed shareholders.

Acquisitions, Mergers, and Divestitures   **407**

knowledge of the product and industry were not essential. This led to some poor decisions and compounded problems with personnel who had this knowledge.

Recognition by management of what occurred in the 1960s has led to a series of divestitures and spin-offs in the 1970s. While multiple reasons are usually cited, many of these companies would have been stronger and more profitable operations if they had followed more closely the guidelines for acquisition research and planning.

Going Public or "Private"

Many companies went public in the 1960s. A few were successful in the 1970s. Going public means selling shares of a company to investors who were not founders or managing partners in the business. It also means establishing a market place for buying and selling these shares on a regular basis. A brokerage house can act as the market place when shares are traded within a state, or the over-the-counter market and stock exchanges can provide the opportunity to trade shares on an interstate basis. Sale of Powerite stock mentioned on page 49 provides an example.

The motivations for going public are: (1) owners can realize cash from sale of their shares, and this cash reflects company growth under their direction. Dependency on the business as their source of wealth is lessened and the sale is a form of personal diversification; (2) the value of shares of a successful company traditionally increases after going public, thereby increasing the wealth represented by shares retained, and (3) the value of privately held companies in the opinion of these shareholders, has been appraised unsatisfactorily by tax authorities in the case of a death and inheritance of the shares. A price established daily on a stock exchange circumvents this problem.

Despite these reasons for going public, some firms are buying their own shares wherever they are traded. A few have completed the cycle and are completely private. The primary reason for this change in direction is avoiding a takeover by another firm or large scale investors such as the Arab oil producers. When stock prices are very depressed (in the mid-1970s shares of well-known companies traded for a fraction of their working capital), solid firms are targets for investors who would want to have membership on the board of directors and to influence management.

An example of vulnerability would be the Chrysler Corporation on June 30, 1974. On that day, book value per share was $46 and its shares closed at $12. A tender offer of $15 might have attracted sufficient shares to gain over 50% ownership for less than $500 million. Another example of vulnerability is the fact that every share publicly traded in England in late 1974 could have been bought for the amount of one quarter's payments by western buyers to Saudi Arabia and Iran for crude oil.

Another reason for going private is that depressed stock prices mean wealth retained in shares of the company is far below the company's estimate of true value. Executive management has decided, in many cases, that extreme understatement of value should not be permitted to continue. Also, as the company buys its stock and shares become scarce, the stock price increases. In some cases, the acquisition of a majority of shares which prevents a takeover and the improved stock price has influenced management to stop short of going wholly private.

Two reasons for going all the way are first, the time and costs of reporting to shareholders and complying with laws and regulations protecting small investors. Second, conflict of interest is cited by service companies such as accounting firms and advertising agencies. Management decisions based on industry practices or company guidelines resulting in the refusing of certain kinds of business could be detrimental to the investor.

SOME FUNDAMENTALS FOR NEGOTIATING

In the buying and selling of company assets, millions of dollars ride on the negotiating skills of executive management. While this skill comes naturally to some individuals, most managers do not have this capability and are thrust into their first negotiations with inadequate training and experience. This discussion covers some of basic points to assist in clarifying the bargaining process.

The Need to Complete the Transaction

The primary point in negotiating is to be realistic about how badly you want or need (most always different from desire) to complete the transaction. Will the business fail or be seriously hurt if the deal is not made? Or, is there another possibility which will accomplish the same purpose? Or does the firm buy several companies per year and this possibility is not essential to any component of the company plan.

There is diminishing want and/or need in the three examples. If you are a buyer and there is a theoretical asking price of $1,000, you can expect to pay close to the asking price if the acquisition is considered very important to your business. When it is not critical to your business, it may be possible to buy for considerably less than $1,000.

Some negotiators, especially buyers who have an active acquisition program, will be able to extract optimum terms from a transaction regardless of how desperate the situation is. This emphasizes that negotiating is an art between seller minimum and buyer maximum. The skill can be partly learned, but much comes from instinct.

Preparation

The study undertaken (buyer research) to determine the advisability of proceeding with the transaction is the cornerstone for negotiations. It is usually initiated, as a result of direction provided by short- and long-range plans, strategies formulated to achieve specific objectives in the plans, and screening research which identifies specific alternatives for the sale or acquisition. This study gives the information for two types of preparation normal in major contracts: (1) definition of minimum and optimum terms and (2) indications of the other party's position.

Definition of Your Position

Books have been written on preparing for negotiations. *Creative Business Negotiations* by Gerard I. Nierenberg is particularly good. In this chapter it is sufficient to cover the steps leading to discussions.

1. Study the facts, opinions, and forecasts to decide on the maximum price and the methods of payment. The optimum situation and number of alternative methods will depend on your flexibility.
2. Identify nonprice terms that must be in the contract. Subsequently, isolate other desirable features that management would prefer in the contract putting priorities on the items for bargaining purposes.
3. Experiment with strategies by writing down approaches and comparing the ideas to your appraisal of the situation. Select a starting strategy with a proposed agenda retaining the other possibilities for approaches to counter tactics by the other negotiator.
4. Know your company's position on tactics such as misleading statements, misrepresentation of facts, and so on. Know your own position so that no incompatibility arises from differences in ethics, integrity, and honesty.
5. Review peripheral factors which could be significant such as

the place for initial negotiations, who is negotiating, timing, and similar items.

6. Consult with specialists in your company to be certain all items have been considered. This includes lawyers, the experts, marketing personnel, technical specialists, and appropriate staff.

When the negotiator has completed each of the six steps, the individual should review them again. There is always a point overlooked or a helpful term to be added. Thoroughness in preparation will partly overcome shortcomings in bargaining personality and lack of sensitivity in the discussions.

Estimating the Other Party's Position

1. Estimate probable terms including price and method of payment. Use the studies for specific rationales. Be prepared for surprises so that you are not inflexible in the discussions.

2. Augment information with intelligence from appropriate sources such as banks, competitors, suppliers, and customers. Special services are sometimes retained to obtain information in a way that cannot be traced to the negotiator. This occurs often when a family is the principal owner and there is little public data.

3. Reassess your assumptions on the other party's position. Consider every detail from the opposite point of view including the peripheral factors such as place, timing, agenda, and so on. Consider possibilities needed to close the deal including phasing of payments or delaying takeover.

4. Develop a list of concessions that could be important to the other party but are less meaningful to your company. Also identify those which are important but might be traded for high priority points in your list of terms.

Professional negotiators are thorough. They avoid careless mistakes by writing down information on each of the 10 steps. It is time consuming but the payout is a better contract than what would have occurred without the preparation.

Tactics

Chance plays a role in putting negotiators together. The stage is set for an able seller to extract the maximum from the buyer or the reverse. However, chance is less of a factor than the seller often realizes. Negotiators employed by aggressive buyers take advantage of every opportunity and their experience permits them to recognize advantages others would not.

Once discussions have begun, a number of tactics are used to gain concessions. These are often classified as follows:

BLUFF   Characteristically, the bluff involves threats to go it alone, hold up the zoning, and so on, or the "we must have a minimum of" types of statements. Deliberate lies and deception seem to be always uncovered and hurt relationships. However, negotiators can make a true statement in a dozen different ways to convey a dozen different meanings. The fundamental point in the tactic is to err on the side of audacity rather than temerity.

SURPRISE   Many negotiations have been converted to a rout by springing an important unanticipated factor at the right time. The buyer could know that the seller just defaulted on an interest payment to a bank or that a property is worthless because of hitherto unknown factors. Unethical negotiators have used personal situations against owners such as a mistress or gambling debts. It is essential that a negotiator maintain composure when hit with unexpected information. The individual can regain the offensive by adroit handling of the maneuver.

THEATRICS   Table pounding, walk-outs, and keeping people waiting are examples. Experienced negotiators have learned to remain stoic during most of these attempts at psychological maneuvering, but a knowing smile that penetrates the tactic has also been effective. Composure can gain stature at a time such as this and reverse the effect attempted by the other party.

GIMMICKS AND GADGETS   Hidden tape recorders are used to give a word-by-word record of the negotiations. A tone of voice, an undetected reaction, or background voices with important information can be detected by replaying the tape. In some cases both sides agree to recordings, but frequently it is done secretly. The place where negotiations are held can be critical if the other party has a hidden speaker which permits specialists to listen and prepare counter points. Some negotiators use pictorial displays to emphasize points. Most avoid any tactics that could jeopardize the relationship.

When a negotiator resorts to tactics instead of straight bargaining, it is usually indicative of a problem in the discussions. Probing to find out the critical point can sometimes improve the atmosphere and result in more constructive negotiating.

Reaching An Agreement

It is advisable to establish the correct negotiating environment at the beginning. Professionals will prepare thoroughly, develop a strategy including an agenda, and have priority lists for terms needed

Figure 11-7. Good Contracts

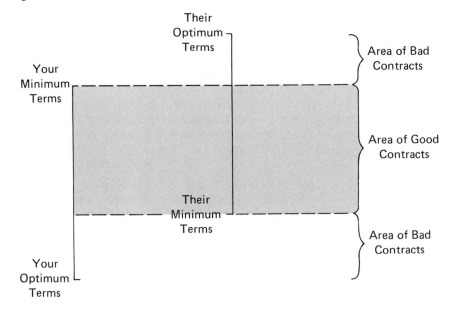

and possible concessions. When a negotiator enters the room, it is quite possible the individual will employ an entirely different strategy because of a change in people, a casual statement, or some other factor that has altered judgment of the situation.

As discussions progress it is prudent to record agreements. The negotiator should also log concessions along with the other party's concessions, sensitive points, new information and attitudes revealed in the discussions, and terms which may be difficult to attain. This log will permit the negotiator to study the progress of discussions and identify points that may be significant in reaching a successful agreement.

Figure 11-7 illustrates the concept of a fundamentally good contract. In either "bad contract" area, the party who is potentially injured will usually seek to: (1) live by the letter of a contract and not be generally cooperative or (2) attempt to break the contract. The objective of an agreement should be to meet the primary goals of both parties, achieve a balance of compromises on secondary goals, and avoid terms that place the agreement in the "poor contract" area.

SUMMARY

The activity of buying and selling assets is a critically important management technique.

Acquisitions provide a means of accomplishing company goals for growth. Three points are essential for success: (1) the amount of investment is compatible with estimates for earnings and minimum return on investment; (2) operations of the acquisition are complementary to the company's plan and will combine with existing operations to realize company objectives, and (3) handling of the transition period is carefully planned and organized to gain full support of personnel in the acquired firm as well as to absorb operations smoothly. Thorough research by the buyer before serious discussions will overcome many of the disappointments in acquisition performance cited by experienced businessmen, but errors of judgment and changes in the strategic variables will still cause problems.

Mergers are often acquisitions in disguise. There are four questions that when answered can clarify the situation, and this can be important to an individual's career. Motivations for merging are both offensive and defensive, including strategic gains or company survival. Mergers usually involve some form of exchange of shares to avoid taxation of shareholder. Because of the magnitude of merger transactions, companies normally use a checklist with the six major points given in the text.

Divestitures occur most often because of government decrees but there are a number of other motivations including overcommitment and need for financial reorganization. Spin-offs became popular as a means of regaining capital from acquisitions by gathering together unwanted segments and selling them for unusual prices in some instances. Going private is occurring more often in business, and is mostly motivated by depressed stock prices and the need for defense against takeovers.

Negotiating skills are fundamental to realizing the objective of growing through the addition of going concerns or proven ideas. Preparation is critical and can overcome limitations in bargaining skills. Tactics used in negotiations include bluffs, surprises, theatrics, and gadgets, but the optimum results for both parties come from less gamesmanship and more straightforward discussions. An extra margin can be gained by maintaining a log of the bargaining to know exactly what has occurred as a basis of identifying the optimum terms within the limits of a good contract.

DISCUSSION QUESTIONS

1. What conditions would favor a company's growth through internal development? External sources such as acquisition and mergers? Describe how you would achieve a balance.

2. How does an acquisition program of a conglomerate differ from that of a firm seeking to diversify?
3. How can a company acquire the assets of another company without acquiring its shares? How would "buyer research" enter into this decision?
4. Describe a situation in which an exchange of shares with a seller would be bad for the buyer.
5. Identify five examples of reasons for a divestiture and/or spin-off. Clarify the difference between the two in your examples.
6. Relate an acquisition/merger program to SROP and long range planning. Use one transaction to trace progress from one plan to another. Could a strategy be involved?
7. Examine Figure 11—8. If you are buying 100% of the shares and the seller will not be a factor in operations after the closing why not pay the lowest possible price?

SUGGESTED READINGS AND BIBLIOGRAPHY

Ackerman, Robert W. and Lionel L. Fray. "Financial Evaluation of a Potential Acquisition," *Financial Executive.* October, 1967, pp. 34—54.

Anderson, Harry B. "You're Out . . . Boss," *Wall Street Journal.* January 10, 1973.

Barmash, Isadore. *Welcome to Our Conglomerate—You're Fired!* 1971.

Boulden, James B. "Merger Negotiations: A Decision Model," *Business Horizons.* February, 1969, pp. 21—28.

Graichen, Raymond E. "Buying, Selling, and Merging Corporate Businesses," *Financial Executive.* November, 1965, pp. 36—53.

Haner, F. T. *Multinational Management.* February, 1973.

Healy, Robert E. "How To Size Up a Merger Candidate," *Business Management.* December, 1968, pp. 43—46.

Hershman, Arlene. "The Age of Un-Merger," June, 1970, pp. 30—33.

Hexter, Richard M. "How to Sell Your Company," *Harvard Business Review.* September—October, 1968, pp. 71—77.

Kilmer, David C. "Growth By Acquisition: Some Guidelines for Success," *Business Horizons.* pp. 55—62.

Lovejoy, F. A. *Divestment for Profit.* 1971.

Kraber, Richard W. "Acquisition Analysis: New Help From Your Computer," *Financial Executive.* March, 1970, pp. 10—15.

MacDougal, Gary E. and Fred V. Malek. "Master Plan for Merger Negotiations," *Harvard Business Review.* January—February, 1970, pp. 71—82.

McCarthy, G. D. *Acquisitions and Mergers.* 1963.

Nierenberg, Gerard I., *Creative Business Negotiations.* 1971.

Nierenberg, Gerard I., *The Art of Negotiating.* 1968.

"New Breed: The 'Deconglomerates,' " *Financial World.* January 6, 1971, pp. 13–28.

Prokop, Trudy. "Acquisitions Light the Way for LCA Expansion," *The Philadelphia Inquirer.* January 12, 1973.

"Roadblocks Slow The Urge To Merge," *Business Week.* September 10, 1966, pp. 183–188.

Rockwell, Willard F., Jr. "How To Acquire a Company," *Harvard Business Review.* September–October, 1968, pp. 121–132.

Shick, Richard A. "The Analysis of Merger and Acquisitions," *The Journal of Finance.* 1970, pp. 495–501.

Stern, Louis W. "Acquisitions: Another Viewpoint," *Journal of Marketing.* July, 1967, pp. 39–46.

"The Sharp New Line On Antitrust," *Business Week.* June 21, 1969, pp. 120–122.

"Why They Turn To Divestiture," *Business Week.* August 15, 1970, pp. 97–98.

Case: The Rise and Fall of Ling Temco Vought, Inc.

Techniques are developed. In addition, some of the problems which confronted the conglomerates are identified. The case offers the student considerable opportunities for "second guessing" executive management.

James Ling is a man dedicated wholly to business objectives. Work and pleasure are one, and rest is taken only when his physical condition demands it. To him success depends on how much of himself he is willing to apply toward defined goals. Defeat in one endeavor is only a signal to begin again.

Born in Hugo, Oklahoma, Ling quit school when he was 14. He worked at odd jobs until enlisting in the Navy during World War II where he served as an electrician's mate until the end of the war. After discharge from the service, Ling pooled his entire worth (nearly $3,000) and went into business for himself as an electrical contractor. By the end of 1947, the small Ling enterprise was grossing $70,000 annually. By the end of 1951 billings exceeded $1.5

million. In 1955 Ling sold shares to the public at the Texas State Fair, and this capital provided the means for beginning the conglomerate which had sales of $3.75 billion in 1969.

LING'S ACQUISITION TECHNIQUES

Ling built his corporate empire on acquisitions and spin-offs. His primary asset is his strong desire to succeed coupled with: (1) a very acute financial mentality; (2) an intuitive capability of sensing opportunity, and (3) the courage to follow his intuition.

His aggressiveness has been generally criticized because rarely does he withhold significant company assets as a reserve against the possibility of recession or Defense Department cutbacks. Instead he applies them to high-risk options that theoretically produce greater returns. He believes that classical management techniques cannot substitute for entrepreneurship ("caretakers vs. entrepreneurs") and that there has to be one predominant owner. This attitude may be the source of both his strength and his weakness.

Ling's acquisition technique involves selecting candidates with accumulated cash or assets convertible to cash. This added capital becomes a means of strengthening his equity position in future deals. To accomplish his acquisition objectives, Ling employs leverage, not only in the form of long-term debt but also nonvoting equity, thus obtaining management control from a relatively small cash investment. In addition, he uses what he calls "20/20 hindsight,"[1] which is a method of analyzing each step that has been taken for errors and ideas. Ling also attempts to design his deals with enough flexibility to allow him to ease out of a troublesome situation.

Perhaps his most practical strength lies in his ability to take a company apart, retaining the cash and the attractive portions of the business, and sell off the less profitable areas. In doing this, Ling appeared to be a master of acquisitions, spin-offs, financial design, organizational realignments, share

[1] This concept seems to have been abandoned in the late 1960s, and also later with Omega-Alpha, Inc. (his post-LTV venture): errors were repeated and ideas were overlooked.

exchange offers, and divestitures during the decade beginning in the mid-1950s.

The first step in Ling's technique involves borrowing under the most attractive terms to maximize leverage. The company selected for acquisitions must earn enough to service the debt and yield a reasonable return, all on a relatively small amount of equity.

The second step is to split the company into distinct and autonomous parts. The theory is that the smaller the company, the more efficient and competitive it can be.

Once these divisions are functional, the third step is for Ling to spin off those which are not part of his long-range plans. He then uses the cash from these sales to reduce the long-term debt and start the cycle all over again.

The Rise of L-T-V

Ling realized $738,000 from his unorthodox sale of 450,000 shares at the Texas State Fair in 1955. With these funds he strengthened his contracting business and in 1957 Ling was able to purchase a small California company manufacturing vibration testing equipment. (See Appendix A for a log of Ling's acquisitions and spin-offs.) Soon after, he bought Altec-Lansing, a manufacturer of high fidelity sound equipment. In 1960 Ling sold his remaining interests in the original electrical contracting business and merged Ling-Altec Electronics, Inc., with Temco Electronics and Missiles Co. The combined sales of the new company were $148 million. (See Appendix B for financial details.)

Chance-Vought was added to the combination in August, 1961 through use of warrants and convertible debentures. The purchase of Temco had put Ling into the aerospace business in direct competition with Chance-Vought. This company not only competed for military contracts, but shared the same building with Temco. Ling decided to buy Chance-Vought and eliminate this source of the defense contract competition, a move opposed by Attorney General Robert F. Kennedy. Soon after the acquisition, he began to trim the low profit components from that organization which was originally comprised of 24 divisions and 700 management personnel. When Ling was finished, Vought was operating with 11 divisions and 166 management people. However, even with this streamlining L-T-V stock was only about nine times earnings in 1964.

Ling decided at that time to split the Ling Temco Vought components into a parent holding company and three subsidiaries. The purpose of this split was four fold. *First,* it was necessary to erase the image of a dependent defense contractor which would look bad to the public in times of government cutbacks. *Second,* by splitting L-T-V the shares of subsidiaries in electronics would be in a position to command a higher market price than other industries. *Third,* if the first two moves were successful, Ling would be able to: (a) pledge more valuable stock to the banks; (b) feed into the market more shares of the now glamorous subsidiaries; (c)

pay off bank loans with new found capital, and (d) create management incentives at the subsidiary level. *Fourth,* with some bank loans retired, Long would be in a better position to finance additional acquisitions. This is exactly what happened.

At the close of 1964 L-T-V operations consisted of L-T-V Electrosystems, Inc. (developed all the electronic gear aboard the Pueblo); L-T-V Aerospace Corporation; and L-T-V-Ling Altec Corporation. Up to this time L-T-V had a high level of debt and profits were comparatively low because of defense cutbacks in the early 1960s.

In 1965 Ling wanted to acquire Okonite Company which was for sale for $31.7 million. In order to achieve this objective, he used the increasingly higher priced stock of the three subsidiaries as collateral and sold additional shares of these now glamorous issues. While L-T-V bought Okonite shares at below book value per share, the stocks sold to facilitate the acquisition were three times their own book value.

It was following this reorganization that Ling formalized what he called "Project Redeployment." This meant dividing each aquisition into parts. In some cases, Ling sold stock of the subsidiary to raise cash. In nearly every situation he spun-off the unwanted division and often made the parts worth more than the price L-T-V paid for the original company. With the purchase of Okonite Ling successfully changed L-T-V from a military contractor into a company predominantly operating in the civilian section.

L-T-V's structure in 1965 was:

L-T-V Aerospace Corp.
sales 230,000,000
% owned 75[2]

L-T-V Electrosystems, Inc.
sales 120,000,000
% owned 75.8[2]

L-T-V Consolidated
sales 460,000,000

L-T-V Altec, Inc.
sales 25,000,000
% owned 84.4

L-T-V Okonite Co. (1966)
sales 50,000,000
% owned 82.4

A high point in Ling's career was the Wilson and Company takeover in 1967. Wilson revenues from meat packing, sporting goods, and drug production were over $1 billion dollars while L-T-V's was $468 million dollars. Hence, it was referred to as a case of Jonah swallowing the whale.

Ling needed about $80 million dollars, but the money market was so tight that United States banks were forbidden to lend cash for the purpose of corporation takeover. Ling performed what he called an "end run" through Philip Shelbourne, partner in N. M. Rothschild in London. Loans totalling $50 million dollars were arranged in Europe and Ling launched "Project Touchdown" (the L-T-V name for the Wilson takeover). William Osborn of Lehman Brothers persuaded non-banking institutions in the United

States (insurance companies and the Harvard and Stanford Universities trust funds) to lend $30 million to complete the financing.

Even before all the financing had been arranged, L-T-V started buying up Wilson stock on the open market which drove up the price. Ling then authorized a tender offer to buy the additional 750,000 shares needed for control at a flat $62.50 per share, 26% higher than the $49.50 stock market price. Stock poured in and 53% of outstanding shares were purchased for $81.5 million dollars. The takeover went so smoothly that Roscoe Haynie, President of Wilson, was not aware of the Ling acquisition until the public offer.

L-T-V acquired the rest of Wilson by offering a special convertible preferred stock valued at $100 and paying a 5% dividend for $93.75 worth of Wilson common which had paid a dividend of $2. To relieve L-T-V of the $80 million debt, Ling transferred the $50 million from European banks into Wilson's books. Of the remaining $30 million, cash from Wilson trimmed this to $6 million, L-T-V's only real investment. Ling then split the company into three divisions:

> Wilson Sporting Goods
> Wilson Meat and Food
> Processors
> Wilson Chemical and Phar-
> maceutical Corp.

This tactic led to Wall Street referring to each segment as the golf ball, the meatball and the goof ball. Regardless, the acquisition of Wilson enabled L-T-V to surpass rival conglomerates Litton Ind., Inc., and Textron, Inc. in sales volume.

---

[2] Recall the 80% required for consolidation of subsidiary operations into a holding company's statements.

The organization consisted of seven major subsidiaries plus a holding company in early 1967. In the same year he began negotiations for the Greatamerica Corp. and the purchase of this bank and insurance holding company in April, 1968 gave L-T-V 31 percent of Braniff Airways. His combined sales at the end of that year amounted to $2.77 billion. Acquisition plans for Allis-Chalmers Manufacturing Co. fell through in 1967–68.

THE TURNING POINT

By mid-1968, the last major acquisition for L-T-V was underway. Ling had made a tender offer for Jones and Laughlin Steel in May and by August had purchased 83% interest in the company. As has been explained, up to this point, Ling had solved L-T-V's financial problems by: (1) breaking up acquired companies into individual operating components; (2) trimming off the management fat, and/or (3) selling them outright. At this time, however, Ling wanted to keep J and L as a single operating entity, reportedly because of being consumed with the idea of bigness. Parallel to this departure from his "project deployment," L-T-V went heavily into debt to purchase control of J and L. Long-term debt had increased by just over one billion dollars by the end of 1968. See Figure 11C–1 for a graphic comparison of these totals. In contrast to previous post-acquisition

Figure 11C–1. Summary of L-T-V Consolidated Performance

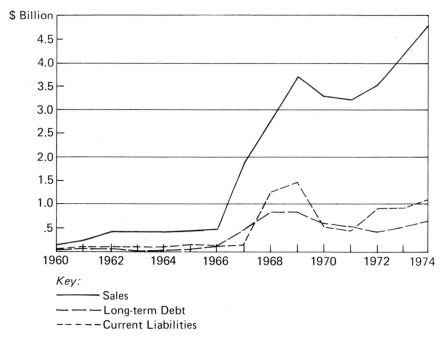

Key:
——— Sales
— — —Long-term Debt
- - - - Current Liabilities

stock performance, the price of L-T-V common dipped to nearly half its value of the previous year (see Appendix B for information on the situation).

Up to the Jones and Laughlin takeover bid, Ling: (1) had the public's confidence; (2) could borrow seemingly unlimited amounts of cash from varied sources; (3) always managed to cut away unwanted low productive units; (4) had always managed to minimize financial drains due to economic fluctuations yet meet his debts, and (5) had invariably managed to ride each crisis and come out the victor. Considering his history of intuitively sensing trouble and correcting the problems before serious results, it is difficult to understand why Ling failed to take into consideration the following:

1. Steel is sensitive to economic pressures and commands huge amounts of capital to sustain it during times of recession. Forecasts of a recession were prevalent early in 1968 well before Ling committed to the venture.

2. A dismal stock market outlook and a distinct down trend in L-T-V earnings during the last half of 1968 were apparent in May when the Jones and Laughlin tender offer was made.

3. The possibility of a profit slump at J and L due to a trucking strike and high start-up costs from unusual technical problems with new processes could have been foreseen in feasibility studies.

4. The management staff at Jones and Laughlin was allowed to hold voting control of its common stock at the time of acquisition on the assumption they would be loyal to L-T-V. However, Jones and Laughlin voted no dividends in 1971 when L-T-V badly needed them.

5. U.S. government agencies were actively trying to curtail the tide of takeovers and mergers in 1968, and the scope of the L-T-V-Jones and Laughlin relationship attracted their active opposition. It is a fact, however, that legal counsel felt that no action would be taken to dissolve the takeover, especially because of his support for the Nixon administration in the 1968 Texas race for President.

6. William J. Stephens, Chairman of J and L, was less than two years from retirement, and he had little interest in the aggressive management expected by Ling.

When L-T-V earnings fell in the latter half of 1968 and early 1969, Ling responded by diversifying. He created a new concern called Jones and Laughlin Industries, Inc., that would act as a holding company for J and L Steel and future acquisitions outside the traditional lines of steel.

The Downward Spiral

Despite the lack of direct control in J and L, Ling began to feel pressure from the Justice Department. The charge was that L-T-V's acquisition of controlling interest in J and L Steel threatened to diminish competition in steel, other related metal markets, and diversified industries. Specifically, the Justice Department pointed out that:

1. L-T-V was a potential competitor before it acquired Jones and Laughlin in steel and other metal lines—specifically copper, aluminum wire cable, and high alloy steel.
2. L-T-V's acquisition of Jones and Laughlin significantly increased the opportunity to engage in reciprocal dealings.
3. This merger would increase substantially the concentration of control of the nation's manufacturing assets and encourage the trend to further concentration by merger.

With Ling's decision to keep J and L Steel the stage was set for L-T-V's downhill slide. In 1969 the company was facing severe financial activity, high interest rates, and the results of the Justice Department suit concerning J and L (no say in company management). To improve the situation, Ling trimmed his corporate staff by 35 per cent and decentralized his top subsidiary, L-T-V Aerospace, into Vought Aerospace Corp., Synthetics, Inc., and L-T-V Education Systems, Inc. This change permitted shares to be tendered for additional cash, yet retain 80% ownership in Aerospace to allow L-T-V to consolidate its federal tax returns.

Meanwhile Braniff Airways, obtained with the acquisition of the bank and insurance holding company in 1967, became financially ill. In an attempt to boost revenues, L-T-V established two new routes: Texas to Hawaii and Florida to Texas. In addition to high start-up costs, the planes flew these routes about half loaded, resulting in high annual losses.

In 1969, Ling attempted to sell $100 million of debentures and failed. Success would have enabled Ling to retire the bank debt obtained to acquire shares in J and L and give L-T-V badly needed working capital. However, with the Justice Department suit in progress, Ling's strategy was not possible and L-T-V found itself in a vise with a $1.5 billion debt requiring $100 million per year in interest on one side and the Justice Department on the other.

After lengthy delays, great expense, and huge amounts of executive time expended by L-T-V in the Jones and Laughlin case, the company consented to settle out of court. The agreement involved retention by L-T-V of Jones and Laughlin providing L-T-V would divest Braniff and Okonite within three years. Also, Ling was forbidden to acquire any company with assets of over $100 million for a period of ten years without Justice Department approval.

The Fall and Resurrection

In May, 1970 a group of local businessmen led by E. Grant Fitts gained control of L-T-V's board. Most of these businessmen had large holdings in the $474 million of 5% L-T-V debentures which were scheduled to come due in 1988. Known as the 5's of '88, the debentures had been issued to finance the purchase of Greatamerica. What particularly concerned Fitts and other debenture holders was that Ling might sell assets to pay the bank debt and there would be too little left to pay off the debentures should L-T-V go under.

The insurgents demoted Ling, and installed Robert H. Stewart III as chairman. A power struggle evolved with Fitts and the debenture holders on one side and the bankers (led by Bank of America) on the other side supporting Ling. Finally on July 9, 1970 Paul Thayer was elected chief executive. Thayer told Fitts that if he was going to be chief executive, he was going to run the entire show—chairman, chief executive, and president—and Fitts agreed.

Thayer, who had been the head of L-T-V Aerospace, is an operating man. His first step was to hack the corporate staff to the bone. He moved some people down from the parent company into the divisions and simply fired others. Eventually he sold off four of the company's seven subsidiaries—Okonite, Ling Altec, L-T-V Electrosystems, and Braniff—and portions of Wilson.

In May of 1971, Jones and Laughlin's mangement refused to vote cash dividends and L-T-V lost a source of sorely needed cash. In an attempt to generate working capital, management arranged to increase ownership of L-T-V Electrosystems (before divestiture) and L-T-V Aerospace to 80% compared with 69% and 63% respectively. They then consolidated statements and offset the profits from these subsidiaries with losses from others. This avoided corporate income tax of approximately $15 million/year. The method by which the two subsidiaries achieved consolidation involved creating a new class of voting nonconvertible preferred stock at $100/share which paid 4%. This stock cost $13.8 million and increased voting control of these subsidiaries to 80+ per cent. The lenders provided the 13.8 million contingent on the subsidiaries turning over to L-T-V cash saved on taxes for immediate repayment of the loan.

In compliance with the Justice Department's decree to unload Okonite and Braniff, L-T-V resurrected one of Ling's ideas. L-T-V owned 10,564,000 shares of Braniff (class A) stock. To avoid lengthy legal procedures resulting from selling the stock to another airline, L-T-V transferred control of Braniff to an investor group. The first phase of this plan sold 4.5 million shares of Braniff and retired $27.8 million in 9¼% collateral notes. This move also improved the L-T-V cash flow by eliminating $4 million in annual interest payments.

The second phase applied $32 million from the $40.5 million sale of Okonite to Omega/Alpha Corporation (a new Ling enterprise) to other debt and this released the remainder of L-T-V Braniff shares from pledges as collateral. Within the time permitted under the Justice Department decree, the lenders disposed of the final Braniff shares.

Thayer reunited the remaining Wilson Companies after sale of the sporting goods and pharmaceuticals, and saved $2 million in annual overhead.

The biggest financial problem in 1971 was Jones and Laughlin rolling over $75 million in bank loans every 90 days. Thayer persuaded William J. Stephens, J and L chairman and chief executive, to retire President William Getty, and promote the company's most obvious comer, William

R. Roesch. Roesch retired or fired all but 2 of J and L's 14 vice presidents, reduced the staff by 20% and placed more responsibility at the operating level.

L-T-V's immediate financial worries were then behind it. No long-term debt comes due until 1977. Thayer has trimmed the total debt by $314 million, or 40% and cut fixed charges by more than half. Even with this progress the company still must find some way to raise cash or increase the value of L-T-V's own stock in order to gain 80% of J & L. On December 31, 1972 the company had a negative net worth of $101 million; by the end of 1973 this was decreased to $55 million.

JAMES LING AND OMEGA-ALPHA

In 1969−71 Ling had seen his L-T-V empire wrested from his grasp, his personal fortune of nearly $100 million tied up in L-T-V stock diminished to a value of nearly zero, and his $3 million Texas mansion sold for debt payments. Nevertheless, Ling was far from being defeated. The remnants of his personal fortune consisted of the $800,000 consulting contract with L-T-V and he used this as security to form Omega-Alpha, Inc. (Omega representing the end of one career and Alpha the beginning of another.) This is James Ling's comeback vehicle, which he began assembling five months after he lost control of L-T-V.

With $18 million borrowed from Texan friends, equity from sale of shares, and other leading sources, Ling's first big acquisition in May, 1971 was Okonite Corporation, which he bought from L-T-V for $32 million cash and an $8,500,000 note. Using what he now calls "corporate redevelopment," (similar to his previous strategy called "project redeployment") Ling has divided Okonite into two subsidiaries, the Okonite Company and General Felt Industries, Inc.

In March of 1972, Ling acquired Transcontinental Investing Company and also split it into two subsidiaries, Transcontinental Music Corp. and North America Acceptance Corp. Ling realized when he bought T.I.C. that he was buying a problem company. However, after the auditors had reconciled inventories and disputed accounts with creditors, T.I.C.'s operating loss was $34 million, over a period of 27 months on sales of $170 million. This means that a company for which he had paid $51 million (in cash and stock) had net tangible assets of less than $10 million.

In its first two years, Omega-Alpha has managed to lose a significant amount of money—$47,837,000 on total sales of $374,395,000—while amassing $178 million in debt.

The price of its stock has reflected this performance. Originally offered to the public at $5.50 in August, 1971. Omega-Alpha rose to $6.50 per share in early 1972. But as news of the company's huge deficits came out, the price dropped sharply, and by December was down to $1.50. At this time Ling arranged for a reverse one-for-ten split, but the stock continued to drop, going from

$12.50 to $3.50 in mid−1973. This is equivalent to $.35 on the original $5.50 share.

It is clear that Wall Street first judged James Ling as a financial genius, but now investors are looking at numbers which are dismal. Omega-Alpha has yet to show a profit, and its net worth is a negative $31 million. The best that Ling did in 1973 is reduce its operating losses. In 1974 shares and warrants listed on the American Stock Exchange were barred from trading due to failure to submit a statement on conditions in the company. During that year the company explored bankruptcy as a means of solving its financial problems.

STUDENT PROBLEMS

1. Outline the elements in Ling's normal approach to acquisitions. How would you have changed Ling's methods in the late 1960s? Is strategic planning visible at L-T-V during any period?
2. Look up the present condition of L-T-V and Omega-Alpha and compare these totals with latest information in the case.
3. Refer to the book, Ling (The Rise, Fall and Return of a Texas Titan), and research the events leading to his present financial position. What personal characteristics, in your opinion, led to this position?

Appendix A. Log of Acquisitions and Spin-offs By James Ling and L-T-V Corporation.

Year	Acquisition/Merger	Divestiture/Dissolved
1947	Established electrical contracting business. $3,000+	
1957	Acquired IM Electronics, Inc. through $1.3 million in common stock and convertible debentures.	
1958	Merged Ling Ind., Inc. & Subs & American Microwave Corp. & Electronic Wire & Cable Co. & Subs & acquired United Electronic Co. (entire ca. stock) for $750,000 cash/65,000 common shares.	Dissolved — United Electronics Co. 8/58.
1959	8/58 acquired Calidyne Co. for $150,000 cash — $170,000 5¾ 6% notes & 922,500 convertible debentures due 1970.	Sold — Electronic Wire & Cable Co.
	3/59 — Purchased entire stock of Altec Companies, Inc., on a share for share exchange although 2x Ling's size.	
	4/59 — Purchased University Loudspeakers, Inc., for $2,300,000.	

Year	Acquisition/Merger	Divestiture/Dissolved
	9/59 — Purchased Continental Electronics Manuf. Co. for $3,250,000 cash, 125,000 5% notes & 10,000 common shares.	
1960	7/60 — Acquired assets of Temco Aircraft Corp. for exchange of .48 common & 12/12 preferred share for each Temco share. Made top 500 businesses; moved away from electronics goal.	Sold — Grady-Ling Electronics, Inc.
1961	1/61 — Merged Fenske, Friedrich & Miller, Inc., with Temco Electronics & Missiles Co., a subsidiary, & acquired Ed Friedrich, Inc., & Friedrich Refrigerators, Inc.	
	2/61 Acquired National Aeronautics & Space Engineering, Inc. Sales merged into Temco.	
	8/61 Acquired assets of Chance-Vought for exchange of C-V stock for company debentures and warrants at a rate of 1 share of C-V for 43.50 convertible debentures 5½s and 5 year warrant for 1/5 additional share at 40.00 per.	11/61 Sold — investment in National Data Processing Corp. (former sub. of C-V)
1962	1/62 acquired all stock of Kentron Hawaii L.T.D.	3/62 Sold investments in Vought Ind., Inc., (former sub. of C-V). Loss of $8.7 million.
		4/62 Sold portion of Information Systems, Inc., (former C-V sub.) for 324,815 of 1,266,000 in rights offerings to stockholders. Loss of $6.34 million.
		7/62 Sold assets of Crusader Finance Co. (former C-V sub.)

Year	Acquisition/Merger	Divestiture/Dissolved
1963	8/63 Acquired Ganset, Inc.	1/63 Sold capital stock of United Electronics Co.
		2/63 Sold assets of L.T.V. Industrial Division.
		4/63 Sold remainder of Information System, Inc., merged with Scam Instrument Corp., an affiliate of Harbor Boot Building Co. (former sub. of C-V)
1964	4/64 Acquired 70% interest in Saturn Electronics Corp. also L-T-V redeployed its business & operation by forming 3 new sub-corporations — L-T-V Electrosystems & L-T-V. Ling-Altec, Inc.	4/64 Sold Ed Friedrich, Inc., & Friedrich Refrigerators, Inc., for $3,000,000 cash, 1,000,000 American Investor Corp. ca stock to represent 1,000,000. 2,000,000 6% subord. prom. note due in 1 yr., chattel mtge. covering all Friedrich machinery & 6,000,000 noninterest bearing note, due 60 days representing balance of total purchase price.
1965	10/65 Acquired assets of Okonite Co. for $31,700,000.	
1967	1/67 Acquired 53% of Wilson & Co., Inc. — aggregate cost of $81,504,653.	
	6/67 Merged company with Wilson by issuance of $5 convertible preferred series A at rate of 1 preferred for each 1.5 Wilson common. Upon completion of merger, company transferred assets of Wilson to form 3 new subs. i.e. Wilson & Co., Inc., Wilson Sporting Goods & Wilson Pharmaceutical & Chem. Corp.	

Year	Acquisition/Merger	Divestiture/Dissolved
1968	4/68 Acquired 95% interest in Greatamerica by exchange for each 10 common or class B common of Greatamerica of $300 principal amt. 5% subordinated debentures due 1/88 and one warrant exp.	6/68 Sold 99.3% in First Western Bank & Trust Co. (former Greatamerica interest) for $62,000,000 cash.
	1/78 to purchase 1 share company common at $115 per share. Under this offer the company acquired all class B common & 90% common. Remaining interest in Greatamerica was later purchased under similar offer following which Greatamerica was liquidated.	6/68 Sold Greatamerica's 100% interest in Stonewall Ins. Co. for $63,000,000 cash.
	6/68 Purchased 63% of Jones & Laughlin Steel Corp. for $425 million cash.	6/68 Sold Greatamerica 57% interest in American-Amicable Life Ins. Co. for $15,000,000 cash, 30,000,000 of notes with warrants to buy 525,000 common in Gulf Life Holding Co.
	8/68 L-T-V & L-T-V Aerospace Corp. formed Computer Technology Corp.	
1969	1/69 Organized Jones & Laughlin Ind. Inc. — a holding company to succeed to the 63% ownership of J & L Steel.	3/69 Sold remaining interest in National Car Rental System. Loss of $3.3 million.
	12/69 Company's sub., Wilson & Co. made exchange offer to its stockholders to redeploy its business and form 4 subs. of Wilson, Sinclair, Certified, Beef & Lamb & Farms.	Sold Computerteck.
1970		Sold interests in Wilson Sporting Goods & Wilson Pharmaceutical.
1971		Company divested itself of Braniff & Okonite (Okonite sold to Omega-Alpha).
1972-3	Acquired the shares needed for 80% ownership of J & L. 1972 statements revised to consolidate finances of the steel company.	Sold L-T-V Electro Systems, L-T-V Jet Fleet, and L-T-V Altec in 1973.

Appendix B. Ling Temco Vought, Inc.

| | | $000 | | $000 | Common Stock Data | | |
| | | Current Liabilities | L.T. Debt | Net Income | Earnings per Share | Price Range | |
Year	Sales						
1947	.070	NA	NA	NA	—	—	—
1955	1,500	NA	NA	NA	—	—	—
1959	48,100	NA	NA	NA	—	—	—
1960	148,450	42,760	14,640	NA	.83	28	-13⅜
1961	192,850	87,620	64,590	NA	d3.33	28⅛	-15⅛
1962	325,440	70,450	64,200	5,418	2.03	17¼	-10
1963	329,000	68,710	34,590	3,904	1.42	12¼	-9
1964	322,860	57,560	37,010	4,295	1.21	13½	-9¾
1965	336,210	125,290	40,270	3,616	1.87	38⅝	-11½
1966	468,250	126,290	95,776	5,809	4.02	53⅝	-25⅛
1967	1,871,530	371,220	205,100	9,578	7.08	169½	-109¼ (1)
1968	2,769,740	823,850	1,236,690	14,976	3.88	135¼	-80 (2) (3)
1969	3,750,260	834,510	1,500,792	28,740	(0.05)	97¾	-24⅛ (4) (5)
1970	3,279,590	689,080	535,580	6,009	(17.09)	29⅛	-7⅛
1971	3,154,000	512,300	362,700	(57,840)	(9.35)	27¼	-9⅝
1972	3,416,582	467,815	953,800	8,838	.73	14¾	-9
1973	4,150,638	512,245	912,882	49,880	5.16	13½	-7½
1974	4,768,010	647,416	1,042,978	111,692	10.32	12½	-7⅞

Notes on Specific Stock Prices of L-T-V:

(1)	Takeover Greatamerica	150+	2/67
(2)	Tender offer for J & L Steel	140	5/68
(3)	Four-stage refinancing plan	75+	8/68
(4)	Antitrust suit L-T-V — J & L	70	3/69
(5)	Corporate Reorganization	30+	8/69

BIBLIOGRAPHY

"An L-T-V Alumnus Graduates Into Trouble," *Business Week.* July 29, 1972, p. 23.

Bulban, E. J. "Banker Replaces Ling At L-T-V," *Aviation Week.* May 25, 1970, pp. 26–27.

"Battered Ling Tries A Comeback." *Business Week.* December 25, 1970, pp. 23–24.

Brooks, John. *The New Yorker,* July 2, 1973, p. 44.

Brown, S.H. "Jimmy Ling's Wonderful Growth Machine," *Fortune.* January, 1967, pp. 136–138.

Brown, S. H. *Ling.* 1972.

Butkus. "Will Jimmy Ling Do It Again?," *Duns.* September, 1971, pp. 38–42.

"Fate Worse Than Bankruptcy?," *Forbes.* August 15, 1970, pp. 17–18.

"How Ling Engineered A New Beginning," *Business Week.* May 29, 1971, pp. 76—79.

"How Paul Thayer Runs Ling's Old Empire," *Business Week.* January 8, 1972, pp. 70—71.

"How to Grow," *Economist.* August 12, 1967, p. 567.

"Hungry L-T-V Aims for Lean Look," *Business Week.* August 23, 1969, pp. 27—28.

"Jim Ling Turns To Demerging," *Business Week.* February 28, 1970, pp. 36—37.

"Jim Ling's Chess Game," *Forbes.* September 1, 1966, p. 18.

"Jim Ling's Instant Conglomerate," *Forbes.* November 1, 1967, p. 42.

Kaufman. "Today Ling Would Be A Loser," *Iron Age.* April 24, 1969, p. 87.

"Ling Finds A New Twist," *Business Week.* February 8, 1969, p. 34.

"Ling Starts Swinging In His L-T-V Style," *Business Week.* May 13, 1972, pp. 54—55.

"Ling-Temco-Vought," *Moody's Industrial Manual.* 1971, pp. 2083—87.

"Ling-Temco-Vought," *Moody's Industrial Manual.* 1972, pp. 3270—73.

"Ling-Temco-Vought," *Preliminary Prospectus.* October 25, 1972.

"Ling-Temco-Vought," *Standard & Poor's Corp.* September 16, 1970, p. 179.

"Ling's Latest Tremor Splits Top Subsidiary," *Business Week.* October 4, 1969, pp. 31—32.

"Ling's New Lesson In How To Go Public," *Business Week.* January 9, 1971, p. 21.

"Ling Tries His Wings Once More," *Fortune.* June, 1973, p. 139.

"L-T-V Blitzes Its Way Into The Ranks Of The Giants," *Business Week.* March 18, 1967, pp. 178—180.

"L-T-V's Flight from Bankruptcy," *Fortune.* June, 1973, p. 134.

"L-T-V Rejoins Civilian Ranks," *Business Week.* October 23, 1965, p. 96.

"L-T-V Resurrects Ling Game Plan," *Business Week.* March 20, 1971, pp. 30—31.

"L-T-V Trims Down The Room At The Top," *Business Week.* July 1, 1972, p. 19.

"L-T-V's Busy Jimmy," *Economist.* May 25, 1968, p. 91.

"L-T-V's Lost Year," *Fortune.* May, 1970, p. 275.

McManus. "What Will L-T-V & J & L Spell?," *Iron Age.* June 20, 1968, pp. 61—62.

"Omega," *Economist.* November 17, 1973, p. 136.

"Sudden Concern For The Small Investor," *U.S. News & World Report.* October 16, 1972, pp. 76—78.

"Swinging without Ling," *Barrons.* January 7, 1974, pp. 9, 21—22.

Wright. "Unorthodox L-T-V Follows Style in Wilson Move," *Mag. Wall Street.* April 29, 1967, pp. 20—22.

Multinational Operations

The nature of multinational corporations is described. Reasons for doing business outside the United States are identified. Selected fundamentals in establishing new operations and approaches to relating them to plans and strategies are summarized. Management techniques required for success in other countries are outlined. The purpose of this chapter is to focus on this increasingly important portion of business and to point out differences from American practices.

Many American companies are conducting international business on a regular basis. Some have expanded to the point of global operations and employment of several nationalities in top management. Figure 12–1 shows the range of involvement from the multinational corporation at one extreme to a firm dealing in occasional exports or imports at the other.

12

THE MULTINATIONAL CORPORATION

The model of a fully evolved multinational corporation (MNC) has the characteristics shown in Table 12–1.

Very few, if any, American corporations resemble the model in all respects. Members of the executive management will usually place patriotism, personal ethics and integrity, and ethnocentric preferences (preferring one's own kind) before profits. Also, while it is more and more possible to find competent nonAmerican managers, prejudice of various types usually precludes true multinationality in top management during the 1970s. In addition, power to affect the

Figure 12-1. Range of Multinational Operations

economics and monetary policies of some countries has led to restrictive measures around the world to restrain corporate attack capability. Regulations on currency flow, duties, prices, wages, and so on, combine to keep the MNC in line.

It is important to distinguish between: (1) a large corporation having extensive international operations but also having strong national ties, called a MNO in this book, and (2) the fully evolved MNC. Both can have equally large global operations, but the firm closely aligned to a single country such as many American and Japanese corporations are much more vulnerable to restrictive legislation than the true MNC. The latitude of decision making in conducting international business is less now, and is very likely to be narrowed in the future.

Bad publicity in the early 1970s focusing mostly on ITT (political maneuvering) but including oil companies (energy) and others swayed public attitudes about MNO's and assisted the AFL–CIO and legislators like Representative Burke in California, and Senator Hartke in Indiana, in their quest for restrictive laws and regulations in the United States. Such actions, however, are viewed as contrary to national interests by most business analysts, and this factor could lessen the impact on international business.

Important Issues

Competitors to American firms are seeking markets in Japan, European countries, and other industrialized nations. This source of competition is being supported by subsidized transportation, low-cost long-term loans and other means of assisting both exports and foreign investments. National strategies exist to gain commercial and industrial power throughout the world. The basis of the decisions to interweave profits and national policy is the need for countries to protect their currencies, secure sufficient energy and raw materials, advance technologically, and improve living standards.

The American approach up to this time has been based on independent companies, no formal link with national policy, and limited support from the U.S. government. This is now changing.

Table 12-1. Fully Evolved Multinational Corporation

---

1. A placelessness pervades the organization. The headquarters could be in any country that provides modern functional telecommunications, superior air connections, political stability, an overall environment that is not detrimental to operations nor retaining quality management, and adequately trained support staff. Tax avoidance is a primary consideration. No patriotism nor loyalties to particular countries are involved.

2. Management personnel could be from any country. Competence based on consistent performance is the standard for advancing, leveling or terminating. Clusters of individuals from a single nationality who work well together are possible, but prejudice based on creed, origin and/or sex are not normal. Part of the performance standard is placing corporate goals before those of the individual. The overall ethics and integrity in decision making reflects the individual's need to achieve corporate goals.

3. Ownership is dispersed among many countries, and shares may be traded on several stock exchanges. It is probable that management is not influenced by stated preferences of major shareholders representing an issue or a country.

4. Corporate performance is based on after-tax earnings and is measured by achieving a consistent rate of annual growth before inflation such as 8%. This means optimum financial management without regard for influence on individual currencies unless these transactions have potential affect on operations such as retaliatory government action. "What is a problem for one is an opportunity for another," is one precept of this financial management.

5. The corporation is an entity which must protect itself. This means using wealth and power to keep assets functioning profitably. If an opposing force such as a government, quasigovernmental institution*, banking organization or competitor takes a damaging position, the multinational corporation will use its resources through every legal means to change this position or render it ineffective.

6. Issues such as social and consumer responsibility must be judged on the basis of their impact on profit performance. Compliance with laws and regulations is mandatory, but discretionary diversion of resources into programs and projects which are below profit standards must be balanced by those which exceed those standards. Moral and ethical aspects are to be considered along with earnings expectations if appropriate.

---

*Quasigovernmental institution refers to institutions such as the Inter-American Development Bank, the International Monetary Fund and other similar organizations.

Some Aspects of American Firms With Multinational Operations

The American market is immense and this size gives sufficient scope to operations headquartered in this country to be competitive in most industries outside the United States. Foreign investments are supported by comparatively efficient administration and technological innovation. Other important reasons for the strong American position abroad include this country's political power, relative strength of the dollar, and banking support.

Most members of executive management are not usually an asset when expanding outside the United States. The major problems are that executives are monolingual, and have limited knowledge of other cultures and business practices. Sophisticated international managers tend to counterbalance these people in day-to-day operations, but it is necessary to be constantly concerned about communications between these two extremes of attitude which could exist within a company. The diagram in Figure 12−2 portrays the potential problem.

ADVANTAGES TO THE COMPETITIVE POSITION OF THE UNITED STATES The American MNO has a reservoir of proven personnel who can identify, structure, develop and operate foreign businesses effectively. This talent enables them to offer economic expansion and jobs to the host country, but primarily it also facilitates design of the

Figure 12−2. A Shortcoming in American Knowhow

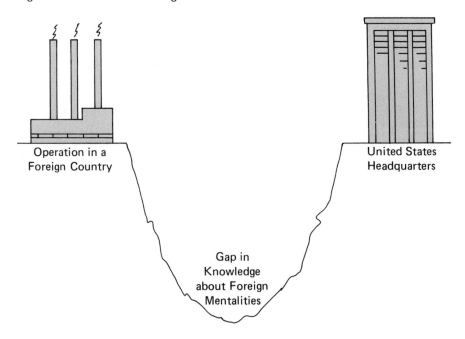

Operation in a
Foreign Country

United States
Headquarters

Gap in
Knowledge
about Foreign
Mentalities

organizational structures and financial packages which minimize dollar outflow from the United States and maximize remittances to this country. Consequestly, these companies have a substantial positive contribution to the balance of payments.

Size, financial strength, negotiation specialists, and inter-company trading possibilities between countries give the American MNO's more bargaining power than smaller firms. This improves their leverage within the global banking community and tends to improve terms of contracts with suppliers, governments, labor unions and partners. As a result, these American companies have superior capacity to withstand pressures of nationalism and other adverse changes in a business environment.

The scope of the American MNO's means that forced or voluntary withdrawal from a country does not threaten the firm's capacity to continue in international business. Also, on-going business in the region enables it to assess sufficient improvement to gain maximum advantage in moving back into operation. This type of financial and geographic diversification protects the American investor from major losses in most instances.

Profitability of products and services will usually be at its maximum if the life cycle is extended through operations in other countries. Different stages of development offer markets for concepts which have reached maturity in the United States. This means gains for both the U.S. government and the investor.

CRITICISMS OF AMERICAN MNO's   The basis of most criticisms of American firms with multinational operations is the result of discretionary actions by individual executives rather than inherent defects in the concept. However, regardless of the source of the problem, the following areas of criticism have been directed at American MNO's:

1. *Currency Speculation.* Most companies have, according to U.S. government investigations, hedged against losses based on devaluations and/or downward drifts in value after a currency float but have not speculated against the dollar. The latter would involve a partial shift of the $175 billion± in short-term holdings by private parties (vs. $100± billion in the hands of governments) from dollars to another currency thought to be undervalued for the purpose of a trading gain.

2. *Political Embarrassment.* Interference with the normal process of government, use of financial resources to influence policy and the results of elections, and decisions on operations that are contrary to U.S. government preferences are examples of actions actually taken by MNO's. While not applicable to the majority of firms, repetitive

occurrences have been a factor in the restrictive legislation passed in several countries in the 1970s.

3. *Balance of Payments.* The net effect has been favorable rather than creating an additional drain on the dollar. The net positive contribution is usually between $3-8 billion per year. Nevertheless, anti-MNO's in government and labor claim that this total would be greater by 20% if these companies would move funds into American financial centers instead of other alternatives such as London, Singapore, and Zurich.

4. *Loss of Jobs.* The three assumptions given in the 1973 U.S. Tariff Commission report are on page 443. The AFL−CIO has other statistics showing significant losses. IBM claims one out of every eight jobs in its American plants would not exist if it did not produce abroad. The statistical battle will never be settled because of indefinite assumptions necessary to analyze historical data.

5. *Technology Transfers.* The 1973 U.S. Tariff Commission report says, "MNC's[1] do not, on balance, export their first-line technology either to their own affiliates or to unrelated foreigners. Rather, first-line technology tends to be retained in plants at home to generate new exports and compete effectively with imports in the same class." Logic would support this statement since foreign markets provide a means of extending the life of products and services. Some instances have occurred, but they are rare exceptions.

Conclusions for the Future

"It is better that the American MNC's[1] be ours rather than some other country's." This unidentified quote in one of the Senate Committee Hearings capsulizes one aspect of the situation. If legislation in the United States limits efficiency of operations and increases taxes payable, there is a threat that creative corporate minds will work at shifting operations away from this country. Patriotism in this case will be outweighed by the challenge of performing.

The change most needed involves greater cooperation between government, labor and company management. Increasingly competitive markets in all countries including the United States, require optimum efficiency and part of this improvement will stem from positive attitudes rather than those resulting from accusations and counter-accusations. A form of nationalism is needed in which all three recognize that global operations are basic to achieving this country's objectives.

The laws and regulations governing MNO's will depend on the decision making of their executives in the 1970s. If Congress is

---

[1] Under the definition of MNC's in this book, this abreviation would be MNO, or firms with multinational operations.

motivated by additional instances of interference in politics or excessive profits from maneuvers hurting the American public, harassment will occur. If the press is not provided with extreme cases, it is probable that government, labor and company management can improve their cooperation. Certainly, competition from MNO's outside the country will provide continuing incentive.

Examples

The major MNO's are given in Table 12–2. The years 1972 to 1974 are used to minimize distortions created by price increases in petroleum products. The percentage of profits on sales provides interesting comparisons, particularly the averages for American and foreign based companies.

A sharp increase has taken place in the commercial and industrial power of foreign based MNO's as indicated by the number included in the top 25. In the 1950's most of these firms were fighting to gain a greater portion of markets in their own parts of the world. In the 1960s exports to areas previously dominated by Americans became a major factor. During that decade and the early 1970s foreign companies displaced Americans in vulnerable markets within the United States.

Generation of immense quantities of hard currency from expanded operations and devaluation of the dollar in the 1971–73 period led to another stage for the foreign based MNO. Direct investment in this country (excluding portfolio investment of less than 25% share ownership and short-term transfers) has increased to over $16.5 billion, up 40% in five years ending with 1973. In addition to these firms which contribute jobs and technology to the American economy, serious concern has developed about the use of the "petrodollar" being generated by oil sales. Takeovers by Middle Eastern powers would be a major setback to American flexibility in global operations.

REASONS FOR DOING BUSINESS OUTSIDE THE UNITED STATES

When many countries and mentalities[2] are involved in a company's operations, the major common denominator is profits after taxes remitted across borders to a bank of the company's choice. The avenues for achieving these profits are summarized in the following sections.

[2] Mentality means the summation of a people's characteristics, standards of value, tastes, traditions, traits and other common attitudes that individuals share in an area of the world.

Table 12-2. Top 35 Multinational Corporations

Company	Country	1972-74 Annual Avg. Net Profits	1972-74 Annual Avg. Net Sales	Profits as % of Sales
Exxon	USA	$2,372.4	$29,365.1	8.7
General Motors	USA	1,837.0	32,594.3	5.6
Royal Dutch/Shell	Netherlands/ Britain	1,700.0	20,844.3	8.2
IBM	USA	1,564.1	11,067.9	14.1
Texaco	USA	1,255.9	14,451.8	9.4
Mobil Oil	USA	823.6	13,161.8	6.4
Ford Motor	USA	712.5	22,276.7	3.2
Gulf Oil	USA	687.3	10,369.9	6.4
British Petroleum	Britain	681.1	10,480.1	6.4
Standard Oil (Indiana)	USA	618.7	6,334.9	9.5
Eastman Kodak	USA	609.7	4,032.3	15.2
General Electric	USA	574.4	11,742.6	4.9
Standard Oil of California	USA	505.7	10,260.8	8.6
ITT	USA	487.4	9,964.7	4.9
Du Pont	USA	467.9	5,517.2	8.8
Imperial Chemical	Britain	408.5	5,314.6	7.4
Unilever	Britain	359.5	10,766.8	3.4
Procter & Gamble	USA	298.4	4,111.1	7.3
Philips	Netherlands	291.0	8,430.6	3.5
Continental Oil	USA	246.8	3,485.4	5.1
Nestle	Switzerland	224.2	5,230.3	4.3
Westinghouse Electric	USA	213.9	5,751.7	2.3
Bayer	Germany	188.7	5,747.2	3.4
Goodyear Tire & Rubber	USA	178.4	4,667.2	3.9
BASF	Germany	177.5	5,155.1	3.2
Siemens	Germany	154.7	5,558.4	2.8
RCA	USA	151.7	4,226.4	3.6
Chrysler	USA	141.3	10,834.9	1.5
Nissan Motor	Japan	132.2	4,648.8	2.9
Nippon Steel	Japan	119.7	6,636.1	1.8
International Harvester	USA	108.3	4,217.2	2.6
Daimler-Benz	Germany	99.8	5,193.8	.8
Fiat	Italy	39.5	3,995.6	1.0
British Steel	Britain	(3.6)	3,758.9	(.9)
Volkswagen	Germany	(65.5)	6,097.2	(.8)

USA Companies (3 year average of 20 companies) — 6.6% Profits on Sales
Foreign Companies (3 year average of 15 companies) — 3.4% Profits on Sales

Sources: *Fortune Magazine*, May, 1973, May, 1974, and May, 1975. *Moody's Industrials*, 1973, 1974, and 1975. *Business Week*, July 14, 1975.

The worldwide search for petroleum is an example of companies being forced to go where the needed raw material is located. Ores for aluminum, copper, nickel, tin, iron, and rare metals are other examples. Without a major breakthrough in technology that permits use of a material abundant in the United States, more and more American companies explore and develop what is needed in their business in other countries. In some cases the choice is discretionary, and foreign operations slow the depletion of American materials. In other situations there is no choice.

Most of the companies placed in this position go through a predictable cycle. *First*, they are welcomed by the host country as a source of foreign currency, a major employer, a means of upgrading the country's skills, a stimulant to the economy and a catalyst to attract other investors. *Second*, after a few years pressure increases on the firm to process in addition to only extracting the material. This often leads to a second phase of investment by the company and more benefits to the country. *Third*, the company is now sufficiently dependent to be vulnerable to a request to have local participation in ownership, either through private parties or directly by the host government. *Fourth*, nationalization advances to a takeout stage after more years of evolving relationships, usually involving compensation for assets and some arrangement on management. *Fifth*, recalling the primary reason for the original investment was a source of materials, and recognizing that government owned operations are almost always ineffecient, the company is forced to pay increasing prices and turns to alternative sources if they exist.

Usually, large amounts of capital are involved in developing, extracting and refining basic materials. This means that companies dependent on foreign sources are constantly trying to lengthen the time in each of the early stages just described and, if possible, eliminate the last three. Nevertheless, considerable risk is involved in investments with huge fixed assets. Even in more industrialized countries such as Australia, where the "takeover" type of nationalization is not probable, changes in taxation and other regulations have squeezed earnings of foreign operators after major commitments were made on other assumptions.

Market Opportunities

Figure 12—3 shows the typical evolution from occasional exports to integrated manufacturing in a foreign market. The geographic definition of a market can range from a group of countries associated through a formal agreement such as the European Economic Com-

Figure 12-3. Evolution of Supplying a Foreign Market

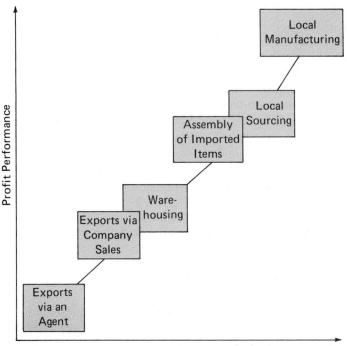

munity to a region of a country such as a metropolitan cluster of buyers.

In the 1950s it was usually possible for American firms to service foreign markets from the United States because of shortages and the near absence of competition from other countries. Since that time it has become increasingly necessary to locate manufacturing within the market in order to have the lowest feasible cost structure. Eighty percent of investment outside the United States other than mining and petroleum operations has been in developed countries where intensive economic activity takes place, and $0.75 of capital has generated $1.00 of sales as compared to local companies requiring $1.25 for the same sales. While wages are higher in industrialized countries than in developing countries, the minimization of transportation expense and losses from damage en route to the market more than offset labor cost differential. Also, in time some companies are successful in developing a local image which helps sell the product.

In addition to manufacturing, service companies such as engineering and franchising firms have taken advantage of markets for American expertise. Cash investment is minimal in most of these instances. Another motivation for getting involved in foreign business is operating equipment systems that are becoming obsolete in the

United States but have additional life in selected countries. Older machinery replaced by new concepts can be a trap because competition from other countries with the latest technology may be able to displace the operation from the market. However, this approach is sometimes successful in lengthening the time over which the original investment yields a return.

Cheap Labor

The labor unions in the United States are attempting to slow what they claim to be "the exportation of jobs". The controversy started in the early 1970s with concern about the real impact of American firms setting-up manufacturing and assembly plants in places such as: China (Taiwan), Hong Kong, Ireland, Korea, and Singapore. The purpose of going to these countries is a net reduction in the cost of labor and flexibility in introducing new production line methods. Wages, company-paid benefits and freedom to hire and fire are involved in the cash cost. Productivity is the critical factor, and this is a combination of worker ability, attitude and investment in automation by the company. Naturally, capital investment should be minimized wherever prudent so detailed studies have been made by American firms producing electronic units, toys, and so on, on the use of cheap labor considering their product, markets, and management methods.

The 1973 U.S. Tariff Commission report on corporations with multinational operations analyzed what had happened to American employment in recent years under three assumptions:

1. American exports would have retained all of the markets served by the MNO's. This resulted in a loss of 1.3 million jobs through 1972. Even the labor unions regard this assumption as unreasonable.

2. American exports would have retained 50% of the markets served by the MNO's. This resulted in a loss of 400,000 jobs. Most economists studying the variables feel that this is too high a percentage of retention.

3. American exports would have retained only the share of markets held in 1960–61, a good export period for this country. This resulted in a net gain in American jobs, estimates ranging up to 500,000. The Tariff Commission calls this the most realistic assumption.

It is reasonable to conclude that American firms have not "exported jobs", and that without profit motivated decisions to operate from the lowest cost base, the American economy would have suffered.

Many unions recognize the need for cooperation with management in reducing or eliminating factors lessening productivity in this country. Parallel to improvement in some industries such as steel (see the case in Chapter Eight), prosperity and inflation have shrunk the advantages of locating in countries formerly having clearly cheap labor. In fact, with inflation and the shift in the expense of energy, many companies will find the United States as the low cost base.

Other Reasons for Multinational Operations

Mergers and acquisitions have resulted in having a business in another country which came along as an extra in addition to the primary reason for the transaction. Some firms spin them off for a partial recovery of capital. Others build on this base. A few are left to struggle outside the "main stream" of company operations, and this is an indication of poor management if the status quo remains for a sustained period.

Obligations to foreign governments can result from negotiating for favorable terms of entry into the country or subsequent expansion. Some examples include mining companies developing agribusiness such as poultry, electronic firms running resorts, and joint ventures with nationals in another industry such as farm implements. The government wants to use the resources of the American corporation and its initial bargaining power to accelerate economic development, especially in regions that might lag behind those with obvious attractions.

Licensing is a contractual agreement between a company and a foreign entity permitting the latter to use technology developed by the former. For an initial fee and a continuing royalty, the foreign entity commercializes the product or service. This is a low-risk means of exploiting markets. However, the disadvantages are: (1) a loss of a substantial portion of potential profits through sharing with the licensee; (2) less expertise by the foreign entity in realizing the opportunity; (3) vulnerability to losing control and termination of the contract by the foreign entity after it has full knowledge, and (4) the creation of competition by providing the expertise for foreign firms to begin exports and foreign expansion. The most sophisticated use of licensing is by high technology companies in dynamic markets that can sell-off operating concepts over the peak of their usefullness in the United States. The licensing agreement, in this case, extends the economic life of the concept without threatening the operating base of the American firm.

Management contracts are another form of licensing, and can range into franchising if a name and/or a system goes with the contract. The hotel chains such as Hilton, Sheraton, Holiday Inn, and so on, are examples. Many of the facilities bearing their names are only managed, not owned, by the American company.

FUNDAMENTALS IN ESTABLISHING THE OPERATION

Three stages are involved in setting-up a business in another country: (1) Development of alternatives, screening of the alternatives, and relating them to plans and strategies, (2) Analysis of the venture to determine profitability relative to risk, (3) Negotiations, organizational details and start-up of the operation.

Development and Screening of Foreign Investment Alternatives

Leads can come from internal research or outside parties. Usually companies depend on a combination of the two if they are actively building multinational operations. *Internally generated* investment alternatives are based on project specifications stemming from formal long-range plans. Variables include political risk, composition and growth rate of the country's economy, operating requirements, geographic location, special financing necessities, and infrastructure needs such as harbors, telecommunications, and so on.

Many of the alternatives can be eliminated by "desk research" and this eliminates a portion of the expensive process of on-site evaluation. Some of those remaining will appear more attractive than others, but analysts experienced in international business know that parameters defined too narrowly might eliminate what could prove to be good investment alternatives. Only through on-site screening research by someone with background in the work is it feasible to make good decisions on those with potential and those to be eliminated.

Outside parties supplying leads, in order of normal reliability, are:

1. Investment banking firms including merchant banks.
2. Consulting firms with a good reputation in their field, and other reliable professionals such as accounting and law firms.
3. Commercial banks and their subsidiaries abroad, the International Finance Corporation of the World Bank and other financial institutions.
4. Suppliers of machinery, other equipment, product components, and so on and competitors not interested in the situation.

Multinational Operations   **445**

5. Governments including departments and agencies of the American government.

6. Brokers, promoters, other intermediaries, and those having a financial interest such as individuals and organizations having property, a license, a going concern, and so on.

Once it is known that a company is interested in investment alternatives, a flow of proposals from various sources will begin. Figure 12–4 shows the number of leads typically handled by managers responsible for developing multinational operations at successive stages of progress.

Figure 12–4. Developing New Business Abroad

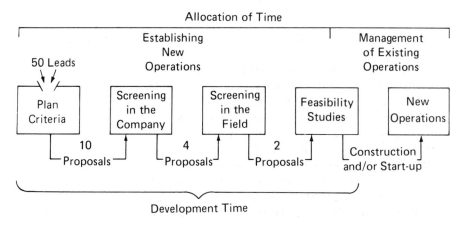

One phenomenon that occurs frequently is the creation of an investment possibility different from the lead which originally led the executive to the country. It is important for executives to recognize that this could happen while discussing alternatives. Otherwise, the people proposing the original lead could cause complications and bad feelings that might jeopardize other investment possibilities.

Analysis of the Venture

Some leads are sufficiently attractive to justify detailed investigation. The amount of time and money to be committed to venture analysis depends on the scope of the project. For example, an investment of $3 to $10 million might justify spending $20 to $25,000 on a feasibility study, whereas $25 to $50 million might necessitate $100,000 to estimate profits from operations. After agreement by executive management that the potential investment meets project specifications, particularly profits vs. risk comparisons, venture analysis goes through five stages.

Content can be divided into: (1) operating variables; (2) strategic variables including risk assessment, and (3) requirements for setting up business in a way which results in the maximum after-tax profits (including United States obligations). Special attention has to be given to potential deviations from American practices or experiences in other parts of the world. Even within common markets such as the European Economic Community, conditions can vary substantially and serious mistakes in the analysis can stem from assuming pertinent and decisive information is the same as other regions in which the company operates.

Level of accuracy expected in each component of the analysis must be defined. If time and money must be limited, data with a wide margin of error such as $10\% \pm$ must be tolerated. If the investment is large or the decision is strategically important, more accurate estimates will be necessary. Certainly, in estimating taxation through selection of the most effective company entity, its ownership (for example, a company subsidiary in the country with the most advantageous double taxation treaty) and related factors can be critically important.

Network models controlling the progress of components of the analysis become vital to achieving deadlines. The stages of preparation, field work and report completion compounded by company analysts and consultants in marketing, production, accounting, and so on, or audits of potential acquisitions, need to be coordinated. Figure 12-5 gives a simple example of the approach commonly used by venture analysis managers (VAM).

Selection of Staff

Normally the best people for the study team are viewed as necessary for the success of other operations. As a result, priorities must be established to assure that the best talent is assigned to the team analyzing the venture. One important criterion in addition to competence in familiar surroundings is the likelihood of the analyst adapting to a wholly new environment in which to conduct research. Many talented people have performed poorly because of their inability to function effectively in a strange environment outside the United States.

Outside consultants are a logical solution to filling voids in the venture analysis team. Sometimes individuals or firms do the complete feasibility study for the client, and in this case, the experience gained in conducting the research is communicated only through the written and oral reports. As a result, considerable know-how about the environment in which the proposed investment might operate is

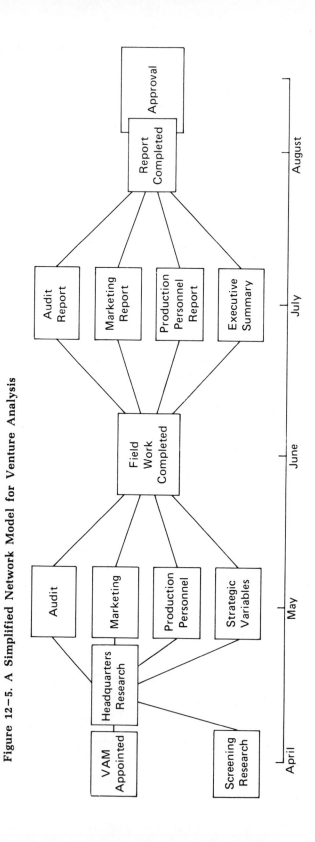

Figure 12–5. A Simplified Network Model for Venture Analysis

lost because company personnel are not participating in the study. The best approach is to prepare job descriptions for each expert essential for the work. This will facilitate assessing the talent available and the need for outside help.

If there is a decision to use outside consultants, two fundamentals are needed in any agreement: (1) experts represented to be in the consulting firm actually conducting the research rather than junior members of the organization, and (2) penalty clauses for not adhering to scheduled completion dates assure necessary information being available on time. Serious problems are possible without attention to these points.

A redesign of the venture analysis may be necessary at this stage to balance costs, timing costs, timing and quality. This step is nearly always required to adjust budgets for decisions on personnel and consultants.

Implementation

Orientation of the venture analysis team and the results expected is basic. In addition, communicating the importance of the research will motivate the individuals involved and improve the quality of input.

It is likely that 50%± of needed information will be available from published sources, and most of it can be obtained before departing for the country or immediately upon arrival. Another 30%± must be developed by the study team through interviews and interrelating miscellaneous pieces of information. There is always some unknown information relating to the investment decision; some very efficient venture analysis teams will reduce the percentage from a normal 20%± to approximately 10%±. The hope is that only unimportant information remains uncertain or unknown, and that executive management is receiving good recommendations. However, the true opportunity can only be judged after the commitment has been made and a year or two of operating experience has been logged. Even then, poor management in the initial stages can cloud the true assessment completed by the venture analysis team.

Some factors affecting research are common to all venture analyses. First, team members should fill their daily calendars and develop 3 to 4 sources for the same key information to crosscheck for misleading facts and opinions. Second, written notes and summaries should be prepared at the close of each day of research in the country. Third, team members must exchange details on what occurred each day in the event they can help each other. Fourth, feedback to executive management during the research will prepare them for major decisions such as possible termination of research if results uncover fatal information. Finally, the venture analysis manager

(VAM) should also be certain each team member is consistent in his comments on why questions are being asked in case the situation is confidential or sensitive.

A preliminary draft of the report section for which each analyst is responsible should be attempted before leaving the country. This is a discipline that assures major voids are identified and filled before departure. Research conducted in the last few days as a result of this early writing has generated the most resourceful research and estimates with the highest probability of being accurate in many instances.

Completion of the Report

A summary should go to the VAM as soon as possible upon return to base headquarters. This gives him an indication of the viability by synthesizing market estimates, capital and operating costs, financing possibilities and the remainder of related factors. It also forces the experts to pull their thoughts together and make the necessary important decisions. Figure 12–6 gives the structure of a typical report to executive management and the probable member of the venture analysis team responsible for each section.

Most organizations are part political in their operation. Consequently, the VAM must take the time to sell study conclusions to his boss. This can be accomplished in several ways, but it is best achieved through good communications and feedback throughout the course of the research. However, more convincing arguments might be necessary once the facts are condensed into an "executive sum-

Figure 12–6. The Structure of a Venture Analysis Report

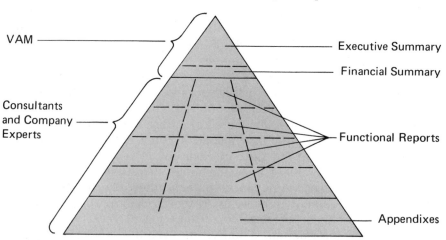

mary". Assuming the VAM is successful, the executive must then develop support from other members of executive management and, if appropriate, the board of directors. Usually this is done by informal meetings at breakfast and lunch rather than visits to the person's office. Exchanges, suggestions and disagreements can best be uncovered in their early stages, and countered if possible in a relaxed environment. It can be generalized, "the less structured the setting, the more open the meeting."

The most delicate aspect of reporting on a venture analysis is the amount of general knowledge assumed at the executive management level involved. Problems, for example, can arise if VAM does not give adequate background and environmental facts to orient the decision maker. On the other hand, an executive can become very impatient to get to the "heart of the matter" in a report with too much detail.

Structuring of the Investment Decision

Most companies have investment standards against which to measure the venture. The long-range plan usually provides the basis of judgment, although sometimes a particular strategy will justify variation. Usually the discounted cash flow method is applied to ventures with no historical record.

If executive management or a board of directors is not "sold", the matter is (1) terminated; (2) postponed until there is change in conditions, or (3) sent back to the VAM for clarification. The latter two are part of a tactic commonly used by those who are not favorable but who do not wish to take a negative stand. It is a problem for those supporting the venture because international business has the extra variables of distant political climates, different laws and regulations, and financial and operational uncertainties provide a negative element that the decision-making group can seize to block approval.

If approved, the next step is to establish negotiating parameters in cases where the following are involved: (1) joint venture partners; (2) governments; (3) banks and other sources of financing, and (4) operating relationships including suppliers, customers, transporters, and parts of the distribution chain. Guidelines are established within which the manager has approval to reach an agreement.

Negotiation, Organization, and Start-up of the Venture

Many of the principles of negotiating were discussed in Chapter Eleven. Some points, however, are particularly applicable to multinational operations.

1. The earnings after taxes must exceed the assessment of risk which is a more formal and exacting step than a comparable assessment in the United States.

2. Management control by component of the organization is important and sensitive if other parties are involved; a defined position on minimum position and compromise is needed to avoid setbacks.

3. The probability of negotiating tactics previously unencountered or unethical by American standards is quite high. Intelligence on what might be expected could save expensive reactions.

4. Hidden issues are much more likely to occur such as "black" profits (net cash unknown to tax authorities), over-/under-stated inventories and receivables, and liabilities to third parties. A minor case of paranoia is recommended even after the venture analysis.

5. Deviation from preliminary agreements which were contingent on studies and board of director decisions could cause a confidence crisis. The psychology of approach is critical to subsequent success.

6. Evidence of bonafide authority could be important. Americans have poured their strategy on a person not authorized to sign a contract. This is an effective tactic for exposing a company's real position.

7. The place to negotiate could be interrelated to unusual tactics. Microphones leading to convenient interruptions is an example of the possibilities.

8. Good health could be dependent on controlling the urge to be a tourist while on business. Drinking, nightclubbing, and testing new foods are the normal causes of problems.

A professional approach involves ranking points of concession into no major impact, important to the seller and minor impact on buyer, major impact on buyer, and terminal position. With clarity on the affect a concession would have on profitability or other key issues, the negotiator is a step closer to being prepared.

Some executives advance preparedness by filling in a matrix in which alternative strategies feasible by both parties are identified and arranged by the optimum ploy and counterploy. The matrix provides rough guidelines for choosing the initial strategy and paths of gain or retreat.

Points for Americans to keep in mind include:

1. Keep time open. Do not place a burden on negotiating capacity by needing to catch a plane or meet someone else.

2. Legal representation is critical in the negotiations. New approaches arise, and if agreement is to be concluded, the legality and soundness of new proposals must be confirmed.

3. Writing down the course of discussions and concessions in the midst of negotiations is essential to assure an overall result that is not detrimental to the company even though individual points do not appear damaging.

4. Being placed on the defensive for a sustained period when there were means of regaining the initiative in negotiations can cost millions of dollars in major investments and loss of important points in other commitments. Tactics which anticipate such contingencies and favorably shift the momentum are used by professionals.

Organization

The report, on which decisions and contracts with third parties were made, is the basis of setting up a network model to complete the pre-operations period on schedule. Most managers will use an approach similar to that which controlled the venture analysis shown in Figure 12–5.

The details depend on the company and industry. An important point to consider includes a means of expediting within the country(s) involved. Many firms use a national with possibilities for line management or a key staff job. By employing someone with good contacts, total language capacity, and a mentality compatible with the American approach, the processing of paperwork and logistics of getting men, material and machinery on the job is accelerated.

Formation of the formal entities may be vital to obtain financing, work permits, trademarks, licenses, leases and similar documents. Local personnel can assist, but company executives at headquarters are obligated to make decisions on the entities involved as rapidly as possible. Integral with these decisions is the taxation structure which minimizes exposure all the way back to the American shareholder.

At this stage it is also important to make decisions on management. The people at the top have to be in their positions in order to build the remainder of the organization in the country and finalize decisions best made at the local level.

Start-up

The venture analysis probably allowed for contingencies in penetrating the market, achieving optimal costs, and so on. Managing these problems is usually in reverse relationship to experience a new manager has with the country and its method of operations. This is a primary reason for problems in the early stages of a venture.

Figure 12—7 indicates that it might take eighteen months in completing the organization stage and as much as 32 to 36 months from receipt of a lead to start-up in an uncomplicated manufacturing business.

Figure 12—7. Evolution of an Investment

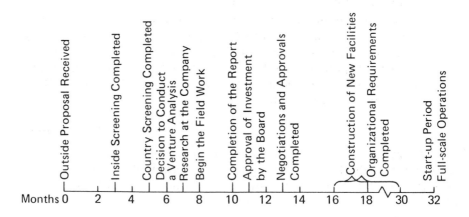

The most consistent problem in making progress is time pressure on top of management. In big companies, important, but postinvestment, decisions are often delayed for only "press of business" reasons. The performance of operating managers can be hurt by indecision.

SIGNIFICANT MANAGEMENT TECHNIQUES

This discussion involves aspects of management in multinational operations different from practices in the United States, and important to achieving plans and strategies.

Accounting

More than one set of books conjures an image of wrongdoing. However, there are two legitimate reasons for having more than one set of books. *First,* laws and regulations on accounts in most countries outside the United States do not permit compiling the same data in a form useful to management. Therefore, it is necessary to compile financial information one way for the government and another way for decision making. *Second,* reporting to headquarters or a regional control center sometimes requires a different format than that which is needed to manage the business. As a result, a third set of books (government, local management and headquarters) is kept to satisfy the parent company.

One of the most difficult situations for American accountants to handle in an acquisition or joint venture is "black" profits. These are earnings not reported to tax authorities, and are a tradition in most countries. Nationals do not feel they are dishonest — it is a game between them and the government which adds zest to the business. Also, they are usually powerful enough to avoid prosecution if caught. The systems created to circumvent detection are quite elaborate, and Americans sometimes never learn about the "black" profits.

In most instances there is disclosure to avoid any embarrassment at the time of audits. The complication is that Americans normally prefer to report on operations completely and rely on ingenuity to minimize the impact of taxes. This policy has backfired in some cases, but the normal problem is the transition from practices controlled by the nationals, to reporting under new management.

Monitoring Receivables and Payables

The occurrence of 120 to 180 day receivables in the overseas operations of an American MNO is much less frequent than in other foreign firms. However, it happens because individuals and companies outside the United States are characteristically slow payers. Governments are even worse in paying for products and services and have actually caused undercapitalized firms to fail due to extended delays. Much more attention is needed to expedite outstanding invoices in other countries and a full range of local contacts is sometimes needed to get the cash on schedule. In fact, if inflation is a serious problem, earnings could be wiped out without prompt action.

Payables are, of course, the other side of the cash flow situation. It is essential that Americans control the urge to eliminate their obligations by using standards in this country. If money does not come in as fast, it should not go out as fast. This is not a recommendation to shift to the practices of foreign businessmen; however, the controller has to seek the proper point between two extremes.

Cash Management

Another form of managing cash flow is use of short-term money markets to: (1) earn interest, and (2) hedge against inflation. While this is common business practice, the methods to accomplish this are often different outside the United States and require a flexible attitude on the part of an American given the assignment. Considerable study of the methods used locally is needed for consistent success.

Applications to the Ministry of Finance, if required to convert the local currency to dollars or another international currency, must be carefully managed in the same thoroughness as handling the money itself. Constant attention is necessary to get both approval and have the liquidity to remit. Local banking relationships may be very important in these situations.

Finance

The use of financial leveraging (much more debt as compared to equity invested) is common in ventures outside the United States. In fact, development loans given in areas where the foreign government wants economic stimulation and other extended terms can transform an unattractive investment into one that is highly profitable when measured against the money actually committed by the company. Table 12—3 shows the possibilities with a simplified example.

Structuring the financial composition of an investment is a talent developed from experience. Maximum use of local currency loans, for example, gives the operation the flexibility to repay these obligations during periods in which it is difficult to obtain approval on remitting to headquarters. Another technique involves including a major foreign bank having dealings with the government as a partner, or the International Finance Corporation of the World Bank, in order to spread risk and minimize the possibility of nationalization, and so on. The power of these financial institutions has an influence on the government.

Guarantees purchased, or given, by the parent company have enabled some MNO's to borrow the entire capital required for a new operation or the expansion of an existing business. Professionals in the merchant banks of Europe are extremely helpful in putting together

Table 12—3. Use of Leveraging

Case 1		Case 2
$1 million	Capital Required for the Investment	$1 million
$200,000	Equity Invested	$800,000
800,000	Long-term Loans	200,000
$80,000*	Seven-year Average for After-tax Profits	$100,000
40%	Simple Rate of Return	12½%

*Adjusted for interest payments.

the financial package with the lowest cost sources and the latest tax exposure. Americans have greatly increased their capability to provide this service to companies interested in multinational operations in recent years.

Marketing

Sales are the primary source of cash inflow, and Americans are globally recognized as having the expertise and creativity to optimize cash return from a product or service. Nevertheless, some aspects of marketing abroad require special attention.

Pricing

Inflation in this country beginning in the early 1970s gives an indication of the problems of operating in areas where consumer and industrial price indexes are increasing at 1% + per month. In some countries, such as Brazil, the rate is even higher but the mechanism for adjusting prices to changes in costs is reasonably efficient. In most instances, adjustments must be made which bypass controls. This involves handling, transportation, insurance, warehousing and losses from damage and/or pilfering enroute to the buyer. Policies become flexible to reflect the companies' current position relative to costs and capacity to raise the price.

In many countries a cartel sets the price of a product, and individual firms must comply. Usually this arrangement is endorsed or tolerated by the government. Since this practice is against the law in the United States, American companies sometimes feel uncomfortable about participating in monopolies. Government endorsement is usually based on reasonable profit margins and lower prices to the buyer than competition would provide because of savings in advertising, distribution costs and direct selling expense. Exploitation of the buyer is sometimes a problem, and extremes in unit profit margins have opened the door to new methods and materials in several countries.

Venture analyses which are not sufficiently thorough can fail to take the full impact of taxes into consideration. Bilateral and multicountry treaty agreements could favor competitors. Also, major employers and export-oriented firms sometimes receive special tax concessions. A lower cost base can be lost and profit margins are narrowed as a result of tax advantages held by others.

Selling, Promotion, and Advertising

Many times product preferences in other countries are significantly different than American tastes. While we have influenced the choice of products and services around the world, some factors such as size, appearance, "gimmicky" options and quality are different. The choice of color on package or shape of a trademark can have an impact on sales performance.

A customer's capacity to buy is often difficult to determine. Companies that appear to have no financial standing are the means used by wealthy families to avoid tax inquiries. Poor countries such as Portugal are large markets for luxury goods because of the distribution of wealth. Outdated credit ratings fail to reflect critical gains or losses in recent months. Appearances are misleading and the marketing manager must be especially careful to avoid loss of sales to good risks and making sales to bad risks.

More sales are made through personal and family relationships in other countries than in the United States. Contacts are extremely important. Superior products may lose out because someone knows somebody. Nationals as sales representatives can be both helpful and harmful because of attitudes, feuds, and mentality factors not apparent to Americans. Employment of the wrong person becomes very important when you consider it is difficult to terminate such a person.

Advertising content, intensity and media must be chosen for the buyer in the foreign country, not because it is effective in the United States. Controversial aspects could be clever in one situation and gain the loyalty of the buyer. In others, not only might the buyer be alienated but the government might react against the campaign.

Distribution Including Transportation and Warehousing

Competitiveness in pricing is affected by the number of middlemen needed to distribute products and market services effectively. The mark-ups at each stage could be magnified by double border crossings and damage from multiple handling by manual systems. Careless design of the distribution phase of the business can cost a significant portion of the profit margin.

Transportation can seriously complicate timing. Some mentalities regard the importance of meeting deadlines with indifference. This attitude is compounded by actual delays at borders and breakdowns. Another transportation problem is condition of goods on arrival, and constant attention is needed to minimize damage from the method of packing.

Warehouse facilities in most countries will range from excellent to unbelievably poor. Another uncertainty is knowledge of the supervisor about the necessary atmosphere being cool or dry or away from the sun, and so on. Access to a warehouse is sometimes difficult because of crowded streets near docks and terminals. Finally, stacking techniques may be unknown and cause losses due to lack of structural strength.

Most of these problems can be resolved with minor changes and planning, but unfortunately many American companies learn the hard way.

Staff Functions

The differences between business practices in this country and those abroad increase the need for control systems and problem-solving services. However, there is not a tradition of staff managers outside this country, and nationals with the capability to administer sales or develop new money saving concepts are scarce. The alternative of Americans living in other countries with their families is very expensive. The net result is that some problems are not solved until they become glaringly acute.

Production and Industrial Relations

The workforce can be a blessing such as in Singapore or a nightmare such as in Great Britain. Unions become a political tool, and the best conceived labor relations policies and programs will not overcome manipulations to create unrest or harass foreign investments. However, plant managers can reduce unrest through a feedback system that permits planned actions and explanations and minimizes the basis of complaints.

Inventories can be a problem if there are extended distances between the supplier and the operation. This could lead to major capital commitments in both material and components for manufacturing and parts and spares to keep production lines running. Quality control is a major cost in many situations because of indifference to specifications. Supervision is critically important and an investment in training can pay off handsomely.

Accuracy in the sales forecast is more important to the production manager abroad because he has less latitude in being able to respond to major changes in demand. When this is combined with limitations in staff capability, "second guessing" involving arbitrary cutbacks is often a cause of product shortages.

SUMMARY

The fully evolved multinational corporation (MNO) has six characteristics that tend to place loyalty to company before country and other traditional standards. No American firms conform with all of these characteristics, and are called MNOs (firms with many operations abroad) in this book. Publicity about political interference, the energy crisis and accusations about "exporting jobs" developed a poor image for MNO's among large portions of the public.

MNO's are comparatively efficient and have made major contributions to the balance of payments. Problem areas cited most frequently by critics include currency speculation, political embarrassment, balance of payments, loss of jobs, and technology transfers. It is likely that four of the five areas are an asset rather than a problem. Political complications must be expected in multinational operations. Generally, American MNO's should not be encouraged to find headquarters in other countries by restrictive legislation. It might be necessary, however, to limit share holdings by foreigners who are not experienced in business such as oil-rich Middle East investors.

American companies are being forced to search for sources of raw materials and energy outside the United States. The extractive phase of these operations is usually followed by pressure to process in the host country. After several years a wave of nationalism then leads to the government wanting local ownership. This is followed by takeovers in a few instances.

Market opportunities and cheap labor have also played a major role in motivating American companies to establish multinational operations. The lowest possible cost base is needed to remain competitive in today's market conditions. Loss of jobs in the U.S.A. does not appear to have occurred because of these investments.

Other miscellaneous reasons behind multinational operations includes mergers, acquisitions, obligations to foreign governments, licensing opportunities, and management contracts.

Specific operations originate with both internally generated leads and those proposed by outside sources. The screening process sometimes produces alternative approaches which are better than the original lead, and management must be careful about premature commitments. The five stages of venture analysis to estimate investment viability are: (1) study design; (2) selection of staff; (3) implementation; (4) completion of the report, and (5) the decision and its structure. Eight points for negotiating strategy on approved ventures outside the United States are identified along with four additional suggestions for controlling the bargaining. Once necessary contracts have been signed, organizational decisions must be made as rapidly as possible, and indecision by busy members of executive management can cause harmful delays.

Management techniques cited are those required by differences between American practices and those in other countries, and facilitate executive management successfully fulfilling their responsibilities. Examples are given in accounting, finance, marketing, personnel and production. The emphasis is on cash flow and achieving profit expectations.

DISCUSSION QUESTIONS

1. The statement has been made by government and labor union officials that MNO's export jobs. Do you agree? Defend your position using library research as required.
2. Discuss the cycle of industrial involvement in foreign countries. Using five stages as your base, analyze each for benefits and disadvantages.
3. Are government owned operations always less efficient?
4. Distinguish between the MNC and a large national corporation doing international business.
5. Define "Venture analysis." What factors are common to all venture analyses in foreign countries?
6. "Most members of executive management are not usually an asset to expansion outside the United States." Discuss this point and how business can best expand to other countries.
7. Multinational operations involves working with people of different values, traditions, attitudes, etc. Discuss what effect these differences might have on profit performance.
8. Can you foresee sufficient laws and regulations adopted in this country to force MNO's, or those with a major portion of their business abroad, to move their headquarters to another country?

SUGGESTED READINGS AND BIBLIOGRAPHY

"A New Growth Industry: Studying the MNCs," *International Finance.* December 17, 1973, pp. 7—8.

"A Reprise for the Ailing Dollar," *Business Week.* July 14, 1973, p. 24.

"Australia's Investment Climate-Sunshine and Showers," *Business International.* March 23, 1972, p. 93.

Bluhdorn, Charles G. "A Case for American Nationalism," *Business Week.* September 1, 1973, pp. 8—9.

Blumenthal, W. Michael. "Needed: A GATT for Investments," *Business Week.* August 18, 1973, pp. 12—14.

"Burke-Harte Blues," *Nations Business.* May, 1972.

Campbell, Walter J. "Is There Still Time . . . To Save U.S. Industry?" *Industry Week.* October 4, 1971, pp. s1—s2.

Carley, William M. and Ulman, Neil. "ITT Europe Rings Up Profits; a Low Profile Keeps Troubles Minor," *The Wall Street Journal.* January 18, 1974, p. 1.

"Drawbacks of Japanese Management," *Business Week.* November 24, 1973, pp. 12—14.

"Everybody's Favorite Target," *Forbes.* March 1, 1972.

"First, Catch Your Multinational," *The Economist.* September 1, 1973, pp. 61–62.

Gannon, James P. "Increasing Investment in U.S. by Foreigners Irks Many in Congress," *The Wall Street Journal.* January 22, 1974, p. 1.

"Global Companies: Too Big to Handle?" *Newsweek.* November 20, 1972.

Haner, F. T. *Multinational Management.* Charles E. Merrill Publishing Co., 1973.

"How Investments Abroad Creates Jobs at Home," *Harvard Business Review.* September, 1972.

"Japan's Foreign Investment Machine," *Business Week.* March 24, 1973, p. 52–57.

Levine, Richard J. "America's Dependence on Imported Metal Seen Leading to New Crisis," *The Wall Street Journal.* December 26, 1973, p. 1.

"MCN's on Trial," *Harvard Business Review.* May, 1972.

"Multinational Corporations and Nations," *Current.* September, 1972.

"Multinational Corporations vs. Nations," *Current.* April, 1972.

"Multinationals," *U.S. News & World Report.* May 21, 1973, pp. 65–66.

"Multinationals: A Step Toward Global Bargaining," *Business World.* October, 1972.

"Multinationals: Giants Beyond Flag and Country," *N.Y. Times Magazine.* March 3, 1973.

"Multinationals in Trouble," *Business Week.* June 9, 1973, p. 110.

"Multinationals: Resisting Tax Hikes on Foreign Profits," *Business World.* December 10, 1972.

"Multinationals: The Public Gives Them Low Marks," *Business Week.* June 9, 1973, pp. 42–44.

"Multinationals Win Some Points; Senate Finance Committee Hearings," *Business Week.* March 3, 1973.

"New Dollar Diplomacy, 1972 Style," *Newsweek.* April 10, 1972.

Northrup, Bowen. "Consortium of Banks Multiply in Europe; Some U.S. Banks Join, Others Shy Away," *The Wall Street Journal.* May 25, 1973, p. 28.

Obstacles and Incentives to Private Foreign Investment, 1967–1968. Volume 1: Obstacles. National Conference Board, Inc. New York, New York, 1969.

Pearson, John. "Domesticating the Multinationals," *Business Week.* May 26, 1973, p. 15.

"Philips: A Multinational Copes with Profitless Growth," *Business Week.* January 13, 1973, pp. 63–69.

Robock, Stefan H. and Simmonds, Kenneth. *International Business and Multinational Enterprises.* Richard D. Irwin, Inc., 1973.

Scheibla, Shirley, "Taxing the Multinationals," *Barron's.* April 30, 1973, p. 5.

Sommer, N. B. "The Multinational Challenge of the Chemical Industry," February 28, 1973, pp. 1–12.

Stabler, Charles N. "Many Critics Charge Multinational Firms Create Money Crises," *The Wall Street Journal.* April 19, 1973, p. 1.

Stobaugh, Robert B., et al. "U.S. Multinational Enterprises and the U.S. Economy," Boston, Harvard Business School, 1972.

Symposium with Michele Sinsona on the Role of Multinational Corporations, *Journal of World Business,* Summer, 1973, pp. 44–48.

Teuson, Geoffrey E. "Common Market Wants to Create International Firms," *The Christian Science Monitor*, March 27, 1973.

"The International Investment Position of the United States Developments in 1972 and U.S. Direct Investments Abroad in 1972," *Survey of Current Business*. August and September, 1973, pp. 18–34.

The Multinational Corporation as a Force in Latin American Politics—A Case Study of the International Petroleum Company in Peru. 1973.

"The Multinationals Win Some Points," *Business Week*. March 3, 1973, pp. 19–20.

"The New Competition from Foreign-Based Multinationals," *Business Week*. July 7, 1973, pp. 56–65.

"The Scramble for Resources," *Business Week*. June 30, 1973, pp. 56–64.

"The Worldwide Impact of Multinational Companies," *International Finance*. p. 7.

Turner, Louis. *Invisible Empires: Multinational Companies and the Modern World. 1970.*

Ulman, Neil. "Multinational Firms Face a Growing Power: Multinational Unions," *The Wall Street Journal*. April 23, 1973, p. 1.

"U.S. Companies Turning to Overseas Licensing of Industrial Know-How," *American Bulletin of International Licensing*. September and October, 1972, pp. 6–7.

"Who is Going to Build the Eurocompanies?" *The Economist*. December 30, 1972, pp. 51–52.

"Why 'Multinationals' Are Under Fire at Home, Abroad," *U.S. News & World Report*. May 21, 1973, p. 64.

"World Council of Employees: A Challenge to the Supranational Corporation?" in *Western European Labor and the American Corp.* Alfred Kamin (ed.) Washington Bureau of National Affairs, 1970.

Case: Occidental Petroleum Corporation

Fundamentals necessary in developing business abroad are illustrated by the decisions of Armand Hammer. In addition, many of the problems and frustrations of multinational operations resulting from strategic variables are also described.

In 1957 Occidental Petroleum Corporation was a sleepy little California oil exploration company that had not made sufficient profits to pay a dividend in nearly 20 years. They raised funds for exploration by soliciting wealthy investors willing to put up high-risk money in return for a large share of the profits if the company found oil. In its search for investors, the company was directed to Dr. Armand Hammer, a self-made millionaire and entrepreneur who had recently retired and moved to California.

ARMAND HAMMER

While studying medicine at Columbia University, Armand Hammer made his first million dollars by transforming his father's faltering drug supply business into a highly profitable wholesale operation. Upon graduation in 1921, he bought a surplus Army field hospital and set out on a mercy mission for the Soviet Union, which was still recovering from the ravages of the Revolution. Upon arrival, he found the major problem was lack of food, not medical attention. He began bargaining with the government and arrived at an agreement to trade American wheat in return for caviar, furs, and hides because the Soviet government had an extremely limited supply of foreign exchange.

This transaction began Dr. Hammer's career in international business and his philosophy of creatively filling the needs of foreign countries in his business dealings with them. Lenin was so impressed by the young doctor that he gave his personal letter of approval for all Hammer's business deals. With this personal advantage, Armand Hammer set himself up as the Russian sales agent for a number of large American firms. In 1925 the Russian government informed him that they intended to handle all importing to the country and offered him any manufacturing concession he wanted as compensation. He saw a need for pencils, which at the time were 100% imported. Within a year his factory was built and operating at a profit of over a million dollars a year. In 1931 the government also nationalized this business and paid Hammer with promissory notes. He left Russia taking with him a vast collection of art treasures which he had accumulated during his stay.

Other entrepreneurs who had been paid off by the Russian government in promissory notes were not as confident as Hammer that they would be honored when due, so they sold him millions of dollars worth of them for as little as 30% of face value. When the notes came due several years later, the Russians paid in full with all interest earned.

In 1933 Dr. Hammer learned that brewers, just starting up again after prohibition, would be dependent on the Soviet Union for seasoned oak barrel staves for several years. He bought up the entire Russian output for the next two years and began using them to make his own barrels. Shortly thereafter, he entered the whiskey business and began selling 100 proof bourbon at discount prices.

He continued as a very successful business executive for the next 20 years, finally selling his various businesses for $9 million in 1953 and retiring to the easy life in southern California at the age of 54.

Like many successful business executives, he thrived on the excitement of running a big business. After four years of retirement he was ready to return to the business world. When he was first approached by Occidental Petroleum in 1957, he put up $50,000 for exploration. When the company found oil, they returned to him for an additional $500,000 of financing. Dr. Hammer agreed, with the option to buy a controlling interest in the firm. In 1959 he exercised this option, and as the company's largest shareholder, assumed its presidency.

Early Expansion Moves by Hammer

The company grew fast under the leadership of Armand Hammer. His first major move after joining the firm was the acquisition of an oil and natural gas drilling company and the purchase or leasing of large amounts of land in California. Through ingenious financing, the company was able to continue expanding its reserves and acquiring other small oil companies without any long term debt. With its successes in locating oil and its strong financial position, the company's stock became a favorite among oil investors. Its price rose from about $.20 per share in 1959 to over $9.00 per share by 1963.

In a major expansion effort in

1963, the company used its high stock price to acquire three more companies. Seeing the opportunity to diversify into another growth industry using oil depletion allowances to shelter income, Occidental acquired Best Fertilizer Co., Jefferson Lake Sulphur Co., and International Ore and Fertilizer Corporation. Dr. Hammer felt Occidental was too small to challenge the major oil companies at their own game, and found another niche which could use company capabilities.

FERTILIZER OPERATIONS

Fertilizer has four basic ingredients: ammonia (derived from natural gas), sulphur, potash, and phosphates. Best Fertilizer had an ammonia plant at the edge of one of Occidental's new gas fields and was thus a natural integrative acquisition. Following a policy of controlling all aspects of its fertilizer operations, the company hoped to realize even greater synergies than it had with the limited integration of its oil operations.

Jefferson Lake Sulphur Co. was the next acquisition and the third largest domestic sulphur producer. Its 69% owned subsidiary, Jefferson Lake Petrochemicals, Ltd., was the second largest Canadian sulphur producer. Occidental, thereby, had direct control over two of the four basic fertilizer ingredients from the start.

International Ore and Fertilizer Corporation followed as the largest marketer of fertilizer in the world, accounting for over 50% of American fertilizer exports in 1963. With branches in 23 countries and sales in 59 different countries, Interore was respected not only for its strong sales force but also for its pioneering mining operations in many parts of the world. Combined with Armand Hammer's 40 years of international experience, this gave Occidental a strong foothold for international expansion in fertilizers.

Realizing that success is not dependent solely on size, but on the economies and technological advancements which largeness often allows, Occidental Research and Engineering Corporation was formed to coordinate R and D efforts for the whole company. One of its first accomplishments was the development of a commercial process for making superphosphoric acid out of phosphate rock. As an advance over the existing phosphoric acid process, it allowed phosphates to be shipped in a more concentrated and less corrosive form. It also brought about a revolution in the fertilizer industry by creating the means for producing new types of fertilizer never before possible.

This discovery helped Occidental to offer a unique fertilizer product especially suited to tropical climates. It also made feasible low-cost transport of phosphates and helped lead the company to one of its most successful master strategies. This strategy was to: (1) extract and semiprocess raw materials at the point of origin; (2) move these to consumer markets in the most concentrated form feasible, and (3) convert them into end products in the consumer market.

By following this strategy, Occidental became the first truly multinational fertilizer company. It had technological and organizational expertise and was not limited by national boundaries. With domestic fertilizer demand forecast to increase 15% to 20% per year and foreign demand 25% to 30% per year over the next decade, the company began an all out effort to expand both its sales and its control of basic raw materials.

Foreign Joint Ventures

With the help of the United States Agency for International Development (AID), many underdeveloped countries were able to purchase fertilizer needed for agricultural development. AID also insured investments made by American companies in these countries. By tailoring its offers around the particular needs of the countries in which it wished to set up extractive and production operations, Occidental soon gained a reputation among foriegn governments as a very good American company with which to do business.

The first joint venture in which the company participated with a foreign government was for the mining and processing of phosphate rock in Morocco. The newly developed superphosphoric acid process made the phosphate rock deposits in Morocco very attractive. Phosphates could be economically shipped from the country's ports on the Mediterranean and Atlantic Ocean to anywhere in the world. Before

negotiations began with the Moroccan Office of Phosphate Monopoly, a detailed study of the Moroccan economy was made and analyzed in terms of what the company could offer the Moroccan government in addition to the standard royalties.

The results showed that construction of the mining and processing facilities would bring in badly needed foreign exchange and provide new employment. When the production facilities came on-line they would provide not only employment, but also training of skilled workers. Agricultural development could be aided by the construction of a fertilizer complex in addition to the phosphate plant, and this complex could also profitably serve other areas in North Africa.

Finally, the study showed there was a need for well managed Western type hotels to aid the Moroccan tourist trade. Further studies showed that this final point was common to several other countries in which the company hoped to set up future operations. Consequently, an agreement was reached with Holiday Inns of America, Inc. for overseas joint ventures to give Occidental additional strength at the bargaining table.

The final agreement called for the construction of mining and processing facilities which would produce $30 million in net sales in the first year of operation and be gradually expanded to produce $150 million per year in net sales. A small fertilizer complex was to be built to serve the country's agricultural needs and eventually expanded to serve other North African countries.

In addition, a modern hotel complex was to be built and managed by the Occidental-Holiday Inn group.

This agreement in March, 1964 gave the company substantial control over three of the four basic fertilizer ingredients and fertilizer plants on two continents. To gain control of sources of the remaining ingredient, Occidental acquired a 50% interest in large potash lands in Saskatchewan, Canada and began negotiations with the government of Tunisia for operations in that country.

To strengthen its R and D operations in potash mining and processing, the company acquired the highly respected Garrett Research and Development Co. A study similar to the one undertaken in Morocco was made in Tunisia and resulted in similar findings. Occidental's offer included the extraction and processing of potash, the building of a modern hotel in the capital city of Tunis, and the import of fertilizer from the nearby plant in Morocco. In addition, the company would seek new uses and processing methods for other saline minerals found with the Tunisian potash. The agreement was signed in 1965, and operations began in 1968.

To complement its North African phosphate and potash operations, the company also reached an agreement in 1965 with Petromin, an agency of the Saudi Arabian government, for the construction of an anhydrous ammonia plant. As a result of the company's thorough research before negotiations and investment, Occidental had gained an excellent reputation in foreign countries. Consequently, the Saudi government was anxious to have the firm's expertise and offered to provide full financing for the project. This was important to the company, for with its rapid expansion and continued growth, it needed to conserve capital. The final agreement called for Occidental to manage construction and production for a 20-year period and for the Interore Division to market the entire output. For its part, the government was to provide full financing, provide all the natural gas *free*, and give the company 10% of net profits for management and 5% commission on gross sales.

Investments in the Americas

Fertilizer operations were also expanded in North, Central, and South America. In 1964 the company opened the world's largest phosphate rock mine in Hamilton County, Florida. Using the superphosphoric acid process, the firm was able to cover the entire world market from its two major phosphate rock mines. In 1965 domestic market coverage was increased by the acquisition of three Midwest fertilizer companies. In South and Central America the company followed the same strategy it was using in Africa and the Middle East.

In joint venture with Corporacion Venezolana de Guayana, a company owned by the Venezuelan Government, Occidental took advantage of the country's natural resources (natural gas and abundant hydroelectric power) to build an ammonia and chemical complex which would produce the lowest cost ammonia in South America. From the Guayana region of Venezuela, this low cost ammonia could be shipped to satellite plants throughout the continent to be combined with phosphates from the Florida mines and other ingredients. Operations started in 1968 after five years of studies, negotiations, and construction.

Typical of these satellite plants was the one built in Corinto, Nicaraugua. A separate corporation, Interore International, S.A., was formed; ownership and control were by Nicarauguan farmers and business executives. A 50/50 joint venture between this new entity and Occidental was then arranged, to build a $5 million fertilizer plant.

PETROLEUM OPERATIONS

While it was becoming one of the world's largest and most profitable fertilizer companies, Occidental never forgot its heritage. Throughout the 1960s it continued to increase its domestic oil and gas reserves, and continued its integration in the oil industry by acquiring two crude oil gathering and marketing companies: Permian Corp. in 1966 and McWood Corp. in 1967. In addition to its domestic expansion, the company made its entry into international oil production.

Libyan Concessions

In 1965 King Idris I announced that his government would begin entertaining bids for new oil concessions. Total Libyan oil reserves are among the largest in the world and the best fields in the country were not yet tapped. All of the major oil companies were represented in the bidding. Occidental was much smaller than the oil giants it was competing with, among them Mobil, Shell, and Standard of New Jersey.

Only after a stormy board of directors meeting was Armand Hammer able to get approval to go ahead with bidding for the Libyan concessions. His arguments were persuasive. Unpublicized geological and economic studies of the country had been carried out under this direction since 1961 in anticipation of the time that new lands would be opened. Occidental's small size, he argued, would be an advantage in winning concessions from a country which did not want to become controlled by a few large corporations. Also, the Libyan oil was very low in sulfur content, which would become increasingly important in the future.

Using the same techniques which had been so successful in negotiations for foreign fertilizer operations, the company prepared an elaborate proposal that called for 5% of its Libyan oil profits to be devoted to the agricultural development of Libya, a pet project of the king. It also provided for an intensive search for water to bring more land under irrigation, using the company's geological expertise, and the creation of an oasis near the ancestral home of the king. In addition, it included a feasibility study for a fertilizer complex using natural gas found with Libyan oil. As a final touch, one typical of the thoroughness with which Occidental prepared its proposal, the company's bid was tied with a red, green, and black ribbon—the Libyan national colors.

In early 1966 the awards were announced. Occidental received all four of the concessions on which it had bid, among them two of the most sought after parcels, which had been bid on by over 30 different companies. In anticipation of the awards, the company had taken the risk of signing on a $60,000 per week exploration crew in Libya. Within weeks after the announcement of the awards, the crew had made a major find—long before any of its competitors. This was extremely important because, under Libyan law, existing pipelines owned by one company must be leased to other companies on a first come, first served basis if any excess capacity exists, and Mobil had the only existing pipeline in the areas of Occidental's concessions.

Although the company was able to use the excess capacity in Mobil's pipeline, to be able to take full advantage of its production capacity required a major new pipeline. Industry experts predicted it would take three years to complete the 40-inch, 135-mile pipeline to the port of Zutitina. Occidental, using its highly developed international information gathering apparatus found a California turbine manufacturer ready to turn out the pumps needed and an Italian pipe company which had just finished producing 40-inch pipe and had its tooling ready to begin immediate production. Using a sophisticated and computerized

network model, the company was able to avoid bottlenecks and complete the entire project in under a year. By 1968, production capacity was over 500,000 bbl. per day. Having become a major world producer, the company continued its integration by acquiring the European refining and distribution operations of Signal Companies, Inc.

European Refining and Distribution

The original agreement with Signal Companies called for that company to market Occidental's Libyan oil throughout Europe on a commission basis. This agreement included an option for Occidental to acquire Signal's European operations. On February 20, 1968 they exercised this option for $100 million in stock. This gave the company direct control of the product from the wellhead to the consumer's gas tank. The major refineries were located in Belgium and Germany, turning out asphalt, heating oil, diesel fuel, and gasoline to be distributed throughout Europe under the OXY brand name.

The company began expansion of its refineries and expansion of its distribution network through the acquisition of small independent chains.

The Tanker Fleet

Included in the acquisition of the European refining and distribution operations were four tankers used to transport crude oil across the Mediterranean. Unlike most oil companies, which charter tankers at short-term rates determined by demand, Occidental had its tankers on long-term rates which were fixed. Predicting a rise in short-term charter rates and wishing to have convertible tankers which could be used to transport not only oil but also many of the company's other products, the firm purchased several tankers outright and increased its long-term charter fleet to 22 ships.

Chemical Operations

With the price of its stock at an all time high, reflecting its successes in Libya, Europe, and around the world, the company setup a wholly-owned subsidiary to merge with Hooker Chemical Corporation and became full owner of the chemical company in one of the largest financial transactions of its kind. On July 24, 1968 Hammer's firm exchanged nearly one billion dollars worth of its stock for Hooker's, and gained $365 million in sales and $25 million+ in after-tax earnings from the investment.[1] This move also gave the company an aggressive young management team, a new direct outlet for its petroleum, and the opportunity to use its international expertise to expand Hooker's foreign operations. As a result, Occidental saw profit potential beyond the basic numbers.

Political Troubles in Libya

Until 1969 the company seemed

[1] Information reported by Hooker Chemical in the year ending December 31, 1967.

to have a golden touch. Nearly everything had been a great success. But Occidental had made a serious miscalculation about the political stability in Libya and the company's ability to withstand pressure from the government. When the government of King Idris I was overthrown by the Revolutionary Command Council, under Mu'ammar El—Qadafi, the safety of the company's investment became highly suspect.

Colonel Qadafi, hoping to bring about a united Arab nation and expel foreign oil interests, soon began squeezing by setting arbitrary production limits. Occidental was smaller than the other oil companies, like Esso, Mobil, Texaco, Shell, and Standard of California. However, Occidental was almost totally dependent on its Libyan operations. Over 80% of its proven reserves were in Libya, and it had no other foreign oil production.

At this stage, Occidental had developed a concept for European operations as shown in Figure 12C—1. During 1969 and 1970, the company was able to meet its delivery obligations to the beginning of this complex by purchasing Middle East crude oil from other producers and reselling it. Realizing its vulnerability because of dependence on its Libyan holdings, the company started extensive exploration the world over.

OCCIDENTAL IN THE EARLY 1970s

For 11 years the company increased profits every year. In 1970, it had earned $175 million after taxes. In

Figure 12C—1. European Cluster Model

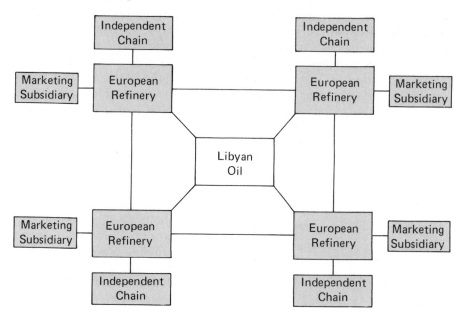

1971, a recession year, Occidental was confronted by: (1) production cutbacks in Libya; (2) soft demand and lower prices for oil, sulphur, fertilizer, and petrochemicals; (3) abnormally depressed short-term charter rates caused by an oversupply of tanker capacity, and (4) a mild winter. The combination led to a $67 million loss for the year.

Working capital was insufficient to finance all the oil exploration plans that had been made. As a result, the only substantial find outside of Libya was the Piper field in the North Sea, in which Occidental had a 36½% working interest. The company's share in this find doubled its total non-Libyan reserves. Although exploration rights had been granted in many areas of the world: the Middle East, Nigeria, Peru, Venezuela, Ghana, and the Gulf of Mexico, financing for these projects was generally unavailable because of the company's highly leveraged position.

In 1972, the company barely managed to break even. As a result, its foreign expansion, which had proceeded in leaps and bounds for nine years ground to a halt. See Appendix A for a synopsis of Occidental's financial history.

U.S.S.R. Trade Agreement

In 1971, the company and Dr. Hammer began heavily publicizing negotiations with the Soviet Union. An agreement in purpose was reached which provided for future negotiations in the areas of:

1. Exploration, production, and refining of oil and natural gas.

2. Agricultural chemicals and fertilizers.
3. Metal treating and plating.
4. Hotel design and management.
5. Solid waste processing and disposal.

In return for its expertise in these areas, the company would receive compensation in the form of oil, gas, nickel, chromium, and fertilizer raw materials.

Although the agreement in purpose was signed, no definite project agreements have been made, nor has the company been able to secure financing for its proposed projects. Because many of the statements made by the company about these negotiations tended to be misleading about the degree of actual commitment, the SEC sued Occidental in 1971 and again in 1973, forcing Dr. Hammer to sign a consent decree which prevents the issuing of misleading statements.

Other Developments

In 1973, the Libyan government carried its confrontation with Occidental one step further. Bowing to pressure, the company agreed to accept $135 million as compensation for a 51% nationalization of its Libyan assets. This was considerably less than their book or market value. In return for this loss of control, the company was assured of a continued and increased supply of oil. This increase has yet to be seen, however, since shortly after the nationalization of the company's operations, oil production for all companies was curtailed throughout the Arab world.

One of the few bright spots since 1970, has been the development of a method for extracting oil from shale. Deposits in Colorado, Utah and Wyoming offer the United States potential independence from Arab oil, and, with oil prices at their June, 1975 levels, this might become a commercially feasible process. However, as with many Occidental opportunities, considerable financing will be required to put it in operation.

STUDENT PROBLEMS

1. Are Occidental's problems in the mid−1970s indicative of a company with lasting difficulties, or will they emerge? Develop a strategy for growth in the next five-year period using information from research on Occidental's current situation.
2. Judging from information in the case, and details from other research, was the Libyan crude oil venture a prudent investment? Did subsequent moves in Europe and the merger with Hooker Chemical based on successes in Libya offset the problems subsequently encountered in that strategy?
3. Based on your assessment of food supplies and current emphasis on agribusiness, how do you estimate the future profitability of fertilizer operations? (See Appendix B for the names and dates of firms acquired to estimate the scope of this part of Occidental.)

Appendix A. Financial Statistics

	$		Millions				$
	1974	1973	1972	1971	1970	1969	1965
Sales and Revenues:							
Oil and Gas	3287.5	2090.0	1635.1	1682.1	1465.6	1241.2	467.0
Chemical	1688.6	1064.7	830.6	706.0	658.0	625.3	450.3
Coal[1]	561.4	301.0	255.1	247.1	262.1	192.5	109.9
Total[2]	5578.2	3455.7	2720.8	2635.2	2385.7	2059.0	1027.2
Net Income	280.7	79.8	10.4	(67.0)	175.2	174.8	51.0
Cash Flow	410.2	221.7	120.3	150.6	282.0	247.5	11.2
Total Net Assets	3325.5	2871.0	2562.0	2580.0	2656.0	2213.5	204.7
Long-term Debt	1040.3	1100.8	995.8	898.7	863.0	718.2	103.4
Net Working Capital	464.6	313.9	253.2	237.9	351.8	306.5	51.5

[1] See Appendix B for the company which generates this domestic income.
[2] Total includes a fourth category of income from sources such as saved interest so that sales and revenues from operations do not add to the overall total in 1974 only.
Sources: Annual Reports for 1972, 1974, and 1975 for the Occidental Petroleum Corporation.

Appendix B. Major Acquisitions

1959	Gene Reid Drilling Co.	Integration, enter drilling operations
1961	Signet Oil & Gas Co.	Expand American gas and oil interests
1963	Best Fertilizer Co. Jefferson Lake Sulphur Co. International Ore and Fertilizer Corp.	Become an integrated fertilizer company
1965	Green Belt Fertilizer Co. Summers Fertilizer Co. Ashkum Fertilizer Co.	Expand domestic fertilizer operations

Appendix B. Major Acquisitions cont'd.

1966	Garrett Research and Development Co.	Expand and upgrade R & D
	Permian Corp.	Entered crude marketing and gathering
1967	McWood Corp.	Expand crude marketing and gathering
1968	Signal Companies, Inc.	Integration, obtain European refining and distribution operations
1968	Hooker Chemical Corp.	Outlet for crude, entry into new markets
1968	Island Creek Coal, Inc.	Expand toward the goal of being a "total energy supplier."

BIBLIOGRAPHY

Art News. April, 1973, p. 20.

Business Week. March 23, 1963, p. 66; November 2, 1968, p. 150; February 22, 1969, p. 86; December 18, 1971, p. 79; February 26, 1972, p. 24; July 22, 1972, p. 20; May 19, 1973, p. 50; December 1, 1973, p. 28; February 9, 1974, p. 68.

Economist. September 21, 1968, p. 66; November 16, 1968, p. 46.

Forbes. June 1, 1968, p. 24; August 1, 1970, p. 18; November 15, 1971, p. 31.

Life. February 18, 1966, p. 71.

Magazine of Wall Street. August 2, 1969, p. 16.

Moody's Industrial Manual. 1960–1972.

Occidental Petroleum Corporation, *Annual Report.* 1959–1972.

Occidental Petroleum Corporation, Presentation before the New York Society of Security Analysts. September 12, 1973.

Standard & Poor's Corporation, *Industrial Report.* 1973, pp. 57–83.

Standard & Poor's Corporation, Standard N.Y.S.E. Stock Reprints, Occidental Petroleum Corp. August 1, 1973.

Stevenson, John S. *Occidental Petroleum Corporation: Analysis of Corporate Strategies 1959–1972*, University of Delaware research report.

Case: Trenton Industries, Inc.: an Expansion Outside the United States

Trenton Industries is typical of smaller firms interested in expanding outside the Unites States. The student, with background on the company given in Chapters Three and Six, can increase understanding of the process of establishing operations in other countries.

BACKGROUND

In this situation Hank Trenton is interested in expanding the company in another country initially, if the profit opportunities are superior to expansion in the United States. Executive management is using growth in after-tax profits as a measure of performance, and the successful new location at Wichita plus approvals on policies and formal planning have strengthened the organization.

THE DEVELOPMENT PHASE

The core of this proposed international expansion is the self-propelled combine. (See Figure 6C−1.) Therefore, the countries to be considered had to have broad expanses of land under cultivation in grains which could be harvested by the combine. Preliminary research in Omaha, and a trip to Washington to talk to the U.S. government and several foreign embassies, indicated that Argentina, Australia, Canada, Brazil, South Africa, and Venezuela justified an on-the-spot trip to screen possibilities.

John Hotchkiss, director of planning and development, visited Canada, Venezuela and the southern hemisphere countries to explore the possibilities for Trenton Industries in late 1976. One consideration was that a single operation thousands of miles from headquarters might be difficult to manage effectively. Hank Trenton thought that the first international investment should have neighboring countries with potential, so that a cluster could be developed, and regional administration could reduce the overhead burden on any one operation. Also, money management is critically important in most countries in order to avoid loss of profits in erosion from inflation and inability to convert local currency to dollars.

Preliminary Investigations

The results of John Hotckkiss' screening trip are summarized here:

ARGENTINA   Real economic growth averaging 2%; Bahia Blanca is a functional port, a center of large scale farming on the immense Las Pampas, and a good location for manufacturing; political stability is questionable with guerrilla activity continuing in the cities and foreigners a target for ransom; discussions with the local government officials indicate excellent long-range potential; geographic location compatible with a location in Brazil.

AUSTRALIA   Real economic growth of 5%; Perth location in western Australia is the best possibility; no language problem; no possibility of expansion into a second country in that area of the world; government is tending to be nationalistic; while Americans are well received, competition is established in the country.

BRAZIL   Real economic growth of 9%; a Belo Horizonte location northwest of Rio de Janeiro is the center for supplying large scale farming in the interior; government is

selective about new foreign investments but enthusiastic about agribusiness operations; Brazilian manufacturers can supply local content requirements and pricing will bear added costs of these components; Portuguese language would be a special requirement.

CANADA   Real economic growth of 3%; a Calgary, Alberta location to service the vast western plains; established competition; buyers and market situation very similar to Midwest U.S.A.; potential supplies from existing plants possible; also, administrative support from Omaha; generally stable political environment, but very sensitive about American investments.

SOUTH AFRICA   Real economic growth of 5%; a Bloemfontein location south of Johannesburg would be a good location to supply farming in the country; no language problem; government supports the investment, particularly if it can be located in one of the neighboring black homelands and local black labor can be used; no apparent problems with black unrest but there could be criticisms in the United States from those opposed to Apartheid; potential expansion country if Brazil progresses.

VENEZUELA   Real economic growth of 5%; political shift to nationalization of foreign facilities or majority Venezuelan ownership; tremendous potential in the Orinoco River basin but sufficient large-scale farming is years away; some cattle operations being squeezed by Government regulations; eliminate from consideration despite proximity to the United States.

Proposal to the Board of Directors

The success of Trenton Industries since Hank Trenton's appointment as executive vice president in 1974 has led to him being the top day-to-day executive beginning in 1977. His father comes to the office only one or two days per week and travels to golf courses in various parts of the United States much of the year.

The senior Trenton and Board members were not enthusiastic about foreign expansion, but they saw more and more foreign equipment in the United States, and recognized that international business is common everywhere. Also, Hank Trenton had been thorough in each of his major steps and the Board had confidence in both his competence and judgment. This led to a willingness to give the idea a fair hearing, but the general attitude was, "The numbers better be pretty fancy."

Upon returning to Omaha after five weeks of research, John Hotchkiss felt he had learned enough to know that much more information was needed to make a final recommendation on committing millions of dollars to international operations. The physical plant could be established nearly as easy as at Wichita, but important details about marketing, financing, and legalities were much more complex. It was a challenging business opportunity but you could make serious mistakes. Consequently, they proposed the following:

1. The concept of an investment cluster will be important for Trenton Industries to realize the full profit potential because of the cost of: (a) financial expertise to manage pre-tax earnings and convert them to hard currencies; (b) high safety stocks for parts of both production equipment and imported components, and (c) proven competence for administration, research to adapt to local problems and other required staff. If more than one investment within three years is not feasible, the idea will be tabled.

2. A detailed feasibility study should be conducted in Brazil. In addition, South Africa should receive more investigation to determine future potential. Some economies will result from a coordinate study team working in both areas. John Hotchkiss would lead the team which would include company personnel and consultants.

3. Conservative estimates for the discounted cash flow rate of return will be the basis of judging the concept of international operations. The company standard of 14% must be exceeded by a minimum of 3 to 5% in order for management to recommend the venture.

Hank's father and the remainder of the Board received a thorough presentation of results from the trip. Businesslike slides included maps (none had a clear picture of where South Africa is). At the close they were satisfied with this approach. A budget of $55,000 in direct expenses was authorized. In addition, Hank Trenton could make temporary assignments to cover company personnel selected to participate in the studies.

Selection of a Consultant

John Hotchkiss called four consulting firms with a good reputation for international studies to determine interest in submitting a proposal. Sometimes consultants want full responsibility, and Trenton was proposing that the consulting firm provide expertise on the country and venture analysis in foreign countries while the company provides expertise on the business. In this way Trenton would gain a knowledge of their expertise and train their own personnel.

Three visited Omaha in February, 1977, and the bid from Richard E. Young Associates in Indianapolis was accepted. Young would provide two experienced American analysts with knowledge of Portuguese at $6,000 per man/month for 3½ months plus itemized expenses. Their representative in Sao Paulo would also join the team in Brazil for one month at $3,000 per man/month plus expenses, and Michael Chapman in Bahia Blanca would assist on the Argentina research at the same rate.

Results of the Feasibility Studies

The team returned to Omaha in late May, 1977 and had draft reports for Hank Trenton by mid—June (they were partially prepared before arrival). Notes for remarks prepared for a special July 1 Board meeting by the executive vice president summarize the results:

1. *Brazil.* DCF = 23%[1] on $2.25 million in equity and 17% on $4.25 million total capital, including major deficit in first half on Year 1, breakeven in the last half, and 70% potential in Year 2. Plant with rail siding available January 1978 due to pending failure of undercapitalized business. Labor available but very limited in skills; workers responsive to training; productivity estimate 80% of Omaha. Market penetration via established distributors eager for Trenton line; position sufficiently strong to expect maximum 120-day payment. Financing an asset due to attractive cruizeiro terms if a Brazilian bank joins as minority partner: inflation at 24% but manageable under the hedging system. Major problems: Management potential of nationals is good but they are very expensive (110% of the United States) and in short supply; cruizeiro conversion usually takes 75 days; Brazilian manufacturers are highly unreliable on delivery dates, and expediting is an art requiring expense and patience. Recommendation: Proceed immediately with investment, staffing and the multitude of other steps to be operating in the country by year-end 1978.

2. *Argentina.* DCF = 20%[2] including a deficit in Year 1 and breakeven in Year 2. Work force skills good and trainable (learning curve allowance is one portion of first year deficity); productivity estimate 80% of Omaha. Market penetration potentially more rapid

[1] Cash remitted to and received by Trenton Industries' bank in the U.S.A. or Switzerland.

[2] Cash remitted to and received by Trenton Industries' bank in the United States or Switzerland.

Figure 12C-2. Organizational Design for Overseas Operations

*Note that management of production will eventually be given to a national in 2-3 years after assembly systems have operated successfully for an extended period.

than forecasts; "giro" system of customer payment[3] permits quick recovery of cash in local currency. Also, 25% subsidy to farmers mechanizing is an important factor. Recommendation: Table concept of plant similar in size to Omaha until the political situation stabilizes.

3. *South Africa.* Analysis terminated on the basis of racial policies.

THE INVESTMENT RECOMMENDATION

Personnel

Hank Trenton and John Hotchkiss felt that the company should employ an outsider experienced in international operations as a vice president to start the division. He would work at Omaha for the remainder of 1977 and, assuming he could be found and employed in three months, it would

[3] A "giro" is a formal promissory note which can be taken to a bank and discounted for only the current interest rate rather than a premium amount.

give him some time to become oriented to Trenton Industries and its capabilities.

John Hotchkiss would initiate action on the basic things which would have to be done no matter who would be in charge. This would include legalities involving corporate entities, import permits, utility installations, and licenses. Also, financing negotiations could be advanced to near agreement. Discretionary decisions such as selection of employees would be left to the new vice president.

Anticipated sources of personnel are given in the organization chart shown in Figure 12C-2. This concept was presented to the board of directors.

Screening of Trenton Industries' candidates would be handled by picking those who would be capable of adjusting to the transition of living abroad in addition to required competence. Assignments would be for three years. During this time replacements would be hired and trained. Opportunities for advancement would be created in each case so that an international position is a road to promotion rather than something to be avoided.

Investment and Financial Return

The table gives the anticipated progress if Trenton Industries goes ahead, and the profits remitted to New York.

The profit "pipeline" from Brazil, should be full in 1981 (delays in remittances offset by previously processed applications), and expected performance in 1982, when the market position is fully established will be $5.5 million in net sales per year and $1.05 million flowing to New York annually. After adjusting for taxes paid in Brazil and Country X (likely Argentina) the net earnings after U.S. taxes would be $.85 million±.

STUDENT PROBLEMS

1. Place yourself in the position of a board member at Trenton Industries. You are being asked by management to approve the following agenda items at the meeting on July 1, 1977. Prepare your position based on the information in this case and those that have preceeded it.

a. The international division, and a total investment of $4.25 million divided between $2.25 million in equity and $2.0 million in loans to finance operations including working capital.

b. If approved, the choice of Brazil as compared to other countries; how would you rate Canada?

c. If approved, a 20% banking partner in Brazil; theoretically, the bank would provide cruzeiro loans under favorable terms, discounting of receivables in the form of duplicates at prime interest rates, and contracts helpful in operations and remittances to the United States.

d. If approved, the appointment of a new vice president to head the division.

e. If approved, adjustments in the American organization to provide personnel according to Figure 12C−2.

2. Assume the role of John Hotchkiss. What country would be your choice for the second location (update details on the countries considered originally as a start)?

	½ 1977	1978		1979		1980		1981	
		1st ½	2nd ½	1st ½	2nd ½	1st ½	2nd ½	1st ½	2nd ½
Personnel	Mgr.	—	U.S. Staff	Local	Full	Full	Full	Full	Full
Construction:									
Brazil	—	Site	Renov.	Instal.	Start	Full	Full	Full	Full
2nd location	—	—	—	—	—	—	Site	Plant	Plant
Financial:									
Sales (Mil.)	—	—	—	—	$0.50	$1.00	$1.35	$2.50	$2.65
Profits	—	—	—	—	(0.25)	—	0.10	0.30	0.55

Executive Management in a Period of Inflation and Shortages

Management techinques to cope with inflation and shortages and achieve profit goals are discussed. Important management issues in this environment are indentified.

It is apparent that the period of raw material abundance in American business history is over. As dependence on foreign deposits increases, and control of these deposits decreases, the supply and price of key raw materials is uncertain. Global conditions in crude oil and the situation described in the steel industry case are examples. Furthermore, the problem has expanded to include components which companies had produced in formerly low cost areas such as Portugal; prices have escalated seriously and political conditions are often uncertain. However, business will continue and executive management will be expected to overcome these difficulties.

During the first 20 years after World War II companies concentrated on marketing strategies, financing innovations and cost reduction programs to achieve profit objectives. In the 1960s pressure for recognition of social responsibilities began to build, and management started allocating an increasing portion of resources to investments that service community needs but usually earned a low rate of return. A parallel wave of consumer advocates produced a series of improvements in goods and services which increased their inherent value to the buyer.

In October, 1973 imported petroleum products became four times more costly. Energy experts were also predicting the shortages of natural gas which have occurred. These developments were compounded by the Arab embargo based on American support for Israel.

13

This energy crisis induced a "conserve or be laid-off" situation. Despite the serious economic decline in the mid-1970s, and consequent leveling of demand for oil and its derivatives such as many plastics, some shortages persisted. Wood, metals, fibers and minerals also have a high probability of being scarce and expensive in a period of economic expansion.

Each company must take short- and long-range steps to avoid or overcome the effects of scarce materials.

NECESSARY STEPS IN SROP

More attention of top company executives to short-range operating problems will be required in the 1970s and 1980s. Up to the present, authority to handle planning and purchasing of materials was delegated to lower management levels. Now, due to the impact on profit performance caused by increased and/or fluctuating prices and shortages, these decisions warrant and need the best minds in the business. Major policy changes are likely to be required, and aspects of the following four areas must be considered.

Availability

Energy, raw materials and components from suppliers must be available at a reasonable cost or operations cease. Achieving this goal in periods of inflation and shortage can mean higher inventory levels and commitment of more capital. Avoiding these developments has induced significant efficiencies in achieving greater output from the same volume of materials, and contingency stockpiling has been kept to a minimum in many instances. Long-term contracts to assure supply will be common, and whenever possible, relationships will be established which allow emergency sourcing.

New issues in labor relations are possible as a result of efforts to "stretch" supplies. For example, a company may be able to function at 100% of capacity if it can maintain office and plant temperatures at 60°F instead of 70°F. Scarcity of lubricants, heating oil, natural gas, propane and other petroleum products could necessitate greater flexibility in the number of days per week and hours per day in the work week.

Productivity and Cost

Many companies have initiated studies and established incentive systems to uncover wasteful and uneconomic practices. These firms have found that, while the "house cleaning" in 1970–71 recession identified jobs which could be eliminated, less attention was concentrated on operating practices. Also, substitutes that have been costly relative to materials and components in current use are found to be feasible alternatives, and in the long run open the door to new technology and business opportunities. Research will be continuously exploring ideas, some of which had been previously disregarded and others that are wholly new.

Caution is advisable in decisions to shift to another material or supplier based on current prices because a reliable, continuous source may be more important than savings based on short-range conditions. The possibility that other users might be shifting should also be considered, and simulation might be prudent to estimate the situation under the worst possible conditions.

Cost analysts will become more alert to new economics in operating factors such as increasing quality control to reduce rejects, security precautions to reduce pilfering, and environmental controls to minimize deterioration. All of these steps designed to assure the continued profitability will, however, add to cash outflow, and the adverse affect on profit margins increases pressure on executive management.

Consultants working with a variety of companies are beginning to write about the successes of organizations with a good flow of information and creative use of computerized methods which are able to cope with the upward spiral of costs effectively despite the complexities. Management, which has performed competently in the past, may find they are no longer able to cope with the future without investment in advanced systems because of the need for speed in decision making based on a maximum of applicable information.

Pricing

The natural affect of scarcity is an increase in prices, and this is reflected in rising costs. A period of cost–push price increases is being augmented by demand–pull based on shortages. In addition, there have been arbitrary increases in prices by countries controlling key resources. Inflation resulting from the three-fold pressures has led to business controls in many countries, and these regulations around the world have limited the latitude of management in decision making on pricing. This government intervention has made essential coordinated programs in marketing, cost control, and cash control through SROP.

Executive management must participate to a greater degree in:

1. Analyzing the fundamentals of classical price theory (cost, profit, demand, supply, competition, and customer expec-

tations) for their inpact on the company's current and anticipated situation.

2. Assessing the relationship of these price fundamentals to the company's present technological position.

3. Evaluating future technological advantages expected to flow from research and development, particularly for justifications to increase prices as new features are added to an existing product, or for motivations to replace the product to gain an improved profit margin.

4. Estimating product life cycles and turning points for each item, and allow for the possibility of "step pricing" which anticipates smaller margins and more competition at the end of a cycle by establishing very good margins at the beginning and narrowing the margin in "steps" as required.

5. Determining at frequent intervals the cost of inventories at each stage of production, and properly reflect cost fluctuations in the prices of goods being sold.

Each of the five points must be reviewed much more often than in the past. This is time consuming, and there is jeopardy that top management could neglect the future of the firm while solving operating problems.

Marketing management will be looking for other ways to increase revenues despite governmental controls. Traditional practices are being eliminated in many instances. Examples include services formerly free being changed to a fee basis, handling charges added, and items such as transport which are not under control increased. Federal and state officials will clarify whether a new approach is legal and they should be consulted.

Continuous price analysis by product is critical under conditions of inflation and shortage. Cost will vary unexpectedly, both up and down. Profit margins could change sufficiently to change the attractiveness of various products significantly. The performance of a company could fluctuate alarmingly without almost daily attention to costs, prices and resulting margins, and the modification of previously effective policies.

Product Mix

More frequent review of the product lines in a company is necessary in order to maximize current profits and establish priorities in the event of cutbacks. While this is usually the highest unit profit combination, strategic and operating factors could necessitate a product-mix which is not the optimum from a comparison of margins under current volumes. Marketing may need to offer a full line in order to retain customers. Operations may be able to demonstrate sufficiently lower unit costs with another combination of output to change unit profit margins.

Speed of decision making on the best product mix can make a significant difference in profit performance, and systems suggested in earlier chapters willl assist in adjusting product lines. The steps involved are:

1. Eliminate the products which are at the end of their life cycle.
2. Identify extreme situations where, for example, 25% of products in a line account for 75% of profits (usually measured in pre-tax profit contribution).
3. Determine the optimum mix from the positions of key components of the organization in order to identify different perspectives on the products with the lowest costs, best outlook for availability of materials and components, greatest price flexibility, customers with acceptable paying records, availability of worker skills and similar factors affecting SROP.
4. Select the optimum mix for the overall company or division.

Figure 13—1 summarizes the necessity of having top caliber management in decisions on availability, cost control, pricing and product mix in the 1970s.

Figure 13—1. Necessary Steps in SROP

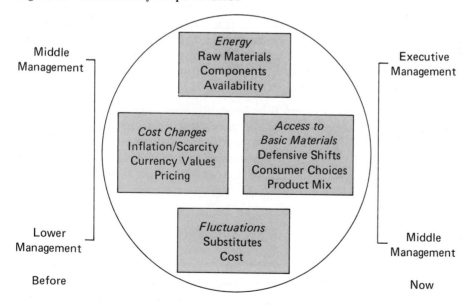

Executive Management in a Period of Inflation and Shortages **487**

Organizing for Shortages

Special organizational steps are likely to be needed on either an active or standby basis:

1. *Vice President or Director, Product-line Management.* This senior staff position monitors the product mix to present recommendations to top level decision makers on deletions needed to optimize profit performance during a specified time period, and additions by operations and research personnel.

2. *Purchasing Task Force.* Though the individual has a permanent position in the organization, he is placed on a standby task force to buy specific items through personal calls on suppliers. Information on developments in these items is regularly forwarded to the individual while he is on his normal job. The task force is alerted as a situation becomes critical.

3. *Materials/Cost Analysts.* With or without #1, specialists are assigned to monitor the costs of groups of materials or components. Comparisons are made with substitutes to have relative position reports, and these are issued at frequent intervals. The facts about a changeover to a substitute are thereby current and accurate. (The likelihood of competitors considering the same step makes the final decision a top management judgment.)

4. *Energy Coordinator.* Alternative sources are secured to keep operations going within specified cost limits. This position involves negotiations and regular outside contacts rather than statistical work on lowest cost sources that can be provided by cost analysts.

5. *Profit Margin Analysts.* An individual becomes the focal point of information and ideas on costs, prices and means of sustaining or improving profit margins. By not dividing responsibilities between two to four people, better recommendations result from knowledge being accumulated in one place.

In addition to creating jobs, executive management must be certain that modifications are made in the organizational structure to be certain full benefits result from additions. Information must flow to the new people and their recommendations must reach decision makers. Figure 13−2 gives a portrayal of the possibilities.

LONG-RANGE PLANNING CONSIDERATIONS

Adjustments for inflation and shortages in SROP assumes a company has limited latitude to change the composition of its business. In the

Figure 13-2. An Example of Organizing for Shortages

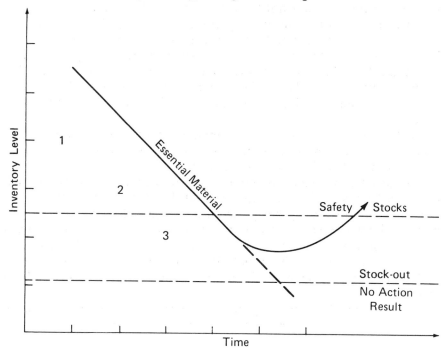

1. Purchasing Task Force Appointed as a Contingency Option
2. Energy Coordinator Appointed, Cost Analysts Added to Support Purchasing
3. Purchasing Task Force Placed in Operation

period covered by the long-range plan, new operations can be added and existing ones can be sold, abandoned, or transformed. When lasting shortages of materials and components become evident, or are judged to be lasting, prudent management will take the steps required to achieve acceptable profit performance in future years under these conditions.

Vertical Integration

Big corporations such as General Motors have investigated the feasibility of captive oil operations. Consortiums of American firms have joined to develop and extract from ore bodies that are in countries with high political risk in order to assure supplies and spread the risk. Power companies are joint venturing on large-scale storage facilities for gas and acquiring coal mines for supplementary reserves. Many of these investments will necessitate coordination

Executive Management in a Period of Inflation and Shortages   **489**

with the Justice Department and other U.S. government agencies monitoring for possible antitrust activities in business.

It is a serious step to allocate resources to securing the needs of existing operations instead of using them for expansion projects. Sometimes this decision can add substantially to profitability. However, it would be a critically poor decision if the supply situation changed, and materials and/or components became available at a cost comparable to or less than that which the company could supply itself.

Different industries and companies will take different approaches to overcoming shortages. It is a period when good management can perform above expectations and mediocre management can cause bankruptcy. Decisive action based on reliable information will enable a firm to make the right move at the right time, and the right time may not always be hasty action to become the first company to make a change. Because of uncertainty in many instances, executives have the obligation to have adequate information and advice so that the judgment has a high probability of being accurate. Simulations will assist top management in defining the benefits of vertical integration.

Acquisitions to secure supplies of materials and components or to improve quotas for energy are becoming increasingly common.

Buying Cooperatives

Many buying co-ops existed in building materials before serious shortages became apparent. They were formed to give small regional firms sufficient volume to reduce the cost of items purchased. Now they serve the purpose which is applicable to a broad range of companies:

Buying strength to improve ability to obtain needed items at a reasonable price.

Time is needed to organize buying co-ops although shortages plaguing an industry might motivate increased cooperation. The government is always informed about the organization to prevent allegations of collusion, price fixing, and other monopolistic practices.

Diversification

Materials research could lead some companies into new product lines that are reasonably secure from shortages. This could occur through acquisitions of going concerns, development of new concepts within the company to meet the needs of existing customers, and combinations of the outside/inside approach such as acquuisitions to provide production capability for ideas conceived internally.

Changing processes and/or materials instead of product lines is a new form of diversification. This allocation of resources is motivated by deciding to service the same customers with products composed of different materials or with processes which circumvent supply and/or cost problems.

Some observers claim that R and D in this country is facing cutbacks in the allocation of funds by executive management because of uncertainty about the direction projects should take and their priority. This is unlikely. Applied research will be the backbone for programs to cut costs or avoid increases. Basic research will seek new concepts for meeting customer needs, new product lines less vulnerable to shortages, production methods utilizing less energy or scarce materials, and practical approaches to complying with pollution controls. In summary, the need for solutions based on scientific research will accelerate. In fact, staying ahead of global competition will depend on full use of our technology base.

Changes in Life Styles and Buying Patterns

Buyers on both the industrial and consumer level will be changing what they purchase in the years ahead, sometimes involuntarily. Part of the shifts in buying patterns would be expected because of planned and technological obsolescence. However, dramatic changes will result from shortages, converting from one material to another, and the dropping of certain product lines. Steps recommended under SROP in this chapter will lead to narrower lines and fewer options.

When the results of these trends are applied to industrial supplies, it will be important not to be dependent on low-volume components with profit margins that might influence a supplier to drop the product. The make or buy decision is assuming new dimensions. If a buyer has other attractive orders to place, it will likely be possible to retain a marginal item in the package. Otherwise, long-range planning must anticipate the possibility of: (1) making components in jeopardy because of material shortages; (2) altering designs to permit a component to be used in several products, thus increasing unit volume through standardization; (3) less production of some products, and/or (4) sharp increases in cost. Selective vertical integration may be necessary, but the impracticality or reluctance to allocate resources toward such projects could have a bearing on companies dropping product lines.

Regarding consumer buying patterns, the proliferation of models, styles and options for clothing, white goods, brown goods, food products and other items is ending. In a period of shortages it is more economical for the producers to limit the variety common in the 1960s and early 1970s, but the consumer also becomes more cautious. Consequently, market research on what will be accepted in volume will have to be carefully analyzed by top management.

Buyers will have fewer alternatives from which to choose, and a mood to conserve will reflect on industry back to basic raw materials. In this climate it may be necessary for companies usually planning five years into the future to change to three years. A narrow time gap between SROP and the long-range plan, or no gap at all, may make both plans a more practical guide to future operations.

Government Action

The resources needed for American business are often found outside this country. Global competition for scarce resources has become international in character and more than profit oriented, privately owned companies are involved. This means that there is a major role for the federal government to play in assisting American corporations in their quest for oil, ores and minerals, in the same way that other governments will be developing strategies for their companies to gain power and competitiveness through control of these resources.

The stakes in this battle are: (1) export capability and strength of currency; (2) the capability to supply domestic industry and generate growth in employment and the standard of living; (3) political power, and (4) strategic military materials. The United States cannot afford to ignore this struggle for resources, nor can it gamble on private business making the correct decisions for the country as a whole. Some joint planning between government and industry and incentives designed to motivate individual companies into carrying out the plans and strategies, seem to be inevitable.

Concern about the availability and price of energy has interjected emotion into an issue which needs cold American logic and ingenuity. When combined with the anti-MNO[1] and anti-big-business attitude common in Washington D.C., the national needs in obtaining raw materials from other countries have a high probability of being confused with aiding large corporations.

[1] See Chapter Twelve for definitions of multinational corporations (MNC's) and firms with extensive multinational operations (NMO's).

Organizational Adjustments

The questions in long-range planning are: "What positions are going to be important in achieving profit objectives in future years?" "What present structure is going to provide qualified personnel needed for the structure in that future period?" "What authority is needed to make the manager functional?" In a period of inflation and shortages obtaining answers to these questions require changes in evaluation standards conventional in the 1960s.

For example, marketing may become less important while operations (production planning, inventory control, and so on) becomes critical to a successful business. The head of international could be responsible for overseas sourcing fundamental to output. Each company will have to assess its own requirements in this context to make necessary changes.

Possibilities for new positions resulting from inflation and shortages have been suggested. Priorities established in plans will clarify the decisions that should be made in redesigning the organization. It is important to make these decisions as part of the planning process to identify the means through which the plan will be carried out.

Financial Implications

Allocation of financial resources becomes a series of delicate decisions because of the need to protect future operations with supplies of materials and components while having to show acceptable growth in profit performance. In addition to striving for the correct balance, the company will be confronted with:

1. Uncertainty about cash flow because of sudden changes in the price of items purchased and the resultant impact on profit margins.
2. Competition for acquisitions (going concerns, rights to new processes and quotas for needed items, property, and so on) and consequent upward spiral in capital required.
3. Greater escalation and contingency allowances in estimates for new operations due to potentially sharp increases in prices due to demand/supply disbalances.

Although financial executives have always been expected to have standby borrowing capability, it will be critical to refine techniques for providing the lowest cost money on short notice. Conditions will be more fluid than in the past. Figure 13–3 summarizes the aspects of long-range planning affected by inflation and shortages.

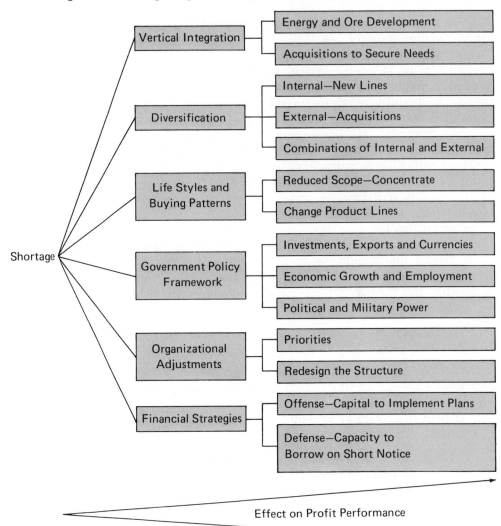

Figure 13-3. Long-Range Planning for Inflation and Shortages

MAJOR ISSUES CONFRONTING EXECUTIVE MANAGEMENT

In reviewing the first 12 Chapters some important points stand out as major issues confronting the management of American companies. These are summarized here in order to underscore the realities that challenge those running businesses in the years ahead.

Studies[2] indicate that large American companies averaged 10% after taxes on invested capital during 1971–73. Average real growth in earnings of these firms in the ten year period ending at the close of 1973 was 4½%. Is this combination enough to attract new capital? It will take 15+ years for the average company to double its earnings at a 4½% growth rate. ITT wants to grow 10% annually, and IBM has exceeded the ITT standard consistently. As a result, these corporations and others demonstrating better than average growth will attract new capital in addition to plowing back after-tax cash flow.

It is essential that new money flow into a broad spectrum of business operations. To attract this investment, the primary criteria of appreciation in share value and dividends must be more than safe places for capital such as savings accounts or tax-free municipal bonds.

With inflation and interest rates high compared to the 1960s, and with the challenges of shortages and other factors such as social responsibility, management will have difficulty in guiding their companies to performance which exceeds the averages. Sometimes earnings will appear sufficiently satisfactory to attract capital, but when adjusted for inflation, profit performance is much less impressive.

Creative incentives for professional managers based on profit growth which supplement personal standards and competitive instincts may be required to inspire the management contributions needed in the 1970s.

The Relative Cost of Profits

A means of measuring for social earnings per share was suggested in Chapter Two. Such a measure would not substitute for the profit performance and cash generation needed to compete for new capital. Consequently, one of the most complex problems confronting today's executives is earning respectable profits while complying with public pressure to make decisions which exhibit concern about the community and its needs.

Several strategic and operating variables including inflation and shortages have been cited which will keep an average firm from performance which would attract investors. Laws and regulations such as those on pricing, pollution and acquisition/mergers are limiting the latitude of companies to outmanage their competition. Changes in

[2] Statistical analyses were undertaken by the author utilizing the *Fortune* list of the 500 largest companies, the U.S. Tariff Commission's report on Multinational Corporations and miscellaneous sources.

the composition of management from white males to combinations of other talented people are occurring in the midst of the many complications. It is understandable that top executives could be tempted to: (1) by-pass modifications in products, services and advertising which would satisfy consumer advocates but narrow profit margins, and/or (2) avoid spending on socially responsible projects which divert funds from growth programs.

It is unrealistic to expect management to comply voluntarily to all the demands of consumer advocates and community leaders. Even the reasonable requests will likely meet with some resistance as a result of pressures arising from strategic and operating variables. On the other hand, corporations, particularly MNO's, are very conscious about the image exposed to the public because of the potential impact on sales, litigation, legislation, and bargaining with outside parties such as labor unions and local governments.

Judgment in estimating the future effect of business variables on a company's operations, in combination with variables caused by community and consumer needs, will distinguish between average and superior management in the years ahead.

Modern Management Systems

The business climate anticipated in the future necessitates use of proven management systems. There is little room for error. Yet, it will be a transition period between: (1) true computer capability as limited by return on money and time invested, and (2) actual management usage of the capability in strategic decision making.

Considerable time has elapsed without significant improvement in use by executive management. Most of the applications at this level are the result of a few enthusiasts who have risen in the organization — not on the basis of general use by top executives in the firm.

Reasons for forecasting accelerated use of computerized systems for making key decisions are:

1. The vast number of strategic and operating variables in selecting a course of action.
2. The penalties for poor decisions by top management.
3. The complexities and interrelationships of strategic variables.

Management is confronted with awesome scope in their planning and strategy formulation. Defining the causes of problems instead of dealing with symptoms, developing adequate alternative solutions instead of those apparent using traditional techniques, and selecting the alternative with the highest probability of being correct instead of using pure intuition is an increasingly difficult task as the individual progresses up the organization and as the company increases in size.

In addition, systems such as those discussed in Chapters Five and Nine simplify the process of using advanced concepts. By not requiring much more than reading a directory which gives a code reference to specific information and dialing an instrument similar to a pushbutton telephone (rather than interfacing with the computer through a terminal), top management can access what they need in both tabular form and graphics.

Figure 13—4 summarizes the three issues.

Figure 13—4. Major Issues Confronting Executive Management

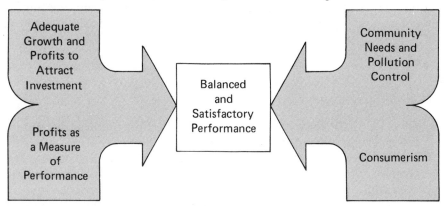

SUMMARY

The likelihood of lasting shortages in many materials, sources of energy and components necessitates the introduction of refinements in management techniques to keep operations going and to achieve profit objectives. In addition to availability, short-range considerations include cost control becoming crucial as prices paid fluctuate and substitutes are considered. Pricing of company products becomes a variable needing almost day-to-day attention. Product mix will change throughout the economy, and decisions by basic producers could affect availability and price all the way to the end consumer.

Some organizational requirements might be required to cope with shortages. Purchasing task forces, a senior staff position to monitor product lines for needed changes, addition of cost analysts, and an energy coordinator are examples of those who might be appointed.

Long-range considerations involve the advisability of vertical integration, diversification to bypass insurmountable problem areas, forecasting changes in life styles and buying patterns, the freedom of management to make decisions considering future laws and regulations, organizational adjustments and financial requirements to implement plans and defend against sharp declines in cash generation.

Three critical issues are confronting executive management: (1) Will the expectations for growth and profits in the years ahead attract sufficient new capital into American business? (2) Should profits retain the position as the primary measure for management performance or will social pressure change the system to permit lower profits and more investment in the needs of communities? (3) Will advanced management systems utilizing the potential of computers in strategic decision making cope with the complexities of business and result in adequate company performance?

DISSCUSSION QUESTIONS

1. Given a SROP for a company, identify the relevant areas of potential revision caused by shortages and inflation.
2. Pick an important resource needed by industry in this country, but which is located in another country; outline a plan involving cooperation between the U.S. government and a consortium of American companies to secure rights to exclusive development of the resource.
3. Select a specific company in your area. Which product lines are most vulnerable to shortages and inflation? List them in order of vulnerability, and defend your decisions.
4. Relate a period of shortages and inflation to social responsibility by giving three possible impacts on social progress.
5. What are the long-range financial implications of shortages and inflation for a firm, and what must executive management do to attract new capital?

SUGGESTED READINGS AND BIBLIOGRAPHY

Ford, James C. "The Executive's Primer on Research and Development Project Selection," Department of Management Science, The Pennsylvania State University. January, 1974.

Hieronymus, Bill. "As Scrap Values Soar, All Sorts of People Start Collecting and Selling What Used to be Garbage," *The Wall Street Journal.* January 31, 1974, p. 30.

Paine, Thomas O. "The Energy Crisis: Some Causes and Solutions," GE reprint. November 15, 1973.

"Pricing Strategy in an Inflation Economy," *Business Week*. April 6, 1974.

Reddish, Jeannette Mabry. "What to Buy for 2001," *Financial World*. November 7, 1973, pp. 18−30.

Stinson, Richard J. "Energy Crisis: Who is Helped, Who is Hurt?" *Financial World*. November 28, 1973, pp. 18−27.

"The EPA Compromise on Clean Air Rules," *Business Week*. January 26, 1974, pp. 21−22.

"The Squeeze on Product Mix," *Business Week*. January 5, 1974, pp. 50−55.

Trezise, Philip H. "How Many OPEC's in Our Future?" *The New York Times*. February 10, 1974, p. 3.

Case: Powerite's Constructo Line: Sourcing Components

The impact of changing supply and cost conditions becomes evident from the problems encountered by Powerite. Profitability of a potentially attractive line is jeopardized in the case.

The response to hand tools in the Constructo Line exceeded expectations throughout 1976. An increase in construction industry activity assisted in achieving a 14% greater than plan performance in volume. However, inflation added $345,000 to the cost of purchased components, or 23%. As a result, the cash flow loss of $410,300 predicted in Table CC-2 (pp. 376-7) of the comprehensive case at the conclusion of Part II was actually $365,000; the fourth quarter's pre-tax profit was slightly better than the forecast.

The market outlook for 1977 is excellent. Operations has shifted to a Kevlar™ housing which is lighter and stronger than the metal used in 1976. Availability of the material is assured by duPont, and the change permits subtle design modifications that make the hand tools more functional and attractive. The forecast has been increased from 105,000 units to 120,000 units. Kevlar™ will also be used for components of the stationary tools being introduced in March, 1977.

An emergency has developed, however, in obtaining motors for the units. A contract for supply had been signed in November, 1975 with Asahi Electric in Osaka. Volumes were according to Table CC-1. No problems were encountered when 11,000 units were added to production in 1976, but a cost escalation clause overlooked by Plant Manager Mohlen resulted in motors being responsible for 70% of the budget overrun for components. Volume at the Japanese firm was only just beginning to recover from the 1974—75 economic difficulties during 1976; however, commitments to Japanese and other Far East customers during 1977 will limit supplies to a maximum of 95,-000 motors for the hand tools and 30,000 larger motors for stationary tools. Furthermore, 25% cost increases are expected under the contract which terminates at the end of the year.

COST DEVELOPMENTS AND PRICING DECISIONS

Operations Vice President Allan was less concerned about motor sourcing than escalation of costs. In 1977 wages and salaries will go up 12% more than the planned increase; materials and supplies other than components is predicted to rise 18% more than predicted. The Operations segment of costs excluding components was expected to be $2,233,400 in 1977; instead, the revised estimate is $2,428,400, up $195,000.

In addition, Controller Les Chadwick had reported that administration and overhead charged to the Constructo line during the year would be $85,000 more than planned. Finally, Charley Bobzin had re-quested an extra $75,000 for advertising and promotion to assure support for the choice of Kevlar™ for the stationary tools.

Overall, $355,000 is expected to be added to internal costs plus $320,-000 to produce the added 15,000 hand tool units. Finally, escalation in purchased components will force this total upwards by $455,000 (the $365,-000 in 1976 plus 25%). Based on the planned 1977 unit volume of 120,000 hand tools and 37,000 stationary tools, the increase in unit costs would be $3.80 and $7.25, respectively (see Table 13C–1). Vice President and General Manager Middleton feels that inflation could have an even greater impact before the end of the year, and that 1978 could see a serious erosion of the line's profit margin.

George Middleton is considering a $6.00 increase in the hand tool line to $69.50 before the new Kevlar™ units are distributed. Also, he has a proposal from his stationary tool Product Manager to go to $114.00 per unit immediately before the line goes to the public. The rationale is that Powerite Tools exposed its price structure on hand tools during 1976, and is obligated to be restrained in the increase. However, the company has the opportunity to anticipate the

Table 13C–1.

| | 1976 | | 1977 | |
	Original Budget	Actual	Original Budget	Forecast
Hand Tools	$64.81	$64.30	$43.14	$46.94
Stationary Tools	—	—	66.06	73.31

impact of inflation in the ready to be introduced stationary tool line. In addition, the new Kevlar™ concept adds to the creditability of the suggested prices.

The prices to buyers would increase to $110+ for hand tools and $150+ for stationary tools. In 1975 the less than $100 price was thought to be significant, but escalation everywhere is now reasoned to be justification for going above the "magic" price. $150 is still within the thought to be critical range for the stationary line in the feasibility study. George Middleton has to decide on these prices as soon as possible.

SOURCING MOTORS

Vice President Allan in operations must find the motors. The Asahi Electric problem has gained top priority. In fact, the gravity of the situation has created pressure for Bob Allan to take personal charge of the search to both obtain: (1) 25,000 motors for hand tools (and 7,000 motors for stationary tools) in 1977, and (2) a reliable supplier with better than prices expected from Asahi in 1978 and beyond.

Bob Allan is considering the following:

1. Retaining Asahi for part of the requirement if the price loophole could be closed and some rollback of prices expected by the end of 1977 could be negotiated.
2. Reverting to 100% American sources of motors assuming the suppliers could quote something similar to the end of 1976 Asahi price.
3. Turning to European alternatives including France and/or Italy which had quoted in 1975.

The three broad types of sources seem to cover all known possibilities. It is now necessary to get quickly to specific quotes on price, timing, quantity, and quality. Vice President Allan is planning to be cautious about clauses on price increases or the right to change other negotiated terms after signing.

STUDENT PROBLEMS

1. Assume the role of George Middleton and decide on your pricing policy for the two Constructo lines.
2. Assume the role of Bob Allan and lay out an action plan with a timetable for solving both the immediate and long-range problem in sourcing motors.
3. Do you think Dick Foster and Joe Huggins should be involved in either Problem 1 or 2?

People in Executive Positions

Managerial success factors, common characteristics of top management, and executive living patterns provide insight on the human factors that can affect company performance. Information on salaries and benefits of top executives and perspective on the motivation to achieve such a position. Finally, the increasing presence of women and minority races in executive management is discussed in this last chapter.

Members of executive management are extremely busy people. The saying "The organized person has the most time" is offset by an equally true proverb, "Creative minds are never idle." Twelve-hour days are common. Spare moments in trains, planes, restaurants, meetings, and so on are occupied with problem solving. Lower level employees may be just as busy, but their decisions usually do not have the serious impact on the company as those made by executive management.

14

SIGNIFICANT FACTORS IN ATTAINING A POSITION IN EXECUTIVE MANAGEMENT

Most people want to be "successful," and one measure of success is being promoted to executive management. It is a sign that the individual has:

1. Performed previous assignments satisfactorily, indicating adequate technical training and experience in the functions involved.

2. Demonstrated skills in leadership by motivating and directing subordinates and relating well to others at all levels in the organization.

3. Developed and optimized technical and "people" skills, thereby creating a reputation within top management that the individual is a competent, reliable executive with creative problem-solving abilities.

Making your way to the top of the organization through consistently outstanding performance earns the label of "success." Figure 14–1 summarizes the concept of competition and the need for excellence, increasing as the number of management stratas above the individual decreases.

Another factor in success is being prepared to sacrifice the amount of time and attention an executive gives the family. An individual's personal life can become secondary to business as the person takes on increasing responsibilities.

Finally, an important factor for an executive moving up through

Figure 14–1. Competition and Competence to Reach Executive Management

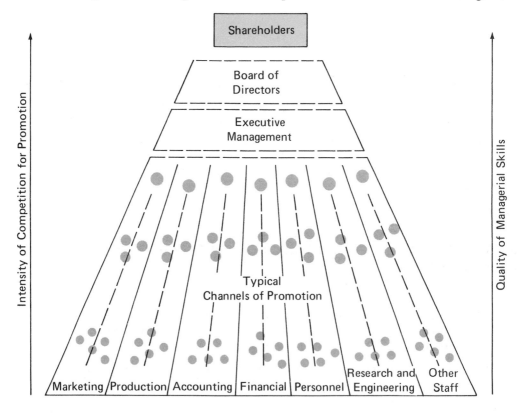

the organization is recognition that the tasks to be performed become increasingly intangible. For example, the executive must convince others of his or her ideas but most often there is no certainty that the other people have accepted the individual's point of view. It is important that the executive be able to communicate, but rarely is there assurance that the information has been received as intended. The executive must evaluate, assess, criticize, or channel the work of others. Problems can arise when an individual that has been promoted to top management finds greater job satisfaction from jobs like directly making or selling a product. Intangible skills are refined by experience, and an executive can limit a successful future by not consciously developing these skills.

Characteristics Needed to Achieve Success

It is important to understand what is involved in "success." In addition to the skills usually required to become a member of executive management, there are specific characteristics and trade-offs in living patterns to be considered. The primary characteristics are:

1. *Pride and Pride Control.* Executives usually want to be the best at what they undertake. They possess high self-esteem and readily accept challenges. They have a strong drive to compete and to demonstrate their superior combination of skills. On the other hand, success is often dependent on controlling an excessive need for ego satisfaction. Good managers give credit to others, work hard at developing peer and subordinate relationships, and usually claim a team effort as the basis of successful accomplishments.

2. *Business Ethics.* It is vitally important that executives maintain personal integrity. Managers with corruptible standards are dangerous, unreliable people in any organization. While it is true that a few companies have deceived their customers and the government and damaged the reputation of business by unethical behavior, these situations are the exception.

3. *Adaptability.* Business executives must cope with a constantly changing environment. They must adjust their living patterns, friendships, and physical surroundings each time they are transferred or promoted. There will be times when top executives must work with personalities that are annoying and with people they find incompetent. Adapting and not allowing their emotions to gain an upper hand is important.

4. *Perseverance.* Managers encounter the realities of business when confronted with their first major setback. They might be passed over for a promotion or fired for being part of a management

takeover attempt that failed. Failure of their own judgment in an important situation is a shock. However, successful individuals in top management do not lose confidence in their abilities. They must be able to bounce back from setbacks and problems which can easily damage the careers of the "weak of heart."

5. *Risk Exposure.* Companies grow most rapidly when led by people who will mix good judgment with some personal risk. Taking a chance on an unpopular strategy or investment in which the executive has confidence can result in either promotions or career setbacks. An individual's willingness to deviate from tradition and accepted practices is a factor in identifying this person as a candidate for top management.

6. *Other Characteristics.* Much has been written about the important attributes of the person who rises to the position of being a leader. To describe fully a member of executive management it is usually proper to include: (a) mental capacity; (b) imagination; (c) character; (d) initiative; (e) human understanding, and (f) self-discipline.

Summarizing, a person with these significant characteristics and technical, people, and optimizing skills has a high probability of reaching the executive management level.

Living Patterns

At one extreme, men and women view their careers as a means to an end—earning sufficient cash to enjoy life outside of business. The other extreme involves people who become consumed by business life. They enjoy the challenge of team assignments and individual responsibilities. Increased status and other rewards such as money drive them toward more involvement. Somewhere between these two extremes is the normal, talented manager who enjoys the job and has succeeded in advancing to the level of executive management. The individual has a continuous struggle to balance the time devoted to an expanding career and to a demanding home life.

Travel

Most business executives are required to do some traveling as part of the job. Usually, it is no more than occasional day or two per week. Problems usually begin with the one- and two-week trips that build up a backlog at the office and at home. Accumulated work, important decisions, delayed meetings, and so on require long hours upon return. Evenings and weekends are often needed for catching up. The following problems are also part of executive travel.

1. The living standard on the road is high for people in executive management, and it is easy to become accustomed to the special service and accommodations offered by luxury establishments. When this type of travel is combined with involvement in the challenge of a job, time away from home sometimes increases to the point of jeopardizing personal relationships.

2. The question of what is a deductible expense is closely scrutinized by the Internal Revenue Service (IRS) and, therefore, by company managers charged with the responsibility of financial reporting. There are times when habits and circumstances force people to spend more on a trip than is allowable. While many executives will absorb this extra amount as a personal responsibility, quite a few are tempted to "bury" questionable items to recover all money spent on a trip.

3. Some firms permit key managers to take their spouses on business trips. The IRS has guidelines for the portion allowed as an expense and payments on behalf of the couple, which are income subject to income tax. Sometimes spouses see fewer of the hardships of travel and become accustomed to the luxuries and conveniences of business trips. A problem arises when the privilege becomes expected and the subject of complaint when it is not received.

Figure 14—2 summarizes the pressures of business travel on the people in executive management.

The Commuter

Few individuals have homes minutes away from the office by car or public transportation. The remainder must commute long distances often requiring an hour or more, especially if their office is in a big city. These executives become part of the "new nomads" described in Alvin Toffler's *Future Shock*.

Two distinct lives develop for those who have families. Home is in a suburb with activities completely unrelated to conditions in the city. Community and social relationships sometimes develop which could be beneficial to the executive's business life, but they are often unconnected. Many people prefer the distinction between home and office to avoid personal friendships complicating business decisions.

Use of a company chauffeur is usually restricted to the level of chief executive officer. In large companies it often includes those who report to this executive directly. Even with this privilege, many commute by train and use the driver for appointments in the city, commuter connections, and transportation to airports and train stations. The remainder of executive management struggles to link the office and home.

Commuting time can be very productive if the executive can get

Figure 14-2. Travel Decisions and Pressure

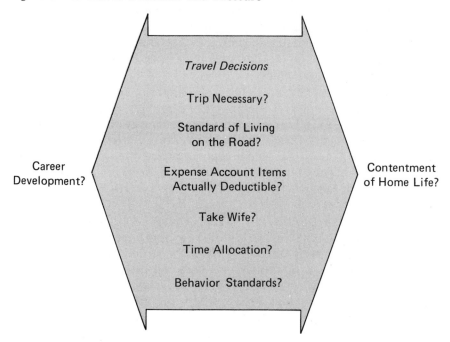

Career
Development?

Travel Decisions

Trip Necessary?

Standard of Living
on the Road?

Expense Account Items
Actually Deductible?

Take Wife?

Time Allocation?

Behavior Standards?

Contentment
of Home Life?

comfortable and does not have to drive a car. Loose ends are completed and report writing is kept on schedule. However, wherever this situation exists, real estate costs are high because of demand for homes in a limited geographic area. Suburbs in Connecticut and New Jersey with good commuter trains are examples.

Most people in executive management are either forced to drive or suffer the inconveniences of crowded public transportation. This commuting time is not only lost, but rushing and frustrating delays start and end the day with tension and dissatisfaction. Top executives have changed jobs to minimize the inconvenience and improve their lives. As a result, companies are moving offices to the suburbs to gain better morale and tax advantages, and to avoid the distractions of city environments.

Business Entertainment

Another demand on the time of top management is entertainment of customers, board members, visiting dignitaries, employees from other locations, and so on. If it were possible to isolate each occasion and not consider the collective impact, the majority would be pleasant luncheons, dinners, and parties. However, problems arise when these obligations are combined with travel and commuting. The more successful people are, the more demands are placed on their time. In fact, others in the organization could measure their success by the amount of time top executives are willing to give them.

Community Obligations

A person accumulates obligations in the community. Charity drives, pollution issues, good government campaigns, and tens of other organizations could use the help of successful executives. However, due to business and family responsibilities, often they do not have the time. Other parents have kept the Scouts going, aided the school system, and coached the little league. Younger members of executive management have an average of two teenagers, and this means some community assignments.

One sign that a manager has the skills to reach the top is the ability to plan. An important application of this ability is arranging one's own life so that business, family, and community obligations can be fulfilled with a high standard of performance. Figure 14−3 illustrates the delicate balance involved in achieving this objective. Critically important changes in life style can result from these decisions, and permanent adjustments in relationships may be needed.

"People" Relationships in Gaining the Threshold

To advance and to survive in executive management, the individual must be able to get along with other people. This involves common sense, diplomacy, and alertness in the game of company politics. It also involves attention to planning "people" relationships. These fall into four categories:

1. *Superiors.* There must be concern about the upper levels of management because there it is decided whether an individual will progress in the firm. These decisions are made on the basis of: (a) impressions of the person's managerial capabilities developed from day to day encounters; (b) tangible evidence such as reports and successful transactions, and (c) the availability of openings that offer more responsibilities. The evaluation process is rarely precise and can be strongly biased by personal relationships.

2. *Peers.* Within a company there are men and women with similar ambitions. Many cautious executives regard all people on the same approximate level in the organization as competitors because they are theoretically eligible for the same important promotions. As a result, these managers maneuver to gain an advantage over others in the quest for promotion. This involves: (a) defensive tactics such as avoiding assignments with a low probability of success; (b) offen-

Figure 14-3. Selecting the Emphasis in an Executive's Life

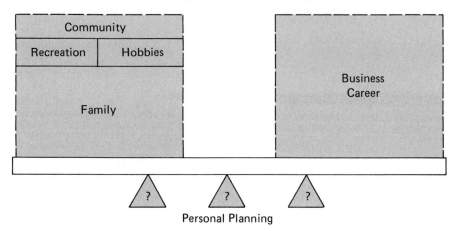

Personal Planning

1. Allocation of Time to the Community
2. Personal Diversion
3. Maximizing Time with the Family

1. Performance on the Job
2. Personal Career Decisions
3. Business Traveling

sive tactics such as obtaining assignments with high visibility, and (c) alliances to keep informed and cope with competitors.

3. *Subordinates.* As an executive progresses, the number of employees on whom the person depends for support, information, performance, and so on increases. Consideration of their feelings and acknowledgement of doing a good job, in addition to formal relationships, are examples of actions that build job satisfaction and an atmosphere conducive to superior performance.

4. *Outsiders.* There are a variety of contacts outside of the company who can: (a) help a manager to achieve outstanding performance by assisting him with getting business, a loan, and so on, and (b) influence bosses to view the person as a prime candidate for promotion. These relationships become essential when approaching the threshold of executive management because, as indicated in Figure 14-1, competition for the few available important positions is intense.

Companies are criticized for poor planning and reacting to maneuvers by competitors instead of implementing their own strategies. Individuals are subject to the same criticism. It is essential for a manager to develop personal plans for a career, which include factors affecting it both favorably and unfavorably. The individual must then formulate strategies to achieve objectives and overcome problem areas.

Some top executives insist that personal planning should be completely in the mind. This is a very questionable practice. There is merit in keeping a business diary that also includes the components of a career plan currently in effect, memory "joggers" on important "people" relationships, observations on developments affecting the plan, such as probable modifications, applicable comments by others, and sources of information who keep the individual informed about the tactics of others. The reluctance of many executives to write down important details is based on the disaster that might occur should the diary fall into the wrong hands.

The advantages of a written, detailed personal plan include: (1) the individual can make better assessments of alternatives and necessary tactics as a result of the discipline of writing down the points and seeing them on paper; (2) the recording of details reveals significant patterns such as widely spaced but consistent remarks by members of top management about a position that is obsolete or divisions that should be merged; (3) the diary provides a place to put ideas for better performance, innovations, and approaches to problem solving, and (4) a log of activities is essential when specific details become important such as in litigation by the government or a competitor.

The individual executive must judge for himself about the needs for security and the advantages of written plans, logs of events, ideas, and so on. Many separate the diary from personal planning files kept with other valuable documents. This necessitates transferring details from bits of paper periodically, and forces a review and updating of the plan. Keeping the plan current is important to long-range success.

To summarize, developing "people" relationships and personal career planning are vitally important to gaining the threshold of executive management. Taking these steps will supplement skills and characteristics and lead to better decisions. Figure 14—4 illustrates the factors just discussed.

BENEFITS AT THE TOP

Important benefits can compensate for the stress and strain of being a member of executive management. Professor Herzberg[1] correctly states that man is motivated to work by more than just money. However, the financial obligations of most individuals in management make this benefit a good starting point to describe why executives accept increasing responsibilities.

[1] Herzberg, Frederick; *Work and the Nature of Man*; World Publishing Co.: New York, 1966.

Figure 14-4. Factors in Career Development

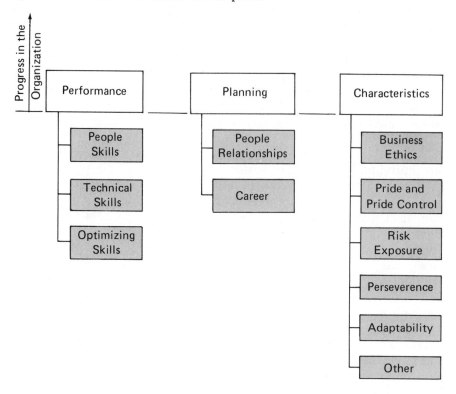

The Compensation Package

Salary ranges and compensation plans vary widely by industry and organizational design. Table 14-1 gives salaries of three top positions in 48 very large companies. The remainder of the data in Table 14-1 is the result of a survey of people in medium and small firms.

The cost of living and taxation in major urban clusters such as New York and Chicago have a serious impact on salaries. Some examples might help interpretation of the problems confronting both the individual and company. An executive in the steel industry earning $36,000 per year in Pittsburgh took a job in New York paying $50,-000 per year. The family found a home in New Jersey similar to the one they had left, but the price was $20,000 more and property taxes were double. After New York income taxes, higher prices and com-

Table 14–1. Salary Guidelines (1975 Dollars)

	Large Corporations	Small Corporations
Chairman of the Board (Chief Executive Officer)	$300,000	$48,000–72,000
President (Frequently Chief Executive Officer)	240,000	
Executive or Senior Vice President	180,000	42,000
Vice President — Line	72,000	36,000
Vice President — Staff	50,000	30,000
General Manager, Division A (Reports to a Corporate Vice President)	42,000	24,000
Director — Staff (Reports to a Corporate Vice President)	36,000	20,000

muting expenses, the change in position resulted in a reduction in their standard of living despite almost a 40% raise in salary.

Another typical situation involves someone being promoted from a line job in less densely populated areas such as Flint, Michigan or Baton Rouge, Louisiana to a boom atmosphere. Atlanta, Georgia, for example, has become a headquarters location for operations in the southeast. An executive can receive a promotion to executive management as general manager of a division in this city and find it will take $75,000 to duplicate a $50,000 house. A private school might be necessary, and so on. In summary, companies often have to increase the executive's salary by 35 to 40% for the individual to gain financially from the promotion.

Incentive compensation in cash is a means of augmenting base salaries and motivating top management. The package could depend on: (1) individual performance based on operating plans; (2) departmental and divisional performance and contribution to profits; (3) overall company performance, and (4) combinations that reflect capacity to pay bonuses.

Compensation in Forms Other Than Cash

Listed here are categories of compensation offered by companies which exclude cash. Variations are often attempted by companies to minimize executive taxation. The Internal Revenue Service counters by establishing guidelines for each method.

1. *Shares in the Company.* Bonuses are often given in shares.

They represent income to the receiver and will probably cost only the amount for taxes although extra equity is gained. Stock options permit an executive to buy shares in the company at a fixed price within a given period of time. A newer approach has recently become popular called "performance shares." This arrangement calls for common stock to be earmarked for future payment to an executive if the person achieves a predetermined performance objective. There are also cash purchase plans where the company buys a number of tax paid shares for you equal to what you buy for yourself. There are variations, and tax liability varies with the firm.

2. *Car or Car and Driver.* This saves the capital required to buy a car, including monthly payments, insurance, and maintenance. Most of the expenses are paid, even some that are not business and will not be challenged by the IRS.

3. *Clubs, Social and Athletic.* Paid memberships in convenient and important clubs are common practice. The memberships are usually in the name of the firm and assigned to the individual. They are used mostly for business entertaining, but it is normal for the family to have access to the facilities. Personal expenses are identified and the executive is billed by the firm. A few companies have exclusive facilities in resorts, large cities, and places to "escape" which are available to top management. Others permit sabbatical leaves to update knowledge about techniques.

4. *Creative Combinations.* Participation in tax shelters, property with mortgage arrangements, low interest loans, paid life insurance, access to boats and planes, complimentary executive luncheons, payment of credit card bills, and so on are conceived as means to avoid taxation.

Many people obtaining jobs in executive management develop a sensitivity about their level of taxation, and place some creative energy into legal ways of minimizing local, state, and federal taxes. Tax avoidance is legal; tax evasion is not. The tax on $30,000 taxable income is $9,030 plus 53% over $26,000, or a total of $11,150. This level of taxation leads people receiving a high income to look for ways to be paid which increase: (a) cash actually available after personal taxes are paid; (b) conveniences that significantly improve one's standard of living, and (c) personal wealth arising from the compensation package.

Psychic Income

People in executive management value the symbols of success. These indicators provide psychic income because of the recognition that results and the practical benefits that lead to better performance. While symbols will not directly substitute for cash, they are a strong motivation to forget some of the problems such as job pressure and limited time with the family.

Status Symbols

Most managers readily admit that receiving recognition is an important part of achieving success. Some of the major categories not included in the compensation package are given here.

1. *Title.* Behavioral scientists have interviewed several managers who have answered "yes" to the question, "Would you accept $5,000 less in annual salary to have the title 'vice president' in your company?" While titles are sometimes used as a means of appeasing managers being transferred to unattractive areas or minimizing the cost of reorganizing the firm, most of the time there is no subtlety involved in being given a better title. It is a true symbol of having been promoted, and others in the company recognize your progress.

2. *Office.* The "pecking order" for offices is usually well defined. The corner office with two sets of windows, a washroom, an adjacent conference room, and a secluded alcove for staff assistants is designated for a key member of executive management. The best view of the outside landscape goes to the highest ranking executive. Within large companies the floor on which your office is located may be very important. Acceptance as a member of top management may depend on assignment of an office of minimum size, location, and facilities.

3. *Appointments.* An example will describe the seriousness with which some of these symbols are taken. A controller was appointed for the western region of a major oil company. He was assigned a large corner office. However, the lush carpet was replaced by a less expensive area rug and a 3½ by 6 foot desk top was substituted for the previous 4 by 7 foot top because the position did not warrant the symbols reserved for top corporate management.

4. *Privileges.* The location of a parking space may be very important. An executive washroom may actually exist, and certainly special dining rooms are provided for top management. The opportunity to fix your own working hours could identify your status. Another success symbol is being able to "inform" your boss about a major decision instead of having to request approval, although employing the diplomatic gesture of "getting his thinking" in advance could continue. Other symbols apply in specific companies such as the right to two secretaries, chauffeur driven company car, or having an "assistant to."

Some of the symbols are practical and representative of an individual having been delegated major responsibilities. Others are petty and indicative of highly structured companies that might have vertical communication problems. Being overly concerned about type of rug, size of desk, the view, and so on has hurt many careers. Most business executives recommend ignoring symbols unless they directly affect your capacity to perform the job.

Convenience

The difference between status symbols and conveniences is mostly a matter of attitude. Many executives do not care about parking space location, where they go to the bathroom, and so on. However, they are concerned about conveniences that will save time and help them do a superior job. Being met at the airport by a chauffeur may be a top management privilege, but it might also provide an extra hour's preparation for a meeting. Two secretaries and an "assistant to" may be essential to the executive's information system and effective output of paper work. In summary, the good manager views achieving symbols as means of gaining efficiency.

WOMEN AND MINORITIES IN EXECUTIVE MANAGEMENT

In the mid-1960s two laws were passed by the federal government which started changes in who will evolve to positions in executive management. The Equal Pay Act of 1963 requires equal pay for equal work by women and minority races, and is intended to prevent serious discrepancies in level of compensation. In 1964 the Civil Rights Act was signed, and this necessitates qualified men and women of all races to be given equal consideration for a job.

Some Recent History

A landmark case occurred in 1972 when American Telephone and Telegraph agreed to pay about $15 million in restitution and equal pay claims to 13,000 women and 2,000 male minority race employees. Even more important, the agreement specified that women and minorities would get credit towards seniority for time spent on other jobs with the company as well as time in higher paying positions. Before this was resolved, ATT work rules had discouraged these workers from seeking promotions. Those taking a new job would be the first to be laid off because they lost the seniority gained in the former job.

Progress in Equal Employment Opportunity is now increasing in momentum. Top management will occasionally admit to being uncomfortable about women, blacks, and other minorities in key positions. However, pressure from special interest groups monitoring company decisions on employment and promotion has changed the commonplace situation of passing over these managers.

Women as Managers

Executives usually have assumed that talented women would get married, have children, and quit. Therefore, it made no sense for a company to count on a woman advancing to top management because it was improbable that she would stay long enough to justify investment in her future. This "a women's place is in the home" attitude is still prevalent in a large portion of the male population. However, progress has been made in the 1970s to tap the underutilized source of talent that women offer.

During the 1945–70 period, business thought women went to college to find a husband with similar interests and background. If that did not work out, they would get a job that paid for rent and clothes, and eventually get married. A few had training that could be used, such as chemistry, computer programming, and languages. However, a woman seriously undertaking a business career was a sufficiently rare occurrence to be generally ignored. Table 14–2 indicates an increasing number of working women. While many women in the statistics are still "passing through," more and more want a career with executive management potential.

Problem Areas Cited in the Past

The points usually cited by antifeminists in addition to marriage and children are:

1. Sexual complications in the office and when traveling.

Table 14–2. Women as a Percentage of the Work Force

	Male Workers (Millions)	Female Workers (Millions)	Women as a Percentage of Work Force
1955	44.5	20.5	31.8
1960	46.4	23.2	33.3
1965	48.3	26.2	35.2
1970	51.2	31.5	38.1
1972	54.1	34.1	38.7
1974	57.2	36.9	39.2

2. Emotional reactions to business problems.
3. Lack of stamina, physical strength, and competitive drive.
4. Lack of mobility due to a family.

Women who want careers in top management are working to change male attitudes by consistently displaying superior job performance. The 1970s have shown women overcoming these obstacles in a number of ways.

MEDICAL ADVANCES   Today, it is possible to plan a family. As a result, a woman's career need not be affected by the physical variables that traditionally limited her potential. Some employers cite, however, that this does not change the fact that the woman has the baby when a couple decides on parenthood, while a male is not subject to work interruption. A female candidate for an executive position has to generate confidence that her life is adequately planned to avoid career interruptions and other family interferences that could affect her performance.

PROFESSIONAL BEHAVIOR   Prejudicial treatment of males, emotional reactions to problems, and avoiding travel and transfers are "roadsigns" indicating whether women should be promoted to important positions. Successful female executives work with facts, unbiased judgments, and the opinions of other qualified workers. They retain their composure. Professional behavior at this stage in the feminist movement is fundamental.

TRAINING   Education is an important factor. Graduate schools turning out students with training applicable in business during the 1945−70 period were either 100% male or totally dominated by male students to the extent of having only one or two female per graduating class. Lately the total for women graduates has reached 10% ± in some major universities and 4% throughout the country. This progress is important because a woman usually has to be very well qualified to compete with a man for an opening usually filled by a male.

The Progress of Women

The results of changing attitudes towards women in top management are summarized by Figure 14−5. Attitudes are also changing among the people who influence overall thinking such as sociologists who write more frequently about children of working mothers not being emotionally affected, the potential of successful marriages with both partners having a career, and similar research projects.

Up to the mid-1970s women made more progress in changing attitudes than in actually obtaining executive management positions. Many companies can document extensive searches to find women candidates for openings that developed during 1972−74. Some companies restructured their requirements in order to increase the number of

Figure 14–5. The Progress of Women in Executive Management

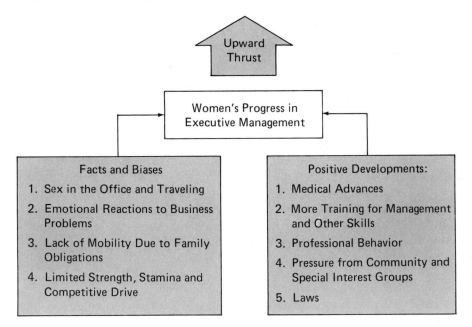

women in key jobs. However, others continued to hire the person with the greatest potential and most of the time it was a man. The reasons cited by executive recruiters are:

1. The increased flow of women candidates with MBA's and other graduate training is just beginning to reach middle management. It is still a trickle compared to male candidates.

2. Experience to prove skills and confirm characteristics required for top management has been offered to few women in past years. As a result, their credentials are often not competitive with the male candidate.

3. Prejudice is still a fact. Many men resist having women in executive management. There are instances today when a woman may lack a degree of specific line experience, but have superior overall potential in comparison with male competitors, and in many instances she will not get the position.

4. Frequently, women do not see themselves as hard-driving executives. Male characteristics are identified with top management positions in the minds of many women with the skills to handle the responsibilities.

Despite setbacks and shortcomings, the important facts are: (1) attitudes toward employing women for managerial positions has improved sharply; (b) the number of fully qualified applicants with plans for a life style that will not hinder her progress up the organization is also increasing significantly; (c) these women managers will greatly increase the number of candidates for executive management positions in the late 1970s and 1980s; and (d) community acceptance and support for these trends had been established by the feminist movement. Consequently, by 1980, it is feasible to expect three to five women in executive management out of every hundred positions.

BLACKS IN EXECUTIVE POSITIONS

John D. Rockefeller, III, in his "The Second American Revolution"[2] says, "Young blacks have differed primarily in being less willing to compromise, to live by myths and double standards. This has proved to be infectious." Mr. Rockefeller believes the ground swell of capable young black Americans who will be candidates for top positions began in 1954 with the Supreme Court ruling overturning the separate but equal doctrine of education.

The mid—1950s timing of this decision and the delays in implementing desegration highlight a problem confronting companies in the 1970s. There are not adequate numbers of qualified blacks to fill the positions that are potentially open to them. The factors involved are:

1. Prejudice eliminated most of the candidates for managerial positions in the pre—1970 period. However, this level of exeperience is needed to gain sufficient overall experience to make it to the top. Many of the black executives who could be cited as successful through the 1960s were athletes, entertainers, and professors converted to business executives.

2. The educational system is changing slowly, but it is still very difficult for black students to enter college with the study habits and motivation needed to excel. Some succeed despite limitations in early schooling, but the majority are handicapped in getting the most out of undergraduate and graduate education.

3. A psychological result of prejudice and a poor education is loss of drive to compete and succeed in business. The required confidence is at a low level. This means blacks who are qualified often do not try.

The shortage of blacks in management is confused by companies reacting to pressure for more black executives in three general ways:

[2] Rockefeller, John D., III. *The Second American Revolution: Some Personal Observations.* Harper & Row, Inc., New York, 1973.

(1) employing a "board room"[2] black or two, limiting their true power, and publicizing outwardly progressive policies; (b) avoiding and ignoring pressure from outside sources, limiting black participation in management to lower levels, and maintaining an unwritten racial policy; and (c) adopting an aggressive development and promotion program for qualified black executives, discouraging any signs of prejudice. Variations and compromises are common, and reflect the spectrum of human reaction to blacks in top management.

Summarizing, there is a mid—1970s shortage of black candidates for executive management positions. However, there is a positive indication for the future of black students and managers. The opportunities are real and growing in number.

Perspectives for Potential Black Managers

There are some practical points from the black student's point of view which will help develop a career to the optimum:

1. *Avoiding Oversensitivity.* After years of prejudicial treatment and being told about prejudicial treatment, it is a human reaction to see a white racist "behind every water cooler." It is equally human to react when racial prejudice is obvious in decision making and day-to-day affairs. The average black executive must, by necessity, exercise self-control, if he or she is going to succeed in a white-dominated business environment.

2. *Choosing an Issue.* Even at the executive management level there is a legal and organizational framework for a black executive to submit a grievance. The safe driving ad that says "Don't be dead right" is very applicable in the corporate environment. If blacks want to reach top management in a company, they must carefully choose issues in order to avoid labels such as "agitator," "chronic troublemaker," and so on.

3. *Training.* Aside from a few words, the section on women applies almost exactly. However, one additional point is important. Because of pressure on companies to meet racial quotas at all managerial levels, many blacks are getting opportunities that are beyond their training and experience. This will not continue into the 1980s, and it is important that black candidates for management positions be competitive with other applicants.

Creating better job opportunities for minority race members is making more rapid progress than ridding business of racial prejudice, as illustrated in Figure 14—6 Superior performance will be the basis on which myths are disspelled.

[3] A "board room" black is business jargon for promoting or employing black managers for important sounding positions to demonstrate a progressive attitude. Usually this is a tactic with no depth to the policy.

Figure 14–6. Forces Working to Overcome Racial Prejudice in Business

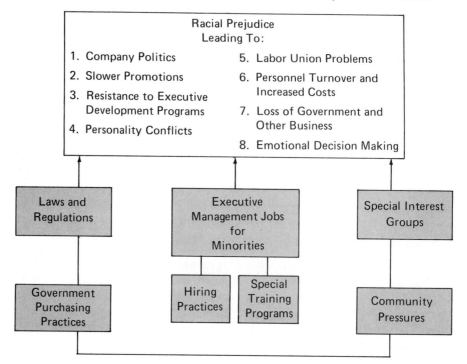

SUMMARY

Progress up through the organization to the level of executive management is a measure of success in an individual's career. Competition for promotions intensifies as you approach this level. The probability of succeeding increases with development of the three skills (technical, "people," and optimizing) and five characteristics (pride control, business ethics, adaptability, perseverance, and risk exposure).

The life of an executive is complicated by conflicting demands on time. Travel, though a necessary part of the job, takes time from the family and responsibilities at the office. When combined with commuting, business entertainment and community obligations, pressures build and performance required to succeed is jeopardized. Careful career planning is needed to optimize use of time and avoid unnecessary setbacks.

Establishing good "people" relationships is fundamental to reaching executive management. This should not be left to chance and becomes another important part of career planning. It is more efficient if the relationships are organized into the four categories: superiors, peers, subordinates, and outsiders.

The benefits of success are: (1) the compensation package which involves salary, shares, creative combinations to avoid taxation such as low interest loans, clubs, and company cars, and (2) psychic income including status symbols such as title, office appointments and special privileges, and conveniences that improve performance.

Women, blacks, and other minorities are gaining a foothold in executive management. Numbers continue to be comparatively small in the 1970s because of tradition, some continuing prejudices, and the limited number of women and minorities with adequate training and experience in the pre-1970 period. Attitudes are changing, however, and genuine opportunities are being offered to the few candidates presently qualified. Many more will be trained in the 1970s and have adequate experience to compete for top management positions in the 1980s.

DISCUSSION QUESTIONS

1. Is adaptability as important a characteristic of success as the others mentioned in the chapter? Why?
2. Why is business entertainment important to the successful executive and the company?
3. Discuss the possible effects of travel on the executive concerning the person's career plans and family life style.
4. Explain why community obligations can complicate the life of an executive in management.
5. Companies compensate executives in forms other than cash. If given a choice, which form of compensation would you choose (express your answer in percentage form such as 80% cash and 20% other)? Why?
6. What has contributed to the increased number of blacks and women in management?

SUGGESTED READINGS AND BIBLIOGRAPHY

Battalia, O. William and John J. Tarrant. "And the Man on the Treadmill," MVA—May, 1973, pp. 29–31.
Blaustein, Arthur I. and Geoffrey Faux. "Black Capitalism—The Star-Spangled Hustle," MBA—January, 1973, p. 10.

Boyle, M. B. "Equal Opportunity For Women is Smart Business," *Harvard Business Review.* May, 1973, pp. 85−95.

"Changes in the Labor Force Status of Women," *Monthly Labor Review.* August, 1973, p. 76.

Dalaba, O. G. "Misuses of Compensation as a Motivator," *Personnel.* September, 1973, pp. 30−37.

"Executive's Compensation: Who got most in '72," *Business Week.* May 5, 1973, pp. 42−55.

"Feminist Consultants: Sifting out the Instant Experts," MBA—March, 1973, p. 9.

Gleason, Richard D., "Planning the Way to the Top," *Business Horizons.* June, 1971, pp. 60−62.

Haner, F. T. and James C. Ford. *Contemporary Management.* February, 1973.

"HBS Management Internships for Women," MBA—March, 1973, p. 48.

Herrick, J. S. "Work Motives of Female Executives," *Public Personnel Management.* September, 1973, pp. 380−387.

Jett, Michael. "The Return of Rosie," *The Wall Street Journal.* April 16, 1973.

"Job Agencies Control 1 of Every 3 Jobs, Break Anti-Bias Law," *The Delaware Spectator.* May 24, 1973.

Lyle, J. R. "Empirical Study of the Occupational Standing of Women in Multinational Corporations," *Labor Law Journal.* August, 1973, pp. 458−468.

Malkiel, B. G. and J. A. Malkiel. "Male-Female Pay Differentials in Professional Employment," *American Economic Review.* September, 1973, pp. 693−705.

Palmer, W. J. "An Integrated Program for Career Development," *Personnel Journal.* June, 1972, pp. 398−451.

"Progress in Role of Women is Steady and It is Sure," *U.S. News & World Report, Inc.* May 14, 1973, pp. 66−69.

Rees, Thomas G. "Is an M.B.A. Worth the Bother," *Industry Week.* December 18, 1972, pp. 25−31.

Reeves, Elton T. "So You Want to be a Manager," *American Management Association.* 1971.

Rockefeller, J. John D. 3rd. "The Second American Revolution," *Business Week.* April 7, 1973, p. 14.

Schoonmaker, Alan N. "Executive Career Strategy," *American Management.* 1971.

"Sex Equality: Impact of a Key Decision," *U.S. News & World Report.* May 28, 1973, p. 69.

Simon, W. "Management in the Future," *Conference Board Record.* March, 1973, pp. 44−47.

Sullivan, J.F. "Indirect Compensation: The Years Ahead," *California Management Review.* Winter, 1972, pp. 65−76.

"The Woman Who Wasn't There," *Dun's.* June, 1972, pp. 63−64.

"White Males Complain They Are Now Victims of Job Discrimination," *Wall Street Journal.* February 28, 1974.

"Women in Business," *Journal of Small Business Management.* January, 1973.

"Women's Rights and Women's Lib," *The Christian Science Monitor.* April 16, 1973.

Case: Creation Corporation— A New Product Line

The case highlights the difficulties being experienced by women in achieving top positions. It also expands on chapter material such as success factors and career planning.

Leadership in the cosmetic industry is measured by innovations in advertising, promotion, distribution, and merchandising. Wall Street analysts have long considered this business an attractive sector of the consumer products market because it has shown excellent consistent growth and, for successful companies, a high return on shareholders' equity.

COMPANY BACKGROUND

Creation Corporation is in its 63rd year of manufacturing feminine aids to beauty. It is a leader in the cosmetic industry and legendary for its phenomenal success, not only in the United States but through the world.

It is one of the best known and most respected business names in the 151 countries where its products are sold. In 30 of these countries there are company owned branches or subsidiaries.

Creation was incorporated under Delaware laws in 1931 as a successor to a small business founded in 1913. Headquarters are now located in Trenton, New Jersey. It manufactures and distributes: (1) make-up and other cosmetic products; (2) perfumes and colognes; (3) men's toiletries; (4) hair care products, hair pieces and wigs; (5) pharmaceuticals, and (6) (through acquisition of Coronet Chemical in 1967) ethical drugs, and diagnostic tests. Table 14C—1 indicates sales of $200 million and after tax earnings of $18.4 mil-

Table 14C–1. Creation Corporation, Consolidated Income Statement

June 30,	$000 1975	1974	1973	1972	$000 1971
Net sales	200,104	192,439	187,511	170,526	159,337
Cost of sales	61,101	58,695	59,695	51,328	49,841
Expenses	106,222	101,696	96,254	87,288	82,731
Oper. profit	33,781	32,048	31,804	31,910	26,765
Other income	1,210	1,094	757	616	712
Total income	34,991	33,142	32,516	32,526	27,477
Income tax	16,510	15,767	16,061	16,513	13,821
Net income	18,481	17,375	16,500	16,013	13,656

lion in 1975. Both totals established new records for the sixth consecutive year.

The Road to Success

An advanced system of research and development has created a flow of innovative products. This flow is guided by the unusually talented marketing personnel with years of experience. These ingredients have been the basis of Creation's success story.

The president and chief executive officer of Creation Corporation, Albert Gilmore, attributes much of the company's profit performance to it's product-oriented marketing organization and advanced strategy involving market segmentation. (Albert Gilmore once was a Creation executive product manager who made a big seller out of a slow moving perfume.)

"The purpose of developing 7 different lines of cosmetics and 18 fragrances is to appeal to all major segments of the cosmetic market in relation to age, interests, needs, im-age, and price. As each line develops into a fully mature business, the company plan is to create a separate management with its own organization and total profit responsibility for its particular line. All this leads to the ultimate Creation goal: a Creation product for every consumer cosmetic need."

Mr. Gilmore also has noted the company's record of near perfect timing, when introducing new products to meet changing tastes of significant market segments. "We keep an eye on the young people especially, and if we spot a solid trend developing that warrants the introduction of a new product, we assign a product manager. R and D goes to work and the new team calls in our ad agency to develop a campaign that will introduce the new product, associate it with the trend, and reinforce the change of taste involved."

"Nine Lives"

"Sure Magic" is a product line directed at the younger cosmetic con-

Table 14C-2. Position Description, Creation Corporation

Title:	EXECUTIVE PRODUCT MANAGER

This position is responsible for profit performance and all other matters pertaining to marketing, production coordination, cash control policies, and personnel assigned to the product line designated "   ". Specifically, the Executive Product Manager undertakes the following duties:

1. Formulates marketing strategy for "   ". This involves creation of the advertising and promotion campaign, sales methods to the consumer, and retailer and other outlets, distribution procedures and policies, market research, and competitor tactics.

2. Coordinates production for "   ". This involves regular communications and negotiations with plants under the authority of Manufacturing Directors producing products for other Executive Product Managers to assure flow of "   " to warehouses and other outlets.

3. Establishes a short range operating plan which acts as the framework for operations in the approaching twelve months. This involves conforming with corporate reporting requirements and the companywide format for plans, but approach and supplements to the plan are within the discretion of the position. Programs and projects in strategies are included in the short range operating plan.

4. Establish a long range plan for a typical calendar year three to five years after the period covered by the short range operating plan. This involves portraying trends in markets for "   " and developing strategies to optimize profit opportunities in the period.

5. Monitor operations, evaluate trends, and initiate actions to adjust for market and other developments. This involves immediate decisions and revisions to plans.

6. Identify ways and methods to optimize day-to-day performance in the areas of cash control, employee relations, incentive programs, product distribution, and contractual obligations. Acquisition, disposition, and divestiture of assets is a corporate decision.

Reports to:	Vice President, Corporate Marketing
Office Location:	Corporate Headquarters, Trenton, New Jersey
Compensation:	Salary Range of $36,000 to $54,000 Eligible for Executive Incentive Bonus Program Corporate Executive Compensation Package—Level 5

sumer, which has become well established nationally within the past three years. The newest addition to this line is "Nine Lives," Creation's new eyeliner—mascara product that does not smear or come off while swimming. One factor that led to its development was a survey taken by a Creation research team that found that eye make-up, which for a while had been a neglected cosmetic area among the youthful buyers, is now back in heavy demand. About 96% reported a strong desire for mascara, eyeliner, and eye shadow being used by parents and friends.

Creation's sales in this area had only increased moderately. Therefore, the "Nine Lives," development was a direct response to loss of market share to early entrants in that field.

The new water proof make-up (a good example of product differentiation) is scheduled for test marketing in Florida in March. "Nine Lives" is expected to become an important contributor to the company's sales.

Mr. Louis T. Firestone, vice president of corporate marketing, has decided the time is right to set up a separate organization for "Nine Lives." In January, 1976 he requested the personnel department to review potential candidates within the company for the position described in Table 14C−2. Rather than initiating a search in the cosmetics industry, Creation has maintained a policy of promoting from within whenever possible.

Personnel submitted the names of two candidates to L. T. Firestone in February. Both were well qualified for the position of executive product manager (the word "executive" is added to the title to connote profit responsibility and participation in a special incentive bonus).

Comments on the Position of Executive Product Manager

The position has general mana-ger responsibility for profit performance. However, authority is limited by the following features of the company's organizational design:

1. The "Nine Lives" product line is produced in plants managed by manufacturing directors who report to the vice president, corporate manufacturing. Creation gains the economies of scale resulting from the output of several product lines under one roof. Also, the features of this system have proven extremely beneficial when demand for one of the lines dropped off sharply as the consumer shifts from one brand to another. However, operating problems are caused for the Executive Product Manager of "Nine Lives" because he does not have full authority to respond to geographic demand, sudden surges in sales and other shifts in market complications.

2. All cash is controlled at corporate headquarters. Requirements are supplied according to the short-range operating plan and adjustments forwarded twice per month by the Controller for "Nine Lives." The profit center is credited for cash generated in excess of the plan at the prime rate of interest, and shortages result in debits at the same rate. This system retains tight control at headquarters, but forces the Executive Product Manger to justify cash requests for each major decision.

3. Approval must be obtained for long-range facility commitments. As a result, decisions based on

standard procedures and limited knowledge about the product line could adversely affect the Executive Product Manager's performance for reasons not related to "Nine Lives."

Summarizing, consistent performance will depend on the individual's ability to persuade and influence Creation personnel outside his range of authority. It will also depend on establishing a flow of information from these components of the organization in order to formulate realistic proposals.

THE CANDIDATES

The personnel department forwarded the background summaries given below to L. T. Firestone as a supplement to company records and a basis for personal interviews.

JOHN R. LAWTON   Age 34. Married. Three children, 2, 4, and 5 years old. Wife is not employed. Family lives in Stamford, Connecticut. Graduate of the University of Southern California in Marketing; winner of three letters in basketball, team captain in his senior year. Honor graduate of the ROTC program; four years in the army; attained the rank of Captain; two years in Vietnam where he commanded an artillery battery. No graduate training.

Employed after discharge for four years by Beauty Pride, Ltd., a competitor; regarded as an outstanding sales representative. Joined Creation in 1970 in a sales position; im-

mediately exhibited leadership skills and ability to work well with others; promoted to assistant product manager of "Sure Magic" line which developed into a hot item, and gave him exposure to a broad scope of administrative responsibilities. Now located at "Sure Magic" headquarters in New York City.

All tests, interview records and performance ratings confirm that J. R. Lawton is a potential member of executive management. Family situation stable; normal outside activities including little league and fund raising for the Democratic Party.

M. LYNN CRAWFORD   Age 39. Married. Two children, 14 and 15 years old. Graduate of the University of Pennsylvania in marketing; M.B.A. from the same university in management; honor student and valedictorian of her class. No military service. Husband is employed as Senior Accountant, Kelley Industries, Inc.; now located at Philadelphia headquarters and considered to have potential up to the level of assistant controller. Family lives in Haddonfield, New Jersey.

Employed after graduation by Monroe Cosmetic Co.; successive positions as sales analyst in corporate sales administration, assistant manager in sales administration of the firm's second largest product line, and assistant manager of marketing services in the same line. Rated as top management possibility after four years with Monroe.

Joined Creation in 1968 to gain line sales experience in a new product (Lilt Hair Sprays); after three years promoted to product manager of specialty products (items for Christmas and Easter promotions); four year of reasonable success in this position confirms ability to obtain the complete cooperation of executive product managers participating in the promotions; rated as hard working, good under pressure, and creative in problem solving.

All tests, interview records, and performance ratings confirm that M. L. Crawford is a potential member of executive management. Family situation stable and husband supports the proposed promotion; his position would not be affected. Outside activities indicate well developed sense of community responsibility; active in teenage drug control, P.T.A. committees and hospital volunteers recruiting.

The Interviews

Mr. Lawton impressed L. T. Firestone with his ideas for expanding cosmetic sales into noncosmetic outlets. He described a minicosmetic display unit that would occupy only 40 square inches of counter space in fashion stores. He explained the basis of concept. "The place where the 18 to 35 year old woman makes her fashion decisions on color should include the opportunity to buy her color accessories at the same time." Mr. Firestone invited John Lawton to lunch with several of his staff to explore the idea and expose him to personnel who will help with his decision.

Ms. Crawford was also impressive and attractive. Her approach in the interview was to outline some imaginative and practical ideas for administration of a new product line including coordination with personnel in production and cash management. Mr. Firestone was left with the feeling she could handle the responsibility involved in the promotion. However, when inviting her to lunch to meet the staff he had a strange feeling that he was asking an attractive woman for a date. On the day when the group got together, her professional approach to presenting her ideas gave him confidence about her overall abilities. She was a persuasive as well as competent woman.

The Decision

L. T. Firestone and his staff agreed that both candidates were "about equally qualified on paper." Mr. Firestone, however, felt that a man could better relate to outside organizations involved in advertising and promotions, distribution channels, and representation of sales outlets from foreign countries. The turning point came when one of the staff said that, while Creation was willing to accept a woman in a position traditionally held by a man, in his opinion persons in other companies were not.

One additional point that revived the feeling he had when asking Ms. Crawford to lunch was the overnight trips required of the Executive Product Manager with the sales force. Mr. Firestone was certain that this would cause problems sooner or later. In late February, 1976, John R. Lawton was told he had the promotion.

An Unexpected Development

Lynn Crawford was informed of the decision by L. T. Firestone who confirmed his remarks to John Lawton's capabilities in handling the job. Nothing was mentioned about the possibility of receiving the next opportunity. She calmly asked him to reconsider his decision and, upon hearing that he would not, requested a better explanation of the decision in order to assess her future with Creation. Mr. Firestone complimented Lynn Crawford's performance and said she had an outstanding future with the company; however, he would not talk about specific avenues of promotion.

The following day Mr. Firestone received the letter given below. Recognizing the possibility of problems with the Equal Opportunity Employment Commission[1] and feminist pressure organizations, Mr. Firestone agreed to weigh all the factors once again before announcing the decision and to give her the benefit of this analysis.

Dear Mr. Firestone:

I would appreciate an appointment with you at your earliest convenience to discuss further your choice of Mr. Lawton for the position of executive product manager for the "Nine Lives" line of cosmetics.

My qualifications are superior in all categories to those of your appointee and, therefore, I have no alternative but to believe that your selection was not based on qualifications.

Very truly yours,
M. Lynn Crawford

[1] The EOEC is the government agency enforcing Title 7 of the 1964 Civil Rights Act.

STUDENT PROBLEMS

1. Do you think that either candidate was more qualified than the other? Give the criteria on which to judge and the reasons for your choice.
2. Would you say that Creation Corporation chose the man over the woman for the reasons that were stated or because they themselves are not ready to accept a woman in an executive management position? Considering the current emphasis on hiring and promoting minorities, do you feel that Lynn Crawford should receive the promotion regardless of comparative qualifications?
3. Develop a course of action for L. T. Firestone which deals with the implied threat of legal action, and the requests made by Lynn Crawford to review the decision and explain the basis for the final choice.
4. What points will be raised by Ms. Crawford in the meeting at which she will be told the decision? Do you consider her tactic to be shrewd or suicidal?
5. If the outcome is reversed, how would you explain Ms. Crawford's promotion to John Lawton? Develop alternatives for L. T. Firestone concerning John Lawton's future with Creation Corporation.

BIBLIOGRAPHY

"Cosmetic's big need is self expression," *Advertising Age.* November 20, 1972, p. 34.

"Cosmetics '73: A look at what the industry can expect," *Chemical Marketing Reporter.* February 26, 1973, pp. 25–40.

Firestien, Alfred. "Women are the same the world over," *Nations Business.* February, 1972, pp. 86–87.

Kotler, Philip. *Marketing Management.* pp. 286–288.

"Max Factor in Mahoney's life," *Business Week.* November 18, 1972.

"Max Factor merger deal seen helping NSI abroad," *Advertising Age.* February 26, 1973, p. 43.

Moody's Industrial Manual 1971. 1972.

Norton Simon Inc. Interim Report to Shareholders, 3 months ended September 30, 1972.

"Product managers as influence agents," *Journal of Marketing.* January, 1972, pp. 26–30.

Raltera, L. "Fashion and cosmetic marketers clash over who creates those new trends," *Advertising Age.* December 25, 1972, p. 3.

Raltera, L. "Something for everyone is Revlon's marketing credo," *Advertising Age.* November 20, 1972, p. 26.

"World of beauty club aims at uncommitted brand buyer," *Advertising Age.* February 16, 1973, p. 140.

Index

Fayol's bridge
definition, 88
Feedback, 14
Force majeur, 342
Full-resource planning, 180
Functions
definition, 88
Future Shock, Alvin Tofler, 507

GIGO ("Garbage in, garbage out"),
341−342

Hiring and developing practices,
334−335

Inflation
long-range planning, 488−493
necessary steps in SROP, 484, 487
Information, company accumulated,
132, 134−143. *See also* Company accumulated information
Information, executive accumulated,
132, 134−143. *See also* Executive accumulated information
Information, special studies. *See also*
Special studies information
Information systems
company accumulated, 132
companywide, 132−149
comparative computerized,
149−153. *See also* Comparative computerized information systems
executive accumulated, 132
special studies, 133
the unknown, 133, 148−149
International operations, 97
Intracompany variables, 265
IMI (Information Management International, Inc.) concept,
317−320

IMSR (investments to meet social responsibilities), 311

Ladder
definition, 102
Line positions
definition, 88
Long-range planning, 342−343
adjustments for inflation and shortages, 488−493
allocation of resources, 221−223
contingency planning, 218−219
master strategies, 219−221
objectives, 216−217
personnel participation, 223−224
planning department, 225−226
strategic variables, 217−218
time period, guide to, 213−215
updating, 215−216
variables in the design, 230−231

Management
bottom-up, 102
Management competence, 330−335
Management information system (MIS)
centralized, 138
decentralized, 138
definition, 132
Manning table, 271, 272
Marketing management
responsibilities, 58
Matrix
definition, 102−103
Maximin, 33
Mergers, 387
business definition, 388, 397
checklist, 403−404
motivation, 398
price of shares, 399−400
Microfilm display systems, 137
Microfisch display systems, 137
Minimax, 33